Educating Children and Youth
with Autism

Educating Children and Youth with Autism

Strategies for Effective Practice

Edited by
Richard L. Simpson
and
Brenda Smith Myles

pro·ed
An International Publisher

8700 Shoal Creek Boulevard
Austin, Texas 78757-6897

This book is designed in Italia and New Century Schoolbook.

Production Director: Alan Grimes
Production Coordinator: Karen Swain
Managing Editor: Chris Olson
Staff Copyeditor: Suzi Hunn
Art Director: Thomas Barkley
Designer: Lee Anne Landry
Reprints Buyer: Alicia Woods
Preproduction Coordinator: Chris Anne Worsham
Project Editor: Susan E. Carter
Production Assistant: Dolly Fisk Jackson
Publishing Assistant: John Means Cooper

Printed in the United States of America

2   3   4   5   6   7   8   9   10   02   01   00   99   98

Contents

Contributors

Stacey Jones Bock, MS
Doctoral Candidate
Department of Special Education
University of Kansas Medical Center
4001 HC Miller Building
3901 Rainbow Boulevard
Kansas City, KS 66160-7335

Judith K. Carlson, PhD
Courtesy Assistant Professor
Department of Special Education
University of Kansas Medical Center
4001 HC Miller Building
3901 Rainbow Boulevard
Kansas City, KS 66160-7335

Debra Galvin Cook, MS, OTR
Assistant Professor
Department of Occupational Therapy
    Education
University of Kansas Medical Center
3901 Rainbow Boulevard
Kansas City, KS 66160-7335

Julie A. Donnelly, PhD
Autism Resource Specialist
Columbia Public Schools
Blue Ridge Elementary
2801 Leeway
Columbia, MO 64202

Winnie Dunn, PhD, OTR, FAOTA
Professor and Chairperson
Department of Occupational Therapy
    Education
University of Kansas Medical Center
3901 Rainbow Boulevard
Kansas City, KS 66160-7335

Theresa L. Earles, MS
Director
Autism Resource Center
Department of Special Education
University of Kansas Medical Center
4001 HC Miller Building
3901 Rainbow Boulevard
Kansas City, KS 66160-7335

Linda Garrison-Harrell, PhD
Assistant Professor
Department of Reading and Special
    Education
Southwest Missouri State University
901 South National Avenue
Springfield, MO 65804

Taku Hagiwara, MS
Doctoral Candidate
Department of Special Education
University of Kansas Medical Center
4001 HC Miller Building
3901 Rainbow Boulevard
Kansas City, KS 66160-7335

Colleen M. McMahon, PhD
Assistant Professor
School of Education
University of California
Riverside, CA 92521-0128

Brenda Smith Myles, PhD
Assistant Professor
Department of Special Education
University of Kansas Medical Center
4001 HC Miller Building
3901 Rainbow Boulevard
Kansas City, KS 66160-7335

Billy T. Ogletree, PhD
Assistant Professor
Department of Human Services
Western Carolina University
Cullowhee, NC 28723-9043

Janine Peck, PhD
Assistant in Research
Department of Child and Family Studies
MHC2113A
University of South Florida
13301 Bruce B. Downs Boulevard
Tampa, FL 33612

Colleen Quinn, PhD
Program Administrator
*Autism Training and Family Support
    Program*
6 North 6th Street, Suite 403A
Richmond, VA 23219

Gary M. Sasso, PhD
Professor
Department of Curriculum and
    Instruction
University of Iowa
N259 Lindquist Center
Iowa City, IA 52243

Richard L. Simpson, EdD
Professor
Department of Special Education
University of Kansas Medical Center
4001 HC Miller Building
3901 Rainbow Boulevard
Kansas City, KS 66160-7335

Sally Morgan Smith, PhD
Principal
Golden Oaks Educational Center
North Kansas City School District
3100 NE 46th Street
Kansas City, MO 64117

Luke Y. Tsai, MD
Professor, Child Psychiatry
    and Pediatrics
Director, Developmental Disorders Clinic
University of Michigan Medical Center
Child and Adolescent Psychiatric
    Hospital
Taubman Center, Room 3887
1500 East Medical Center Drive
Ann Arbor, MI 48109-0390

Preface

Children and youth with autism and pervasive developmental disorders span a wide range of qualities and functioning levels. Indeed, these individuals' variable and unique characteristics combine to create the quintessential challenge for professionals and parents. Over the past several years this challenge has even been further intensified because of a notable increase in the number of children and youth identified as having autism and pervasive developmental disorders, as well as a seemingly ever-changing classification and diagnostic system. Further contributing to the complexity of effectively serving the needs of individuals with autism and pervasive developmental disorders is an unprecedented and dramatic increase in intervention and treatment options for this population. That a number of these purported methods have proven to be less than effective, and that there is significant controversy over the outcomes of using various intervention strategies, have further intensified debate over how best to address the needs of children and youth diagnosed with autism and pervasive developmental disorders.

The aforementioned factors combine to yield an undeniable conclusion: Persons who educate and treat children and youth with autism and pervasive developmental disorders urgently need current information and guidelines. Regrettably, few current resources are available to satisfy this growing demand for information and strategies. It was this need that inspired this book.

The books consists of 11 chapters, beginning with our overview of characteristics, definitions, and conceptualizations of autism and pervasive developmental disorders. Chapter 1 also focuses on current trends and issues affecting the education and treatment of children and youth with autism and pervasive developmental disorders.

In Chapter 2, Carlson, Hagiwara, and Quinn discuss assessment and evaluation methods for children and youth of various ages and functioning levels, focusing on assessment for effective educational planning. In Chapter 3, Earles, Carlson, and Bock discuss instructional strategies and methods for students with autism and pervasive developmental disorders that are based on use of best-practice academic support methods and curricula. In Chapter 4, we describe a variety of behavior management methods and strategies appropriate for use with children and youth with autism and pervasive developmental disorders. The discussion includes individualized and group options for a variety of students. Ogletree focuses on the important topic of communication in Chapter 5.

His discussion includes a variety of methods and procedures for students with varying degrees of verbal and nonverbal language abilities.

In Chapter 6, Sasso and his colleagues present information and methods related to improving the quality and quantity of social interactions of children and youth with autism and pervasive developmental disorders. Their behaviorally based strategies offer teachers and other practitioners a number of best-practice options for improving the social performance of their students. Cook and Dunn address the topic of sensory integration in Chapter 7. They offer professionals and parents a variety of ways of incorporating programs based on sensory integration with children and youth with autism and pervasive developmental disorders.

Chapter 8, which we authored, deals with the issue of inclusion of students with autism and pervasive developmental disorders in general education settings and other normalized environments. Included as a part of the chapter are suggestions for facilitating responsible inclusion. In Chapter 9, Smith and Donnelly focus on the topic of transition. Their discussion includes information and suggestions for facilitating the successful transition of youth from home and school settings to adult life. Chapter 10 provides information related to medical interventions for children and youth with autism and pervasive developmental disorders. Writing for nonmedical readers, Tsai offers insight into various medical methods commonly used with persons with autism, especially pharmacological treatments. Finally, our Chapter 11 examines controversial treatments used with children and youth with autism. In this chapter we examine the legacy of using unproven methods to intervene with children and youth with autism and offer suggestions relative to the use of such interventions.

A number of people contributed to this project. Indeed, seven of the 11 chapters were written by individuals other than ourselves. We are deeply grateful to the contributions of these colleagues. We are also grateful for the editorial support of our colleague Kirsten McBride. And finally, we acknowledge the clerical support of Ginny Biddulph and Carol Simpson, without which this project would not have been possible.

Richard L. Simpson and Brenda Smith Myles

Understanding and Responding to the Needs of Students with Autism

1

Richard L. Simpson and
Brenda Smith Myles

E ven among difficult-to-understand disabilities, autism is the quint-essential enigma. Children and youth identified as having autism and/or pervasive developmental disabilities present highly individualized characteristics that frequently set them apart from their normally developing and achieving peers as well as their peers with other types of disabilities.

A significant range of functioning levels also makes individuals with autism a unique population. Some have near- or above-normal cognitive and language systems, with evidence of their disability manifested in the form of subtle social peculiarities. Others have severe cognitive impairments, limited or no expressive language, and severe behavioral and social aberrations. That individuals with autism sometimes demonstrate isolated unique abilities and highly developed splinter skills (Berkell, 1992) only adds to the mystery of the syndrome. Finally, fierce debates over the causes of autism, intervention choices, and educational programming features have been consistent elements in the history of autism (Biklen, 1993; Lovaas, 1987; Quill, 1995). In fact, many parents and profession-als perceive autism to be such a unique disability that they recommend that students with this exceptionality receive specialized autism-oriented intervention methods, curricula, and programs (Hart, 1993; Olley & Rosenthal, 1985).

More recently, a variety of educational reform and restructuring proposals and movements have been having a dramatic influence on children and youth with autism, as is the case with every other student in this country (Carnegie Forum on Education and the Economy, 1986; Fuchs & Fuchs, 1994, 1995; Smith, 1995). Predictably, these developments (e.g., inclusion, modified expulsion and suspension policies for students with aggressive behavior; Shapiro, Loeb, Bowermaster, & Toch, 1993; Skrtic, 1992; Zigmond et al., 1995) have resulted in an intensive search on the part of both families and professionals for strategies to continue to develop and maintain high-quality and effective educational and treatment programs for students with autism.

To meet professionals' and parents' need to understand the nature of children and youth with autism within a changing educational and social context, this chapter starts out with an overview of characteristics of autism and pervasive developmental disorders, including definitions and conceptualizations. The chapter also discusses several issues and factors that are significantly influencing educational programs and procedures for students with autism.

Defining Autism and Pervasive Developmental Disorders

In his seminal work, Kanner (1943) described a unique group of children whose behavioral anomalies made them qualitatively different from other children with identified disabilities. According to Kanner, these children manifested similar abnormalities from infancy or early childhood, including (a) an inability to relate normally to other people and situations; (b) delayed speech and language development, failure to use developed language for communication purposes, and/or other speech and language abnormalities, including echolalia, pronoun reversal and misusage, and extreme literalness; (c) normal physical growth and development; (d) an obsessive insistence on environmental sameness; (e) an extreme fascination and preoccupation with objects; and (f) stereotypic, repetitive, and other self-stimulatory responses. The characteristics of autism as first described by Kanner over half a century ago have been revised, refined, and broadened in recent years. Nonetheless, current definitions and conceptualizations of autism continue to reflect many of Kanner's original observations.

Current commonly used definitions of autism include those contained in the *Diagnostic and Statistical Manual of Mental Disorders* (4th ed.; DSM–IV; American Psychiatric Association [APA], 1994) and the definition advanced by the Autism Society of America (1995). These and other definitions of autism are presented below.

DSM–IV Definition of Autism

The most widely used definition of autism is that advanced in the DSM–IV. DSM–IV, an extensively used clinical practice guide, classifies autism as a pervasive developmental disorder. In this context, children and youth identified as having a pervasive developmental disorder "are characterized by severe and pervasive impairment in several areas of development: reciprocal social interaction skills, communication skills, or the presence of stereotyped behavior, interests, and activities" (p. 65). Such behavioral patterns are demonstrated in the first few years of life and are clearly abnormal relative to a given child's mental age or developmental level.

Subcategories of pervasive developmental disorders include autistic disorder, childhood disintegrative disorder, Rett's disorder, Asperger Syndrome, and pervasive developmental disorder not otherwise specified.

Autistic disorder, as per DSM–IV guidelines, is reserved for individuals who display social interaction impairments, communication impairments, and repetitive, stereotypic, and restricted interests and activities prior to 36 months of age. In the vast majority of cases, children diagnosed as having autistic disorder are moderately to severely impaired, most having IQs in the range of moderate to severe mental retardation. Specific DSM–IV diagnostic criteria for autistic disorder are shown below.

DSM–IV Autistic Disorder Diagnostic Criteria Summary

DSM–IV criteria include qualitative social interaction impairments as shown by at least two of the following characteristics:

- significant impairment in the use of nonverbal behaviors, including eye-to-eye contact, facial expression, body postures, and social interaction gestures

- inability to develop developmentally appropriate peer relationships

- failure to spontaneously seek opportunities to interact with other people (e.g., by a lack of identifying objects of interest)

- poor social or emotional reciprocity

DSM–IV criteria also include qualitative communication impairments as shown by at least one of the following characteristics:

- delay in, or total lack of, spoken language development (not accompanied by an attempt to use alternative modes of communication such as gestures)

- in persons with adequate speech, significant impairment in the ability to initiate or maintain a conversation with others

- stereotyped and repetitive language use or idiosyncratic language

- lack of varied, developmentally appropriate spontaneous make-believe play or social imitative play

Finally, DSM–IV criteria include repetitive and restricted stereotyped patterns of behavior, activities, and interests, as shown by at least one of these characteristics:

- marked preoccupation with one or more stereotyped and restricted patterns of interest that is abnormal either in focus or intensity

- inflexible adherence to nonfunctional routines or rituals

- stereotyped and repetitive motor movements such as hand or finger flapping or twisting, or complex whole-body movements

- persistent preoccupation with objects/components

In accordance with DSM–IV diagnostic standards, children identified as having *childhood disintegrative disorder* (also referred to as *Heller's syndrome, dementia infantilis,* or *disintegrative psychosis*) can be expected to have behavior patterns similar to those of children with autistic disorder. That is, they can be expected to display the same qualitative social interaction, communication, behavior, and interest impairments as children with autistic disorder. The distinction between individuals with childhood disintegrative disorder and those with autistic disorder relates to the age of onset of the disability. As noted earlier, children diagnosed with autistic disorder must display symptoms of pervasive developmental disorder prior to 3 years of age. In contrast, children with childhood disintegrative disorder will experience a period of normal growth and development prior to manifesting social interaction, communication, and behavioral impairments. Thus, following at least 2 years of apparently normal development (but before 10 years of age), children diagnosed as having childhood disintegrative disorder will display "a clinically significant loss of previously acquired skills in at least two of the following areas: expressive or receptive language, social skills or adaptive behavior, bowel or bladder control, play, or motor skills" (APA, 1994, p. 73). Prognosis for children identified as having childhood disintegrative disorder is guarded. Specifically, DSM–IV notes that the "social, communicative, and behavioral difficulties [of childhood disintegrative disorder] remain relatively constant throughout life" (p. 74).

The DSM–III–R (APA, 1987) pervasive developmental disorders classification system did not include individuals with Rett's disorder. However, this relatively rare disorder of females is one of the five subcategories of pervasive developmental disorders in the DSM–IV. With onset typically occurring by age 1 to 2 years, girls diagnosed with Rett's disorder usually develop in an apparently normal fashion during the first 5 months of age. Onset of the disability is characterized by head growth deceleration; loss of previously acquired motor skills, including purposeful hand movements; stereotypic hand wringing or hand washing; various motor impairments; and social and communication impairments. Loss of these skills is typically progressive and permanent, and prognosis for individuals with Rett's disorder tends to be poor.

In accordance with DSM–IV diagnostic criteria, the essential feature of Asperger Syndrome is impaired social interaction. Asperger Syndrome was named after the German physician Hans Asperger, who in 1944 identified a group of higher functioning children with autistic-like symptoms. Asperger Syndrome was largely ignored in the United States until recently, with professionals and parents in this country relying instead on the work of Kanner (1943) and his successors. However, there has been increased interest in the work of Asperger (1944). This renewed interest has at least in part been stimulated by expansion of the conceptualization of autism to include individuals with autism-type symptoms who are able to function at a relatively high level.

Frith (1991) observed that children with Asperger Syndrome "tend to speak fluently by the time they are five, even if their language development was slow to begin with, and even if their language is noticeably odd in its use for communication" (p. 3). Frith further observed that "as they grow older they often become quite interested in other people and thus belie the stereotype of the aloof and withdrawn autistic child. Nevertheless, they remain socially inept in their approaches and interactions" (pp. 3–4). Although the exact prevalence of Asperger Syndrome is unknown, it appears to be a relatively common form of pervasive developmental disorder/autism. Indeed, many schools are reporting significant numbers of students with this diagnosis entering their programs (Koegel & Koegel, 1995). DSM–IV diagnostic criteria for Asperger Syndrome are summarized as follows:

1. Qualitative social interaction impairment as shown by at least two of the following characteristics:

   - marked impairment in the use of nonverbal behaviors, including eye-to-eye contact, facial expressions, body postures, and social interaction gestures

   - inability to develop developmentally appropriate peer relationships

   - failure to spontaneously seek opportunities and interact with other people (e.g., by a lack of identifying objects of interest)

   - poor social or emotional reciprocity

2. Repetitive and restricted stereotyped patterns of behavior, activities, and interests as shown by at least one of the following characteristics:

   - marked preoccupation with one or more stereotyped and restricted patterns of interest that is abnormal either in focus or intensity

   - inflexible adherence to nonfunctional routines or rituals

   - stereotyped and repetitive motor movements such as hand or finger flapping or twisting, or complex whole-body movements

   - persistent objects/component preoccupation

   - clinically significant impairment in social, occupational, or other areas of functioning

   - clinically significant general language delay (e.g., communicative phrases used by age 3 years)

   - an absence of a clinically significant cognitive development delay or an absence of a delay in the development of age-appropriate adaptive behavior self-help skills and curiosity about the environment in childhood

The fifth subtype of pervasive developmental disorder identified in DSM–IV is *pervasive developmental disorder not otherwise specified.* This somewhat vaguely defined diagnostic classification refers to children who evidence "severe and pervasive impairment in the development of reciprocal social interaction or verbal and nonverbal communication skills, or when stereotyped behavior, interests, and activities are present" (APA, 1994, p. 77). However, the criteria for other forms of pervasive developmental disorder or other disabilities are not met.

Autism Society of America Definition of Autism

On the basis of a conceptualization and definition originally developed by Ritvo and Freeman (1978), the Autism Society of America, Inc. (1995) relies on the following definition of autism. As noted, this definition is also closely aligned with the criteria used in DSM–IV as well as Kanner's (1943) original observations about autism.

> *Autism* is a severely incapacitating life-long developmental disability that typically appears during the first three years of life. The result of a neurological disorder that affects functioning of the brain, autism and its behavioral symptoms occur in approximately fifteen out of every 10,000 births. Autism is four times more common in boys than girls. It has been found throughout the world in families of all racial, ethnic, and social backgrounds. No known factors in the psychological environment of a child have been shown to cause autism.
>
> Some behavioral symptoms of autism include:
>
> (1) Disturbance in the rate of appearance of physical, social, and language skills.
>
> (2) Abnormal responses to sensations. Any one or a combination of senses or responses are affected: sight, hearing, touch, balance, smell, taste, reaction to pain, and the way a child holds his or her body.
>
> (3) Speech and language are absent or delayed, while specific thinking capabilities may be present.
>
> (4) Abnormal ways of relating to people, objects, and events.
>
> Autism occurs by itself or in association with other disorders that affect the function of the brain, such as viral infections, metabolic disturbances and epilepsy. It is important to distinguish autism from retardation or mental disorders since diagnostic confusion may result in referral to inappropriate and ineffective treatment techniques. The severe form of the syndrome may include extreme self-injurious, repetitive, highly unusual and aggressive behavior. Special educational programs using behavioral methods have proven to be the most helpful treatment for persons with autism. (Autism Society of America, Inc., 1995, p. 3)

Other Definitions of Autism

There currently are (and historically have been) a number of other definitions of autism, virtually all of which emphasize the importance of social and language deficits and behavioral aberrations. Although often not as widely used as definitions promoted by the DSM–IV and the Autism Society of America, Inc., they share significant similarities. Several of these definitions and related diagnostic criteria are shown in Table 1.1

Additional Information and Characteristics of Importance for a Full Understanding of Autism and Related Disorders

Beyond the definitions of autism and pervasive developmental disorders presented above and in Table 1.1, knowledge of certain basic facts and information about individuals with autism can facilitate a better understanding of the disability. More importantly, such information is paramount to planning effective services and programs for children and youth with autism. The following discussion focuses on prevalence, predisposing factors, medical factors, and prognosis, as well as learning and behavioral characteristics.

Prevalence

According to Lotter (1966), autism occurs approximately 4 to 5 times per 10,000 births. However, just as definitions and conceptualizations of autism and pervasive developmental disorders have changed, so have prevalence estimates. Indeed, the Autism Society of America, Inc. (1995) has estimated that 15 to 20 out of every 10,000 children will be classified as autistic. Moreover, an ever-increasing number of children are identified as having autism and pervasive developmental disorders (Schreibman, 1988), with as many as 67 per 1,000 individuals being identified as having autism-related disorders (Ehlers & Gillberg, 1993). The reasons for this phenomenal increase are not completely clear, although it is likely that it is related to increased awareness of autism among parents and professionals and broadening of the DSM–IV conceptualization of pervasive developmental disorders.

Autism has consistently been found to be more common among males than females. Most gender comparisons have suggested that males with autism outnumber females at a ratio of 3:1 to 5:1 (Lord & Schopler, 1987; Ritvo & Freeman, 1978).

Table 1.1

Summary of Autism Definitions and Criteria

Source	Definition/criteria summary
Rimland (1964)	Rimland's analysis includes nine symptoms characteristic of autism. Major significance is given to patterns of social withdrawal and insistence on being left alone in an unchanging environment.
World Health Organization (WHO)	WHO categorizes autism as a form of infantile psychosis; major diagnostic signs of early infantile autism include disturbed interpersonal relationships, impaired language development, and stereotypical behaviors (Rutter, 1969).
Hingtgen & Bryson (1974)	Children with autism are classified on the basis of four frequently occurring traits: (1) They look infrequently at environmental objects, including people. However, when they do look at people, they usually fail to make behavioral responses to indicate that appropriate attention is being given. (2) They often display abnormalities of speech and communication. (3) They fail to interact with their environment and engage in little or no appropriate play with other children. (4) They frequently engage in repetitive activities and nonfunctional manipulation of environmental objects, fixtures, and their own bodies.
Rendle-Short (1978)	Rendle-Short (1978) identified 14 behavioral patterns associated with autism. These signs must be evident at an early age and occur to a marked extent over a long period of time. Rendle-Short also observed that because both normal and nonautistic exceptional children may exhibit some of these behaviors, the behaviors must be *age inappropriate* and *occur at a high rate*. The 14 identifying characteristics are as follows: has difficulty mixing with other children, acts deaf, resists learning, shows no fear of real dangers, resists changes in routine, indicates needs by gesture, engages in inappropriate laughing or giggling, is not cuddly, shows marked physical overactivity, maintains limited eye contact, forms inappropriate attachments to objects, spins objects, engages in sustained odd play, and behaves in a standoffish manner.

Predisposing Factors

Autism has been shown to be associated with maternal rubella (particularly when deafness or blindness is present), phenylketonuria, encephalitis, meningitis, and tuberous sclerosis (Lotter, 1974). Studies have also shown that seizures are common among individuals with autism (Holm & Varley, 1989). However, studies have clearly disproved previous assertions that certain familial and parental interpersonal factors (e.g., "refrigerator mother") influence the development of autism (Powers, 1989; Simpson & Zionts, 1992).

Medical Factors

Children identified as having autism vary widely in terms of their health and medical characteristics. Kanner (1943) described children with autism as exceptionally attractive and healthy and, indeed, a number of individuals with autism fit this mold. However, there are also children with autism who have various medical conditions. One such condition is seizure disorders, which often develops during adolescence. This problem appears to be most prevalent among persons with IQs below 50.

Pharmacological treatments are widely used to ameliorate behavioral symptoms associated with autism. For some children, drug treatments are successful. However, as with other interventions for persons with autism, a great deal remains to be learned about drug and other medical treatments.

Prognosis

In 1980, the American Psychiatric Association estimated that approximately 1 child in 6 identified as having autism can be expected to achieve marginal social adjustment, engage in competitive employment, and live independently as an adult; another 1 in 6 makes only minimal adjustment; and two thirds remain severely impaired and unable to live independently. More recent assessments of prognosis (Koegel & Koegel, 1995; Olley, 1992) suggest that early intervention in combination with a coordinated educational program bodes well for the long-term outlook for individuals with autism.

The long-term prognosis for individuals with autism is difficult to determine due to the diverse symptoms related to the disorder and the variance in the degree of impairment. As noted previously, even though the condition is lifelong, some children and youth with autism become independent adults showing only minimal signs of the essential characteristics of the disability. However, the social awkwardness or ineptness usually associated with autism tends to persist. Thus, the individual's lack of social skills can be expected to continue to result in inappropriate social behavior, which, especially in adolescence and adulthood, is often the critical issue in vocational and independent living success.

Generally, IQ and language skills are most directly associated with long-term prognosis. Researchers have concluded that IQ is generally a good predictor of outcome when assessments are appropriately conducted. When combined with IQ, language use and comprehension also serve as reliable indicators of outcome (Koegel & Koegel, 1995; Waterhouse, Morris, Allen, Dunn, & Fein, 1996). In terms of IQ, stable intellectual development has been reported for children with IQs of less than 50 as they mature; however, children whose IQs are higher tend to be much more variable (Howlin & Rutter, 1987). With regard to language, the best prognosis is restricted to individuals who have never shown a profound lack of response to sounds, who have gained useful speech by the age of 5, and who have experienced only transient echolalia (Minshew, Goldstein, & Siegel, 1995).

Learning and Behavioral Characteristics

Children and youth with autism share characteristics with a number of other students with disabilities. Yet, perhaps more than any other group with disabilities, their unique features set them apart from other atypical populations and create significant challenges for those who serve them. These distinguishing characteristics include stimulus overselectivity, diminished motivation, self-stimulatory and other behavioral problems, unique responses to reinforcement and other consequences, generalization difficulties, and problems of attention.

Stimulus Overselectivity

Stimulus overselectivity refers to limited consideration of environmental cues. Students with autism sometimes respond to only a few of the cues available to them in learning situations (Koegel & Koegel, 1995; Lovaas, Koegel, & Schreibman, 1979). Considering the numerous learning situations that require the ability to respond appropriately to multiple cues, the implications of attending to the environment in a highly restricted fashion become readily apparent. Often students are simultaneously presented with both promoting cues and the stimulus to be discriminated. Such conditions frequently interact adversely with selective attention in learners with autism.

Selective attention may, at least in part, explain the difficulties associated with teaching discrimination tasks to children and youth with autism. This nonproductive tendency has also been suggested to be a factor in students' difficulty in acquiring new behaviors. Through the use of prompts such as pointing, underlining, or emphasizing particular stimuli, educators may attempt to focus a student's attention on a new response. However, if the student selectively attends to prompt stimuli, this approach may actually increase task difficulty.

Diminished Motivation

According to Olley (1992), "One of the most commonly heard comments about people with autism is that they are not motivated to engage in education or treatment programs" (p. 11). Students with autism are often withdrawn and preoccupied, unmotivated to explore new environments, and uninterested in expanding their spheres of interest and testing alternative responses.

Clearly, such lack of motivation creates problems for educators because motivation is key to learning. Moreover, lack of motivation eventually results in a reduction of possible reinforcers (Koegel & Egel, 1979; Koegel & Koegel, 1995): Students with autism may perform so few correct responses that can be reinforced that they may have difficulty associating correct responses with reinforcers. As a result, the reduced reinforcement received from their efforts may further suppress their already limited motivation.

Self-Stimulation and Other Behavioral Problems

Self-stimulation and other behavioral problems are especially common among children and youth with autism. Self-stimulatory behaviors take the form of rocking, hand flapping, light filtering, and myriad other repetitive, stereotyped patterns that appear to have no functional environmental relationship. If given the opportunity, some children and youth with autism will spend the majority of their waking hours in such nonproductive activities. These behaviors tend to interfere with both social acceptance and integration and learning (Simpson & Regan, 1986; Varni, Lovaas, Koegel, & Everett, 1979). Accordingly, decreasing self-stimulatory behaviors and replacing them with more productive responses is often a priority goal for children and youth with autism.

Other behavioral excesses and deficits shown by students with autism are also problematic. Extremely dangerous and potentially injurious behaviors are relatively uncommon, whereas less severe behavior problems such as noncompliance are major issues for professionals and parents. Such problems require significant attention on the parts of both parents and professionals.

Unique Responses to Reinforcement and Other Consequences

Unique responses to reinforcement and other consequences are also characteristics of learners with autism, making stimulus consequences highly individualized. For example, some students with autism may consistently respond to a discrimination task by selecting and then dropping a particular item on a training table in order to obtain auditory feedback. Others appear to understand the connection between a response they make and a contingent reinforcer only when the reinforcer is delivered in a particular fashion. As a result, novel training procedures have been explored for dealing with these issues, including direct reinforcement, sensory reinforcement, and sensory extinction.

Koegel and Williams (1980) defined a *direct reinforcement* as "the target response being directly within the chain of behaviors required to procure the reinforcer" (p. 540). For instance, if a child is being taught color discrimination, a relevant task might be to open the lid of a given colored box containing a desired food. In order to obtain the direct reinforcement, a child must correctly respond within a set chain of behaviors. *Indirect reinforcement,* on the other hand, does not require such a response pattern. Using the same example, if the teacher reinforces a student for opening the correct colored box by handing the youngster a food reward, the reinforcement is indirect; that is, the stimulus situation does not contain a naturally occurring reinforcer.

Individuals with autism frequently learn most effectively under direct reinforcement conditions (Koegel & Koegel, 1995; Koegel & Williams, 1980), presumably because of the increased subject attention and reduced opportunities for irrelevant responses between response and reinforcement offered by this approach.

Sensory reinforcement involves analysis and manipulation of antecedents and consequences that are associated with self-stimulatory behaviors as a means of developing more adaptive responses (Rincover, Newson, & Carr, 1979; Sasso & Reimers, 1988). Some forms of sensory stimulation are highly reinforcing for some individuals with autism. For example, a child may spend extended periods of time watching the blades of a ceiling fan or spinning a soda bottle on a wooden floor. In accordance with this characteristic, contingent sensory rewards such as those derived from permitting a child to listen to tapes of particular sounds or to watch flickering lights may serve effectively as rewards for desired behaviors.

Sensory extinction, a strategy for reducing self-stimulation, is based on the notion that self-stimulatory behaviors are maintained by their sensory consequences (e.g., visual feedback of watching the hands move, kinesthetic movement feedback, sounds associated with repetitive tapping). Accordingly, intervention involves identifying and eliminating sensory reinforcement. For example, students with autism who derive reinforcement from block spinning may be required to spin on a carpeted table, and those who obtain visual feedback from hand flapping may be blindfolded (Koegel & Koegel, 1995; Rincover et al., 1979).

Generalization Difficulties

A major challenge facing educators and others who work with children and youth with autism relates to these students' difficulty in transferring information to novel settings, individuals, and other conditions. Indeed, many persons with autism must be instructed in settings and under conditions needed for actual task performance (Belfiore & Mace, 1994). A child who is able to perform a written task in a self-contained special education class cannot be assumed automatically to be able to correctly perform the same task in a general education setting. Accordingly, considerable time must be spent developing strategies for enabling persons with autism to flexibly use information and skills in novel ways, including practicing skills in community and regular classroom settings.

Attention Problems

It is not uncommon for persons with autism to experience difficulty in attending to and/or focusing on only specified stimulus properties, such as stimulus overselectivity of certain colors and shapes (Dunlap, Koegel, & Burkek, 1981; Koegel & Koegel, 1995; Schreibman, Kohlenberg, & Britten, 1986). As a result of these learning challenges, teachers of students with autism must plan specific programs and strategies for enabling students to attend to tasks and to identify and focus on salient stimulus properties and cues. For instance, a student who consistently responds only to materials of a particular color or shape would be trained in such a fashion as to not permit this pattern of overselectivity to interfere with skill acquisition and generalization.

Trends and Factors Related to Educational Programs and Procedures for Students with Autism

As mentioned, education and other efforts on behalf of children and youth with autism have been significantly affected by a number of recent changes and movements. The following trends, in particular, have significantly influenced programs, procedures, and practices for children and youth with autism: (a) recognition of the benefits of early identification and early intervention programs, (b) acceptance of the role of medical treatments for persons with autism and the need for collaboration among medical personnel and other professionals, (c) support for parent and family advocacy and professional–family collaboration and partnership programs, (d) recognition of the benefits of community support and collaboration programs and multidisciplinary and collaborative strategies for assisting persons with autism and their families throughout the life span, and (e) acknowledgment of the cognitive and social benefits of age-appropriate and community-based instructional methods.

Other more recent trends and developments have also significantly influenced autism-related programs and practices. These factors are discussed below, and include (a) inclusion of students with autism in general education classrooms, (b) widespread use of unvalidated interventions and treatment programs, and (c) issues related to the preparation of qualified teachers and other professionals for students with autism.

Inclusion of Students with Autism in General Education Classrooms

Recently the placement of children and youth with autism in general education settings has dominated most other issues related to students with autism. Specifically, according to some advocates, full inclusion is the next step in the development of appropriate and legally required services for students with disabilities, including those with autism (Dyke, Stallings, & Colley, 1995; Gartner & Lipsky, 1989; National Association of State Boards of Education, 1992; Sailor, 1991; S. Stainback & W. Stainback, 1992). Proponents of inclusion perceive special education services as (a) disrupting instructional continuity (Raison, Hanson, Hall, & Reynolds, 1995; Wang, Reynolds, & Walberg, 1986), (b) reducing students' curricular options (W. Stainback & S. Stainback, 1984; Yatvin, 1995), and (c) impeding knowledge and skill acquisition of students with disabilities (Dyke et al., 1995; Sailor et al., 1989). Accordingly, special education pull-out programs and other segregated models are alleged to contribute to problems for children and youth with disabilities, including (a) lowering self-concept and self-esteem (Rogers & Saklofske, 1985; W. Stainback & S. Stainback, 1991), (b) impairing social skill development (Madden & Slavin, 1983; Thousand & Villa, 1990), and (c) impeding students' postschool success (Reynolds, Wang, & Walberg, 1987; W. Stainback, S. Stainback, & Moravec, 1992).

By contrast, Kauffman and Hallahan (1995) have described full inclusion as "special education's largest bandwagon ever, one having gathered such great mass and momentum that it seems to many unstoppable" (p. ix), and as a crusade whose "size, velocity, and direction have become potentially fatal not only to those on board but to the entire special education community through which it is traveling" (p. ix). Full inclusion has also been characterized as lacking a sound scientific foundation (Kauffman, Lloyd, Baker, & Riedel, 1995; Smelter, Rasch, & Yudewitz, 1994).

Simpson and Sasso (1992) lamented that much of the debate over inclusion of students with autism has been based on "references to 'the moral and just thing to do' rather than scientifically established benefits" (p. 3). Moreover, relative to children and youth with autism, they observed that

> The full inclusion debate has too often been reduced to superficial arguments over who is right, who is moral and ethical, and who is a true advocate for children. Much of this simplistic posturing obscures the real issue (i.e., what is best for children) via claims of moral and ethical "high ground" and denouncements of "nonbelievers" as not knowing what is best and not caring about children and youth with disabilities. While perhaps effective in the short term, this process can lead to results that are directly opposite of those intended, including impediments to maximally effective programs for children and youth

with autism. We are of the opinion that full inclusion for students with autism is the right thing to do only if the benefits students with disabilities, their normally developing peers, or (ideally) if it is beneficial for both groups. That is, "the right thing to do," in our estimation, is that which provides the most benefits, not something that someone or some group deems appropriate because it fits their value system, is congruent with a fashionable trend, or appears to be a suitable, albeit unsupported alternative. (p. 4)

There is little sign that the full inclusion debate will soon subside, but there are indications of tentative agreement on some issues. First, a number of practitioners have discovered that the majority of students with autism can be physically maintained in general education settings. Thus, although debates over the appropriateness and benefits of such placement for some students continue, little doubt exists that given sufficient resources (e.g., paraprofessionals) and tolerance on the part of students, teachers, and parents, most students with autism can be physically accommodated in general education classes.

Second, there is growing recognition and agreement that some students with autism, especially those with severe behavioral problems and overall severe disabilities, represent a major challenge for regular class programs. Accordingly, even strong advocates of inclusion increasingly appear willing to question whether general education classrooms are indeed appropriate for meeting all students' needs. For example, some students with autism may need opportunities to spend time in pull-out programs where they can develop skills that are difficult to train in regular classrooms (e.g., self-care skills; Simpson, 1996).

Increasingly, educators and parents appear reluctant to place a student with autism in full-time regular education setting solely for the purpose of social skill and/or peer relationship development without extensive consideration of a student's overall functioning and need for alternative procedures and curricula. Indeed, educators and parents involved with students with autism seem to accept the notion that although a number of students with autism appear to be well suited for full-time general education placement, others are better suited for more secure and restrictive settings. Moreover, there seems to be agreement that successful general education placement is contingent upon the availability of suitable supports.

In this context, *support* refers to resources and modifications that assist general education teachers and others involved in meeting the specialized needs of students with autism. Necessary supports have been identified as paraprofessionals, reduced class size, adequate teacher planning time, availability of trained related-services professionals, teacher training options and consultants, and programs and measures to ensure supportive attitudes toward students with autism (Myles & Simpson, 1989; Simpson, 1996; Simpson & Myles, 1990).

Widespread Use of Unvalidated Interventions and Treatment Programs

Sasso (1995) identified the following treatment and educational programs for individuals with autism:

Gentle teaching	Links to language
Therapeutic horsemanship	Music therapy
Van Dijk method	Operant/behavioral interventions
Challenge method	Azrin 24-hour toileting
Cognitive behavioral interventions	Social stories
Facilitated communication	Language learning ladder
Full inclusion	Sensory integration
Auditory integration training	Cranial/cerebrospinal therapy
Psychopharmacology	Rhythmic entrainment
Irlen lenses	Vision therapy
Holding therapy	Aromatherapy
Giant Steps	TEACCH
Behavioral support	Higashi method
Early intensive behavioral treatment	Options
Eden program	Picture-exchange communication system

Although not completely comprehensive, Sasso's (1995) list provides a sense of the depth and breadth of procedures and options that have been developed and that are purported to be valid interventions for individuals with autism. Except for a few notable exceptions (i.e., operant/behavioral interventions), these treatments are largely unvalidated (in this context, *unvalidated* does not mean ineffective or spurious; rather, it means that a given scientific utility of the method remains unproven). Indeed, one of the hallmarks of programs and interventions for students with autism has been the never-ending search for interventions or methods, whether proven or not, that greatly accelerate individuals' progress and development and a willingness to rely upon unproven treatments and procedures that will restore an individual to normalcy.

It is not surprising that unvalidated treatments that promise a cure or phenomenal result primarily involve individuals with autism, because autism is the disability we know the least about and about which there is most disagreement. For instance, as revealed in the movie *Rainman,* some persons with autism display highly developed splinter skills and other exceptional abilities that sometimes suggest that they are capable of functioning far in advance of their estimated abilities.

Facilitated communication (FC) is the most visible and discussed among the unvalidated methods for persons with autism, at least in part because it holds unprecedented promises of normalcy. Indeed, through FC, persons with autism are purportedly able to reveal advanced skills and abilities that enable them to communicate and interact in a normalized fashion and to routinely achieve outcomes that far exceed those associated with traditional methods (Biklen, 1993).

It is understandable that many professionals, parents, and family members are willing to support use of and to put faith in undocumented methods that offer hope for improvement well beyond the expectations of more traditional and proven methods. We recognize that many effective methods were originally developed and used in clinical and educational settings long before they were scientifically validated. However, we believe that the current imprudent willingness to embrace unvalidated methods for individuals with autism is counterproductive. Such a willingness undermines the effective and cost-efficient use of limited resources by diverting energy from empirically validated best-practice methods while encouraging use of methods with limited proven efficacy.

Moreover, imprudent use of undocumented methods may persuade parents and families to place so much emphasis on academic goals and procedures that more functional needs, such as development of independent functioning skills, are neglected. Also, reliance on unsupported methods may lead to unrealistic and inaccurate expectations and thus heighten frustration for individuals with autism and their families.

To prevent such misguided intervention approaches, agreed-upon guidelines and policies are needed for evaluating interventions for persons with autism and for aiding parents and other professionals in making prudent choices about the use of interventions and other methods for individuals with autism. Implementation of such a plan is replete with difficulties. Nevertheless, it is irresponsible to proceed without guidelines and policies for evaluating programs and treatments, especially in instances in which purported claims far exceed those of traditional methods. Acceptance of an agreed-upon scientific evaluation policy would deter developers of novel intervention methods from advancing their untested interventions as valid and efficacious without objectively demonstrating their scientific validity (Freeman, 1993; Simpson & Myles, 1995). For a more complete discussion of controversial therapies and interventions with children and youth with autism, see Chapter 11 of this volume.

Issues Related to the Preparation of Qualified Teachers and Other Professionals for Students with Autism

There is currently a shortage of teachers and other professionals trained to work directly with students with autism (Bullock & Simpson, 1990; U.S. Department of Education, 1994). This shortage will likely become greater in coming years.

Because education personnel are the most significant variable accounting for gains made by persons with autism, the need to ensure availability of qualified professional educators is critical.

This issue is both quantitative and qualitative. That is, there is a need for greater numbers of teachers and other professionals to work with students with autism, and, at the same time, the skill depth and breadth of individuals who work with these students must be enhanced. Indeed, a major limitation of current teacher preparation programs is their failure to provide adequate in-depth opportunities to learn about instructional and management approaches (Goodlad, 1990). Instructional and management strategies must be explicitly taught to enable educators to be effective with students with autism, followed by modeling and practice in field placements with students with autism.

Providing such training is a significant challenge because there is only a handful of legitimate autism preservice personnel preparation programs in the country and because inservice training programs in the area of autism have consistently been limited in scope, content, and availability.

The need for specialized autism-related instructional and management skills and strategies and appropriate field experiences means that training programs cannot adequately respond to the current need simply by adding a single course to an existing generic special education preservice curriculum, offering occasional and limited autism-oriented inservice training. Nor can institutions meet this need by simply decreeing that generically trained general and special education teachers are qualified to teach students with autism. At the same time, it is unrealistic to expect that every teacher who is assigned to work with a student with autism will have completed an entire preservice program specifically in autism.

A more realistic expectation is that teachers and others who work with children and youth with autism will be well-trained special educators, general educators, or related-services professionals who have acquired the requisite knowledge, skills, and experiences needed to teach and work with children and youth with autism subsequent to completing a preservice training program. In accordance with this plan, educators who work with students with autism would be expected to first complete an appropriate generic education training program and then receive additional systematic professional training in autism. Thus, competent educators would be recruited into the profession and subsequently encouraged to participate in a comprehensive autism-oriented preservice and/ or inservice training program designed to develop specialty knowledge, skills, and experiences, which educators would be expected to demonstrate prior to assuming primary responsibility for students with autism. An important element of this plan is the elimination of emergency teacher licensing and other options that involve lowering training requirements.

In today's educational climate, programs designed to enhance educators' skills and knowledge in the area of autism must also carefully consider the needs of general education personnel. Not every student with autism can be expected to be in a general education program, but a significant number will spend at least a portion of their time in a general education classroom. Thus, personnel preparation curricula, experiences, and related training activities must be designed to assist general class teachers in working with children and youth with autism and to provide them the skills and experiences needed to effectively collaborate with special educators and other professionals, including individuals from nonschool systems such as medicine, respite care, daycare, and vocational and community assistance programs.

Implementation of an effective and cost-efficient autism-related personnel preparation program presents a significant challenge. Indeed, it is unrealistic to think that all general education preservice programs or traditional inservice training programs can effectively address this need. A more realistic approach would collectively and collaboratively use college and university training instructors and school district training personnel and resources (e.g., professional development schools) to plan and implement autism-oriented training programs and experiences.

Finally, preparation of personnel for children and youth with autism should be tied directly to desired student outcomes. That is, teachers and other professionals who educate and treat students with autism should be expected to demonstrate that their efforts make a positive difference. Thus, they should be able to identify appropriate goals for their students and subsequently demonstrate progress in these areas. Simpson, Whelan, and Zabel (1993) proposed an outcomes-based special education teacher education model that appears to have utility for preparing teachers of students with autism. Components of their recommended model, as related to autism-oriented preparation programs, include (a) "we believe" philosophical statements, which describe a shared vision for preparing teachers for students with autism; (b) agreed-upon outcomes for students with autism that are based on professional literature and valid professional practices and that are congruent with the "we believe" philosophy; and (c) a clearly articulated model that describes the steps needed to achieve the outcomes.

Increasing the supply of well-trained professionals to serve the needs of students with autism is by any standard a daunting challenge. At the same time, it is an area that holds tremendous potential. Hence, serious attention to this area bodes well for the futures of individuals with autism and their families.

Summary

Successful education of children and youth with autism and pervasive developmental disabilities presents daunting challenges. These individuals have cognitive, linguistic, and social characteristics that challenge even the most skilled and dedicated professional and parent. Yet significant gains among persons with these disabilities can and do occur when appropriate methods are used. As related in this chapter, a first step in facilitating such growth is knowledge among professionals and parents of the characteristics of autism and pervasive developmental disabilities.

References

American Psychiatric Association. (1980). *Diagnostic and statistical manual of mental disorders* (3rd ed.). Washington, DC: Author.

American Psychiatric Association. (1987). *Diagnostic and statistical manual of mental disorders* (3rd ed., rev.). Washington, DC: Author.

American Psychiatric Association. (1994). *Diagnostic and statistical manual of mental disorders* (4th ed.). Washington, DC: Author.

Asperger, H. (1994). Die "Autistischen Psychopathen" im Kindesalter. *Archiv für Psychiatrie und Nervenkrankheiten, 117,* 76–136.

Autism Society of America, Inc. (1995). Definition of autism. *Advocate, 27*(6), 3.

Belfiore, P. J., & Mace, F. C. (1994). Self-help and community skills. In J. L. Matson (Ed.), *Autism in children and adults* (pp. 193–211). Pacific Grove, CA: Brooks/Cole.

Berkell, D. (1992). *Autism: Identification, education and treatment.* Hillsdale, NJ: Erlbaum.

Biklen, D. (1993). *Communication unbound: How facilitated communication is challenging traditional views of autism and ability/disability.* New York: Teachers College Press.

Bullock, L., & Simpson, R. (1990). *Critical issues in special education: Implications for personnel preparation.* Denton: University of North Texas, Department of Special Education.

Carnegie Forum on Education and the Economy. (1986). *A nation prepared: Teachers for the 21st century.* New York: Author.

Dunlap, G., Koegel, R. L., & Burkek, J. C. (1981). Educational implications of stimulus overselectivity in autistic children. *Exceptional Education Quarterly, 2*(3), 37–49.

Dyke, R. V., Stallings, M. A., & Colley, K. (1995). How to build an inclusive school community: A success story. *Phi Delta Kappan, 76,* 475–479.

Ehlers, S., & Gillberg, C. (1993). The epidemiology of Asperger Syndrome: A total population study. *Journal of Child Psychology and Psychiatry, 34,* 1327–1350.

Freeman, B. J. (1993). Questions to ask regarding specific treatment. *The Advocate, 25*(2), 19.

Frith, U. (Ed.). (1991). *Autism and Asperger Syndrome.* Cambridge, UK: Cambridge University Press.

Fuchs, D., & Fuchs, L. S. (1994). Inclusive schools movement and the radicalization of special education reform. *Exceptional Children, 60,* 294–309.

Fuchs, D., & Fuchs, L. S. (1995). What's "special" about special education? *Phi Delta Kappan, 76,* 522–530.

Gartner, A., & Lipsky, D. K. (1989). *The yoke of special education: How to break it.* Rochester, NY: National Center on Education and the Economy.

Goodlad, J. I. (1990). *Teachers for our nation's schools.* San Francisco: Jossey-Bass.

Hart, C. A. (1993). *A parent's guide to autism.* New York: Pocket Books.

Hingtgen, J. N., & Bryson, C. Q. (1974). Recent developments in the study of early childhood psychoses: Infantile autism, childhood schizophrenia and related disorders. In S. Chess & A. Thomas

(Eds.), *Annual progress in child psychiatry and child development* (pp. 231–267). New York: Brunner/Mazel.

Holm, V. A., & Varley, C. K. (1989). Pharmacological treatment of autistic children. In G. Dawson (Ed.), *Autism: Nature, diagnosis and treatment* (pp. 386–404). New York: Guilford.

Howlin, P., & Rutter, M. (1987). *Treatment of autistic children.* New York: Wiley.

Kanner, L. (1943). Autistic disturbances of affective content. *The Nervous Child, 2,* 217–250.

Kauffman, J. M., & Hallahan, D. P. (1995). Preface. In J. M. Kauffman & D. P. Hallahan (Eds.), *The illusion of full inclusion* (pp. ix–xi). Austin, TX: PRO-ED.

Kauffman, J. M., Lloyd, J. W., Baker, J., & Riedel, T. M. (1995). Inclusion of all students with emotional or behavioral disorders? Let's think again. *Phi Delta Kappan, 76,* 542–546.

Koegel, R. L., & Egel, A. L. (1979). Motivating autistic children. *Journal of Abnormal Psychology, 88,* 418–426.

Koegel, R. L., & Koegel, L. K. (1995). *Teaching children with autism.* Baltimore: Brookes.

Koegel, R. L., & Williams, J. A. (1980). Direct vs. indirect response–reinforcer relationships in teaching autistic children. *Journal of Abnormal Child Psychology, 8,* 537–547.

Lord, C., & Schopler, E. (1987). Neurobiological implications of sex differences in autism. In E. Schopler & G. B. Mesibov (Eds.), *Neurobiological issues of autism* (pp. 191–211). New York: Plenum.

Lotter, V. (1996). Epidemiology of autistic conditions in young children. *Social Psychiatry, 4,* 263–277.

Lotter, V. (1974). Factors related to outcome in autistic children. *Journal of Autism and Childhood Schizophrenia, 1,* 124–137.

Lovaas, O. I. (1987). Behavioral treatment and normal educational and intellectual functioning in young autistic children. *Journal of Consulting and Clinical Psychology, 55,* 3–9.

Lovaas, O. I., Koegel, R. L., & Schreibman, L. (1979). Stimulus overselectivity in autism: A review of research. *Psychological Bulletin, 86,* 1236–1254.

Madden, N. A., & Slavin, R. E. (1983). Mainstreaming students with mild handicaps: Academic and social outcomes. *Review of Educational Research, 53,* 519–569.

Minshew, N. J., Goldstein, G., & Siegel, D. J. (1995). Speech and language in high-functioning autistic individuals. *Neuropsychology, 9,* 225–261.

Myles, B. S., & Simpson, R. L. (1989). Regular educators' modification preferences for mainstreaming mildly handicapped children. *The Journal of Special Education, 22,* 479–492.

National Association of State Boards of Education. (1992). *Winners all: A call for inclusive schools.* Alexandria, VA: Author.

Olley, J. G. (1992). Autism: Historical overview, definition, and characteristics. In D. Berkell (Ed.), *Autism: Identification, education and treatment* (pp. 3–20). Hillsdale, NJ: Erlbaum.

Olley, J. G., & Rosenthal, S. L. (1985). Issues in school services for students with autism. *School Psychology Review, 14,* 166–170.

Powers, M. D. (1989). *Children with autism.* Rockville, MD: Woodbine House.

Quill, K. A. (1995). *Teaching children with autism: Strategies to enhance communication and socialization.* New York: Delmar.

Raison, J., Hanson, L. A., Hall, C., & Reynolds, M. C. (1995). Another school's reality. *Phi Delta Kappan, 76,* 480–482.

Rendle-Short, J. (1978). *Infantile autism diagnosis.* Austin, TX: National Society for Autistic Children.

Reynolds, M. C., Wang, M. C., & Walberg, H. J. (1987). The necessary restructuring of special and regular education. *Exceptional Children, 53,* 391–398.

Rimland, B. (1964). *Infantile autism: The syndrome and its implications for a neural theory of behavior.* New York: Appleton-Century-Crofts.

Rincover, A., Newson, C., & Carr, E. (1979). Sensory extinction and sensory reinforcement principles for programming multiple adaptive behavior change. *Journal of Applied Behavior Analysis, 12,* 221–233.

Ritvo, E. R., & Freeman, B. J. (1978). National society for autistic children: Definition of the syndrome of autism. *Journal of Autism and Childhood Schizophrenia, 8,* 162–169.

Rogers, H., & Saklofske, D. H. (1985). Self-concepts, locus of control and performance expectations of learning disabled children. *Journal of Learning Disabilities, 18,* 273–278.

Rutter, M. (1969). Concepts of autism: A review of the research. *Journal of Child Psychology and Psychiatry, 9,* 1–25.

Sailor, W. (1991). Special education in the restructured school. *Remedial and Special Education, 12*(6), 8–22.

Sailor, W., Anderson, J., Halvorsen, A. T., Doering, K., Filler, J., & Goetz, L. (1989). *The comprehensive local school: Regular education for all students with disabilities.* Baltimore: Brookes.

Sasso, G. M. (1995, October). *Choosing instructional strategies.* Paper presented at the Midwest Educational Leadership Conference on Autism, Kansas City, MO.

Sasso, G. M., & Reimers, T. M. (1988). Assessing the functional properties of behavior: Implications and application for the classroom. *Focus on Autistic Behavior, 3*(5), 1–15.

Schreibman, L. (1988). *Autism.* Newbury Park, CA: Sage.

Schreibman, L., Kohlenberg, B. S., & Britten, K. B. (1986). Differential responding to content and intonation components of a complex auditory stimulus by nonverbal and echolalic autistic children. *Analysis and Intervention in Developmental Disabilities, 6,* 109–125.

Shapiro, J. P., Loeb, P., Bowermaster, D., & Toch, T. (1993, December 13). Separate and unequal: How special education programs are cheating our children and costing taxpayers billions each year. *U.S. News and World Report, 115*(23), 46–60.

Simpson, R. L. (1996). Children and youth with autism in an age of reform: A perspective on current issues. *Behavioral Disorders, 21*(1), 7–20.

Simpson, R. L., & Myles, B. S. (1990). The general education collaboration model: A model for successful mainstreaming. *Focus on Exceptional Children, 23*(4), 1–10.

Simpson, R. L., & Myles, B. S. (1995). Facilitated communication and children with disabilities: An enigma in search of a perspective. *Focus on Exceptional Children, 27*(9), 1–16.

Simpson, R. L., & Regan, M. (1986). *Management of autistic behavior.* Austin, TX: PRO-ED.

Simpson, R. L., & Sasso, G. M. (1992). Full inclusion of students with autism in general education settings: Values versus science. *Focus on Autistic Behavior, 7*(3), 1–13.

Simpson, R. L., Whelan, R. J., & Zabel, R. H. (1993). Special education personnel preparation in the 21st century: Issues and strategies. *Remedial and Special Education, 14*(2), 7–22.

Simpson, R. L., & Zionts, P. (1992). *Autism: Information and resources for parents, families, and professionals.* Austin, TX: PRO-ED.

Skrtic, T. (1991). *Behind special education: A critical analysis of professional culture and school organization.* Denver, CO: Love.

Smelter, R., Rasch, B., & Yudewitz, G. (1994). Thinking of inclusion for all special needs children? Better think again. *Phi Delta Kappan, 76,* 231–239.

Smith, F. (1995). Let's declare education a disaster and get on with our lives. *Phi Delta Kappan, 76,* 584–590.

Stainback, S., & Stainback, W. (1992). Schools as inclusive communities. In W. Stainback & S. Stainback (Eds.), *Controversial issues confronting special education* (pp. 29–43). Boston: Allyn & Bacon.

Stainback, W., & Stainback, S. (1984). A rationale for the merger of regular and special education. *Exceptional Children, 51,* 102–111.

Stainback, W., & Stainback, S. (1991). Rationale for integration and restructuring: A synopsis. In J. W. Lloyd, A. C. Repp, & N. N Singh (Eds.), *The regular education initiative: Alternative perspectives on concepts, issues, and models* (pp. 225–239). Sycamore, IL: Sycamore.

Stainback, W., Stainback, S., & Moravec, J. (1992). Using curriculum to build inclusive classrooms. In S. Stainback & W. Stainback (Eds.), *Curriculum considerations in inclusive classrooms: Facilitating learning for all students* (pp. 65–84). Baltimore: Brookes.

Thousand, J. S., & Villa, R. A. (1990). Strategies for educating learners with severe disabilities within their local home schools and communities. *Focus on Exceptional Children, 23,* 1–24.

U.S. Department of Education. (1994). *Sixteenth annual report to Congress on the implementation of the Individuals with Disabilities Education Act.* Washington, DC: Author.

Varni, J., Lovaas, O. I., Koegel, R. L., & Everett, M. L. (1979). An analysis of observational learning in autistic and normal children. *Journal of Abnormal Child Psychology, 7,* 31–43.

Wang, M. C., Reynolds, M. C., & Walberg, H. J. (1986). Rethinking special education. *Educational Leadership, 44,* 26–31.

Waterhouse, L., Morris, R., Allen, D., Dunn, M., & Fein, D. (1996). Diagnosis and classification in autism. *Journal of Autism and Developmental Disorders, 26,* 59–86.

Yatvin, J. (1995). Flawed assumptions. *Phi Delta Kappan, 76,* 482–484.

Zigmond, N., Jenkins, J., Fuchs, L. S., Deno, S., Fuchs, D., Baker, J. N., Jenkins, L., & Couthino, M. (1995). Special education in restructured schools: Findings from three multi-year studies. *Phi Delta Kappan, 76,* 531–540.

Assessment of Students with Autism

2

Judith K. Carlson, Taku Hagiwara,
and Colleen Quinn

A ssessment is an important tool for determining instructional and behavioral programming for all students. For students with autism, this process can present unique challenges. Those with this disability frequently present idiosyncratic response patterns that defy traditional assessment methods. Many commercial assessment measures rely on verbal responding, an ability many children with autism lack. Thus, those who participate in the assessment of students with autism must have a thorough understanding of the syndrome as well as the diagnostic assessment process.

Prescriptive diagnostic assessment is the process of collecting data with the specific purpose of verifying student strengths and concerns. Such data may include a medical history, intelligence and aptitude ratings, academic test scores, and anecdotal records of the student's daily life. This information is collected in order to provide appropriate educational placement, to target goals and objectives, to monitor the student's progress, and to evaluate the quality of the educational services received.

Assessment can focus on academic, behavioral, social, physical, or environmental components. The assessment process contains many components, including referral, screening, classification, instructional planning, and student progress. Additionally, multidisciplinary teams may be created to assess across areas such as occupational and physical therapy, audiology, vision, sensorimotor therapy, and social work.

Basic Assumptions of Assessment

Because assessment attempts to examine and evaluate complex human nature, it is impossible to obtain perfect data. As a result, individuals involved in assessment must be aware of threats to the quality of their data collection and attempt to avoid them in order to maximize the validity of the assessment. Newland (1973) presented five basic assumptions underlying a valid assessment that have held true across time.

1. *The person administering the test is skilled.* Before administering any test to a student, an examiner must receive appropriate training. Specifically, the examiner must be familiar with the content, characteristics, administration, scoring, and interpretation of the test. Although test materials themselves are usually unchanged, the skills or attitudes of the test subject are fluid. Therefore, to maintain reliability, different examiners must possess an approximately equal administration skill level. It is critical that an examiner does not conduct any assessment procedure in which he or she is not qualified.

2. *Error will be present.* As stated earlier, to date no educational or psychological measurement is perfect. For example, differences in the testing environment, variations between examiners, changes in student behavior, or unexpected events during the testing always occur. Moreover, standardized and commercially produced tests are not error free. As much as possible, examiners must attempt to control for errors in testing, and test interpretation should reflect the expected error levels.

3. *Acculturation must be comparable.* This assumption primarily pertains to norm-referenced or standardized tests, which compare a student's performance with that of a normative sample. A normative sample is a group of scores that have been statistically averaged by age and/or grade level. To obtain an accurate score and to make an appropriate interpretation, the student being tested must approximately match the normative sample of the test with respect to gender, race, ethnic culture, and experiential background. Many commercially produced norm-referenced tests were developed using normative samples containing no students with disabilities. If such tests are used with students with autism, scoring and interpretation should be considered accordingly.

4. *Behavior sample is adequate.* In sampling behaviors, more than just the quantity of the data collected must be considered. The quality of the data must also be evaluated. For behavioral assessment, we need to establish both what we observe and how we rate what we observe. For example, suppose we are observing how a male student with autism buttons his shirt. Examiner A might observe the student once and note that he was unable to button his shirt. Examiner B might observe the student on five occasions and note that he could button his shirt only twice. Examiner C, who has observed the student on three occasions, might note that the student correctly buttoned 11 buttons. All examiners viewed the same process; however, the data reported are clearly

quite varied. Examiner A did not observe the student with sufficient frequency, whereas Examiner C rated the behavior on a different scale. If different examination criteria are used, the data are incomparable. Thus, the examiner must plan in advance how much data should be collected to yield valid results and what types of measurement are appropriate for assessing specific behaviors.

5. *Present behavior is observed: Future behavior is inferred.* During the assessment process, we can observe only the student's present performance. From this limited observational data, we go on to make inferences about the student's capabilities and future performance. However, such projections are merely inference. Diagnosticians must recognize that their future predictions are just that. Predictions are in no way a definitive representation of a student's potential level of functioning.

In addition to these five assumptions, numerous other assumptions are of concern for conducting any assessment using a rigorous statistical analysis. Using statistics is a sound way to maintain accurate and systematic data manipulation. However, many novice diagnosticians find statistics intimidating. It is possible to conduct accurate assessment without using complex statistics through careful planning, proper administration, and reliable interpretation.

The basic requirements for appropriate assessment are ample knowledge and sufficient practice. The following sections first look at the necessary training for conducting appropriate and valid assessment. The discussion then turns to types of assessment used with students with autism and ways to translate assessment results into meaningful intervention procedures. The chapter concludes with two case studies.

Training for Assessment

Assessment of students with autism must be conducted by personnel qualified and familiar with the characteristics, response patterns, and idiosyncratic behaviors of this population. Currently, few training programs specialize in assessment of persons with autism. However, it is possible to learn general assessment techniques through many university programs or through workshops and inservice training offered by local school districts or other educational institutions. Many basic assessment techniques are applicable to all types of students. Thus, after learning general assessment techniques, a practitioner can modify the procedures according to the needs of the type of student being assessed. Figure 2.1 provides a framework for learning and practicing assessment of students with autism.

Knowledge of Autism

Before conducting any assessment, an examiner must have a general understanding of autism. Without such knowledge, he or she cannot modify general

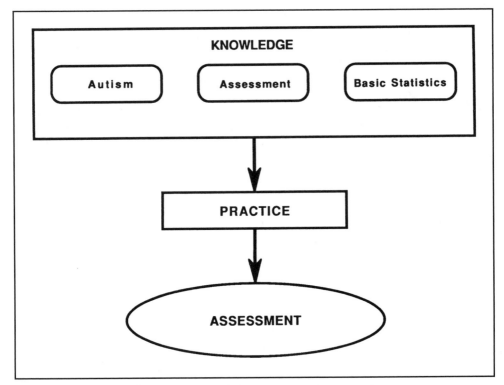

Figure 2.1. Process of assessment training.

assessment techniques appropriately. For example, if the examiner knows how to administer an aptitude test but does not recognize echolalia, a common speech pattern of autism, he or she cannot adequately interpret the unusual verbal pattern observed during testing. Preferably, the examiner would have prior experience in working with students with autism before conducting any assessment.

Knowledge of Assessment

Assessment requires thorough planning. However, such planning cannot be done without an ample knowledge of assessment. Knowledge of assessment includes understanding different kinds of data, observational techniques, formal and informal procedures, scoring, interpretation of data, and trouble shooting.

Basic Knowledge of Statistics

As mentioned, advanced knowledge of statistics is not required for most assessment approaches. However, since assessment handles many types of data, an examiner should, at a minimum, understand the basics of statistics to be able to accurately interpret the results. For example, most norm-referenced tests use the concept of a standard score. Without an understanding of this concept, the test scores received will have little or no meaning for the practitioner. Fortunately, many educational assessment publications, as well as test administration manuals, include information on basic statistics.

Practice

To conduct meaningful assessment, knowledge is not enough. Meaningful assessment requires thorough practice and feedback. Therefore, it is recommended that the practitioner seek opportunities to assist with assessment before attempting solo administration. Furthermore, a mentor to monitor performance during initial assessments can be invaluable. Practice not only assists in developing assessment skills, but also builds confidence in administration and interpretation.

Types of Assessment Used with Students with Autism

Norm-Referenced Testing

Norm-referenced assessment uses standardized tests to collect data. Generally, norm-referenced tests utilize specified questions with directed procedures for administration and scoring. The assumption underlying a norm-referenced test is that every student receives the same questions and the same administration. A norm-referenced test is developed using a *norming group,* which consists of randomly selected students sharing certain characteristics. Items on a norm-referenced test are carefully compiled according to the results of pretests conducted with the students in the norming group. At the same time, scores on the norm-referenced test are statistically determined by the distribution of scores from the norm group. Thus, the basis of the norm-referenced test is that the test taker's performance is compared to the performance of the norm group.

Although the size and nature of the norm group required for a norm-referenced test vary, samples ranging from 1,000 to 2,000 from various populations are customary. Due to the large sample sizes of the norming groups and the complex procedures of test development, most norm-referenced tests are commercially produced.

The manual accompanying a norm-referenced test usually specifies in detail how to administer the test. *The instructions must be followed exactly.* If the examiner violates the prescribed procedures, the scores obtained in that testing are not valid. Since a norm-referenced test compares the test taker's performance to that of the norm group, it is necessary to conduct the test in the same way as the norm group experienced the test.

Usually, a norm-referenced test yields two or more kinds of scores. First, the student's performance on the test is calculated as a *raw score*. Next, the raw score is converted to a *standard score* in order to be able to compare the student's performance with that of the norm group. This is generally done through the use of tables provided with the test. Since the norm group represents the general population from a statistical viewpoint, an examiner can compare a student's performance with that of other similar students in the nation.

The *mean* or *average* of the standard score is typically 100, with a standard deviation of 15. The *standard deviation* is a statistical concept that represents the average dispersion of scores around the mean score of the norm group. Approximately two thirds of scores fall between 1 standard deviation below the mean and 1 standard deviation above the mean. For example, if a student's standard score is 112, the test's mean score is 100, and 1 standard deviation is 15, the student's performance falls within the range of 1 standard deviation above the mean (between 100 and 115). Conversely, if the student scored a standard score of 86, the student's performance is 1 standard deviation below the mean (between 85 and 100). Figure 2.2 illustrates this normal curve and the percentage of expected scores between each listed score.

Extreme caution should be observed when one is using norm-referenced tests with students with autism. Since many norming groups did not contain students with disabilities, it is inappropriate simply to compare the performance of students with autism to that of the norm group of typically achieving students. The diagnostician must consult the manual of the norm-referenced

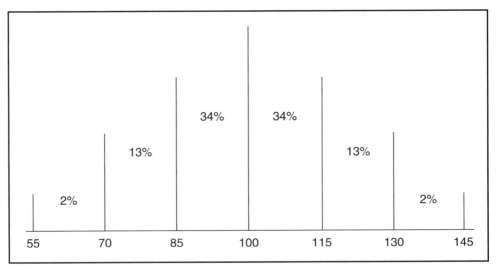

Figure 2.2. Normal curve using mean of 100 and standard deviation of 15.

measure before conducting the test to check whether its norm group is appropriate for the student being assessed.

Commonly used norm-referenced tests for students with autism are categorized into two groups: aptitude/achievement tests and tests of adaptive behavior/social skills.

Aptitude/Achievement Tests

Basically, all general intelligence tests can potentially be used with students with autism (Parks, 1988). There are advantages and disadvantages of using such tests, depending on the skills and capabilities of the individual student. The *Wechsler Intelligence Scale for Children* (3rd ed., WISC–III; Wechsler, 1991) and the *Stanford-Binet Intelligence Scale* (4th ed., Thorndike, Hagen, & Sattler, 1985) are widely used intelligence tests in the fields of education and psychology. Standardized scores yielded by most other norm-referenced tests are comparable with the scores of these two intelligence scales. It is important to note, however, that no students with autism were included in the norming groups for these two tests. It is possible to substitute other standardized measures, which may more directly access the abilities of students with autism. For younger children or those with delayed development, the *Bayley Scales of Infant Development* (Bayley, 1984) can yield valuable information, particularly in the areas of social and language skills. For students who are nonverbal or whose language skills are severely delayed, the *Leiter International Performance Scale* (Leiter, 1969) or the *McCarthy Scales of Children's Abilities* (McCarthy, 1972) may be more appropriate substitutions as these tests require little or no verbal response.

Tests of Adaptive Behavior/Social Skills

Delayed adaptive behavior and social skills are common deficits for students with autism (Wing & Gould, 1979). The *Vineland Adaptive Behavior Scales* (VABS; Sparrow, Balla, & Cicchetti, 1984) is frequently selected to examine behavioral and social skills of children with autism. There are three independent forms of the VABS. Two of the forms, the Expanded Form and the Survey Form, are administered by interviewing the student's primary caregiver. The third form, the Classroom Edition, is conducted with a teacher. All three forms assess the domains of communication, daily living, socialization, and motor skills. The Expanded Form and the Survey Form also contain a maladaptive behavior domain. One concern about the VABS is that it is not scored by direct observation of the student (Parks, 1988). However, administration of this instrument is relatively easy and yields a reliable standard score that can be compared with scores from other norm-referenced tests. Caution should be used in interpretation of this measure for students with autism. Younger children who score in mild ranges on early administration may score much lower as they age. This is because the child with autism frequently does not keep the same developmental pace as typically achieving peers, with the gap widening as years pass.

Another adaptive behavior test that can be used with students with autism is the *American Association on Mental Deficiency Adaptive Behavior Scale–School Edition* (AAMD ABS; Lambert, Windmiller, Tharinger, & Cole, 1981). Like the VABS, this test is administered to an outside party who is asked to rate the student's behavior. Unlike the VABS, which uses a norm group mainly from the nondisabled population, the AAMD ABS was developed based on a norm group from an institutionalized population. This may seem like a strong advantage for use with children with autism; however, controversy exists over the test's applicability. According to Salvia and Ysseldyke (1991), the AAMD ABS suffers from standardization and reliability problems and, therefore, should be used as an experiential device rather than as a norm-referenced measure. Thus, diagnosticians who use the AAMD ABS might consider the results as supplemental information, rather than as a primary assessment measure.

Developmental Assessment

Basically, developmental assessment compares a person's current abilities to an expected scope and sequence of skill acquisition seen in typically developing children. Developmental assessment can yield information useful in creating home, school, or work programs. Knowing a student's score on a standardized test does not answer the question of how that student communicates, organizes the environment, or applies problem-solving skills. By contrast, tests utilizing a developmental approach attempt to answer these important questions.

The belief that all people grow and change, including people with disabilities, is the foundation of developmental assessment. Developmental assessment provides critical information for setting personal goals in areas such as transition, maintenance, generalization, and independent functioning.

Uses for Developmental Assessment

The physical environment, setting demands, task presentation, level of interest, and past learning experience can all influence how well persons with autism demonstrate what they know in a testing situation. Developmental assessment allows the student an opportunity to respond without rigid time constraints or standardized procedures. For example, developmental tests give students a chance to approach problem solving in traditional or nontraditional ways. Since no time limit is specified, the examiner can start and proceed as he or she becomes familiar with the student, allowing time to build rapport.

Designing an assessment to evoke certain behaviors can also provide important information. Is the student able to ask for help or indicate that he or she would like to take a break from the test? If not, how does the student communicate needs? Understanding a student's developmental level can lead to an understanding of how the student approaches tasks and indicates readiness skills in functional academics or social development (Marcus, 1978). Such information can help establish realistic goals, which are crucial for encouraging learning and building success. Setting multiple goal levels—those that the student can readily accomplish, those that are more difficult, and those that are challenging, yet motivating—helps to create an intervention program that is best-practice oriented. Throughout testing, the examiner should identify which tasks are easy or difficult for the student and note which activities, materials, and methods receive the most positive student response.

Myles, Constant, Simpson, and Carlson (1989) listed major areas of consideration for diagnosticians using developmental assessment with students with autism. These areas included (a) stimulus overselectivity, (b) motivation, (c) self-stimulatory behavior, and (d) echolalia. Figure 2.3 displays how these components interact with developmental assessment.

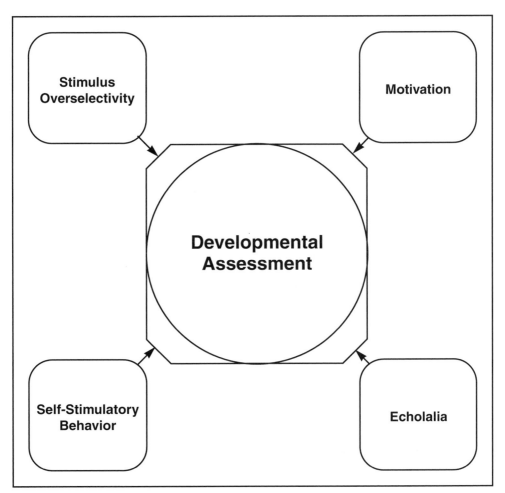

Figure 2.3. Developmental assessment.

1. *Stimulus overselectivity* occurs when a student eliminates all but a few cues in the environment. For example, when presented with word cards with the accompanying verbal instruction, "Point to *exit*," the student with stimulus overselectivity may continually select the card on the left side of the array. This response pattern can easily be disrupted by varying the presentation of the task, the arrangement of the stimulus surface, or the manner in which the examiner requests the information.

2. *Limited motivation* can be confused with an inability to complete a task or a lack of interest in the task. Students with autism frequently require external motivation tied to a task to increase the likelihood of task completion. Prior to testing, it is important to determine appropriate reinforcers, break times, and preferred tasks for the student. Talking with parents, teachers, caregivers, and the student himself or herself can provide a menu of reinforcers to combat limited motivation. These reinforcers can then be paired with task completion using tangible objects, picture boards, or simple token economies.

3. Many students with autism exhibit *self-stimulatory behavior* such as hand flapping or rocking. If these repetitive movements are not interfering with test administration or response, they should be ignored during the assessment. If the self-stimulatory behaviors are disruptive, however, it may be necessary to conduct a brief discrete trial training or other intervention to achieve appropriate response behaviors. Anecdotal records regarding the student's self-stimulatory behaviors should be maintained as they can provide valuable information about the student's frustration levels and coping mechanisms.

4. *Echolalia* can be immediate or delayed. In the case of *immediate echolalia,* the student may repeat a phrase the examiner has just said or imitate a sound made by a test item. With *delayed echolalia,* on the other hand, the student verbalizes something heard previous to the testing session. Delayed echolalia may range from verbalizing a brief phrase to repeating an entire television commercial. Although echolalia may seem random, it can serve a communicative purpose. Take, for example, the case of Tony, an 8-year-old boy with autism. Tony would utter the phrase, "Do you want tartar sauce with those Fisherboys?" whenever he was angry or frustrated. A parent interview revealed that one night while serving fish sticks at home, Tony's mother became upset with his behavior and asked the infamous tartar sauce question in an angry tone of voice. The phrase became Tony's hallmark for signaling his own frustration (T. Earles, personal communication, October 1996). Through interviews with parents and caregivers, the examiner can begin to gain an understanding of how the student communicates. This information should in turn help determine responses that fall into an echolalic pattern and those that do not.

Developmental Measures Appropriate for Students with Autism

Developmental measures provide the examiner with flexibility in both administration style and response pattern. Developmental tests can take into account idiosyncratic learning styles and aberrant behaviors that may be evidenced upon testing a student with autism. Results from developmental assessment can offer detailed, functional, information that allows for the design of appropriate interventions. The following developmental assessment instruments are particularly appropriate for students with autism.

1. The *Psychoeducational Profile–Revised* (PEP–R; Schopler, Reichler, Bashford, Lansing, & Marcus, 1990) is a developmental test specifically designed for children with autism. The information yielded by this instrument can be used for educational and/or home programming. It is best suited for students under the chronological age of 12 years or when significant developmental skills are at or below the first-grade level. The PEP–R divides learning into seven academic areas: imitation, perception, fine motor, gross motor, eye–hand integration, cognitive performance, and cognitive verbal. Behavior is divided into four areas: relating and affect, play and interest in materials, sensory responses, and language.

The academic areas are scored as passing, emerging, or failing, indicating the student's ability to complete a series of developmental tasks. Behavior is scored as appropriate, mild, or severe, based upon the student's interactions with persons and objects in the test environment. The PEP–R allows an examiner flexibility in both item order and presentation mode and incorporates frequent opportunities for nonverbal response. Further, the PEP–R creates an environment in which parents, instructors, and diagnosticians can work together to develop effective and appropriate educational programs for students with autism.

2. The *Adolescent and Adult Psychoeducational Profile: Volume 4* (AAPEP; Mesibov, Schopler, Schaffer, & Landrus, 1988) is a criterion-referenced test designed for persons with autism who are approaching adolescence and/or adulthood. Students of 12 years and older who are functioning intellectually within the moderate to severe range of mental retardation are appropriate for this test. The areas of examination within the AAPEP include vocational skills, independent functioning, leisure skills, vocational behavior, functional communication, and interpersonal behaviors. The AAPEP focuses on work, social, and leisure skills, rather than solely concentrating on developmental skills (Mesibov, Schopler, & Caison, 1989). The concentration on survival skills and functional living activities reflects the increased importance of these skills as a person ages. The AAPEP includes home, school, and work versions and scores this information on separate scales. Data that can assist in the development of life plans and transition goals may be gained from this test.

3. The *Development Therapy Objectives Rating Form–Revised* (DTORF–R; Developmental Therapy Institute, 1992) combines developmental therapy with psychodynamic theory. The DTORF–R identifies skill area strengths and provides a scope and sequence to address underdeveloped skills with the ultimate outcome of enabling students to function as independently as possible in a variety of settings. The *Developmental Therapy–Developmental Teaching* (DTDT)

curriculum, which corresponds with the DTORF–R, attempts to translate theory into educational practice. While concentrating on a student's developmental milestones, the DTDT focuses on the systematic development of skills. Both the DTORF–R and the DTDT can be used with persons with autism ranging from preschool age through high school and across both academic and behavioral components. After completing the DTORF–R with an individual student, the instructor can identify the student's current levels of functioning and specify instructional goals based on areas of need. The DTDT instructional curriculum, divided into the four general areas of behavior, communication, socialization, and (pre)academics, can then be used to develop specific objectives or provide an overall program of developmental sequences.

4. A *scope and sequence approach* can provide similar information to that obtained on the more formalized DTORF–R. With the scope and sequence approach, a skill or concept is broken down into its most basic component parts. The first component in the chain of skills is taught and practiced until mastery is achieved. Then, the next skill in the sequence is taught, and so on. A scope and sequence can be developed for most academic, functional, behavioral, social, and vocational areas.

A scope and sequence is invaluable for programming for persons with autism, especially where splinter skills exist. A *splinter skill* is a specific task that the student can complete, yet the student may not posses the ability to complete prior or subsequent steps. For example, if a student can recite the numbers 1 through 200 yet does not understand the concept of one-to-one correspondence, a scope and sequence approach can target the missing skill steps for intervention. Looking at a math scope and sequence will show where rote counting falls on a continuum of math skills and what skills lie between understanding the concept of one-to-one correspondence and counting numbers.

The *Hudson Education Skills Inventory* (HESI; Hudson, Colson, Welch, Banikowski, & Mehring, 1989) applies the concept of a scope and sequence approach to the assessment process. Developed to assist educators in assessing atypical learning patterns, the HESI is applicable to high-functioning students with autistic disorder. The test is divided into the three core areas of math, reading, and written expression, within which a sequence of skill acquisition, subskills, and objectives is supplied. Although the HESI does not require specialized training to administer, an examiner does need a basic understanding of typical development.

The HESI uses a test-down/teach-up model of assessment. That is, the student is initially exposed to a skill that he or she may not be able to complete successfully. The examiner systematically moves down the sequence of skills until the point where the student achieves mastery. This allows the student to end testing on a positive experience rather than at a negative ceiling due to failure and gives the instructor a clear starting point for intervention and remediation.

When selecting a scope and sequence approach for assessment or intervention, the diagnostician should consider the individual student's learning preferences. For example, students who favor a simultaneous or "big picture" approach to learning do not perform as well using this type of task-analysis method.

Additional Assessment Techniques

Informal Assessment

Informal assessment customarily refers to the process in which practitioners collect, evaluate, and apply information about a student they instruct. The data obtained through informal assessment are frequently used to set goals, identify instructional strategies, and measure outcome behaviors (Guerin & Maier, 1983), Informal assessment procedures add an important dimension to the evaluation process, targeting *how* the student learns, rather than *what* the student knows. As a result, informal assessment data allow practitioners to select instructional techniques that facilitate student learning.

Informal assessment does not require a normed or defined reference group against which to measure a student's performance. Rather, students are compared to their own performance levels within the curriculum and the setting demands of the program or placement. Therefore, much of the data will be collected in natural settings such as the classroom, home, or workplace, rather than a clinic or testing facility. Frequently, information obtained through informal assessment involves ordinary classroom interactions and may be quite idiosyncratic (Guerin & Maier, 1983). For example, interactions that occur in a classroom environment may happen only when a particular teacher is in the room or when the student with autism is hungry or tired. Either of these conditions may not be indicative of the student's typical functioning ability.

Although informal assessment can be used as part of a full evaluation battery, it is best suited for data collection that is ongoing and formative. Revising Individualized Education Program (IEP) objectives, selecting instruction and response mode formats, modifying assignments, setting time frames for performance, and developing individualized curricula are all outcomes that can be enhanced using informal assessment data.

Student Learning Traits

A student's achievement is influenced by a variety of factors. *External factors* such as the bus ride to school or where the student's desk is located in the classroom have an impact that is easy to recognize and observe. *Internal factors,* on the other hand, such as how students perceive or receive information, how they process and store concepts, and how they apply that data to their daily lives, are more elusive. This type of variable must be measured subjectively, through

direct observation of the student, examination of classroom materials and setting demands, and identification of instructional and response preferences. The
indicators that communicate how children learn are called student learning
traits (SLTs).

SLTs may offer insight into how students with autism gain information
across academic areas. For example, a student may respond only to meaningful stimuli and not to rote stimuli. Some students may be sequential learners
and prefer tasks to be presented in a part-to-whole format, whereas others
may favor a simultaneous "big picture" approach. There are as many learning
traits as there are students, and each student possesses specific traits. Student
learning traits have been broken down into three basic categories: learning
style, behavioral patterns/characteristics, and strategies (Myles et al., 1989).

Learning Style

The concept of *learning style* refers to those skills that allow students to focus
their attention and store information. Sequential versus simultaneous processing, stimulus selectivity, and attention to detail all fall under this category.
A student's memory skills, including short-term, long-term, visual, auditory,
rote, and meaningful memory, play a role in creating his or her learning style.
Tasks that examine students' preferences and strengths within these areas
can be contrived and observed for the purpose of shaping teacher instruction.

A student's rate of performance and task pacing also contributes to learning style. Take, for example, the case of Trudy, a young woman with high-
functioning autistic disorder who was being served in a residential treatment
center for adolescents with severe behavioral problems. Trudy was thought to
be stubborn and oppositional by her house staff, teachers, and therapists
because she rarely answered questions or offered input during school and therapy sessions. An examination of Trudy's learning style revealed that she
needed a wait time of 20 to 30 seconds to access and process information, rather
than the traditional 3- to 5-second wait time usually experienced in reciprocal
conversation. When given adequate wait time, Trudy was able to offer insight-
ful information and actively participate in her program goals. Incidental learning, independent work habits, and generalization skills round out the learning
styles category.

Behavioral Patterns/Characteristics

How students act on the information they have retrieved and the unique way
they apply this information to daily functioning reveals their behavioral patterns and characteristics. All types of interactional patterns should be observed,
including adult-to-student, student-to-peer, small-group, and large-group inter-
changes. The student's pattern of response to issues of reinforcement, structure,
stress, and success should be examined. Avoidance behaviors, attention-seeking

behaviors, and self-stimulatory patterns would all be considered part of a student's behavioral profile. Through structured observation of the student in a variety of settings, the examiner can note on-task and off-task characteristics, flexibility in moving from one activity to the next, and the type of events that trigger impulsive or compulsive behavior.

For students with autism, some specific behavioral patterns must be considered. The use of echolalia as a communication tool, the ability to make and maintain eye contact, level of distractibility, and perseverance in task completion are all important links to successful classroom performance. Eye, hand, and foot dominance, as well as the ability to cross midline, must also be examined to determine perceptual abilities and fine and gross motor skills.

These areas can easily be examined by having the student visually track a favorite toy, catch and kick a ball, and draw or write. Midline issues can be addressed by having the student complete a simple shape or interlocking puzzle. The examiner places puzzle pieces on opposing sides of the puzzle board and observes whether the student reaches across him- or herself to place the puzzle pieces. Any patterns of oral or written perseveration should also be noted. Of course, the important issue in examining any behavioral pattern or characteristic is to determine which behaviors affect the student's interaction with academic requirements and social skills.

Strategies

Strategies are the techniques or rules that a student uses to solve problems and complete tasks independently. It is important to determine what types of strategies a student uses and whether the student can learn or develop new strategies. Sometimes a student approaches tasks very strategically but uses strategies that are ineffective or inappropriate for the task. Students with autism frequently persist in using unsuccessful strategies simply because they have no other strategies for the given situation.

Following written and oral directions is another important component involving strategic thinking. Many students with autism are unable to organize or prioritize multiple-level instructions and, therefore, require brief, small instructional steps for successful task completion. It is also important to consider the types of metacognitive strategies that a student applies. *Metacognitive strategies* include skills such as self-talk, self-monitoring, and self-correction. Students with autism frequently do not pass through the developmental stages necessary to develop metacognitive skills. Take, for example, the typically achieving preschooler who is pretending to make lunch for her teddy bear family. As she makes modeling clay sandwiches, she may verbally direct herself aloud, saying, "First I spread the peanut butter on the bread and then I get out the jelly." Children with autism may never have rehearsed these typical developmental activities and, therefore, must experience them through direct instruction.

Diagnostic Teaching

As with student learning traits, the focus of diagnostic teaching is on listening to the student, understanding what he or she feels, and interpreting the subsequent interactions within the learning environment. It is a systematic, clinical process whereby the student is presented with a task or series of tasks that are new or novel. The student is asked to solve a problem or complete an activity while observation notes and anecdotal records are maintained. These notes should describe how the student approaches the task, deals with task frustration, modifies, and self-corrects errors, as well as the problem-solving skills the student utilizes in attempting task completion. As the diagnostic teaching session progresses, the examiner may offer clues or suggestions and even teach small components needed to complete the task.

Another application of diagnostic teaching involves presenting similar tasks to the student using a variety of presentation and/or response modes. For example, six spelling words, all unfamiliar to the student and similar in structure and difficulty, are presented for practice using three different modalities. Two words are practiced verbally, having the student spell the word aloud and then use the word in a sentence. Two different words are rehearsed in a written format, having the student write each word 10 times. Finally, the two remaining words are presented kinesthetically, having the student draw the letters in a box of damp sand. Each practice session lasts for approximately 3 minutes. At the conclusion of the practice sessions, the words are tested using the type of response required in the student's classroom setting. The results are then compared to see if different practice modes facilitated the student's memorization of the spelling words. Some common presentation and response modes used in this type of diagnostic teaching include visual, auditory, tactile/kinesthetic, and combinations of two or more of these modalities.

Diagnostic teaching sessions are usually brief, lasting for 15 minutes or less. Throughout the session, the student's response patterns are observed and areas of strength noted. Working with the student's strengths, deficit skill areas are addressed, compensatory mechanisms are introduced, and home and school environments are rearranged to meet the individual student's specific learning needs.

Functional Analysis

A great deal has been written about the use of functional analysis with children with pervasive developmental disorders (Carr, 1994; Horner, 1994; Repp & Singh, 1990). The purpose of functional analysis is to test a hypothesis about a specific behavior and to find the communicative intent or maintaining variables that support this behavior (Iwata, Dorsey, Slifer, Bauman, & Richman, 1982).

Functional analysis can be used in the classroom, home, clinic, or workplace to examine aberrant behavior of students with autism, such as arm biting or loud screaming. As with all assessment techniques, functional analysis has both advantages and disadvantages. Functional analysis allows the examiner to identify one or more contingencies that are the most relevant to the occurrence of a problem behavior. However, problems can occur in monitoring the consistency of the stimulus condition, collecting systematic data, training data collectors, and obtaining the space and time needed for this detailed process (Iwata et al., 1982).

Traditional functional analysis begins by determining a target behavior for the student (Sasso & Reimers, 1988). Within an organized structure and setting, such as a clinic or classroom, the student is presented differing conditions designed to deliberately provoke the target behavior(s). This is done, in part, to determine the communicative intent of the behavior. Traditional functional analysis examines the effects of sensory reinforcement, negative and positive attention, edible and object reinforcement, and instructional demands on the behavior of the student.

When one is working with students with limited verbal or communicative abilities, it is frequently difficult to interpret the meaning embedded in a behavioral response. These students may not be able to communicate their needs to another person in the same way that someone with verbal skills could relay information. To assess problem behavior for persons with more severe disabilities, several commercial developmental measures may be useful. The *Motivation Assessment Scale* (MAS; Durand & Crimmins, 1988) is a 16-item questionnaire that samples problem behavior in a variety of contexts by asking primary caregivers to answer observation-based questions. A sample question might be, "Does this behavior occur following a command to perform a difficult task?" Areas examined by the MAS include sensory responses, attention focus, escape from task, and tangible responses. The scatterplot recording format (Touchette, MacDonald, & Langer, 1985) is another tool that examines behavioral patterns in students with severe disabilities. The format is a grid composed of time segments that are placed vertically on a graph and day segments that are placed horizontally on the same graph. The occurrence of the target behavior is recorded on the appropriate time/ day intersection. This graphing allows for a visual inspection of the activity, the time of day it occurs, the absence or presence of other people, and the location or setting. Students with mild to moderate disabilities who possess some verbal skills can participate more actively in the process of targeting a behavior and an intervention. The *Problem Behavior Questionnaire* (Lewis, Scott, & Sugai, 1994) utilizes a form that teachers or primary caregivers can fill out to develop a basic hypothesis about a problem behavior. From there, observation is used to detail the specific characteristics of the behavior and interface with the student to identify potential intervention strategies. The form is simple to use and does not require excessive time or training. The *Student-Assisted Functional Assessment Interview* (Kern, Dunlap, Clark, & Childs, 1994) requires the student to complete a form with or without assistance from a caregiver. The form asks the student for personal reflections on behaviors that he or she believes can and cannot be changed or modified. This information can be used in combination with other functional analysis tools to plan effective intervention.

Portfolio Analysis

Recent changes in the paradigm of assessment have led from a reliance on formalized tests to more person-centered approaches (Nolet, 1992; Schutt & McCabe, 1994; Wesson & King, 1992). Many practitioners are concerned that one-shot assessment often does not reveal the small or idiosyncratic gains made by students with autism. Portfolio assessment, which recognizes small changes in performance, can yield valuable prescriptive information for developing student-centered goals and objectives (Hendrick-Keefe, 1995). Portfolio assessment requires students to evaluate their current level of functioning in a specific area while simultaneously requiring the instructor to review educational programming to ensure that goals directly address the students' needs (Schutt & McCabe, 1994). Therefore, portfolio assessment promotes accountability for both student and instructor. Portfolios provide a full picture of a student's abilities by concentrating on strengths and gains, rather than deficit skills (Swicegood, 1994). Additionally, students who prepare portfolios gain management experience and acquire ownership in their product by determining, with the instructor, what will be included within their portfolio.

Although definition, type, and quality of portfolio assessment vary, most researchers agree upon the following components:

- a table of contents or sections detailing what is included in the portfolio
- an explanation of the included materials and why they were selected
- behavior and adaptive functioning data
- strategic learning and self-regulation data
- academic or functional academic data

Furthermore, samples for the portfolio should be selected from a variety of settings and procedures, using both raw data and evaluation feedback. Finally, the portfolio should be housed in a container such as a binder, a folder, or a notebook (Hendrick-Keefe, 1995; Swicegood, 1994; Wesson & King, 1992).

Critics of the portfolio approach to assessment claim that there is a lack of empirical evidence demonstrating that portfolio assessment is an effective evaluation tool. A lack of guidelines for use and an absence of information about its effects on learning and about its impact on student motivation are frequently cited (Nolet, 1992). Although little research has been conducted to date on using portfolio assessment with students with autism, the combination of quantitative and qualitative data it yields may offer an interesting perspective on a student's functional ability. In addition, portfolios may initiate positive interactions between student and instructor, while providing students with valuable decision-making opportunities (Hendrick-Keefe, 1995; Swicegood, 1994).

Students with severe disabilities may have difficulty verbally stating goals or information to be included in their portfolio. However, they should still be an integral part of the overall portfolio process. Begin by determining goals for the student with the aid of a parent or caregiver. Observe the student to determine what types of materials would demonstrate progress or mastery of the selected goals. Provide opportunities for the student to make choices about which materials to include in the portfolio. For example, if one goal is to use a microwave oven, the student could choose between including a videotape of him- or herself using an oven or a photograph of him- or herself holding a finished meal. Realize that more functional academic or behavioral goals may be present in the portfolio of a student with a severe disability. Try to decide upon goals and approaches to those goals that will assist the student in obtaining independence.

Students with mild to moderate disabilities will most likely be able to participate verbally in the development of their portfolio goals. They may provide more traditional input in choosing the materials and describing their experiences in the portfolio. These students may benefit from an interview on videotape to include in their portfolio. For example, an instructor or employer could ask the student questions regarding school or work tasks, such as the following: "Did you like the class or job?" "What made it easy or hard?" and "What would you like to do in this area in the future?"

Portfolio assessment can also be a valuable tool for students who are transitioning from school into the adult community. In this case, items are selected to create a career portfolio. A career portfolio can be used to (a) display informal vocational assessment data, (b) start a discussion about what type of vocational or academic program would benefit the student, (c) develop transition goals in the IEP, (d) teach a student how to match the portfolio to a job description, or (e) visually demonstrate a student's abilities and strengths. The career portfolio can be updated, just like a resume or vita, as the student gains new skills (Bernhardt, Cole, & Ryan, 1993; Sarkees-Wircenski & Wircenski, 1994).

Ecobehavioral Assessment

Ecobehavioral assessment provides information about a student's behavior through manipulation of the environment and other ecological factors (Kamps, Leonard, Dugan, Boland, & Greenwood, 1991). That is, ecobehavioral assessment examines both the behavior and the environmental components that support the behavior. One technique of ecobehavioral assessment is behavior acceleration (Greenwood, Carta, & Atwater, 1991). With behavior acceleration, a student's behavior is assessed within the varied demands of the classroom setting, the work setting, and the student's place of residence. The materials that are used for instruction, as well as the attitudes of and interactions with the instructors, are examined. Behavior acceleration looks at desired behaviors and the skills necessary for success in each specific situation. The resulting information allows for development of interventions that will accelerate the target behavior and/or improve the instruction. Ecological assessment requires a great deal of examiner time but can yield useful information regarding instructional practices and setting demands that can significantly impact a student's level of success.

Translating Assessment Results into Meaningful Procedures

After conducting observations, scoring protocols, and analyzing results of tests, the diagnostician must synthesize the collected data to clarify the student's current performance status. *Synthesis* is the interpretation and integration of findings or information. Synthesis of assessment results describes the meaning of the results of tests or observations and provides insight into how this information can affect instructional strategies. The process of synthesis may well be the most important aspect of any assessment battery. It is customary for this synthesis to be presented in a written report format along with information such as anecdotal observation records, tests scores, and recommendations. Although the format of the synthesis is flexible, depending on the components of the assessment, certain groupings are helpful in organizing a report for a student with autism:

- cognitive and motor skills
- communication and language skills
- behavior and social/emotional development
- problem-solving skills

Three basic types of statements should be included in the assessment report: informational statements, inferences, and judgments (Moran, 1995). *Information* is specific and verifiable. It states only the facts that occur during testing and observation. Information should be stated as quantifiable outcomes or in observable terms such as "hit," "kick," and "bite" rather than the more general "aggressive behavior." A statement such as "Andy bit the examiner's right hand three times while attempting the puzzle activity" is an example of information. *Inferences* are less specific than information statements. They may include interpretive comments that go beyond the observable facts. Therefore, inferences are more subjective than information and cannot be directly verified. The majority of the synthesis in an assessment report will consist of inference statements. For example, if David did not complete five out of six items on a particular subtest, the examiner could infer that David did not possess the needed skills to perform this task. *Judgment statements* are usually contained in the final section of the assessment report. They are both general and subjective. Judgment statements may be recommendations or diagnoses that combine inferences and information. For example, a statement of judgment might be,

"Diane should receive reading instruction in a one-on-one setting specially designed for students with autism." Figure 2.4 shows an overview of how to incorporate these three statement types throughout the assessment process.

Identifying Student Strengths and Concerns

An assessment report should include a section detailing the student's areas of strength and concern. This section includes a specific and clear list of statements. For the list of strengths and concerns, the recommended format is a table consisting of two columns. In one column, the specific strength or concern is listed; in the other column, evidence of those qualities is provided. For example, when the examiner puts "recognizes complex parts of a whole" in the column of concerns, he or she provides direct evidence for the concern in the other column, such as "unable to complete interlocking puzzle." This procedure enables readers of the assessment report to instantly recognize specific strengths and target behaviors for the student. Table 2.1 provides a sample listing of strengths and concerns with evidence.

The detail on the student's strengths is especially helpful in developing an educational plan that fosters knowledge and skills. For example, if a student can recognize single-word directions such as "sit" or "drink" during testing, the examiner can directly utilize this strength when making recommendations at the conclusion of the assessment report, such as "Provide Juan opportunities to follow a variety of single-word directions, then gradually shift this pattern of commands to include two or more words."

Owning Assessment Results: Students, Teachers, and Parents

The final step in the assessment process is the dissemination of the testing results. The benefits of assessment should be shared with the students themselves, their parents, their teachers, and others involved in the student's educational life. It is suggested that the examiner meet directly with the student, the parents, and other professionals to overview and interpret assessment results.

Before this meeting, the examiner must prepare the assessment report. If the examiner determines that additional information might be helpful in developing interventions for the student, copies of articles or other documents can be attached to the report as appendixes. The examiner also plans an appropriate agenda for the meeting. When this preparation is finished, the examiner schedules the meeting with the appropriate parties.

At the meeting, the examiner should create a positive, interactional atmosphere. According to Moran (1995), all parties at the meeting should (a) have a mutual respect for each participant's competency, (b) realize that each person has a unique but equally valuable skill to offer, (c) regard all participants

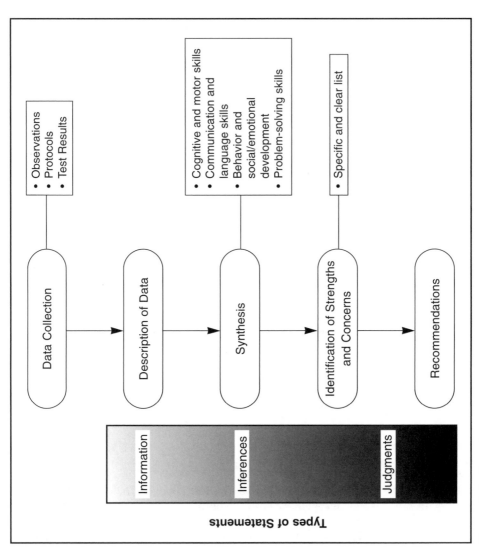

Figure 2.4. Translating assessment results.

Table 2.1

Sample Listing of Strengths and Concerns with Evidence

Strengths	Evidence
Demonstrates fine/gross motor skills	Stringing beads, jumping
Gestures for help	Opening jar
Demonstrates gross motor skills	Clapping hands, standing on one foot
Responds to simple commands	"Sit down," "finish"
Speaks single words or two-word phrases	"Done," "go away"
Concerns	**Evidence**
Demonstrates self-stimulation	Heavy breathing, flipping objects
Is frustrated or distracted easily	Sitting down for short period of time, screaming
Demonstrates knowledge of basic concepts	Identifying geometric shapes, colors, or letters
Interacts with others	Requesting only
Demonstrates eye–hand coordination	Copying shapes

as equals, and (d) remain flexible about considering recommendations. Participants may have difficulty understanding specific terminology related to the assessment process and the different disciplines represented at the meeting. The examiner can avoid misinterpretations by promptly clarifying the meaning of terminology and avoiding professional jargon as much as possible. Although the examiner will most likely assume a leadership role, presenting strengths, concerns, and recommendations based on an interpretation of the assessment data, it is important that all participants feel comfortable and welcome to make suggestions and discuss personal perspectives.

By having a meeting to discuss the assessment results, all participants can share information and gain mutual direction for future educational planning for the student with autism. For professionals, the assessment interpretation can be a valuable tool for creating individualized interventions. For parents, the meeting may help alleviate anxiety about their child's disability and build an understanding of how professionals will work with the student. Finally, owning assessment results among all of the persons related to the education of the student with autism, including the student him- or herself, provides an atmosphere of a team working to assist the student to overcome the challenges of autism.

Developing Assessment-Based Intervention Strategies

Students with autism demonstrate a wide range of discrepancies in skills and capabilities. Many have limited abilities of generalization and unique information processing functions. Teachers and other professionals are required to provide educational services that are precisely matched with the individual's needs. When an assessment allows for a thorough investigation of a student's strengths and concerns, it becomes a useful tool for developing these educational intervention strategies. For students with autism, assessment provides a direct link for establishing quality service models, since many students in this population do not function well in the classroom without individualized curricula. Therefore, integration of educational intervention and thorough and ongoing assessment enable highly individualized educational services for students with autism.

It is not a simple task to establish a routine of assessment-based intervention in daily school life. On the basis of a student's areas of strength, short- and long-range objectives are established to address deficits. Feedback on preferred teaching styles and response modes is used to select and develop curriculum and instructional procedures. The process concludes where it began, by continually reexamining the individual's skills and abilities and making modifications to the intervention procedures. Thus, the cycle of testing, teaching, and modifying continues throughout the student's educational life. Figure 2.5 shows how these components interface to provide a framework for developing instruction and intervention.

The following two case studies are presented as an illustration of practical applications of the various assessment tools and techniques discussed in this chapter. These studies depict two students with different diagnostic classifications, ages, skills, and needs.

Two Case Studies

 Jason

Jason is an 8-year-old student with high-functioning autistic disorder (HF-AD). He is placed in a third-grade general education classroom. Jason is very bright and possesses amazing memorization skills. For example, he is able to memorize lists of up to 50 items instantly and can accurately draw a cartoon character he has seen only once. Jason rarely initiates conversation spontaneously; however, he answers quite normally when asked questions. In spite of Jason's amazing memory skills, he does not obtain good grades in subjects that require creative or abstract thinking. Additionally, he is very inattentive to how he dresses. Occasionally, he returns from the restroom with his pants undone or not completely

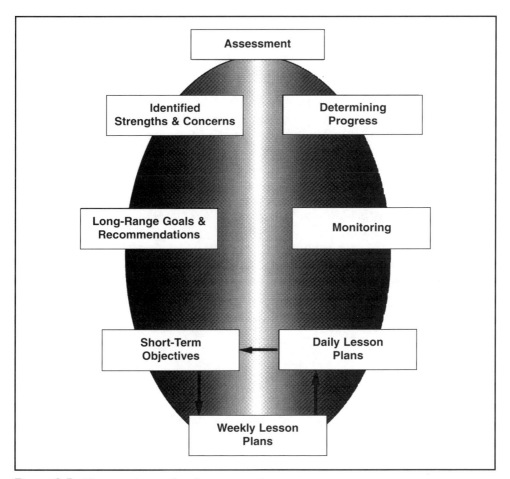

Figure 2.5. The ongoing cycle of assessment.

pulled up. Although Jason's peers are superficially friendly, mostly because of his ability to draw any requested superhero, he is usually a social outcast in day-to-day activities.

Jason's teacher was uncertain as to whether Jason's needs were being adequately addressed in her classroom. It was decided to assess Jason in order to determine his strengths and concerns in both academic and social areas. Since Jason appeared to have expressive language abilities, his examiner selected the WISC–III and the VABS to begin the assessment process.

Jason's scores on the WISC–III revealed that many of his skills fell within the expected range for a student of his age. An area of exception was those skills that required abstract thinking, such as comprehension, similarities, and picture arrangement. On these subtests, Jason's scores fell more than 2 standard deviations below the mean, indicating severe problems. The examiner recommended that Jason receive direct instruction in abstract thinking, using activities such as summarizing and drawing conclusions about stories. A scope and sequence assessment was selected to pinpoint the exact areas where Jason's reasoning skills were breaking down. This was supplemented with diagnostic teaching activities to determine which instructional and response models would enhance Jason's academic performance.

Scores on the VABS indicated that Jason's limited capabilities in communication and socialization were significantly impacting his interactions with teachers and peers. An ecobehavioral assessment was conducted to determine the various setting demands under which Jason was asked to perform social interactions. Peer-to-peer contacts were found to be highly difficult for Jason. A social skills training program, which included the use of social stories and peer buddies, was recommended to help Jason begin to develop peer relationships. In examining teacher instructional style, it was discovered that Jason responded more positively to concrete objects and gestures than to verbal directions. Therefore, it was suggested that the teacher pair visual and auditory stimuli when presenting new materials in class, along with implementing a visual schedule for Jason. A cue card was recommended to address Jason's toileting behavior, with external reinforcement provided for proper dressing before leaving the restroom.

 Winita

Winita is a 15-year-old girl with traditional autism. She is placed in a self-contained classroom for students with severe mental retardation and works 2 hours each day at an area sheltered workshop. Winita appears small for her age, and her general functions are immature compared to those of her nondisabled peers. Winita's language skills are very limited, although she can follow a few single-word directions such as "sit" or "quiet." Winita uses no expressive language, but consistently makes babbling utterances such as "boo-bah." Winita responds best when communicating using icons. At school, her teachers are working on increasing Winita's ability to use icons or gestures to communicate. Currently, when Winita wants teacher attention, she bites her own arm or hand.

Due to Winita's limited verbal abilities, the examiner chose the Leiter International Performance Scale *to assess her intellectual functioning. Winita's scores indicated that her development was significantly delayed. Although all her skills were below the expected range, Winita's daily living and motor skills were a relative strength. As transition goals were important for Winita, the AAPEP was administered to provide her teachers with developmental information that would help them determine if her current curriculum was too easy or too diffi-*

for building upon Winita's strengths to increase her daily living and functional academic skills were gained from this assessment information.

A traditional functional analysis was conducted in the school setting to determine any possible communicative intent of Winita's self-abusive behavior. Winita was taught a communication alternative to biting herself. She was given a small wooden clapper to shake when she wanted to obtain teacher attention. Teachers were requested to come to Winita's assistance as rapidly as possible each time she shook the clapper. The clapper was chosen because it was minimally disruptive to other class members; it was also important that the initial replacement behavior be as or more communicatively powerful than the aberrant behavior to ensure Winita would accept and use it. As Winita realized that she could obtain teacher attention with this method, the clapper would be faded for a less noisy alternative and wait time for teacher interaction would gradually be increased. This communication alternative served the same purpose but was more socially acceptable than her biting behavior.

Recommendations for Winita included staff training at school and the sheltered workshop to develop a greater understanding of her need to communicate and to increase sensitivity to her communicative attempts. Staff were also counseled to keep instructions brief, with limited verbiage around a simple command. It was also suggested that verbal directions be paired with icons or pictures to help Winita understand the intent of each activity. Communication cards containing icons for simple requests such as "bathroom" or "snack" were placed on a metal ring that Winita could wear on her belt loop and present when she desired certain activities.

Summary

As this chapter has shown, there are many different types of assessment procedures available for students with autism, enabling professionals to select a battery of measures most appropriate for each individualized student. Norm-referenced tests and developmental assessments are suitable for initial diagnosis, periodic comprehensive overview, and summative evaluation. Techniques of informal assessment can be chosen for daily or ongoing formative evaluation of student skills. Functional analysis provides insight into student behavior and communication, whereas portfolio assessment offers an ongoing collection of student growth, as well as a useful tool for career planning and development. Ecobehavioral measures allow for physical and interactional modifications to the learning environment. Together, these tools can provide a comprehensive picture of a student's abilities and needs, allowing practitioners and families to work collaboratively to create the optimal learning environment for the student with autism.

References

Bayley, N. (1969). *Manual for the Bayley scales of infant development.* New York: Psychological Corp.

Bernhardt, G. R., Cole, D. J., & Ryan, C. W. (1993). Improving career decision making with adults: Use of portfolios. *Journal of Employment Counseling, 30,* 67–73.

Carr, E. G. (1994). Emerging themes in the functional analysis of problem behavior. *Journal of Applied Behavior Analysis, 27,* 393–399.

Developmental Therapy Institute. (1992). *The developmental teaching objectives for the DTORF–R: Assessment and teaching of social–emotional competence* (4th ed.). Athens, GA: Author.

Durand, V. M., & Crimmins, D. B. (1988). Identifying the variables maintaining self-injurious behavior. *Journal of Autism and Developmental Disorders, 18,* 99–117.

Greenwood, C. R., Carta, J. J., & Atwater, J. (1991). Ecobehavioral analysis in the classroom: Review and implications. *Journal of Behavioral Education, 1*(1), 59–77.

Guerin, G. R., & Maier, A. S. (1983). *Informal assessment in education.* Palo Alto, CA: Mayfield.

Hendrick-Keefe, C. (1995, Winter). Portfolios: Mirrors of learning. *Teaching Exceptional Children, 27*(2), 66–67.

Horner, R. H. (1994). Functional assessment: Contributions and future directions. *Journal of Applied Behavior Analysis, 27,* 401–404.

Hudson, F. G., Colson, S. E., Welch, D. L. H., Banikowski, A. K., & Mehring, T. A. (1989). *Hudson education skills inventory.* Austin, TX: PRO-ED.

Iwata, B. A., Dorsey, M. F., Slifer, K. J., Bauman, K. E., & Richman, G. S. (1982). Toward a functional analysis of self-injury. *Analysis and Intervention in Developmental Disabilities, 2,* 3–20.

Kamps, D. M., Leonard, B. R., Dugan, E. P., Boland, B., & Greenwood, C. R. (1991). The use of ecobehavioral assessment to identify naturally occurring effective procedures in classrooms serving students with autism and other developmental disabilities. *Journal of Behavioral Education, 1,* 367–397.

Kern, L., Dunlap, G., Clark, E. S., & Childs, K. E. (1994). Student-assisted functional assessment interview. *Diagnostique, 19*(2/3), 29–39.

Lambert, N., Windmiller, M., Tharinger, D., & Cole, L. (1981). *American Association on Mental Deficiency adaptive behavior scale–School edition.* Monterrey, CA: CTB/McGraw-Hill.

Leiter, R. G. (1969). *General instructions for the Leiter international performance scale.* Chicago: Soelting.

Lewis, T. J., Scott, T. M., & Suigai, G. (1994). The problem behavior questionnaire: A teacher-based instrument to develop functional hypotheses of problem behavior in general education classrooms. *Diagnostique, 19*(2/3), 103–115.

Marcus, L. M. (1978). Developmental assessment as a basis for planning educational programs for autistic children. *Behavioral Disorders, 3,* 219–226.

McCarthy, D. (1972). *Manual for the McCarthy scales of children's abilities.* San Antonio, TX: Psychological Corp.

Mesibov, G. B., Schopler, E., & Caison, W. (1989). The adolescent and adult psychoeducational profile: Assessment of adolescents and adults with severe developmental handicaps. *Journal of Autism and Developmental Disorders, 19,* 33–40.

Mesibov, G. B., Schopler, E., Schaffer, B., & Landus, R. (1988). *Individualized assessment and treatment for autistic and developmentally disabled children: Adolescent and adult psychoeducational profile: Volume 4.* Austin, TX: PRO-ED.

Moran, M. R. (1995). *Teacher assessment for instructional planning.* Unpublished manuscript.

Myles, B. S., Constant, J. A., Simpson, R. L., & Carlson, J. K. (1989). Educational assessment of students with higher-functioning autistic disorder. *Focus on Autistic Behavior, 4*(1), 1–13.

Newland, T. E. (1973). Assumptions underlying psychological testing. *Journal of School Psychology, 11,* 316–322.

Nolet, V. (1992). Classroom-based measurement and portfolio assessment. *Diagnostique, 18*(1), 5–26.

Parks, S. L. (1988). Psychometric instruments available for the assessment of autistic children. In E. Schopler & G. B. Mesibov (Eds.), *Diagnosis and assessment in autism* (pp. 123–138). New York: Plenum.

Repp, A. C., & Singh, N. N. (1990). *Perspectives on the use of nonaversive and aversive interventions for persons with developmental disabilities.* DeKalb, IL: Sycamore.

Salvia, J., & Ysseldyke, J. E. (1991). *Assessment* (5th ed.). Boston: Houghton Mifflin.

Sarkees-Wircenski, M., & Wircenski, J. L. (1994). Transition planning: Developing a career portfolio for students with disabilities. *Career Development for Exceptional Individuals, 17,* 203–214.

Sasso, G. M., & Reimers, T. M. (1988). Assessing the functional properties of behavior: Implications and applications for the classroom. *Focus on Autistic Behavior, 3*(5), 1–15.

Schopler, E., Reichler, R. J., Bashford, A., Lansing, M. D., & Marcus, L. M. (1990). *Individualized assessment and treatment for autistic and developmentally disabled children: Psychoeducational profile–Revised.* Austin, TX: PRO-ED.

Schutt, P. W., & McCabe, V. M. (1994). Portfolio assessment for students with learning disabilities. *Learning Disability Quarterly, 5*(2), 81–85.

Sparrow, S., Balla, D., & Cicchetti, D. (1984). *Interview edition of the survey form manual: Vineland adaptive behavior scales.* Circle Pines, MN: American Guidance Service.

Swicegood, P. (1994). Portfolio-based assessment practices: The uses of portfolio assessment for students with behavioral disorders or learning disabilities. *Intervention in School and Clinic, 30*(1), 6–15.

Thorndike, R. L., Hagen, E., & Sattler, J. (1985). *Stanford-Binet intelligence scale* (4th ed.). Chicago: Riverside.

Touchette, P. E., MacDonald, R. F., & Langer, S. N. (1985). A scatterplot for identifying stimulus control of problem behavior. *Journal of Applied Behavior Analysis, 18,* 343–351.

Wechsler, D. (1991). *Wechsler intelligence scale for children* (3rd ed.). Cleveland, OH: Psychological Corp.

Wesson, C. L., & King, R. P. (1992). The role of curriculum-based measurement in portfolio assessment. *Diagnostique, 18*(1), 27–37.

Wing, L., & Gould, J. (1979). Severe impairments of social interaction and associated abnormalities in children: Epidemiology and classification. *Journal of Autism and Developmental Disorders, 9,* 11–29.

Instructional Strategies To Facilitate Successful Learning Outcomes for Students with Autism

3

Theresa L. Earles, Judith K. Carlson, and Stacey Jones Bock

Designing an educational program for students with autism can present unique challenges for administrators and practitioners. An effective classroom must include a physical structure that enhances learning opportunities and instructional approaches that facilitate language acquisition, behavior management, social skills, and targeted academic goals. Many of the basic principles of effective instruction used in general education apply to working with students with autism. Certain strategies, however, have proven to be particularly effective with students with autism. These strategies provide structure and predictability to the learning process, allow students to anticipate task requirements and setting expectations, and teach a variety of skills across content areas in the natural environment, enhancing the likelihood of generalization.

This chapter highlights techniques and strategies recommended for use with children and youth with autism. Strategies include ways to create environmental supports to provide students with structure and consistency in the learning environment and techniques for developing behaviorally based communication tools to enhance student attention and on-task behavior. Methods for expanding response opportunities and increasing student flexibility are discussed, as well as specific instructional procedures for teaching students with autism.

Creating Environmental Supports

Environmental supports help organize a student's physical space in ways that facilitate the ability to predict events and activities, anticipate change, understand expectations, and, in general, make sense of the environment. Dalrymple

(1995) defined environmental supports as "aspects of the environment other than interactions with people that affect the learning that takes place" (p. 244). Environmental supports may include the use of (a) labels, (b) boundary settings, (c) visual schedules, (d) behaviorally based communication tools, (e) activity-completion signals, (f) choice boards, and (g) waiting supports. These strategies allow students to respond more appropriately in day-to-day activities by increasing independence and stimulating language development.

Labels

The physical organization of the classroom can be a crucial element for enhancing success. Structure and predictability facilitate the student's understanding of the environment, thus decreasing the likelihood of worry and agitation. This is particularly important for students with autism who tend to react negatively to change and uncertainty in their environment.

Acts as simple as labeling furniture and objects in the classroom can have numerous benefits. A good place to begin is by marking tubs and/or containers with visual representations, such as a miniature object, icon, and/or written label that names the object(s) in the bin. The shelf that houses the bin can also be marked with the same label. Students can then be taught to match the label on the container to the label on the shelf, allowing independence in retrieving or returning an activity to its appropriate place in the classroom.

Classroom labeling promotes language development as well. For example, if the furniture in the classroom is labeled, students have a visual cue to pair with the teacher's verbal cue when given requests such as "Sit in chair" or "Stand by door." Labels can also be used to delineate specific areas of the room. For example, enlarged symbols that represent leisure-time activities, reading, or gross motor skills can be hung above or taped to the area specified for that activity.

Boundary Settings

The use of boundary markers to establish physical space for a specific activity such as playing, reading, or cooking helps students differentiate setting expectations. This method can easily be applied by sectioning an area on the floor with colored tape, rugs, carpet remnants, or other materials that indicate to the student where to remain during a given activity (Dalrymple, 1993). If two or more tasks must be completed in the same area or at the same work space, using a colored tablecloth can distinguish one activity from another. For example, reading could take place with the table uncovered and when it is time for math, a checkered table cloth could be used to signal the change of activity.

Visual Schedules

A visual schedule provides students with an overview of the day's activities and events by depicting general tasks that will occur at specific times. Visual schedules are tools that present an abstract concept such as time in a more concrete and manageable form. The use of visual schedules with students with autism can provide a myriad of benefits. For example, visual schedules allow students to anticipate upcoming events and activities, develop an understanding of time, and facilitate the ability to predict change (Brown, 1991). In addition, visual schedules can be used to stimulate communicative exchanges by discussing past, present, and future events (Twachtman, 1995) and to teach new skills such as self-care and grooming (Thinesen & Bryan, 1981). Finally, visual schedules have been used to increase on-task behavior while enhancing the student's ability to independently make the transition from one activity to another (MacDuff, Krantz, & McClannahan, 1993). A major benefit of visual schedules is that they capitalize on the visual strength exhibited by many students with autism.

Level of Visual Representation

When constructing a visual schedule, the practitioner must make decisions based on the strengths and needs of the targeted student. Using these student characteristics, the practitioner constructs a visual schedule that corresponds to that student's ability to understand visual representation. There is a hierarchy of levels of representation that goes from concrete to abstract. As would be expected, the more abstract the visual schedule, the higher the level of representation. For students who require concrete visual cues to understand upcoming events, an object schedule that uses the actual materials from each of the scheduled activities can be designed. For example, if a math lesson requires the use of colored blocks as manipulatives, then a colored block could be attached to the visual schedule to represent math. If the student is expected to brush his or her teeth after lunch, then a toothbrush could be placed on the schedule to indicate to the student that it is time to brush teeth (Eno-Hieneman, Dunlap, & Reed, 1995). Photographs of the student completing a targeted activity can also be used on the visual schedule with students who require concrete representation. More advanced students may benefit from schedules that use icons, written words, or sentences.

It is important to determine the appropriate level of visual representation for each student and then pair that level with the next higher level. For example, if a student is functioning at the photograph level, a colored drawing can be paired with the photograph to introduce the higher level concept. Similarly, if a student is functioning at the black-and-white drawing or icon level, written words can be paired with the icon. Clock faces can be added to the visual schedule to begin to introduce the concept of time. Table 3.1 lists the levels of visual representation from highest to lowest.

Arrangement of Visual Representation

Schedules can be arranged in either a left-to-right or top-to-bottom format. Although either placement is acceptable, the left-to-right arrangement supports

Table 3.1

Hierarchy of Levels of Representation

Highest	Icon of sign language
	Written phrase or sentence
	Written word
	Icon (black-and-white line drawing)
	Colored drawing
	Photograph
	Miniature object
	Full-sized object
Lowest	Physical gesture

behavior required for reading. Each student's individual needs must be taken into account when one is selecting an arrangement for the visual schedule. Schedules can be constructed in a variety of formats. When selecting a format, consider the length of time the schedule will be used, how durable the materials must be to meet the demands of the individual student, and whether the schedule will be permanently placed or must be mobile. Table 3.2 provides a sample of possible schedule formats.

Student Participation in Creating Visual Schedules

Students may enjoy and sometimes may feel more comfortable when allowed to participate in preparing their visual schedule. This participation can occur first thing in the morning, either when the student enters the room or during morning calendar group. Students can assist in assembling their schedule,

Table 3.2

Sample Schedule Formats

- Place in a photo album or three-ring binder

- Hang on the classroom wall

- Place in a pocket chart

- Write on a white board or chalkboard

- Tape to the student's desk

- Place on hole-punched cards that can hang on the student's belt loop with an O-ring

- Place on a notecard that can go in a belt pouch or the student's wallet

copying it, or adding their own personal touch in some other manner. This interactive time can be used to review the daily routine, discuss changes, and reinforce rules (Hodgdon, 1995). Figure 3.1 shows a sample visual schedule combining icons, words, and clock faces (see Note).

Mini-Schedules and Task Organizers

Mini-schedules complement the daily schedule by providing more specific cues about activities. They allow greater individualization because they can be designed to target specific learning tasks. For example, during the time designated on the daily schedule for math, the student would select the math icon and move to the math table or work area. There the student would find his or her mini-schedule pasted onto a piece of cardboard, placed in a small photo album, or taped to the work space. The mini-schedule would display the same math icon as the daily schedule and would direct the student through the activities that will occur during the math lesson. Figure 3.2 shows a sample mini-schedule for a math lesson.

A task organizer, sometimes referred to as a "cookbook," can be used to add more structure to the lesson or activity depicted on the mini-schedule (Hodgdon, 1995). Task organizers provide a task analysis, or breakdown, of the steps required to complete a specific activity. In the case of the math lesson, a task organizer could be used to further describe the steps within a specific activity, such as writing numbers from 1 to 10. Figure 3.3 shows a sample task organizer.

A mini-schedule can also be designed to provide opportunities for choice making. For example, a mini-schedule for a cooking lesson could direct a student through the stages required for preparing and consuming a snack. At specific points along the mini-schedule, the student would be required to make a choice between two or more items to create the snack. In this application, the mini-schedule provides both the structure and the opportunity for decision making. Figure 3.4 shows a sample combination mini-schedule and choice-making menu. A task organizer can also be added to further structure the activity. Figure 3.5 displays a sample task organizer detailing the steps for making popcorn in the microwave, one of the snack choices on the student's mini-schedule for snack.

Mini-schedules and task organizers should be used only when students need extra structure to understand activities or to provide opportunities for choice and decision making. These tools can be applied in layers, encouraging students to function at their most appropriate independent level. For example, some students require minimal external structure and would need only a daily schedule to keep on task. A student needing more assistance to complete the tasks on his or her daily schedule would benefit from a series of mini-schedules for each major activity on the daily schedule. Finally, for students who need maximum structure to work independently, a combination of daily schedule, mini-schedule, and task organizers would be most effective.

(*text continues on page 65*)

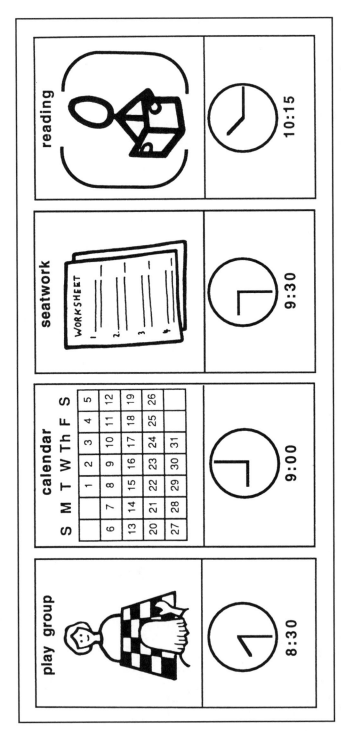

Figure 3.1. Sample of daily schedule. *Note.* The Mayer-Johnson Picture Communication Symbols reproduced in this figure are used with the permission of the Mayer-Johnson Co. Copyright 1981–1997.

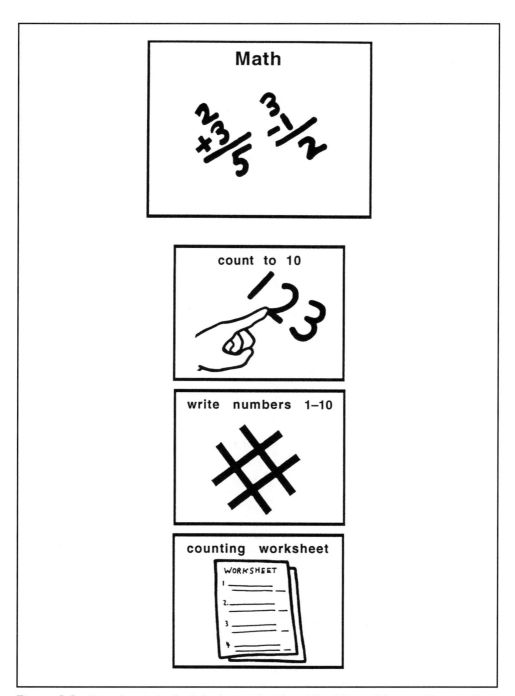

Figure 3.2. Sample mini-schedule for math. *Note.* The Mayer-Johnson Picture Communication Symbols reproduced in this figure are used with permission of the Mayer-Johnson Co. Copyright 1981–1997.

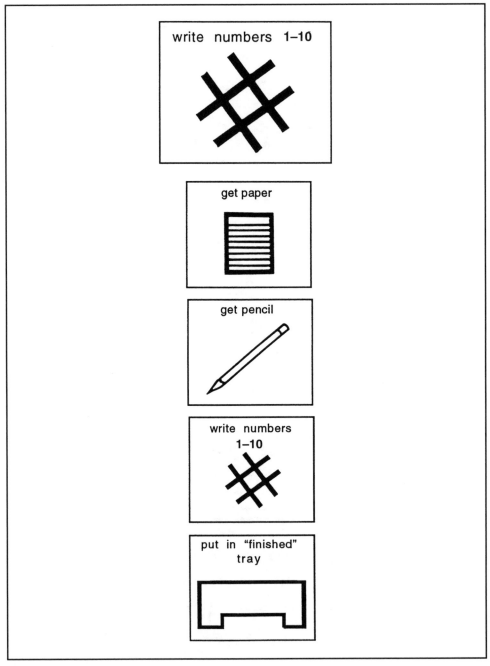

Figure 3.3. Sample task organizer for writing numbers 1 to 10. *Note.* The Mayer-Johnson Picture Communication Symbols reproduced in this figure are used with permission of the Mayer-Johnson Co. Copyright 1981–1997.

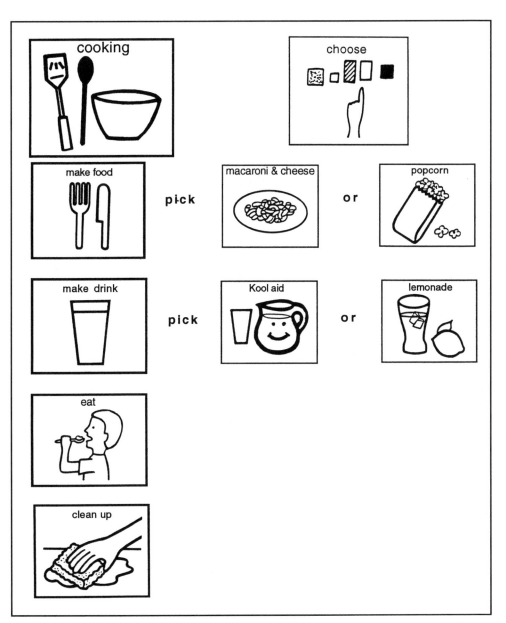

Figure 3.4. Combination mini-schedule and choice-making menu. *Note.* The Mayer-Johnson Picture Communication Symbols reproduced in this figure are used with permission of the Mayer-Johnson Co. Copyright 1981–1997.

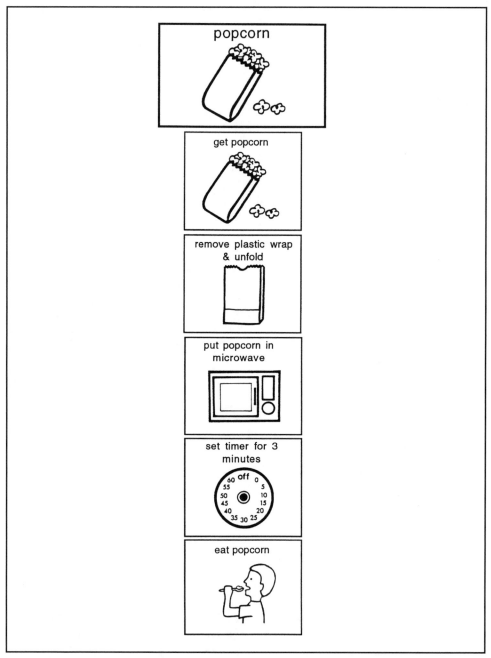

Figure 3.5. Sample task organizer for making popcorn. *Note.* The Mayer-Johnson Picture Communication Symbols reproduced in this figure are used with permission of the Mayer-Johnson Co. Copyright 1981–1997.

Behaviorally Based Communication Tools

Behaviorally based communication tools are teacher-oriented techniques used to enhance communication with students and provide behavioral support. These techniques can help teachers gain and maintain student attention, provide support for on-task behavior, make directions more clear and concise, and encourage basic communication (Hodgdon, 1995).

Picture Card Files

Picture card files are a set of cards in a graphic format that assign different tasks to be accomplished during a specific period of time, such as a transition within a given activity. The teacher gives the student a card that specifically directs what he or she should do during that time. For example, while completing an art project, the student is asked to get crayons. The teacher would pull a picture or icon of crayons from the picture card file and give it to the student as a visual tool. Picture cards help students organize their behavior and remain focused, thereby allowing them to respond successfully to teacher direction (Hodgdon, 1995).

Teacher Minibooks

Teacher minibooks are groupings of pictures and/or words for generic items for student direction that are used throughout the day. Direction pictures or icons are placed on separate pages or index cards and inserted into a small photo album or index card notebook. As the teacher gives the student a direction, he or she also provides a picture that represents the targeted direction. Teacher minibooks can be divided into different categories or academic areas, which may include the pictures for general directions such as "Raise your hand," "Sit in seat," or "Hands in lap." Transition minibooks may also contain directions for lining up, waiting in the hall, and being quiet (Hodgdon, 1995).

Teacher Notebook

A teacher notebook is a three-ring binder containing pages of visuals that are developed for use during a specific activity. The notebook can be laid open on a table or work area and is designed for use with small groups of students rather than individual participants. Oversized visuals can be mounted on cardboard for display with larger groups of students (Hodgdon, 1995).

Activity-Completion Signals

Many students with autism have difficulty knowing how long an activity will last or when they will be asked to switch their focus to another task. Activity-completion signals such as "finished pockets" or a "finished box" can provide support for activity transition. Finished pockets can be constructed using a large manila envelope or cloth pocket hung near the student's visual schedule. When the student completes an activity, he or she removes the representative object, photograph, or icon and places it in the finished pocket. During this time, the teacher may say and/or sign a "finished" phrase such as "Math is finished. Time for recess."

Other types of activity-completion signals may include (a) turning a visual schedule card around so that it is facing backward, (b) placing an object or an icon in a finished box, (c) crossing out a word or phrase written on a chalkboard or wipe-off board, and/or (d) setting timers for a specified period of work time. As with visual schedules, the student's functional level must be considered when determining the level of abstraction for a completion signal.

Choice Boards

A choice board is placed in the classroom to provide students with decision-making opportunities. As such, it displays objects, pictures, icons, or words that represent a menu of activities or reinforcers. It can be constructed using poster paper or any surface to which objects or icons can be attached. Velcro™ provides an excellent medium for adhering materials to a choice board and allows flexibility and ease for moving or switching objects.

The choice board can be placed next to a student's daily schedule. When a designated choice time or break time arrives, the student can select a preferred activity from the board. Additionally, choice boards displaying preferred activities can be placed near the free-time or break area of the room, providing a stimulus for independent selection of an activity. Figure 3.6 shows a sample choice-making menu for leisure-time activities.

Waiting Supports

Waiting is a difficult skill for many children to learn. For students with autism, waiting frequently presents problems because they have limited ability to delay gratification and often do not understand the concept of waiting. Therefore, these students will most likely require specific instruction to develop appropriate waiting behavior. First, role-playing or practice sessions using direct instruction should be provided to ensure that students possess the prerequisite skills necessary to engage in waiting behavior. These simulated activities should be authentic and take place in natural settings. Waiting skills should be taught across a variety of settings to increase the likelihood of generalization. Providing a peer model or peer buddy during waiting times can offer visual support for the desired behavior. Specific physical supports such as placing chairs

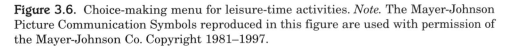

Figure 3.6. Choice-making menu for leisure-time activities. *Note.* The Mayer-Johnson Picture Communication Symbols reproduced in this figure are used with permission of the Mayer-Johnson Co. Copyright 1981–1997.

near the waiting area, setting a timer, or holding a picture representing "wait" may also enhance learning of this concept.

Enhancing Response Opportunities

For learning to take place, it is essential for students to have active involvement with their teachers, their peers, and the curriculum. As students with autism tend to be passive learners, it is necessary to plan activities that require students to become active participants. Creating opportunities for student response is a high instructional priority; research supports a functional relationship between academic performance and the frequency with which a student has the opportunity to respond (Greenwood, Delquadri, & Hall, 1984; Kamps et al., 1991). As rates of active student responding increase, off-task and disruptive behaviors decrease (Carnine, 1976; Miller, Hall, & Heward, 1995; Sainato, Strain, & Lyon, 1987). Specific instructional techniques that increase student response opportunities include (a) direct instruction, (b) choral responding, (c) response cards, (d) motivating objects, (e) choice making, (f) situational sabotage, and (g) silly situations. Each of these techniques is briefly discussed below.

Direct Instruction

Traditional direct instruction is a teacher-led model that provides frequent interaction between teacher and students. These interactions are usually scripted to ensure that teachers know exactly what to say throughout the lesson (Carnine, 1991). The script not only provides a text for teachers to follow, but also indicates specific moments in the lesson when teachers should elicit student response. In direct instruction, all students respond frequently using a variety of verbal and physical response modes, including verbalizing an answer, writing an answer, or performing an action.

Due to the frequent response rate involved in direct instruction, this technique is effective in helping students focus and maintain their attention. Table 3.3 describes 10 steps to consider when using direct instruction with students with autism.

Choral Responding

A simple method to increase student response rate is choral responding (Heward, Courson, & Narayan, 1989; Kamps, Dugan, Leonard, & Dauoust, 1994; Sindelar,

Table 3.3
Ten Steps for Using Direct Instruction with Students with Autism

1. Use a small-group setting of approximately 2 to 6 students.

2. Select specific objectives for each student to master during the lesson.

3. Preplan a structured lesson in which the topic is teacher controlled.

4. Keep the lesson moving at a brisk pace with minimal down time.

5. Actively involve students by asking content-related questions that are primarily factual.

6. Model correct responses and provide additional examples.

7. Provide 3 seconds of wait time for student response.

8. Offer immediate, corrective feedback and probe until correct responses are obtained.

9. Reinforce students for correct responses.

10. Provide opportunities for independent practice after students have achieved an accuracy rate of 90% to 95%.

Bursuck, & Halle, 1986). In choral responding, all students in a group reply in unison to a teacher-posed question. Choral responding is particularly effective for students with autism because it requires direct engagement and provides immediate modeling of the appropriate response. Further, with increased opportunities to respond, students have less unstructured time during a lesson. Students with verbal language skills can provide verbal responses, and students lacking verbal language skills can provide pictorial, signing, or gestural responses.

Heward et al. (1989) proposed a systematic process for conducting an effective and enjoyable choral responding session. The following sample lesson shows how to apply this process to teach students to identify primary colors.

1. The teacher models the response by holding up a color card with a yellow circle and verbalizing, "What is this color? Answer: Yellow." In several trials, the teacher responds in both teacher and student roles.

2. The teacher poses the question to the class, "What is this color?" A wait time of 4 to 6 seconds should occur to allow students to think about their answer. (As students become more proficient in the choral response format, some activities will require a quicker response time.) A clear signal must be given to indicate to students when to verbalize their response. In this lesson, the teacher has selected "answer" as the response signal, but a specific gesture, such as raising and dropping his or her hand to indicate that it is time to verbalize the response "yellow," would be equally appropriate. A clear signal increases the likelihood of unity of student response and must be taught as part of the lesson.

3. The teacher provides feedback for the choral response. This is done by repeating the correct answer, "This circle is yellow," before presenting the next question. This feedback allows students who answered incorrectly to hear the correct response again. To randomly assess student performance, the teacher should call on individual students to repeat or paraphrase the correct response. Throughout the lesson the teacher must maintain a lively and energetic pace. The more items that are presented, the more opportunities students have to respond. Increased response opportunities encourage students to remain focused and on task.

Response Cards

Another method proven to increase active student responding is the use of response cards (Gardner, Heward, & Grossi, 1994; Narayan, Heward, & Gardner, 1990). A response card is any object, such as a sign, an item, or a felt board, that the student can hold up in response to a teacher-presented question. Response cards, like choral responding, increase the opportunities to participate in a group setting and can be adapted to a wide variety of content areas (Heward et al., 1996). For example, response cards could be used in an academic lesson to provide yes/no or true/false responses or in an opinion poll to determine agreement or disagreement.

Three common types of response cards are (a) preprinted cards, (b) write-on cards, and (c) moveable-parts cards. Preprinted cards are hand-held signs that have one- or two-word answers written on them, such as true/false, yes/no, colors, or numbers. The background color or shape of the card can be designed to provide additional distinction between possible answers, such as placing a brightly colored background on the desired response. Write-on cards are blank index cards, wipe-off boards, or small hand-held chalkboards that can be easily erased between question-and-answer trials. Finally, cards with moveable parts include items such as a clock face with moveable hands or a felt board with removable pieces.

Response cards are used in much the same way as choral responding; however, they provide a way to include nonverbal students in the mainstream activity without requiring individual adaptation. Response cards offer the opportunity for higher level responding for all students.

Motivating Objects

Through observing the student in a variety of settings, the teacher can begin to determine which objects appear to be most motivating. Motivating objects can be toys, food, activities, or any acceptable reinforcer from which the student appears to derive a high level of enjoyment. Once a student's motivating objects have been identified, they can then be used to create response opportunities. For example, the teacher can place the motivating object within the student's visual field but out of the student's reach. This will provide the student an opportunity to request the object, item, or activity by pointing or attempting a verbalization. In this way, the object can then be incorporated into the student's lesson. Motivating objects can also be used as reinforcers in the student's management plan.

Choice Making

Making choices is an integral part of daily living. Students with autism must be offered a variety of opportunities for choice making throughout their day. Choice making gives students control over their environment, promotes independence, increases motivation to learn, and allows the teacher an opportunity to provide instruction within the context of the natural environment (Bambara & Koger, 1996; Brown, Belz, Corsi, & Wenig, 1993; Ostrosky & Kaiser, 1991). Opportunities for choice making also facilitate "personal satisfaction and quality of life" (Bambara & Koger, 1996, p. 3). The following section describes strategies for incorporating choice-making opportunities into daily classroom activities and across natural environments.

As discussed, visual schedules can be used to introduce the concept of choice making. A choice-making time can be directly placed into the student's daily routine. An object, photograph, or icon that represents the concept of choice is placed on the student's schedule, with a variety of activity symbols under the choice symbol. When the student reaches this point in the day, he or she may choose one or more of the activities to complete during that period. Choice making should begin with the option of only two activity symbols and increase gradually as the student grasps the concept. Offering the student a choice between a highly preferred item and a nonpreferred item can also be helpful in the beginning teaching stages.

Choice making can also be tied to a student's reinforcement plan. A menu of reinforcers can be developed and a sample selection provided as daily reinforcement options. When the student completes a certain number of behavioral items, for example, he or she may select a reinforcer from the menu. This technique allows for an easy rotation of reinforcers and helps combat reinforcement satiation. Figure 3.7 shows a sample token economy strip for reinforcement. Figure 3.8 provides an example of how to incorporate choice making directly into a token system.

Another method for assisting parents and professionals in increasing student's choice-making opportunities was developed by Brown et al. (1993). The Model of Choice Diversity describes seven categories of choice making that are readily available in most daily routines. These seven categories are (a) "within activities"—the student chooses materials to be used in an activity; (b) "between activities"—the student selects among different activities; (c) "refusal"—the student can elect not to participate in an activity; (d) "who"—the student determines who is included in or excluded from an activity; (e) "where"—the student chooses the location for an activity; (f) "when"—the student determines what time the activity should occur; and (g) "terminate"—the student decides when to end an activity. This model allows parents and professionals to examine the student's daily activities and routines and provides a structure in which to delineate specific occasions when choice-making opportunities can be provided. It should be emphasized that all types of choices should be available within a given routine. Figure 3.9 provides a sample format for The Model of Choice Diversity.

Situational Sabotage

"Situational sabotage" is a teacher-contrived activity designed to elicit a request for help from a student. To create situational sabotage, (a) give the student a familiar activity to complete, (b) leave out an important component of the activity, and (c) instruct the student to complete the activity. For example, the teacher could give the student a coloring sheet to complete and provide all but one or two of the designated colors that the student needs to complete the task. The teacher then observes if the student ignores the need for additional supplies, requests help, or becomes frustrated with the task. These situational responses can subsequently be used to teach or enhance appropriate requesting behaviors (Hawkins, 1995; Kaiser & Hester, 1996; Ostrosky & Kaiser, 1991).

(text continues on page 75)

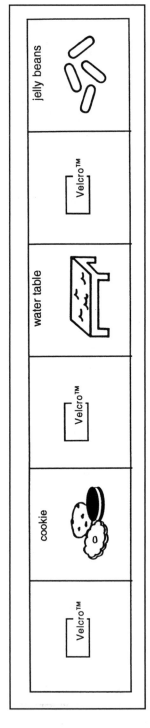

Figure 3.7. Sample token economy strip. *Note.* The Mayer-Johnson Picture Communication Symbols reproduced in this figure are used with permission of the Mayer-Johnson Co. Copyright 1981–1997.

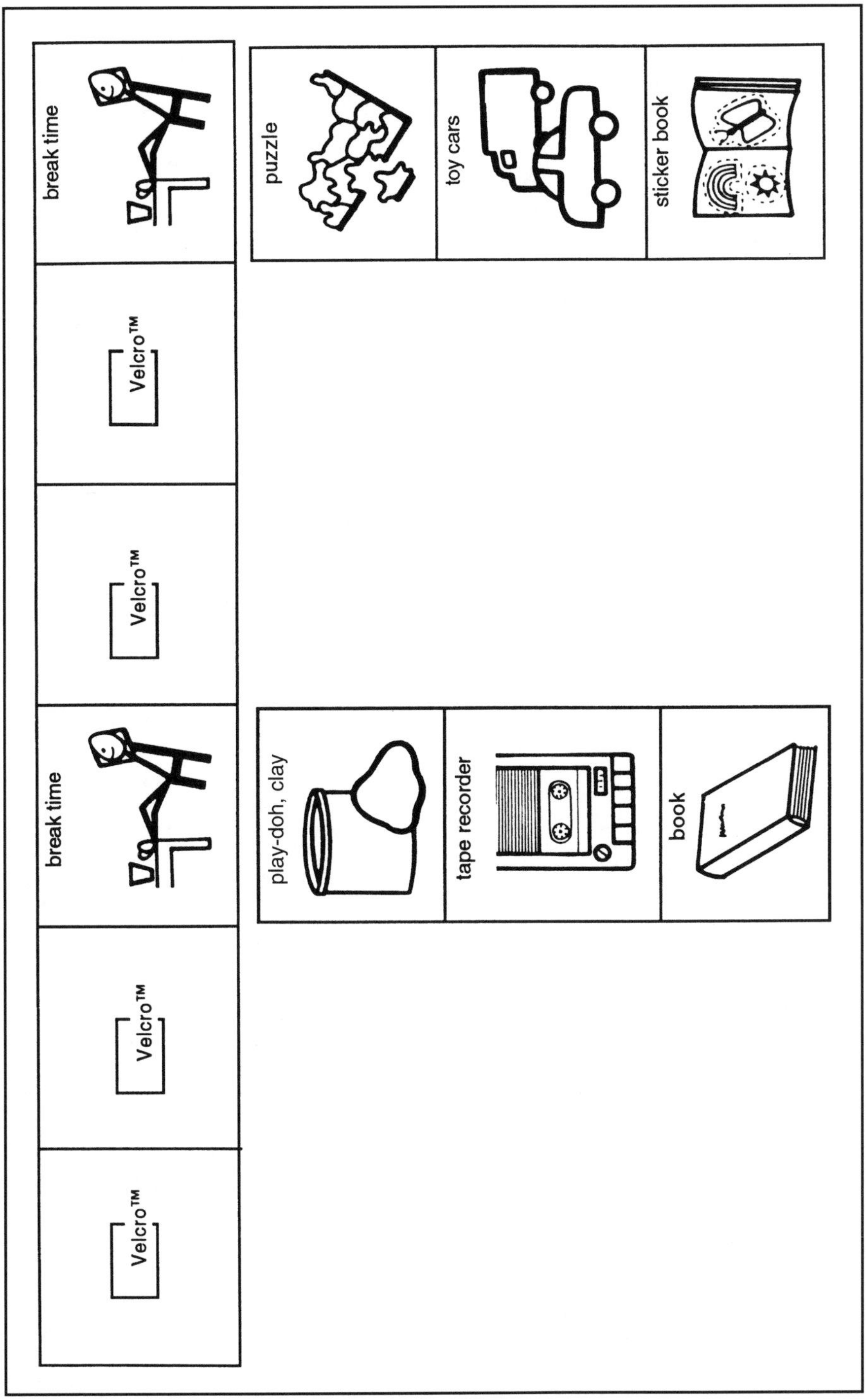

Figure 3.8. Incorporation of choice making into a token system. *Note.* The Mayer-Johnson Picture Communication Symbols reproduced in this figure are used with permission of the Mayer-Johnson Co. Copyright 1981–1997.

CHOICE DIVERSITY

Instructor _____ Learner _____ Setting _____ Review Date _____

CHOICE OPTIONS

Routine	Within	Between	Refusal	Who	Where	When	Terminate
Toilet			"I don't have to go"	"Who's going to take me?"	Which stall	Now or later	Finished
AM Group	Materials	Activity Order		Choose partner	Which seat		Finished
Snack	Drink, food		"No"		Which seat		Finished
Free Play	All available			Choose partner			Finished
Music	Instrument			Choose partner	Which rug		Finished

Figure 3.9. The Model of Choice Diversity. Adapted from "Choice diversity of people with severe disabilities," by F. Brown, P. Belz, L. Corsi, and B. Wenig, 1993, *Education and Training in Mental Retardation, 28*(4), 318–326.

Silly Situations

"Silly situations" are another teacher-contrived activity that stimulates communication. Silly situations are developed by changing or recreating an everyday common experience through adding a humorous or nonsensical component (Ostrosky & Kaiser, 1991). For example, suppose a student brings a daily lunch containing a sandwich, chips, and a cookie. To create a silly situation, the teacher could replace the cookie in the student's lunch box with a plastic cookie. When the student opens up the lunch to eat, he or she will be surprised and have an opportunity for interactive communication with the teacher. Silly situations should be developed on the basis of the abstract abilities of the individual student. Some lower functioning students, for example, might try to eat the plastic cookie. Other ideas for silly situations could include the teacher's trying to pour a glass of juice from a closed container or putting on the student's coat instead of his or her own coat when going out for recess.

Introducing Change and Building Flexibility

Daily living is not a static activity. Students are required to move from one activity to another, adapt to schedule interruptions, and respond to a variety of setting demands. The concept of change is challenging for many students with autism. One effective way to introduce change is through the student's visual schedule. A change symbol, such as the word *change* or a pictorial representation of change, can replace the symbol for the expected activity. For example, if the high school choir is performing and the class will be attending the assembly instead of going to music class, the change symbol could be placed in the time slot usually slated for music class. It is important that the students see or participate in the removal and replacement process. A discussion of what will happen instead of the scheduled activity should also take place. For some students, it may be necessary to visit the location of the new activity or to view the replacement materials while carrying or holding the change symbol. Posting a phrase like "We usually have . . ." at the top of the schedule can help the student understand that change is an expected variation in the routine (Gray, 1995).

Flexibility

Students with autism frequently demand consistency in their environment. If these demands are not addressed, these students may throw tantrums, refuse to participate, or perseverate on the requested change. Although teachers strive to provide structure and predictability in the classroom, it is important to realize that change is an integral part of daily living. Flexibility is such an important characteristic for successful day-to-day functioning that it may be necessary for the teacher to actually plan for changes in the daily routine so that students can practice flexibility. Changes should be very small in the beginning. For example, during math, instead of sorting the colors red and blue, the student may be asked to sort the colors red and green. At lunch, the placement of the student's fork and spoon may be switched so that the student is required to pick them up in a different order. As students learn to accept these small changes, larger changes can be introduced, such as the order of math and reading sessions. Before introducing change as a planned part of the curricula, be certain that students are familiar with the typical schedule and understand how it works.

Transition

Experiencing transition between activities and among different areas of the classroom and school can be difficult for students with autism. For some students, this difficulty may be influenced by an inability to understand what is happening, causing confusion and unpredictability. For others, transition problems may be products of an innate resistance to change, or the student may simply prefer to continue with an enjoyable activity (Groden & LeVasseur, 1995).

All these situations can lead to undesirable or inappropriate behavior. However, supports can be implemented to make transition periods more palatable for students with autism. The primary principle behind these techniques is to provide students with information that will allow them to better understand their environment, thereby reducing the potential for problem behavior (Hodgdon, 1995). These supports include (a) schedules and transition symbols, (b) time limit warnings, and (c) transition routines.

Schedules and Transition Symbols

During transition periods, students can carry a picture or object from their daily schedule as a reminder of the correct destination. If the room is divided and labeled with enlarged symbols, the student can match symbols from the daily schedule to those posted in the activity area. At the completion of an activity, the student can retrieve the symbol, place it in a "finished" box or pocket, and return to the schedule to determine the next activity. This strategy will provide students with transition support and concurrently facilitate independence.

Time Limit Warnings

Giving students warnings regarding the amount of time remaining in an activity can provide a helpful frame of reference. Time limit warnings should be paired with an auditory or visual cue, such as a bell or timer. Periodically throughout the work period, the teacher should verbalize, "Five minutes left. When the timer sounds, _____ will be finished, and it will be time for _____." For students requiring additional support, the verbal cue can be paired with a gesture such as pointing to the timer and manually signing "finished."

When preparing students for the end of an activity that has a natural ending point, such as a game or matching task, the teacher should alert students that a transition is approaching by making a statement such as, "Only a few more cards and then the game is over" (Hodgdon, 1995).

One concrete way to prepare students for transition is to place a colored card or other symbol on the student's desk that will clue the student that an activity will conclude in a specified time frame, such as 5 minutes. Another approach is to lay the numbers 5, 3, 1, and the symbol that represents "finished" on the student's desk. As the timer ticks down, the teacher can remove the corresponding number while verbalizing the time warning.

Transition Routines

Making transitions a planned part of the student's routine can also help students with autism develop the capacity to be flexible in the face of change. Teaching students to put away materials at the completion of a task can function as a natural cue that one activity is ending and another is beginning. If students are reluctant to leave a preferred activity, let them know when they will be able to return. For example, the teacher can state, "You can finish listening to your tape at break," or, "You can play with the ball again at recess." To facilitate smooth transitions, set up the daily schedule using a balance of preferred and nonpreferred tasks. Placing preferred activities after a nonpreferred task encourages students to complete their work in order to move on to the preferred activity. It may be helpful to keep a picture or icon of the preferred activity near the student, where it can be referred to during nonpreferred task completion (Hodgdon, 1995).

Instructional Practices for Teaching Students with Autism

There are numerous instructional techniques for teaching children with autism. A comprehensive listing would be far too long to include in a single book chapter. Instead, procedures detailed here represent a sampling of methods that have been successful with many students with autism. However, as with any educational decision, the characteristics and needs of the individual student will determine which method(s) work best. No *one* method will work for all students. Teachers must be alert and informed consumers when selecting instructional practices.

The specific instructional procedures discussed in this chapter include (a) whole language, (b) incidental teaching, (c) joint action routines, (d) social stories, (e) prompting, (f) discrete trial training, (g) peer-mediated approaches, and (h) icon-based communication systems.

Whole Language

The whole language approach grew out of research on the developmental acquisition of oral language and is based on principles of natural language learning. Whole language uses student interests to develop an array of communicative functions, facilitate the learning of language, and promote achievement of communication goals (Norris & Damico, 1990). Through theme building, planned and systematic implementation strategies, meaningful content, and social interaction, students learn language skills that are both practical and authentic.

The whole language approach is particularly beneficial for students with autism. Prizant (1983) theorized that individuals with autism learn language through a gestalt, or "big picture" format. In contrast to part-to-whole approaches to language, the whole language approach emphasizes this big-picture way of thinking (Twatchman, 1995). Additionally, whole language is based upon the belief that language acquisition is tied to children's experiences; therefore, making learning relevant and meaningful enhances this process. These experiences are subsequently used to develop knowledge and understanding of targeted concepts and vocabulary (Smith-Burke, Deegan, & Jaggar, 1991). This section examines two whole language approaches: language experience activities and thematic units.

Language Experience Activities

One whole language approach is the language experience activity (LEA). LEA has been used with a variety of special needs populations, including students with (a) learning disabilities (Smith-Burke et al., 1991); (b) academic, behavioral, and/or medical difficulties (Peterson, Scott, & Sroka, 1990); and (c) autism (Bock, 1991; Shepherd, 1983). Bock (1991) defined LEA as "an instructional method utilizing children's language (i.e., words, sentences, stories) and experiences as the basis for reading instruction. LEA integrates the development of reading skills with the development of listening, speaking, and writing skills" (p. 1). Because individuals with autism may present unique characteristics and learning styles that differentiate them from other atypical populations (Simpson & Regan, 1986), LEA objectives should not focus solely on reading and writing skills but should encompass skills in the areas of language, behavior, cognitive, and social development (Bock, 1991).

In its most basic format, LEA is a simple process. First, the teacher selects a topic that represents an integral activity or interest in the student's daily life, such as working with motorized gears, eating at a local restaurant, or feeling textures. If capable, the student dictates an experience to the teacher, who transcribes the story using the student's own words. For nonverbal or lower functioning students, a story can be created using simple content drawn from common daily activities. The story is then used for reading instruction, generation of spelling words, language development, and writing activities.

A primary benefit of using LEA is its versatility. For example, with students who are just beginning to read, stories can be developed that pair symbols or pictures with words. Sentence strips can be used as a transitional step to paragraph reading. Students can also use alternative forms for story creation, such as dictating into a tape recorder or videotaping a storytelling session. Nonverbal students can select pictures or icons to create sequencing activities or to teach basic concepts such as "before" and "after."

Thematic Units

Another whole language technique is the thematic unit. A thematic unit uses recurring ideas and themes across a variety of curricular areas. When recurring themes are maintained over days, weeks, and even months, students become highly familiar with the topic and are better able to generalize to other areas (Twachtman, 1995).

Bock (1991) described a seven-step approach to using thematic units with students with autism. A brief description of each step follows. (A sample thematic unit, including detailed lesson plans, has been provided in Appendix A at the end of this chapter.)

1. *Identification of instructional objectives.* Instructional objectives should be created to address multiple skill areas, including language, academic skills, social skills, leisure-time and play skills, fine and gross motor skills, and behavior. Curricular objectives, as well as the student's current Individualized Education Program (IEP), can be used to target specific skills. The use of a scope and sequence instrument such as the *Developmental Teaching Objective Rating Form–Revised* (DTORF–R; Developmental Therapy Institute, 1992) or the *BRIGANCE Diagnostic Inventory of Early Development* (Brigance, 1978) can provide useful information on the sequence of skill acquisition.

2. *Identification of a unit topic.* Unit topics should be chosen on the basis of (a) student interests, (b) available community resources, (c) skills previously taught, (d) topics that build on previous topics, and (e) the cost and ease of unit implementation. Topics should be age appropriate and, whenever possible, linked to the general education curriculum.

3. *Identification of unit activities.* Unit activities should incorporate objectives in the previously mentioned areas of skill development. With older students, transition and vocational goals should be considered. It is possible, with very careful planning, to incorporate goals and objectives from all of the recommended areas into a single unit activity.

4. *Implementation of pretraining activities.* Pretraining activities are developed on the basis of prerequisite skills that are necessary for the student's

successful participation in the unit activities. Pretraining sessions may require one-to-one instruction to ensure familiarity with basic terminology and concepts or to teach specific behavioral characteristics necessary for participation, such as sitting in a group or raising a response card.

5. *Integration of effective techniques with unit activities.* The teacher must plan unit activities on the basis of the individual student's strengths and needs. This includes answering questions such as, Should instruction take place in a group or one-to-one format? What strategies should be used during the instructional process? In what manner will the students respond during the activities? As decisions are made regarding lesson structure, training techniques, and response formats, the design of the unit's activities takes shape.

6. *Identification of skill evaluation procedures.* It is important to know that students are acquiring the desired skills from the thematic unit. Therefore, evaluation procedures should be selected on the basis of individual students' strengths and concerns. Skill evaluation must be both practical and authentic; thus, it should measure not only skill acquisition but also behavior, language, and social development.

7. *Scheduling unit activities.* Unit activities should include skill acquisition, maintenance, and generalization opportunities. Participating staff members must be identified and a schedule of each of their responsibilities developed. It may be useful to design a timetable or grid that describes each activity, individual student's targeted goals, the format under which the activity will take place, and the personnel involved. Table 3.4 provides helpful hints for using a thematic unit.

Table 3.4

Helpful Hints for Using a Thematic Unit

1. Derive thematic unit vocabulary from variety of sources
   - Words that directly relate to the unit
   - Common vocabulary words
   - Survival words

2. Pair written words with a picture or an icon

3. Create unique word banks or dictionaries that use pictures or icons paired with words

4. Take pictures of students for community-based activities

5. Create sentence strips using targeted vocabulary words
   - Begin by forming one-sentence strip
   - Ask comprehension questions
   - Increase number of sentence strips as the student progresses

6. Continue thematic unit until students reach criterion

7. Be flexible

Incidental Teaching

Incidental teaching uses naturally occurring opportunities for instruction throughout the student's day (Cavallaro, 1983). First recognized by Hart and Risley (1968) as a way to teach language to disadvantaged preschool children, incidental teaching is a process that occurs when the natural environment is arranged to attract children to desired materials or objects. The teacher remains available to provide reinforcement and instruction on the topic of immediate interest. This type of procedure is also referred to as "child-preferred instruction" or "milieu teaching" (Cavallaro, 1983).

Research on incidental teaching has demonstrated greater acquisition of skills and stronger generalization of skills across environments than many other traditional teaching procedures (McGee, Krantz, Mason, & McClannahan, 1983). Incidental teaching has also been shown to foster spontaneous use of speech in severely language-delayed children with autism (McGee, Krantz, & McClannahan, 1985).

Conducting an Incidental Teaching Session

Cavallaro (1983) described the basic steps involved in incidental teaching:

1. Observe the student to determine what materials or objects he or she attends to most frequently.

2. Once the student has selected an object or has tried to obtain help or assistance with an object, attempt to gain focused attention. Approach the student, remain silent for a few seconds, and wait for the student to respond. A response can be an attempt at a verbal interaction, a brief glance, prolonged eye contact, or any type of acknowledgment of the teacher's presence. If attention is not gained by this method, initiate verbalization or attempt joint manipulation of the object.

3. Once attention is gained, engage in a brief conversation about the item or object. For example, if the student has a blue truck in one hand and was manipulating the wheels on the truck with his or her other hand, the teacher might say, "Blue truck" or "Tires on truck."

Creating Conversation

Conversation about a preferred object becomes more complex as the student develops language skills. Various types of prompts can be used to elicit higher level student responses. The most basic prompt is a full model prompt such as, "Say blue truck." This type of prompt is used during early acquisition of language skills. A partial prompt provides the beginning sound(s) of the desired response, such as "Say BI . . ." Partial prompts offer a smooth transition away from dependence on full model prompting. The highest level prompt includes demands or requests, such as, "Tell me a sentence" or open-ended questions like, "What do you have?" These prompts are closest to the type of stimuli occurring in the student's natural environment.

Joint Action Routines

Joint action routines (JAR) are social routines that occur in contexts that are familiar and well learned (Reichle, 1994). First presented as a means of facilitating language development for students with severe impairments (Snyder-McLean, Solomonson, McLean, & Sack, 1984), JAR is based on the theory that consistent and familiar routines provide the support required to acquire new responses. Thus, JAR is a ritualized interaction pattern, following a logical sequence, with a clear beginning point. Each participant plays a specific role with preset responses. A "script" detailing what to say and how to respond in a given situation is provided and practiced. The routine allows students to participate in a social situation in which they may not have been able to respond because of their limited repertoire (Snyder-McLean et al., 1984).

Types of Joint Action Routines

Snyder-McLean et al. (1984) proposed three types of joint action routines. Type 1 routines involve the preparation or fabrication of a specific end product. This type of routine allows naturally occurring sequences and roles to be used because the end product is inherent in the routine. One example of this type of routine would be food preparation. In the preparation of snacks, several roles can exist. One role could be the director, who would determine what ingredients were required to make the designated snack. A second role could be an assistant, who would gather materials such as a silverware, plates, cups, and then set the table. A third role could be the cook. The cook would be responsible for combining the ingredients to make the end product. The advantage of the Type 1 routine is that it is broad and flexible enough to allow for age-appropriate roles for multiple levels of participants.

Type 2 routines center around a plot or story line. Sample themes might include "going to the movies" or "eating at a restaurant." During this type of routine, a basic story line and cast of characters are determined. Controlled variations, story modifications, or new roles can be introduced as the story progresses. Themes or plots can be developed to teach community living skills such as shopping or visiting the library.

Type 3 routines focus on cooperative turn taking such as that which occurs in playing a game. This type of routine involves a game requiring interactive play between two or more participants. Cooperative games that require students to act in unison to achieve a specific goal, such as winning the game or meeting a preset criterion, work best for Type 3 routines.

Elements of JAR

Several elements must be in place in order to design or implement an effective JAR (Snyder-McLean et al., 1984). First, the JAR theme should be meaningful and recognizable to all participants. Examples of meaningful themes would be greeting a friend, joining a conversation, and paying for your groceries. The routine should provide students with opportunities to interact and communicate with others. The outcome of the interaction must be clearly defined.

The JAR should designate a minimum of two roles that are easily differentiated and that have corresponding expectations. Each of the roles should be clear and predictable enough for students to be able to perform their role correctly and also determine whether other students are properly executing their roles. The use of two to five different roles is recommended, depending on the ages and levels of the participants. The roles of the JAR should be interchangeable. Roles can be reassigned to different students throughout the routine to provide additional opportunities for learning. Initially, the teacher or other support personnel should participate in the routine to model appropriate behaviors.

The JAR should have a predictable and logical sequence with a clearly marked beginning and ending. Students must be provided with cues as to when the role associated with a particular routine is to be performed. The interactions introduced into the JAR should provide opportunities for students to practice turn-taking skills. Additionally, students should be made aware of the rules and expectations that govern when they are supposed to wait and when they should take their turn.

Introducing planned variations into the JAR will prevent the training of long chains of rote responding and overt prompt dependency. Planned variations will also facilitate the generalization of targeted skills to other social situations.

Social Stories

Social story interventions enhance social skill acquisition for many students with autism. A social story is a "minibook" that describes a social situation and the appropriate social responses. Social stories are individualized for each student and teach a specific, desired response (Gray, 1994). Social stories are written using four sentence types: (a) descriptive sentences, which provide information about the subjects, settings, and actions; (b) directive sentences, which describe the appropriate behavioral response; (c) perspective sentences, which identify the possible feelings and reactions of others; and (d) control sentences, which are analogies of similar actions and responses using nonhuman subjects. A sample control sentence might be, "A puppy barks to get its owner's attention, and Ginny asks to get the teacher's attention."

It is customary for a social story to have two to five descriptive, perspective, or control sentences for every directive sentence in the story (Gray &

Garand, 1993; Swaggart et al., 1995). Writing social stories for lower functioning students or students with stimulus overselectivity may require dropping the control sentence. (Appendix B contains sample social stories for lower and higher functioning students.)

Creating a Social Story

Swaggart et al. (1995) proposed a 10-step process for creating a social story. This process involves all aspects of the social story creation, from identification of a target behavior for change through evaluation of the success of the intervention. A brief description of this social story process follows.

1. *Identify a target behavior or problem situation.* Begin by selecting a social behavior that may result in increased positive interaction or a social learning opportunity for the student. Task-analyze the behavior, breaking it into small sequential steps for completion. The task analysis should be based on the student's strengths.

2. *Define the target behavior for data collection.* Describe the target behavior clearly and concisely. That is, the description should be written so that anyone reading it could precisely identify the desired behavior. It is also essential that the student involved in the social story be able to easily recognize the desired behavior.

3. *Collect baseline data on the target behavior.* Prior to intervention, the target behavior should be measured for a period of 3 to 5 days. This allows the teacher to recognize how frequently the behavior is occurring and provides a basis for comparison for the student's behavior after the social story intervention. Target behavior can be measured by placing tally marks on a sheet of paper each time the behavior occurs or by using a stopwatch to record the length of time the behavior occurs.

4. *Write a short social story using the four sentence types.* Social stories should be written in the first person. The story can describe either a present situation or a social situation that will occur in the future. Select vocabulary and print size for the social story on the basis of the student's developmental and skill levels.

5. *Present one to three sentences on each page.* The format of the social story should be simple to allow the student to focus on and process each specific concept. Presentation of the social story will depend on the individual student. For some students, more than one sentence per page may result in an overload of information. For others, several sentences may be placed on each page.

6. *Use photographs, hand-drawn pictures, or icons.* For students who have limited reading skills, the addition of a photograph, picture, or icon to the social story may enhance understanding of the desired behavior. Be cautious, however, that the illustration does not define the social situation narrowly, as this could result in limited generalization (Gray, 1994).

7. *Read the social story to the student and model the desired behavior.* This step in the social story intervention should become a consistent part of the student's daily schedule. Present the social story several times throughout the day, specifically prior to activities targeted by the story. Students who are able to read independently may do so, and they may share the social story with peers. Nonreading students can follow along or listen as the teacher reads the story aloud.

8. *Collect intervention data.* Using the same procedure as in baseline data collection, record the target behavior throughout the intervention process. Compare intervention data to baseline data to determine if the social story has positively affected the student's social skill development. Do not rely on memory or anecdotal records to assess the effectiveness of the social story.

9. *Review the findings and related social story procedures.* Allow a minimum of 2 weeks to determine if the social story is producing the desired behavior. If it is determined that the story or program must be altered, change only one variable at a time. For example, if a sentence in the story is replaced, do not simultaneously change the time the story is presented or the person who reads it. By changing only one factor at a time, it is easier to determine which factor(s) are affecting the student's skill acquisition.

10. *Plan for maintenance and generalization.* Remember that students with autism frequently do not maintain or generalize skills they have learned. Although you will ultimately want to fade the use of the social story, plan activities to assist the student in generalizing the social story content across persons, environments, and situations.

Prompting

Prompting is a technique that can help students with autism learn new skills or enhance skill development. A *prompt* is basically a cue to elicit a specific behavior from the student. Prompts range from less to more intrusive. Physical prompting or put-throughs are the most invasive type of prompt. In this procedure, the teacher initiates the desired response by physically engaging the child to begin the response pattern. Nonverbal gestures such as pointing or signing to indicate to the student where to look or move are somewhat less invasive to the learning flow. Verbal questions or statements are an even less intrusive type of prompting and consist of a word or brief phrase. Finally, a written prompt, such as a cue card or key word taped to the student's desk, is the least invasive type of prompting procedure.

Prompting can be a useful tool for redirecting a student's attention back to the task at hand. Prompting can also be used to elicit a specific response pattern at a designated time or in a specific situation. As prompting produces errorless learning, it is also effective in promoting a student's sense of achievement.

There are, however, some disadvantages associated with prompting as an intervention for students with autism. For example, consistent delivery of the prompt may be difficult to maintain, causing students to become frustrated when asked to perform without the prompt. Further, prompting can disrupt an ongoing social exchange and, when implemented by peers, can cause an inequity between students. However, the major concern is that the student may develop prompt dependency, a condition that diminishes students' motivation and independence.

Prompt Dependency

A student who has developed prompt dependency is unlikely to perform a task unless the prompt is presented. Prompt dependency can occur when the prompt is used for too long, is consistently administered by the same person, or does not have a preestablished plan for fading.

Certain steps can be taken to avoid prompt dependency. First, determine how much the student knows about a given task. Next, select the least invasive prompt that is likely to be effective and attempt to elicit the desired response. If the response is not achieved, provide more direct prompts in increasing increments until successful task completion occurs. This process establishes a baseline for the level of prompting currently needed. Allow the student to practice the task using the level of prompting currently needed until response appears to be automatic. Then, gradually fade the prompt as mastery of the task is maintained.

Prompt Fading

It is as important to know how to fade a prompt as it is to know how to prompt. The key to prompt fading is to allow the student to respond with increasingly less directive prompts. This can be challenging for teachers and parents, especially in situations in which a student's behavior must be elicited quickly or consistently.

To effectively fade a prompt, select the most natural cue for the required task. For example, physical prompts can be faded using a lighter or briefer touch, and verbal prompts can be faded by using fewer words or a softer voice tone. As the level of prompting is gradually lowered, consistently monitor the student's response pattern. If the student begins performing poorly, fading may be proceeding too quickly. In this case, return to the last step at which the student was able to successfully perform the skill and restart the fading process.

Discrete Trial Training

Some students with autism require a routine to develop certain compliant response patterns, such as a "ready to work" position or a handing or pointing response. The process used to establish this type of routine is called "discrete trial training" or "compliance training." In discrete trial training, the teacher gives a prompt for the student to attend to and a command for the student to perform, and then reinforces the student for the desired behavior (Lovaas, 1987; Scott & Gilliam, 1987). For example, the student is given an oral prompt such as "Look at me," or a nonverbal cue such as pointing to the teacher's eyes. Once this command is given, the teacher waits for compliance to the attending behavior. For some students, it may be necessary to shape attending behavior by pairing the verbal or nonverbal prompt with physical assistance or a put-through. A *put-through* simply means guiding the child physically through the desired behavior, such as lifting the child's chin so the eyes focus on the teacher when the command "Look at me" is given. Additionally, many students will require reinforcement for approximating the desired behavior. In this case, the teacher may choose to reinforce behavior that is similar to or leading toward the desired behavior. For example, when the command "Look at me" is given, reinforcement would occur if the student lifted his or her head briefly but did not maintain eye contact.

Once the student is paying attention, the command to perform is given. Initially, performance commands are simple directives such as "Give me blue" or "Put in box." It is important that the student has the skills required to perform the requested task. If the prompt does not result in the correct response, the teacher can assist the student to complete the task with a put-through. Reinforcement should occur whether the task is performed independently, with prompting, or via put-through. This training step should be rehearsed until the task can be performed at an independent level.

Reinforcement is a major component of the discrete trial training approach. When the student performs or attempts to perform a task at any level of acquisition, immediate reinforcement should be provided. In the initial stages of skill acquisition, reinforcers may need to be edible or tangible to be powerful enough to elicit the desired response. However, the ultimate goal should be performing for social reinforcement.

It is critical to remember that with a discrete trial format, the student is learning a specific response in a contrived setting. Therefore, it cannot be assumed that the student will generalize this response to other skills or settings without teacher-directed activities involving practicing the behavior in a more naturalistic environment.

Certain behavioral characteristics associated with autism should be considered when one is implementing discrete trial training. That is, specific attention should be given to eye contact, stimulus overselectivity, competing responses, and prompt dependency. Each of these characteristics is briefly discussed below.

Eye Contact

It is broadly accepted that many students with autism demonstrate atypical eye contact, including reliance on peripheral vision (Dawson, 1989). Teachers should determine the amount and intensity of eye contact required to perform each specific task in discrete trial training. Some tasks may require little or no eye contact for successful completion. In these cases, eye contact should not be demanded. When training eye contact, teachers should first use a verbal or non-verbal cue. If the desired eye contact is not achieved, physical assistance may be required. Reinforcement should be given at each phase of skill acquisition.

Stimulus Overselectivity

Students with autism may show selective attention to specific items or situations, responding to only a few of the available cues in a learning environment (Mundy & Sigman, 1989). *Stimulus overselectivity* refers to an overt focus on one piece or characteristic of stimuli, disregarding other relevant stimuli. For example, when presented with three choices, a student may always select the choice on the left, or when asked for a verbal response, may always give the final choice offered by the teacher. If it is determined that stimulus overselectivity is present, the teacher may find it necessary to interrupt incorrect responses during discrete trial training to avoid allowing the student to practice the responses associated with stimulus overselectivity (Myles & Simpson, 1990). Redirecting the student's attention to other relevant stimuli can sometimes be as simple as rearranging the presentation of the stimulus or changing the pattern of a verbal prompt.

Competing Responses

Students with autism may display a variety of physical behaviors that interfere with the learning process, such as rocking, hand flapping, or light filtering. Occasionally, decreasing or eliminating these behaviors is a part of the discrete trial training format. There is no set formula for determining whether self-stimulatory or competing behaviors should be eliminated prior to or concurrent with discrete trial training (Myles & Simpson, 1990). If the competing behavior is preventing the child from exhibiting the desired response, it should be addressed. However, if the behavior does not interfere with learning, it may be better to ignore it. For example, if a student engages in hand flapping while focusing on the teacher, but ceases hand flapping when involved in a physical response requiring the use of his or her hands, the teacher could determine that this behavior did not deter the student from completing the discrete trial and, therefore, not target this behavior for reduction or extinction. In some instances, self-stimulatory behavior may actually be useful as a reinforcer for performing a less preferred task (Myles & Simpson, 1990). In such cases, the student is allowed to engage briefly in a noninjurious stimulatory response such as light filtering or dangling a shoestring as a reward for complying with task demands.

Prompt Dependency

Because students with autism frequently lack performance motivation, teachers who engage these students in discrete trial training may find themselves routinely giving excessive prompts and physical assistance (Myles & Simpson, 1990). As discussed previously, this can result in making students prompt dependent. To avert prompt dependency, research recommends that teachers reinforce response attempts or shape new response options (Koegel, O'Dell, & Dunlap, 1988). For example, a student who is socially unresponsive to hugs could learn to enjoy hugs by pairing a hug with a preferred reinforcer. Acceptance of hugs is slowly shaped over time until hugs become an independent reinforcer. It is critical that a plan to fade the prompt be an integral part of the discrete trial training format. Prompt fading should occur in small, incremental steps, such as guiding the student's elbow rather than moving his or her hand during task completion.

Peer-Mediated Approaches

Peer-mediated approaches, also referred to as "peer tutoring" or "peer modeling," have proven to be effective for children with autism. Specifically, peer-mediated approaches have been successful in teaching or facilitating such skills as increased social interactions (McGee, Almeida, Sulzer-Azaroff, & Feldman, 1992); functional community skills (Blew, Schwartz, & Luce, 1985; Haring, Kennedy, Adams, & Pitts-Conway, 1987); acquisition of discrimination tasks (Egel, Richman, & Koegel, 1981); and generalized language learning (Charlop & Milstein, 1989). Peer-mediated approaches offer many benefits for both the student with autism and the peer involved in the instructional technique. Frequently, both students experience an overall increase in academic skill, social acceptance, and general satisfaction (Kamps, Dugan, Leonard, & Carta, 1990).

Kamps et al. (1990) developed a peer tutoring training model for working with students with autism. The model establishes effective rules and procedures for enhancing the tutoring interaction. Figure 3.10 provides a flowchart for the peer tutor training model.

Icon-Based Communication Systems

One of the major goals of a classroom program for children with autism is for all students to have a method of functional communication and ample opportunities to practice these skills. For some students with autism, a communication system that uses alternative forms of expression will be necessary. Some students will require concrete objects, pictures, or icons to make their needs and desires known. One program that addresses this type of communication is the *Picture Exchange Communication System* (PECS; Bondy & Frost, 1994). PECS is a picture-based, augmentative/alternative communication system that was developed within the Delaware Autistic Program. PECS utilizes a step-by-step, six-phase program to teach individuals with autism a means to communicate within a social context. PECS teaches students to approach a communicative

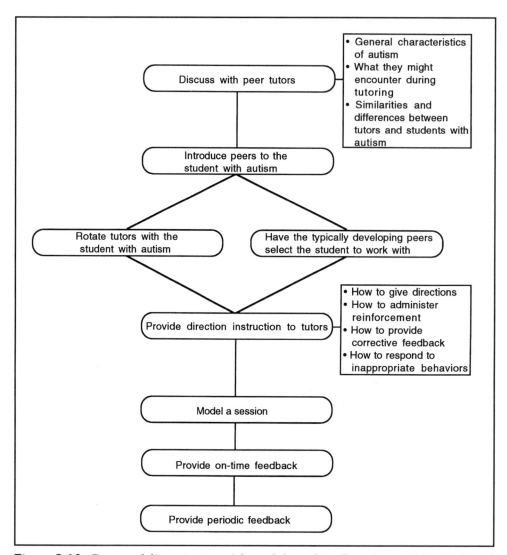

Figure 3.10. Peer modeling strategy. Adapted from *Peer Tutoring and Small Group Instruction,* by D. M. Kamps, E. P. Dugan, B. R. Leonard, & J. J. Carta, 1990, Kansas City, KS: University of Kansas, Bureau of Child Research, Juniper Gardens Children's Project.

partner such as a teacher or fellow student and exchange a picture of a desired item for the actual item. The goal of this approach is to teach initiation of communicative interactions. Behavioral techniques such as backward chaining, shaping, and physical prompts are used to teach the initial phrases of PECS. Verbal prompts should not be given, and physical prompts must be faded during early stages of acquisition to avoid prompt dependency.

The benefits of PECS are numerous. The system not only provides students with a method for functional communication, but also fits easily into the existing classroom program. The same pictures used for PECS can be used in the learning environment to label furniture, shelves, and objects, and to depict activities or routines on the daily schedule.

Summary

Designing an educational program for students with autism requires a gestalt approach that incorporates many different strategies and techniques. This chapter has introduced some of the more successful strategies used in instructing students with autism. Whether you are creating environmental supports, enhancing response opportunities, introducing change, building flexibility, or selecting specific instructional procedures, these strategies will offer support for this challenging group of learners. When choosing an instructional strategy to work with students with autism, you must keep in mind two important factors. First, no one strategy or approach will be right for *every* student. Individualize and customize the curriculum to meet the needs of each student you teach. Second, every student deserves to function at his or her most independent level. Use the techniques and strategies you have learned to give each student a sense of personal responsibility, the opportunity to make relevant choices, and the dignity of independence.

Appendix 3A
Sample Thematic Unit

GOING TO THE GROCERY STORE THEMATIC UNIT

Monday

Play group:

Sample activity: Fruity Memory (memory game with pictures of fruits)

Possible targeted skills:
Name fruits
Matching
Short-term memory

Calendar:

Sample activity: What Is a Fruit?

1. Give each student a fruit name tag.

2. After greetings and/or the hello song, hold up a picture of a fruit, name the fruit, and then ask the group, "Who is wearing this fruit?"

3. Discuss the different fruits (color, shape, etc.).

4. Sing a fruit song where the children are asked to stand when their fruit is named.

5. Hold up two fruits and have students name them. Ask students to close their eyes and hide one fruit behind your back. Ask the students which fruit is missing.

6. Read and discuss *Johnny Appleseed*

Possible targeted skills:
Name fruits
Describe characteristics of self and others (by the fruit)
Recognize colors
Attend to individuals in group and/or book
Short-term memory

Individual work:

Sample activities:
Trace and color different fruits to make a Grocery Store Book.
Cut and paste activities with pictures of fruits.

Do matching activities that require the student to match pictures of fruits.
Do matching activities that require the student to match fruits with their
    appropriate color(s).
Cut out pictures of different fruits from a magazine to make a collage.
Complete worksheet: Color the fruits that are round.

Possible targeted skills:

Fine motor	Recognizing fruits
Tracing	Naming fruits
Coloring	Recognizing shapes
Cutting	Sorting by shape
Colors	Sorting by color

Reading:

Sample activity: Let's Read About Fruits

1. Introduce reading words (e.g., names of fruits, words from Dolch sight
   word list, and survival words such as *exit, poison, women's restroom,* etc.)
   by writing words, one at a time, on a large chart. It may be helpful to
   glue a picture of the fruit next to its written name.

2. Recite and spell words together. Hold up the corresponding picture of the
   fruit as the words are spelled.

3. Lay down word cards in front of each student. Each student should have
   his or her own set of word cards.

4. Hold up one of your word cards, read the card, then ask the student to
   find his or her card that matches or that is the same as yours.

5. Use this same process for each of the vocabulary words.

6. Hold up a picture of a piece of fruit, ask the student to name the fruit,
   and then to point to or find the word that corresponds with the picture.

7. Use the same process for each of the vocabulary words.

8. Give each student a sentence strip and ask him or her to read the sentence. The sentence should contain only words the student knows or is
   currently learning.

9. Ask students comprehension questions about the sentence.

10. When the students have compiled enough sentences, make a class book
    and ask the students to illustrate it by drawing or cutting pictures from
    magazines.

Possible targeted skills:

Naming fruits	Comprehending reading materials
Recognizing words	Following directions

Math:

Sample activities:
Fruity Sums (addition problems using pictures of different fruits)
Fractions with apples
Apple Bingo (Bingo cards in the shape of apples)
Weigh fruit
Fruity Sorting (sorting plastic apples from plastic bananas)

Possible targeted skills:
Addition	Matching numbers
Fractions	Measurement concepts: weight
Recognizing numbers	Sorting by shape or color

Language group:

Sample activities:
Newt the Fruit art project (make a person from fruits)
Make a fruit salad
Color fruit pictures for a Grocery Store Book

Possible targeted skills:
Fine motor	Following directions
Cutting	Naming fruits
Glueing	Recognizing colors

Motor group:

Sample activity: Fruit Hunt (hide a variety of plastic fruits in the classroom or on the playground and ask the student to find the fruits)

Vocational:

Sample activity: Fruity Match

1. Collect pictures of different fruits.
2. Write words of fruits on index cards.
3. Ask students to match the picture of the fruit to the written word.

Possible targeted skills:
Recognizing fruits	Comprehension
Recognizing vocabulary words	Matching

Tuesday

Play group:

Sample activity: Students play with plastic meat toys (e.g., hotdogs, hamburgers, steaks, etc., in the play kitchen)

Possible targeted skills:

Social skills
    Sharing
    Turn taking

Language
Appropriate use of materials
Recognizing meats and breads

Calendar:

Sample activity: Bar-b-que

1. As the children come to calendar, give them a meat or bread name tag.

2. Discuss the meat and bread groups using pictures.

3. Discuss who is wearing each name tag.

4. Sing a song that relates to the meat food group.

5. As the products are named in the song, the child wearing the corresponding name tag should stand up.

6. Read the book *The Sandwichery* by Patricia and Tallivaldis Stubis.

Possible targeted skills:

Recognizing meats and breads
Following directions
Participating in a group

Individual seatwork:

Sample activities:

Color pictures of meats and breads
Cut and paste activities with meats and breads
Matching activities that require the student to match pictures of meats and breads
Cut out pictures of different meats and breads from a magazine to make a collage

Possible targeted skills:

Fine motor
    Tracing
    Coloring
    Cutting

Recognizing colors
Recognizing meats and breads
Naming meats and breads
Matching

Reading:

Sample activity: Reading About Meats and Breads

1. Introduce reading words (e.g., names of meats and breads, words from Dolch sight word list, and survival words such as *exit, poison, women's restroom,* etc.) by writing the words, one at a time, on a large chart. It may be helpful to glue a picture of the meat or bread next to its written name.

2. Recite and spell words together. Hold up the corresponding picture of the meat or bread product as the words are spelled.

3. Lay down word cards in front of each student. Each student should have his or her own set of word cards.

4. Hold up one of your word cards, read the card, then ask the student to find his or her card that matches or that is the same as yours.

5. Use the same process for each of the vocabulary words.

6. Hold up a picture of a meat or bread product, ask the student to name the meat or bread product, and then to point to or find the word that corresponds with the picture.

7. Use the same process for each of the vocabulary words.

8. Give each student a sentence strip and ask him or her to read the sentence. The sentence should contain only words the student knows or is currently learning.

9. Ask students comprehension questions about the sentence.

10. When the students have compiled enough sentences, make a class book and ask the students to illustrate it by drawing or cutting pictures from magazines.

Possible targeted skills:
Recognizing meats and breads
Recognizing vocabulary words
Naming meats and breads
Comprehending reading materials
Following directions

Math:

Sample activity: Recognizing *same* and *different* using identical pictures of breads and meats

Possible targeted skills:
Matching identical pictures
Recognizing "same" and "different"

Language:

Sample activity: Field Trip

1. Take a field trip to a bakery to buy bread and to a deli to buy meat.
2. Make sandwiches.
3. Go to the park for a picnic.
4. Take pictures of this activity for a class book to be used during reading.

Possible targeted skills:

Appropriate behavior	Turn taking
Following directions	Spreading with a knife
Sharing utensils	Eating skills

Motor group:

Sample activity: Meat and Bread Relay (relay race using cut out pictures of different meat and bread products)

Possible targeted skills:

Gross motor skills	Participating in a group activity
Turn taking	

Vocational:

Sample activity: Parts of a Whole

1. Make two puzzles, one of a butcher and one of a hotdog. The puzzles should be of identical shape and should have identical pieces.

2. Put the two puzzles together except for one piece from each puzzle. The unfinished puzzle pieces should be the same.

3. Hand the student the two pieces and ask him or her to complete the two puzzles. The child is required to discriminate by looking at the color and design on the puzzle pieces in order to correctly complete the puzzles.

Possible targeted skills:

Parts of a whole	Visual discrimination
Fine motor	*Same/different*

Wednesday

Play group:

Sample activities:
Vegetable and Fruit Lotto
Vegetable Memory
Go Shopping (similar to Go Fish but using pictures of vegetables)

Possible targeted skills:

Social skills	Recognizing fruits and vegetables
Sharing	Short-term memory
Turn taking	Participating in group activities
Matching identical pictures	Language
Appropriate use of materials	

Calendar:

Sample activity: Vegetable Salad

1. As the children come to calendar, give each student a vegetable name tag.

2. After greetings and/or the hello song, hold up a picture of a vegetable, name the vegetable, and then ask the group, "Who is wearing this vegetable?"

3. Discuss who is wearing each name tag.

4. Discuss the different vegetables (color, shape, etc.).

5. Sing a song that relates to the vegetable food group.

6. As the products are named in the song, the child wearing the corresponding name tag should stand up.

7. Hold up pictures of two vegetables or hold up two actual vegetables and ask the students to name them. Ask the students to close their eyes, then hide one vegetable behind your back. Ask the students which vegetable is missing.

8. Read the book *The Story of Peter Rabbit* by Beatrix Potter.

Possible targeted skills:
Recognizing and naming vegetables
Describing characteristics of self and others by the vegetable name tag (e.g., the teacher can say, "Who is wearing the carrot?" Peers can respond by pointing to or naming the person who is wearing that particular name tag. This skill correlates with Steps 1–6 in the Vegetable Salad Activity)
Recognizing colors
Attending to individuals in a group and/or book
Short-term memory
Participating in a group

Individual seatwork:

Sample activities:

Color pictures of vegetables.
Cut and paste activities with vegetables.
Match word with corresponding picture of vegetables.
Sequence activities using pictures of vegetables.

Possible targeted skills:

Fine motor	Recognizing vegetables
Tracing	Naming vegetables
Coloring	Matching
Cutting	Sequencing
Recognizing colors	

Reading:

Sample activity: Reading About Vegetables

1. Introduce reading words (e.g., names of vegetables, words from Dolch sight word list, and survival words such as *exit, poison, women's restroom,* etc.) by writing the words, one at a time, on a large chart. It may be helpful to glue a picture of the vegetable next to its written name.

2. Recite and spell words together. Hold up the corresponding picture of the vegetable as the words are spelled.

3. Lay down word cards in front of each student. Each student should have his or her own set of word cards.

4. Hold up one of your word cards, read the card, then ask the student to find his or her card that matches or that is the same as yours.

5. Use the same process for each of the vocabulary words.

6. Hold up a picture of a vegetable, ask the student to name the vegetable and then to point to or find the word that corresponds with the picture.

7. Use the same process for each of the vocabulary words.

8. Give each student a sentence strip and ask him or her to read the sentence. The sentence should contain only words the student knows or is currently learning.

9. Ask students comprehension questions about the sentence.

10. When the students have compiled enough sentences, make a class book and ask the students to illustrate it by drawing or cutting pictures from magazines.

Possible targeted skills:

Recognizing vegetables
Recognizing vocabulary words
Naming vegetables

Comprehending reading materials
Following directions

Math:

Sample activities:

Recognizing *big* and *little*. In a group circle, give directions such as "Give me the big tomato," or "Stand by the little carrot."
Sort big and little plastic vegetables

Possible targeted skills:

Recognizing *big* and *little*
Recognizing *same* and *different*
Sorting by size

Language:

Sample activities:

Coloring sheets for Grocery Store Book

Art project: "Mr. McGregor's Garden" (students cut out pictures of vegetables for a collage)

Generic board game (After the students roll the dice, they must answer a question about a picture of a vegetable—"What is this?" "What color is this carrot?"—before they can move their game piece)

Possible targeted skills:

Social skills

    Turn taking

    Sharing

Following directions

Participating in group activities

Recognizing vegetables

Recognizing colors

Fine motor

    Coloring

    Cutting

    Glueing

    Recognizing numbers on the dice

    Counting

Motor group:

Sample activity: Vegetable Walk

1. Place a picture of a vegetable made from construction paper on the playground.

2. Give each student directions, such as "Jump on the tomato," or "Stand behind the carrot."

Possible targeted skills:

Gross motor skills

Turn taking

Participating in a group activity

Vocational:

Sample activity: One-To-One Correspondence

1. Cut out vegetables from construction paper, mount them on tag board, and then laminate them.

2. Write numbers on the pictures of the vegetables.

3. Give the student clothespins and ask him or her to clip the correct number of clothespins on the vegetable that corresponds with the written number.

Number Order

1. Cut out vegetables from construction paper, mount them on tag board, and then laminate them.

2. Write numbers 1–15 on the vegetables.

3. Ask the student to put the numbers in order.

Vegetable Sort

1. Ask the student to sort labels from cans of vegetables that can be purchased at the grocery store.

2. Have students sort vegetables by the beginning sound, such as beans in the "B" bag.

Possible targeted skills:

One-to-one correspondence	*Same/different*
Counting	Sorting
Visual discrimination	Naming vegetables

Thursday

Play group:

Sample activities: T & S Supermarket

1. Set up a grocery store in the classroom. Save food cans, boxes, and so on, price them, and put them on a shelf.

2. Collect grocery store advertisements and coupons.

3. Assist students in making shopping lists by cutting out pictures of foods from advertisements. The foods that the students cut out must be products that are available in the classroom store.

4. Designate student roles (shopper, cashier, sacker).

5. Help children to perform their roles.

Possible targeted skills:

Social skills	Participating in group activities
Sharing	Language
Turn taking	Fine motor
Matching identical pictures	Cutting
Using play materials appropriately	Glueing
Matching objects/labels to words	

Calendar:

Sample activity: Dairy Products

1. As the children come to calendar, give each student a name tag that represents a dairy product.

2. After greetings and/or the hello song, hold up a picture of a dairy product, name the product, and then ask the group, "Who is wearing this dairy product?"

3. Discuss who is wearing each name tag.

Possible targeted skills:
Recognizing and naming dairy products
Describing characteristics of self and others by the dairy product's name tag
(This skill corresponds with Steps 1–3 in the Dairy Products activity)
Attending to individuals in a group and/or book
Participating in a group

Individual seatwork:

Sample activities:
Color pictures of dairy products.
Cut and paste activities with dairy products.
Match word with corresponding picture of dairy product.
Cut out pictures of different dairy products from a magazine to make a collage.

Possible targeted skills:
Fine motor   Recognizing colors
    Tracing   Recognizing dairy products
    Coloring   Naming dairy products
    Cutting   Matching

Reading:

Sample activity: Reading About Dairy Products

1. Introduce reading words (e.g., names of dairy products, words from Dolch sight word list, and survival words such as *exit, poison, women's restroom,* etc.) by writing the words, one at a time, on a large chart. It may be helpful to glue a picture of the dairy product next to its written name.

2. Recite and spell words together. Hold up the corresponding pictures of the dairy products as the words are spelled.

3. Lay down word cards in front of each student. Each student should have his or her own set of word cards.

4. Hold up one of your word cards, read the card, and then ask the student to find his or her card that matches or that is the same as yours.

5. Use the same process for each of the vocabulary words.

6. Hold up a picture of a dairy product. Ask the student to name the dairy product and then to point to or find the word that corresponds with the picture.

7. Use the same process for each of the vocabulary words.

8. Give each student a sentence strip and ask him or her to read the sentence. The sentence should contain only words the student knows or is currently learning.

9. Ask students comprehension questions about the sentence.

10. When the students have compiled enough sentences, make a class book and ask the students to illustrate it by drawing or cutting pictures from magazines.

Possible targeted skills:
Recognizing dairy products
Recognizing vocabulary words
Naming dairy products
Comprehending reading materials
Following directions

Math:

Sample activities: Money Game

1. Cut out pictures of dairy products from grocery store advertisements.

2. Glue the pictures of the dairy products and their price tags onto a piece of poster board in a game format.

3. Ask student to roll a die and then move his or her game piece the appropriate number of spaces.

4. Ask the students to name the dairy product and then count out the amount of money that corresponds with the product's price tag. The students should count out real money.

Possible targeted skills:

Counting money	Participating in group activities
One-to-one correspondence	Counting
Naming dairy products	Language
Turn taking	Following directions

Language:

Sample activities: Banana Split

1. Make a banana split. Talk about the different dairy products, fruits, and so on. Ahead of time, develop a recipe using words and pictures.

2. Take pictures of the activity and develop a class story.

3. Assist students in completing a banana split art project.

Possible targeted skills:

Social skills	Following a sequence (recipe)
Turn taking	Fine motor
Sharing	Coloring
Following directions	Cutting
Participating in group activities	Glueing
Recognizing dairy products	Following a sample

Motor group:

Sample activity: Cheese Toss

1. Cut out a large square from a piece of plywood.

2. Cut holes in the wood to resemble a piece of Swiss cheese.

3. Paint the wood yellow.

4. Attach a board to the back of the plywood to allow the finished product to stand on its own.

5. Paint prices near the holes (e.g., 25¢, $1.00, etc.).

6. Have students attempt to throw bean bags through the holes. Add up the prices that correspond with the hole. The student next in line can add the prices using a calculator.

Possible targeted skills:

Gross motor skills	Addition
Turn taking	Money
Participating in a group activity	Eye–hand coordination

Vocational:

Sample activity: Supermarket

1. Gather four grocery bags and write the name of one of the food groups on each bag.

2. Ask the students to unstock the shelves from the T & S Supermarket and bag the products according to the corresponding food group. For students who may have difficulty with this activity, pictures from grocery store advertisements can be glued to the front of the bag and then students can be asked to match the product to the picture on the front of the bag.

Possible targeted skills:

Categorization
Visual discrimination
Same/different
Sorting
Naming fruits, breads, meats, vegetables, and dairy products
Participating in group activities

Friday

Community-based instruction:

1. Discuss picnics and the foods that will be needed to go on the picnic.

2. Have each student make a shopping list by cutting out pictures from grocery store advertisements, tracing the words, or copying words from the chalkboard.

3. Take a field trip to the grocery store. As the products are put in the shopping basket, assist students in marking the products off their shopping lists.

4. Ask one of the students to use a calculator to add up the prices of the products.

5. Discuss the food groups as the class is walking around the store.

6. Take pictures of the trip.

7. After arriving back at school, ask the students to name the products that were purchased before the sacks are unloaded.

8. Make sack lunches and go to the park for a picnic.

9. Use the pictures from the field trip to make a class book.

Possible targeted skills:

Community involvement
Participation in group activities
Short-term memory
Visual discrimination
Activities of daily living (e.g., making sandwiches for picnic)
Opportunities for generalization

Appendix 3B
Sample Social Stories

 Sample social story for a low-functioning student

Page 1

I like toys.
I can earn my toys.

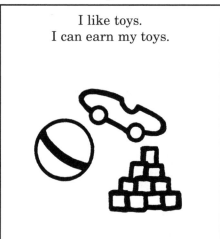

Page 2

When I do my work, I need to
have nice hands and feet.

Page 3

When I do my work,
I should not bite.

Page 4

There are pictures of toys on
my chart. If I hit, kick, or bite,
I lose a picture.

Page 5

After lunch, I can have free time
with my toys if I have at least
one picture to give my teacher.

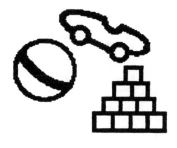

Page 6

When I earn my toys
the teacher will clap and say,
"Good earning your toys, Donald!
You had nice hands and feet,
and you did not bite."

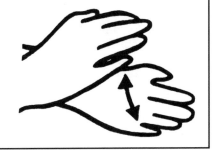

Sample social story for a high-functioning student:
When I Have a Substitute Teacher

Page 1

Sometimes people get sick. Sometimes sick people stay home.

Page 2

Sometimes my teacher gets sick. When she gets sick, she must stay home from school.

Page 3

When my teacher is sick and stays home, there will be a substitute teacher in my class. The substitute teacher may be a man or a woman.

Page 4

When I have a substitute teacher, I need to follow my schedule and do my work. If I need help with my work, I need to ask the substitute teacher by saying, "I need help."

Page 5

I can also ask my friend Jeff for help.

Page 6

When my teacher feels better, she will come back to school. When she comes back to school, she will ask me about my day with the substitute teacher.

Page 7

If I followed my schedule and did my work, I will earn extra time on the computer. My teacher will be happy.

Page 8

A bird sings more than one song. I will work for more than one teacher.

References

Bambara, L. M., & Koger, F. (1996). *Opportunities for daily choice making.* Washington, DC: American Association on Mental Retardation.

Blew, P. A., Schwartz, I. S., & Luce, S. C. (1985). Teaching functional community skills to autistic children using nonhandicapped peer tutors. *Journal of Applied Behavioral Analysis, 18,* 337–342.

Bock, M. (1991). A modified language-experience approach for children with autism. *Focus on Autistic Behavior, 6*(5), 1–15.

Bondy, A. S., & Frost, L. A. (1994). The picture exchange communication system. *Focus on Autistic Behavior, 9*(3), 1–19.

Brigance, A. H. (1978). *BRIGANCE diagnostic inventory of early development.* North Billerica, MA: Curriculum Associates.

Brown, F. (1991). Creative daily scheduling: A non-intrusive approach to challenging behaviors in community residences. *Journal of the Association for Persons with Severe Handicaps, 16*(2), 75–84.

Brown, F., Belz, P., Corsi, L., Wenig, B. (1993). Choice diversity of people with severe disabilities. *Education and Training in Mental Retardation, 28,* 318–326.

Carnine, D. W. (1976). Effects of two teacher presentation rates on off-task behavior, answering correctly, and participation. *Journal of Applied Behavior Analysis, 9,* 199–206.

Carnine, D. (1991). Direct instruction applied to mathematics in a general education classroom. In J. Lloyd, N. Singh, & A. Repp (Eds.), *The regular education initiative: Alternative perspectives on concepts, issues, and models* (pp. 163–175). Sycamore, IL: Sycamore.

Cavallaro, C. C. (1983). Language interventions in natural settings. *Teaching Exceptional Children, 16*(1), 65–70.

Charlop, M. H., & Milstein, J. P. (1989). Teaching autistic children conversational speech using video modeling. *Journal of Applied Behavior Analysis, 22,* 275–285.

Dalrymple, N. J. (1993). *Helping people with autism manage their behavior.* Bloomington: University of Indiana, Institute for the Study of Developmental Disabilities.

Dalrymple, N. J. (1995). Environmental supports to develop flexibility and independence. In K. A. Quill (Ed.), *Teaching children with autism: Strategies to enhance communication and socialization* (pp. 243–264). Albany, NY: Delmar.

Dawson, F. (1989). *Autism: Nature, diagnosis, and treatment.* New York: Guilford.

Developmental Therapy Institute. (1992). *The developmental teaching objectives for the DTORF–R: Assessment and teaching of social-emotional competence* (4th ed.). Athens, GA: Author.

Egel, A. L., Richman, G. S., & Koegel, R. L. (1981). Normal peer models and autistic children's learning. *Journal of Applied Behavior Analysis, 14,* 3–12.

Eno-Hieneman, M., Dunlap, G., & Reed, M. (1995). Predictability, structure and personal control. *Network Magazine, 4*(3), 23–28.

Gardner, R., Heward, W. L., & Grossi, T. A. (1994). Effects of response cards on participation and academic achievement: A systematic replication with inner city students during whole-class instruction. *Journal of Applied Behavior Analysis, 27,* 63–71.

Gray, C. A. (1994, October). *Making sense out of the world: Social stories, comic strip conversations, and related instructional techniques.* Paper presented at the Midwest Educational Leadership Conference on Autism, Kansas City, MO.

Gray, C. A. (1995). Teaching children with autism to "read" social situations. In K. A. Quill (Ed.), *Teaching children with autism: Strategies to enhance communication and socialization* (pp. 219–241). Albany, NY: Delmar.

Gray, C. A., & Garand, J. D. (1993). Social stories: Improving responses of students with autism with accurate social information. *Focus on Autistic Behavior, 8*(1), 1–10.

Greenwood, C. R., Delquadri, J., & Hall, R. V. (1984). Opportunity to respond and student academic achievement. In W. L. Heward, T. E. Heron, D. S. Hill, & J. Trap-Porter (Eds.), *Focus on behavioral analysis in education* (pp. 58–88). Columbus, OH: Merrill.

Groden, J., & LeVasseur, P. (1995). Cognitive picture rehearsal: A system to teach self-control. In K. A. Quill (Ed.), *Teaching children with autism: Strategies to enhance communication and socialization* (pp. 287–306). Albany, NY: Delmar.

Haring, T. G., Kennedy, C. H., Adams, M. J., & Pitts-Conway, V. (1987). Teaching generalization of purchasing behavior across community settings to autistic youth using videotape modeling. *Journal of Applied Behavior Analysis, 20,* 89–96.

Hart, B. M., & Risley, T. R. (1968). Establishing use of descriptive adjectives in spontaneous speech of disadvantaged preschool children. *Journal of Applied Behavior Analysis, 14,* 389–409.

Hawkins, D. (1995). Spontaneous language use. In R. L. Koegel, & L. K. Koegel (Eds.), *Teaching children with autism: Strategies initiating positive interactions and improving learning* (pp. 43–66). Baltimore: Brookes.

Heward, W. L., Courson, F. H., & Narayan, J. S. (1989). Using choral responding to increase active student response. *Teaching Exceptional Children, 21*(3), 72–75.

Heward, W. L., Gardner, R., Cavanaugh, R. A., Courson, F. H., Grossi, T. A., & Barbetta, P. M. (1996). Everyone participates in this class. *Teaching Exceptional Children, 28*(2), 4–10.

Hodgdon, L. A. (1995). *Visual strategies for improving communication: Practical supports for school and home.* Troy, MI: QuirkRoberts.

Kaiser, A. P., & Hester, P. P. (1996). How everyday environments support children's communication. In R. L. Koegel, L. K. Koegel, & G. Dunlap (Eds.), *Positive behavioral support: Including people with difficult behavior in the community* (pp. 145–162). Baltimore: Brookes.

Kamps, D. M., Dugan, E. P., Leonard, B. R., & Carta, J. J. (1990). *Peer tutoring and small group instruction.* Kansas City: University of Kansas, Bureau of Child Research, Juniper Gardens Children's Project.

Kamps, D. M., Dugan, E. P., Leonard, B. R., & Dauoust, P. M. (1994). Enhanced small group instruction using choral responding and student interaction for children with autism and developmental disabilities. *American Journal on Mental Retardation, 99*(1), 60–73.

Kamps, D. M., Walker, D., Dugan, E. P., Leonard, B. R., Thibadeau, S. F., Marshall, K., Grossnickle, L., & Boland, L. (1991). Small group instruction for school-aged children with autism and developmental disabilities. *Focus on Autistic Behavior, 6*(4), 1–18.

Koegel, R. L., O'Dell, M., & Dunlap, G. (1988). Motivating speech use in nonverbal autistic children by reinforcing attempts. *Journal of Autism and Developmental Disorders, 18,* 525–537.

Lovaas, O. I. (1987). Behavioral treatment and normal educational and intellectual functioning in young autistic children. *Journal of Consulting and Clinical Psychology, 55,* 3–9.

MacDuff, G. S., Krantz, P. J., & McClannahan, L. E. (1993). Teaching children with autism to use photographic activity schedules: Maintenance and generalization of complex response chains. *Journal of Applied Behavior Analysis, 26,* 89–97.

McGee, G. G., Almeida, M. C., Sulzer-Azaroff, B., & Feldman, R. S. (1992). Promoting reciprocal interactions via peer incidental teaching. *Journal of Applied Behavior Analysis, 25,* 117–126.

McGee, G. G., Krantz, P. J., Mason, D., & McClannahan, L. E. (1983). A modified incidental teaching procedure for autistic youth: Acquisition and generalization of receptive object labels. *Journal of Applied Behavior Analysis, 16,* 329–338.

McGee, G. G., Krantz, P. J., & McClannahan, L. E. (1985). The facilitative effects of incidental teaching on preposition use by autistic children. *Journal of Applied Behavior Analysis, 18,* 17–31.

Miller, A. D., Hall, S. W., & Heward, W. L. (1995). Effects of sequential 1-minute time trials with and without intertrial feedback on general and special education students' fluency with math facts. *Journal of Behavioral Education, 5,* 319–345.

Mundy, P., & Sigman, M. (1989). Specifying the nature of the social impairment in autism. In G. Dawson (Ed.), *Autism: Nature, diagnosis and treatment* (pp. 3–21). New York: Guilford.

Myles, B. S., & Simpson, R. L. (1990). A clinical/perscriptive method for use with students with autism. *Focus on Autistic Behavior, 4*(6), 1–14.

Narayan, J. S., Heward, W. L., & Gardner, R. (1990). Using response cards to increase student participation in an elementary classroom. *Journal of Applied Behavior Analysis, 23,* 45–59.

Norris, J. A., & Damico, J. S. (1990). Whole language in theory and practice: Implications for language intervention. *Language, Speech, and Hearing Services in Schools, 21,* 212–220.

Ostrosky, M. M., & Kaiser, A. P. (1991). Preschool classroom environments that promote communication. *Teaching Exceptional Children, 23*(4), 6–10.

Peterson, S. K., Scott, J., & Sroka, K. (1990). Using the language experience approach with precision. *Teaching Exceptional Children, 22*(3), 28–31.

Prizant, B. (1983). Language acquisition and communicative behavior in autism: Toward an understanding of the "whole" of it. *Journal of Speech and Hearing Disorders, 48,* 296–307.

Reichle, J. (1994). Developing communicative exchanges. In J. Reichle, J. York, & J. Sigafoos (Eds.), *Implementing augmentative and alternative communication: Strategies for learners with severe disabilities* (pp. 133–156). Baltimore: Brookes.

Sainato, D. M., Strain, P. S., & Lyon, J. R. (1987). Increasing academic responding of handicapped preschool children during group instruction. *Journal of the Division for Early Childhood, 12*(1), 23–30.

Scott, B. S., & Gilliam, J. E. (1987). Curriculum as a behavior management tool for students with autism. *Focus on Autistic Behavior, 2*(1), 1–8.

Shepherd, T. R. (1983). *Using experience language (LEA variation) to teach an autistic-like child with a visual disorder to read (and write and talk).* Carbondale: Southern Illinois University. (ERIC Document Reproduction Service No. ED 243 389)

Simpson, R. L., & Regan, M. (1986). *Management of autistic behavior.* Austin, TX: PRO-ED.

Sindelar, P. T., Bursuck, W. D., & Halle, J. W. (1986). The effects of two variations of teacher questioning on student performance. *Education and Treatment of Children, 9*(1), 56–66.

Smith-Burke, M. T., Deegan, D., & Jaggar, A. M. (1991). Whole language: A viable alternative for special and remedial education? *Topics in Language Disorders, 11*(3), 58–68.

Snyder-McLean, L. K., Solomonson, B., McLean, J. E., & Sack, S. (1984). Structuring joint action routines: A strategy for facilitating communication and language development in the classroom. *Seminars in Speech and Language, 5,* 213–228.

Swaggart, B. L., Gagnon, E., Bock, S. J., Earles, T. L., Quinn, C., Myles, B. S., & Simpson, R. L. (1995). Using social stories to teach social and behavioral skills to children with autism. *Focus on Autistic Behavior, 10*(1), 1–15.

Thinesen, P., & Bryan, A. (1981). The use of sequential picture cues in the initiation and maintenance of grooming behaviors with mentally retarded adults. *Mental Retardation, 19,* 246–250.

Twachtman, D. D. (1995). Methods to enhance communication in verbal children. In K. A. Quill (Ed.), *Teaching children with autism: Strategies to enhance communication and socialization* (pp. 133–162). Albany, NY: Delmar.

Management of Students with Autism

4

Richard L. Simpson and
Brenda Smith Myles

Children and youth identified as having autism and/or pervasive developmental disorders clearly present highly unique behavior, including aberrations of social interaction, self-stimulatory behavior, overactivity, and marked preoccupation with restricted and stereotyped response patterns. Management of children and youth with autism is considered to be of such importance that the central premise of this chapter is that virtually every educational consideration is either related to or secondary to establishing effective management and social interaction programs.

The basic thesis of this chapter is that behavioral procedures are the single most effective means of bringing about desired social and behavioral changes (Farrar-Schneider, 1994; Groden & Baron, 1988; Simpson & Regan, 1988). Indeed, procedures based on behavioral methodology have been successfully used in a variety of settings to

- decrease aggressive behavior (Gardner & Cole, 1990);

- increase social interactions (Simpson, Myles, Sasso, & Kamps, 1991);

- develop communication and language skills (R. L. Koegel & L. K. Koegel, 1995);

- reduce self-injurious behavior (Azrin, Besalel, Jamner, & Caputo, 1988; Iwata, Pace, Kalsher, Cowdery, & Cataldo, 1990);

- reduce self-stimulatory behaviors (Newman, Whorton, & Simpson, 1977); and

- manage a variety of other behavioral excesses and deficits (LaVigna & Willis, 1992).

In addition, these methods have been used successfully by both parents and professionals (Risely, 1968; Simpson, 1996) and with a variety of age groups (Powers, 1992).

On the basis of their proven record of success, behavioral methods are clearly functional, efficient, and versatile tools that can be used as the foundation for effectively managing student behavior and facilitating learning.

This chapter introduces principles and considerations associated with the use of general behavioral strategies with individuals with autism as well as specific intervention methods. Topics related to general principles and considerations include assumptions underlying the behavioral approach and application of basic behavioral principles. In subsequent sections of this chapter, these basic principles and considerations are translated into specific program elements.

Assumptions Underlying Behavioral Strategies

As claimed earlier, behaviorally based approaches constitute the single most effective and efficient strategy for managing the behavior of individuals with autism. The efficacy of behavioral strategies is significantly enhanced when users understand their underlying principles and assumptions, including the following: (a) Operant behavior is learned; (b) understanding and manipulating observable stimuli and behavior are of primary importance; (c) intervention procedures may be independent of diagnoses; (d) the usefulness of intervention methods should be empirically judged; and (e) antecedent and consequent factors are primary determinants of behavior. Each of these areas is briefly discussed below.

Operant Behavior Is Learned

According to Skinner (1953), human behavior can be divided into two general categories: respondent and operant. *Respondent behavior* refers to involuntary responses such as those over which we have little or no control. Examples of respondent behaviors include increased blood pressure and pulse rate in response to anxiety-provoking conditions. Such responses are elicited. That is, a stimulus is presented and a particular response automatically follows (e.g., involuntary tearing in response to a foreign object in the eye).

On the other hand, *operant behavior* is voluntary. Operant responses are emitted; that is, they are within an individual's control and are primarily maintained by environmental antecedents and consequences. Examples of operant behavior include engaging in social interactions and countless other responses over which we have control.

As for everybody, the majority of responses of children and youth with autism are assumed to be learned. That is, most of their day-to-day behaviors are subject to their control. Therefore, when children with autism engage in self-stimulatory behavior or run from their parents, their behavior is typically under their control, even though it may appear that the behavior is associated with some external force. Further, adaptive and maladaptive behaviors are assumed to develop and be maintained in much the same manner.

The educational and clinical implications of this assumption are significant. First, behavioral approaches permit planned change via replacement of inappropriate and nonfunctional behaviors with more appropriate responses. Second, they eliminate the argument that children and youth with autism manifest unusual and nonfunctional behavior exclusively as a function of unobservable or unknown events. Subsequent sections of this chapter emphasize specific methods for managing operant responses of students with autism.

Understanding and Manipulating Observable Stimuli and Behavior Are of Primary Importance

Behaviorally oriented intervention programs focus on systematic application of learning theory principles to increase, decrease, or strengthen specific behaviors in order to bring about changes in specific target behaviors. Consequently, teachers who employ behavioral procedures to manage their students with autism identify and precisely define behaviors for modification, such as staying in seat, complying with verbal directives, and so forth. For example, rather than stating that a child is overactive and prone to excessive movements, a teacher using a behavioral approach might define the target behavior as "having the student's normal seating surface be in contact with his chair whenever he is in the classroom, except when he has permission to be somewhere else."

The emphasis on observable antecedents, stimuli, and responses is also associated with the notion that operant (voluntary) responses are developed and maintained by observable environmental events that precede and follow a given response. That is, the focus is again on those events and stimuli that can be observed, monitored, and potentially modified, and that are part of an individual's present situation rather than historical past. For example, it is typically far more productive for educators to focus on children's reactions to curricula and environmental stimuli such as setting, noise, and so forth, than to base program interventions on unobservable and unproven phenomena such as purported perceptual aberrations associated with a neurological deficit. Although the latter explanation for a behavior might in fact be correct, it is nonetheless far more difficult to base a program on such an allegation than on more observable and controllable variables.

Finally, the flexible nature of behavioral strategies allows for their application by parents, paraprofessionals, and other individuals who interact routinely with individuals with autism. Thus, the model is applicable beyond a single environmental or educational setting, as opposed to psychotherapeutic and similar intervention approaches, which rely on methods that do not easily transfer to other settings.

Intervention Procedures May Be Independent of Diagnoses

A diagnosis of autism is not a prerequisite for using behavioral procedures. Indeed, children, youth, and adults of various types and abilities have been beneficiaries of behaviorally based strategies. Behavioral procedures focus on identifying, analyzing, and developing behaviors that are associated with enhanced social, cognitive, and communication performance. Accordingly, because educators and other professionals are able to use behavioral methods to identify, analyze, and modify observable behaviors, as opposed to labeling a student who manifests them, primary attention can be focused on identifying and applying problem-solving strategies. In summary, behavioral strategies combine the advantage of using diagnostic labels in a circumspect and efficient manner with empirically valid and pragmatic problem-solving strategies.

The Usefulness of Intervention Methods Should Be Empirically Judged

The basic tenet of the behavioral model—that the effectiveness of interventions must be judged empirically—requires that the utility of a given strategy be individually determined through precise measurement methods. No behavioral intervention strategy is assumed to be effective or functional without systematic evaluation. This notion, which is a cornerstone of applied behavioral analysis (Alberto & Troutman, 1990), necessitates use of a systematic approach to teaching and behavior management based on direct observation and charting of student behavior.

Hall, Hawkins, and Axelrod (1975) noted the advantages of careful measurement and empirical validation related to the application of behavior modification procedures. In part they observed the following:

1. Measurement forces the teacher to define target behaviors more precisely.

2. Measurement results in a precise assessment of performance that is a more relevant form of diagnosis than most psychological testing.

3. Measurement focuses the teacher's efforts on the specific behavior and thus is more likely to achieve the desired changes.

4. The frequent, usually daily, measurement and charting of data on a graphic record encourages the teacher to persist with the technique until its effect is adequately tested, rather than to give up when immediate and obvious results cannot be seen.

5. With frequent measurement, the teacher is stimulated to make small improvements in technique and to note the effects. Thus, the technique may achieve much more than the original approach. (pp. 195–196)

Antecedent and Consequent Factors Are Primary Determinants of Behavior

As noted throughout this discussion, operant behavior is largely determined by stimulus events that occur *before* a response, and the consequences that *follow* the response. Accordingly, analyses of variables associated with particular responses are key to their modification.

Although behaviorally based management has sometimes been interpreted narrowly, such as exclusively meaning one-to-one discrete trial training, it is in fact an extremely far-reaching tool with the potential for great flexibility. In this regard, effective interpretation and use of behaviorally based interventions should place as much weight on antecedent conditions such as curriculum and environments as on consequences. Indeed, it is our contention that curricular and environmental considerations are salient antecedent variables related to effective design of management programs. Thus, we cannot overemphasize the importance of selecting appropriate curricula and settings that meet the needs of students with autism.

Application of Basic Behaviorally Based Principles

The application of behavioral strategies with children and youth with autism has produced generally impressive results (Lovaas, 1987). Such evidence has at least in part been the basis for the widespread use of applied behavioral analysis and other behaviorally based strategies. Yet, in spite of the proven efficacy of behavior modification techniques, successful application requires an understanding of and willingness to follow basic protocol. Included are considerations related to reinforcement, extinction, and punishment.

Reinforcement Principles

According to behavioral theory and practice, a reinforced behavior will be repeated. In this context, reinforcement involves presenting an appropriate consequence following a desired behavior. If increases in the identified behaviors are observed, we infer that reinforcement has occurred.

Reinforcement can take either a negative or a positive form. *Positive reinforcement* relies on rewards of positive consequences that increase behavior. *Negative reinforcement,* on the other hand, involves the removal of some event or stimulus an individual dislikes contingent on the performance of a desired behavior. For instance, removing an additional school assignment contingent on a youth's successful participation in a social interaction is an example of negative reinforcement. Positive reinforcers have obvious social and interpersonal advantages over negative reinforcers. That is, it is preferred that educators and parents provide activities and other reinforcers as rewards for acceptable behavior as opposed to removing disliked items.

As noted, reinforcers are consequences that accelerate a behavior, rather than events or conditions perceived to be rewarding. Rewards may be a preferred toy for a student contingent on certain verbalizations. However, such consequences qualify as positive reinforcers *only* if they increase the occurrence of desired behaviors.

Certain conditions must exist in order for a positive consequence to effectively influence a behavior. First, positive consequences must be provided contingent on the occurrence of a desired response. Thus, a consequence must follow rather than precede a desired behavior. For example, it is important to provide a reward of computer time for completing a language activity after, rather than prior to, a student's engaging in the desired behavior.

Second, to be most effective, positive reinforcement should be temporally connected to the desired response. Reinforcers should be delivered *immediately* following a desired behavior. If delays in dispensing reinforcers occur, students may not know why they are being reinforced, or other behaviors may intervene and inadvertently be reinforced. Although important for all children, this consideration has particular significance for children and youth with autism because of their limited cognitive and receptive language abilities.

Third, we must avoid satiating individuals by providing reinforcers in excessive quantities or in insufficient varieties. Once a child has had enough of a given positive reinforcer, performance motivation diminishes. Additionally, we must be careful not to rely excessively on any *one* type of reinforcer.

In addition to being positive or negative, reinforcers are classified as primary or secondary. *Primary reinforcers,* such as food, drink, and preferred activities, do not have to be conditioned for students to want them. *Secondary reinforcers,* on the other hand, are learned, and their reinforcing properties result from association with other reinforcers. Teacher praise, for example, may become reinforcing to a child with autism when presented simultaneously with other reinforcers.

Desired behaviors are most easily and effectively established when reinforcement follows each occurrence of the target response. Such schedules are termed *continuous.* On the other hand, desired behaviors are maintained most effectively under *intermittent* reinforcement schedules, or when reinforcement follows only a portion of the desired behaviors. Many children and youth with autism may require systematic use of continuous reinforcement schedules to establish a desired operant behavior. However, efforts should be made to gradually advance to intermittent schedules. Such reinforcement schedules are not only easier to implement, they are also more resistant to extinction.

Punishment Principles

Just as reinforcers increase a behavior, so *punishers* decrease the occurrence of a behavior. Again, whether an event actually reduces the future occurrence of a behavior is the crucial factor, regardless of how it is perceived by an adult. Further, just as with reinforcers, punishers are most effective when applied immediately and contingent on the occurrence of a target response.

Although reinforcers are the preferred means of bringing about desired behavior changes, such methods are not always effective in all situations. Thus, while punishment may appear to be an inherently undesirable option, it is basic to successful management of students with autism. Consequently, it is our opinion that punishment must be considered a necessary alternative for some persons when positive reinforcement has proven ineffective.

Punishers may take a variety of forms, ranging from contingent electric shock (Lovaas, Freitag, Gold, & Kassorla, 1965) to soft reprimands (O'Leary & Becker, 1968). Professionals involved in managing children and youth with autism generally rely on less extreme alternatives, such as reinforcing responses incompatible with the target behavior and response-cost programs. Although professionals who work with persons with autism should rarely have to use aversive techniques, under extreme conditions, such as self-injury or when behavior is dangerous to self or others, aversive techniques may be considered.

As in the case with reinforcers, punishers are classified as unconditioned or conditioned. *Unconditioned,* or unlearned, consequences include such events as loss of privileges. *Conditioned punishers* acquire their punishing qualities through association with unconditioned consequences. For example, a child may learn to pair a verbal warning with loss of privileges.

Unlike reinforcement programs, which work best on an intermittent schedule, punishers are maintained most effectively when applied each time a target behavior occurs. Hence professionals and parents who apply these procedures must be careful to employ continuous rather than intermittent consequences during both initial and maintenance phases of behavior management programs. Additionally, because of the danger of negative side effects, such as interpersonal problems of persons dispensing punishment, it is recommended that each punishment program include a positive reinforcement component whereby desired behaviors incompatible with the undesired behavior are reinforced.

Finally, when punishing consequences are considered, the option with the highly probability of success should be selected. Professionals and others who work with individuals with autism should not be enticed into selecting a consequence that is less robust than needed for success because of humanitarian reasons. When all other notions have proven ineffective and punishment techniques are deemed necessary, the most appropriate technique should be selected.

Extinction Principles

Undesired behaviors may be decreased not only by using punishing consequences, but also by eliminating the attention that has been observed to follow
the unwanted response. Accordingly, some students' behavioral excesses may
be successfully reduced when attention is the primary contributing factor to
the maintenance of the response.

Even though extinction may be a useful tool for use with many students
with autism, we must recognize that it is not unusual for children and youth
with autism to engage in aberrant behaviors for reasons other than securing
attention. Self-stimulatory behaviors that may be immune to extinction are
commonly manifested by students with autism. Since self-stimulation may
occur regardless of whether someone is attending to the person, ignoring such
behaviors may have little impact. Accordingly, extinction should be used only
when there is evidence that a behavior is primarily a function of environmental attention.

The following considerations should also be given careful thought before
extinction programs are implemented:

- Some behaviors may not be able to be ignored (e.g., striking another
  student).

- Extinction programs are not usually associated with immediate behavior
  changes, but rather with slow improvements, and when improvements do
  occur, they may follow behavioral deteriorations. Such increases in target behavior, known as *extinction bursts,* usually occur as an individual
  increases the intensity or frequency of the behavior to obtain attention.
  Although extinction bursts often suggest that extinction programs may
  have the potential for success, such increases in unwanted behaviors may
  prove difficult to ignore.

- Without consistent withdrawal of prior reinforcement, success is unlikely.
  Thus, persons using such procedures must be able to exercise a high degree
  of control over other adults and over students' peers if these individuals
  have previously provided reinforcement for the unwanted behavior.

In spite of the challenges associated with using extinction programs with
children and youth with autism, extinction should not be discounted as it
offers a viable alternative for many students.

A Model for Designing Behavior
Management Programs

A variety of options are available for developing and implementing behavior
management programs for students with autism. The model presented here is

eclectic, but primarily reflects a behavioral orientation. Elements of a behavior management program include the following: (a) identification of one or more behaviors for change; (b) analysis of environments and other antecedents related to the target behavior(s); (c) identification and analysis of outcomes, functions, and other contingencies associated with the target behavior(s); (d) accurate measurement of the target behavior(s); (e) selection and application of intervention options; and (f) generalization, maintenance, and follow-up activities.

Identification of Behaviors for Modification

The first step in developing intervention programs for children and youth with autism is to identify and define an appropriate target behavior. Although versatile, behaviorally based intervention programs are functional only to the degree to which they are applied to observable and measurable behaviors that have been clearly defined. It is important, therefore, that the behavior selected for modification be defined in such a way that all individuals involved with the student (e.g., teacher, parent, paraprofessional) can reliably observe and judge the behavior. For example, "aggressive behavior" might mean verbal remarks to one teacher, whereas to another it might mean self-hitting. To avoid this kind of confusion and lack of consistency, all participants in behavior management programs must have a common definition and understanding of the target behavior.

It is recommended that an operational definition include the four Ws (Clark-Hall et al., 1976):

- *who* the target individual is,
- *when* the target behavior is to be measured,
- *what* the behavior is, and
- *where* the behavior is to be measured.

For example, take the following operational definition for throwing—"any purposeful movement of the arm by Dawn that propels an object in any direction in the classroom during any scheduled activity." The four Ws can be identified as follows: (a) *Who* refers to Dawn; (b) *what* is the purposeful movement of the arm that propels an object; (c) *where* is in the classroom; and (d) *when* refers to any scheduled activity.

Because children and youth with autism demonstrate a variety of behavioral excesses and deficits, professionals who design intervention programs must establish priority behaviors for change. As a general rule, it is recommended that programs be designed to focus on severe behavioral excesses before attempts are made to ameliorate deficit areas. This recommendation is based on the notion that children and youth who display severe behavioral excesses are not good candidates for deficit training. For example, children who regularly display severe tantrums are poor candidates for social interaction training because of their difficulties in relating to others. This should not be interpreted to mean that *all* behavioral excesses must be dealt with before deficit areas can be addressed; however, the selection of responses for change should be based on an analysis of students' records; interviews with teachers, other professionals, and parents; and behavioral observation and formal and informal assessment. Further, a student's Individualized Education Program (IEP) should prove helpful in establishing behavioral priorities.

Analysis of Environments and Other Antecedents Related to the Target Behavior(s)

Bersoff and Grieger (1971) noted that "obtaining knowledge about environments and situations in which the behavior appears is a necessity" (p. 487). Indeed, successful design of behavioral programs is associated with determining whether a behavior occurs primarily in certain settings or under particular conditions (e.g., during free time following afternoon recess) or whether it is pervasive across environments and situations. Accurate identification of the settings and circumstances that surround a particular behavior should also include an evaluation of those individuals who are associated with particular situations. Accordingly, professionals must analyze whether an individual displays the target behavior only in the presence of a limited number of individuals (e.g., one teacher) or in a more generalized manner. As suggested by Bandura (1969), "Under naturalistic conditions behavior is generally regulated by the characteristics of persons toward whom responses are directed, the social setting, temporal factors, and hosts of verbal and symbolic cues that signify predictable response consequences" (p. 25).

Identification and Analysis of Outcomes, Functions, and Other Contingencies Associated with the Target Behaviors

Because adaptive and maladaptive operant behaviors are thought to be controlled by environmental stimuli (Skinner, 1953), relevant antecedent and consequent events associated with a particular target behavior must be identified. Although it is unrealistic to expect persons developing intervention programs to have a complete understanding of all the variables that influence a child's or youth's behavior, they must be able to identify salient factors associated with particular patterns. Such factors include environmental stimuli that inform a child that conditions are correct for display of a certain behavioral pattern as well as those environmental events that are subsequent to the behavior.

The behavior analysis form shown in Figure 4.1 was developed by Myles and Quinn (1995) to help professionals analyze antecedent and consequent events that may influence a student's behavior. Even though it is an informal tool, it can be used to structure identification and analysis of variables needed for effective management programming. A discussion of how to conduct a thorough and accurate functional analysis is also presented in Chapter 2.

Sasso and Reimers (1988) have also focused on conducting functional assessments of students' behavior as an important part of intervention planning. These researchers identified five basic functional analysis conditions for clinical and classroom analysis: "Alone, Social Disapproval, Tangible, Toy Play, and Demand" (p. 3). Each of these conditions represents a situation in which students are placed for observation and analysis. For example, Alone involves observing a child in a setting without people, toys, or other stimuli as an environment conducive to self-stimulation. Students are observed under each of these five conditions, and based on their responses, intervention programs are recommended. The Demand condition, for instance, can be used to analyze whether or not a child uses a particular behavior to escape or avoid certain instructional demands. Although by no means infallible, use of an effective functional assessment strategy such as that proposed by Sasso and Reimers increases the probability of identifying an appropriate and effective intervention program.

We also recommend using the informal functional analysis procedures shown in Table 4.1. As illustrated, the method involves making informal observations and recordings of interactions between students and teachers in various settings related to occurrences and nonoccurrences of reported management problems. Thus, in the example, two morning observations were made, one in a special education setting where the tasks involved an independent math seatwork activity and a small-group reading activity, and the other in a regular classroom science class.

As shown in Table 4.1, the person making the observations attempted to analyze the interactions that occurred by noting the responses initiated by the student in reaction to various class assignments, and the consequences and student responses that followed. In this example, the *consequences* are the reactions of the student's teachers in response to his various behaviors, whereas the *responses* are the student's reactions to his teacher's consequences. For instance, the observation reflects that while in the general education class scheduled from 9:15 a.m. to 10:05 a.m., the student was thought by his teacher not to be attending. As a result, this teacher verbally reprimanded the student to attend, which resulted in brief attention. However, when the teacher reprimanded the student a second time, the student "talked back," at which time he was sent to the office.

Although the use of an informal analysis method such as the one shown in Table 4.1 in no way universally guarantees conclusive results, it does offer an efficient and effective tool for gaining insight into antecedents associated with

Child's Name _____ Date _____

Brief Description of Behavior _____

_____

Behavior Observation

I.   When does the behavior occur?
___ During structured activities
___ During free choice times
___ During group activities
___ During individual activities
___ During listening activities
___ During quiet time
___ During clean up time
___ During transitions
___ Other _____

II. What happens just prior to the incident?
___ The child is not engaged in an activity.
___ The child is engaged in an isolated activity.
___ The child is playing with another child.
___ The child expresses a dislike for activity.
___ The child is told no by an authority figure.
___ The child has an argument with another child.
___ The child is not able to complete a task.
___ The child does not have wanted materials/toy.
___ Other _____

III. What happens immediately after the incident?
___ The child shows no concern.
___ The child throws tantrums.
___ Another child laughs.
___ The child looks to the adult for reaction.
___ The authority figure reacts in a positive manner.
___ The authority figure reacts in a negative manner.
___ The authority figure ignores the incident.
___ Other _____

IV. Comments _____

_____

_____

Figure 4.1. Behavioral analysis form. *Note.* From *Behavior Analysis Form,* by B. S. Myles & C. Quinn, 1995, Kansas City, KS: University of Kansas Medical Center, Department of Special Education. Copyright 1995 by B. S. Myles & C. Quinn. Reprinted with permission.

Table 4.1

Informal Functional Analysis

Time	Setting	Task	Behavior (B), consequence (C), and response (R) analysis
8:00–9:10 a.m.	Special education	Independent seatwork (math)	**B:** Failure to start assignment **C:** Verbal prompt **R:** Brief attention to task
			B: Complaint regarding assignment **C:** Teacher discusses assignment with student; teacher reminds student of classroom rules **R:** Brief work; head on desk
			C: Teacher reminds student of classroom rules; student reminded of rules **R:** Aggressive verbalizations **C:** Student sent to time-out
		Small group (reading)	**B:** Appropriate behavior **C:** Verbal praise **R:** Continued attention
9:15–10:05 a.m.	General education (science)	Lecture/ full class discussion	**B:** Failure to attend **C:** Verbal reprimand **R:** Brief attention; head on desk
			C: Teacher verbal warning **R:** Talk back **C:** Sent to office

students' successes and problems and hopefully results in a clearer picture of the function and outcome of behaviors.

Accurate Measurement of the Target Behavior

Hall (1970) identified five basic observational options for accurately measuring target behaviors: frequency observation, duration recording, interval recording, time sampling, and continuous observation. *Frequency observation* involves maintaining a count of the frequency with which an individual engages in a particular behavior. Frequency counts can be used to analyze such diverse responses as the number of times a child responds to a social gesture, engages in a particular self-stimulatory behavior, or completes a classroom assignment. In addition, such counts are relatively easy to interpret and can be presented as frequency or rate (the frequency of a response per unit of time) data.

Duration recording requires that the observer determine the amount of time an individual engages in a particular behavior during a set period of time. This observation approach is most suitable when the length of the response is of greatest importance. For example, knowing the number of minutes a child is involved in a social interaction with peers may be more functional than knowing the frequency of the behavior.

Interval recording involves dividing a specified time period into equal segments and recording whether a behavior occurs during each interval. Interval systems allow simultaneous assessment of multiple responses. Even though interval recording systems may not allow for analysis of the frequency of response occurrences among intervals, they are nonetheless a valuable observation option.

Time sampling is similar to interval recording but has the advantage of not requiring that the observer continually observes. Instead, the observer records whether an individual is engaged in a particular response or responses at the end of a set time interval. For example, a teacher might observe a student's attention to task over the course of 50 minutes, noting at the end of each 5-minute period whether the student was engaged in the assigned task. This approach yields reliable behavior samples while allowing observers to be involved in other activities.

Continuous observation consists of keeping anecdotal records of an individual's behavior over a set period of time. Although continuous observation allows individuals to observe a variety of behaviors, it typically lacks reliability and requires a great deal of time and effort. Thus, continuous observations are often a poor observation alternative.

Using one of these observation methods, persons planning behavior management programs for students with autism are able to obtain a pretreatment measure of a target behavior so that the effectiveness of the chosen intervention procedure can be validated. The length of time the baseline is taken should depend on the stability of the behavior. An ascending or descending trend indicates that the strength of a given behavior is changing. Ideally, if the treatment procedure is designed to decrease a given behavior, intervention should start with a behavior indicating an ascending or constant trend. Alternatively, the intervention should begin with a behavior indicating a descending or constant trend if the treatment is aimed at increasing the behavior.

Baseline data may be presented in a variety of forms. The most suitable for assessing the baseline performance of children and youth with autism include the following:

- frequency of events (e.g., frequency of social initiations)
- quantity of time (e.g., minutes of self-stimulation)
- rate (e.g., frequency of social initiations per 60-minute session)

- percentage (e.g., percentage of assignments completed)

- percentage of interval (e.g., number of intervals in which aggressive behaviors were observed divided by the total number of intervals during which observations were made)

Reliability of observations should also be an element of each behavior management program. In this context, *reliability* refers to the accurate observation of a behavior by multiple recorders. Interobserver agreement ensures that observations of the target behavior are accurate.

Specific Intervention Options

In designing effective intervention programs for students with autism, discussions with parents, other professionals, and students themselves, provide important information and input. Moreover, as suggested earlier, direct observations form the cornerstone of effective intervention programs. Thus, functional analysis (see Chapter 2) must be an integral element of any intervention program. Moreover, the value of any intervention procedure must be empirically determined. Thus, in order to evaluate the efficacy of a treatment, its influence on the ensuring behavior must be assessed. Accordingly, continuous and accurate measurement procedures must constitute a basic component of any behavioral treatment program.

The following sections discuss several management strategies for students with autism: reinforcement programs, extinction procedures, punishment programs, and antecedent interventions.

Reinforcement Programs

As noted, reinforcers increase the future probability of a particular behavior. Such an increase may take place in two ways. First, behaviors that are followed by a reinforcing consequence tend to be repeated. For example, an adolescent who significantly increases vocational productivity as a result of receiving contingent computer time can be assumed to be positively reinforced. Second, a response can be accelerated by the removal of an unpleasant stimulus (negative reinforcement). For example, a student may be permitted to miss a social interaction session if his academic performance meets a specific criterion. If this program leads to a significant increase in academic performance, the contingent removal of the social activity can be considered reinforcing. Although negative reinforcers may result in planned response changes, they should be used conservatively because positive reinforcement procedures can typically achieve the same goals in a more positive fashion.

The following positive reinforcement programs have proven effective with children and youth with autism when properly arranged and planned: tangible/

edible reinforcers, contingent activities, social reinforcers, and token economy systems.

Tangible and edible reinforcers may be necessary to obtain initial responses from low-functioning children. Such extrinsic reinforcers should be paired with social reinforcement. Edibles and other tangible reinforcers have been used successfully during language and other one-to-one sessions as well as during more independent tasks to reinforce task completion. Further, edibles can be used for one-to-one continuous reinforcement, as well as for fixed or variable-ratio schedules or group reinforcement.

Edibles and tangible reinforcement may be used throughout the day, provided that care is taken not to satiate a student, thereby rendering a reinforcer ineffective. When one is using edible reinforcers, it is also important to monitor intake to avoid possible food allergies or undesired behavior reactions. Although raisins, dry cereal, and so forth, tend to be most common, more involved events such as meals at fast-food restaurants may be used as primary reinforcers. Overall, the most important consideration in selecting food reinforcers is the student's preference.

Contingent activities involve making certain activities (e.g., free time) contingent on particular types and levels of desired behavior (Mitchell & Stoffel-moyer, 1973). For example, a child might be required to complete a prescribed block of work while displaying specified social behaviors in order to acquire additional computer time. Contingent activities are commonly used across various educational settings, including regular classes, making them a highly desirable procedure for students in inclusive settings.

Although sometimes undervalued as a management tool with students with autism, *social reinforcers* can and should be used routinely. Appropriate social reinforcers include supportive verbal and nonverbal responses made contingent upon desired behavior. Selection of the most effective and appropriate method of communicating approval depends on the findings of functional analyses as well as other evidence regarding particular students' preferences. Accordingly, contrary to the widespread belief that individuals with autism dislike social contact with others, verbalizations, signs, and touching (e.g., hugs) may be used to reinforce desired behavior.

Token economy systems involve the use of tangible, conditioned reinforcers (tokens) that are exchangeable for a variety of desired items. This type of reinforcement requires association with primary (tangible) reinforcement strategies. Thus, a student must understand that primary reinforcement will follow the receipt of a token. Token or backup reinforcers include poker chips, play money, stick-on symbols, and so forth. The appropriate token reinforcement is selected based on a student's age, interests, and abilities.

Token systems offer several advantages:

- Tokens are potent reinforcers and serve to maintain behavior at a higher level than other conditioned reinforcers such as praise, approval, and feedback, which are used independently.

- Tokens bridge the delay between desired target responses and backup reinforcement.

- Tokens can be backed up by a variety of reinforcers and are less subject to satiation than other reinforcers.

- Tokens can be administered without interrupting desired target responses (e.g., a student can be provided a chip for being on task without taking him or her away from the activity).

- Tokens permit using a single reinforcer with several individuals who might otherwise have different reinforcement preferences.

- Tokens permit using portions of reinforcers (e.g., activities) that might have to be earned in an all-or-none fashion.

- Tokens earned provide a quantitative basis on which to evaluate program progress.

As with other tools, however, token reinforcement has certain drawbacks, including the following: (a) With some students, desirable behavior may decline once tokens are withdrawn; and (b) occasionally, tokens may be obtained in unauthorized ways (e.g., stolen) or may be lost.

The following are examples of token programs that have been used successfully in public schools to manage the behavior of students with autism. The first two examples were designed for younger or lower functioning students; the other token programs were designed for older or higher functioning students.

Examples of Token Programs for Younger or Lower Functioning Students

Simpson (1977) used poker chips during receptive language training. The task consisted of having a child identify pants, shirt, shoes, and socks that were placed on a table in front of him. The trainer showed the student a picture of a shoe, pants, and so forth; the appropriate response was the child's touching the correct article, whereupon he received one chip, which he placed on a card that had spaces for four chips. After making four correct responses, the child received an edible. Later, the student was required to point to the correct article when the trainer said its name in order to receive a chip.

A second example of a token program for younger or lower functioning students involved training a primary-age student to walk to a toilet, sit on the stool, and remain there for 6 minutes. The student received one chip after each 2-minute period on the stool. If the student urinated during the 6-minute period, she was immediately allowed to trade the chips for a primary reinforcer. If she failed to urinate during the 6-minute period, she was required to exchange the tokens for the reinforcer at a later time. This program significantly decreased classroom enuresis.

Examples of Token Programs for Older or Higher Functioning Students

Task completion is a type of token system that uses a piece of cardboard onto which different slots are drawn to represent tasks or periods of time. Each time a student successfully completes a task or a period, the slot is filled with a coin or a sticker. The last slot displays a word or picture representation of the reinforcement that the child obtains upon receiving the last token. The system can be adapted to differing levels of functioning, attention span, and age. If capable, the student may fill in his or her own slots, thereby taking responsibility for both behavior and recording.

Another token program appropriate for older or higher functioning students involves the use of play money. As part of a program developed by Simpson (1977), students earned a predetermined amount of play money for completed tasks, acceptable behaviors, and appropriate social interaction with peers and adults. The money was spent for lunch, special privileges, and items in the school store. Students were fined for deviant behaviors such as hitting, threatening peers, spitting, and for being sent to the time-out area. All programs and contingencies were explained and role-played with the students prior to implementation. In addition to requiring students to accept responsibility for their own behavior, the token economy system served as a learning experience. Through activities on individual assignment sheets, students learned and practiced recording starting and finishing times and grades for each completed task. Students also learned to keep balance sheets for money earned and spent, thus requiring that they use skills in addition, subtraction, and making change.

Reinforcement Schedules

A continuous reinforcement schedule is considered most appropriate when a new behavior is being shaped. Thus, each time a student responds correctly, he or she is presented with a reinforcer. However, when higher rates of appropriate responding have been established, an intermittent schedule (e.g., one in which only every fourth correct response is rewarded) has been found more beneficial for the following reasons: (a) The student is less likely to become satiated on the reward, (b) the task can progress more efficiently because the act of reinforcing is not taking time away from instruction, and (c) an intermittent reinforcement schedule is more resistant to extinction than a continuous schedule. Because of the low functioning level and response rates of some children and youth with autism, a continuous reinforcement schedule for extended periods of time may be most effective.

Additional Reinforcement Techniques

Additional reinforcement considerations may be necessary because students with autism may fail to demonstrate desired behaviors or may demonstrate extremely low occurrences of the response. These additional strategies include shaping, prompting, modeling, fading, chaining, and generalization. These strategies are introduced here and expanded on in other sections of this book.

Shaping involves differentially reinforcing successive approximation of a desired terminal behavior until the final behavior is achieved (Hall, 1970). The following steps are typically used in shaping:

1. Define and measure a desired terminal behavior (i.e., what the student should be able to do at the end of the procedure).

2. Identify as a starting point a beginning behavior that the student can perform and that resembles the desired terminal behavior.

3. Break the terminal behavior into steps that the student is able to achieve, beginning with the easiest and ending with the terminal behavior.

4. Teach the student to perform each step, with each step being reinforced as it is successfully accomplished.

5. Divide a given step into smaller steps and reteach if the student is unable to perform a step.

6. Continue this procedure until the student is able to perform the complete behavior.

Prompts are extra reinforcement cues used to facilitate a student's learning a desired behavior. Thus, for instance, a teacher may physically assist a child in matching colors during a one-to-one direct instruction exercise. As with shaping, prompting is most useful when students do not demonstrate or inconsistently demonstrate a desired response.

Modeling involves teaching a behavior by performing the act while the student observes. For example, a child may be shown how to match various colors or shapes as a component of teaching the task.

Fading is used to gradually reduce prompts, models, or other support methods until they are no longer necessary to maintain a newly acquired behavior. For example, as a student begins to acquire a particular skill, fewer and fewer support cues are offered in an effort to assist the individual in independently completing the task.

Chaining involves training clusters of responses that are supportive of one another. For example, consider the behaviors involved in tying shoelaces: (a) A lace is held in each hand, (b) one lace is crossed under the other to form the first tie, (c) a bow is made with one lace, (d) the other lace is wrapped around and through, and (e) the two bows are pulled tight. When broken down like this, the discrete behaviors of tying shoelaces each constitute one act in a behavioral chain. The implications of chaining for the education of students with autism are many. Because it is sometimes difficult to teach these students even simple behaviors, a method that allows for a more efficient training and reinforcing alternative to instructing an individual in independent discrete steps has obvious advantages.

Generalization is critical in the training of persons with autism because of their limited skill transfer. In isolation, a great number of behaviors can be taught to children and youth with autism. However, behaviors taught in isolation do not readily generalize to real-life situations. Thus, students taught to tie shoelaces on a laceboard will likely have trouble transferring the skill to their own shoes, and students who have learned to say "juice" in one-to-one language sessions may remain mute when presented with a juice container in the lunchroom. Accordingly, as noted throughout this book, generalization is a major consideration in planning for students with autism, including developing reinforcement programs.

Extinction Programs

Extinction involves cessation of previously reinforced responses. That is, attempts are made to decrease or eliminate a response by eliminating whatever contingent reinforcement is thought to be maintaining it. For example, a child who yells in order to secure teacher attention would be denied contingent reinforcement. The efficacy of extinction programs has clearly been established (Williams, 1959; E. H. Zimmerman & J. Zimmerman, 1962), particularly when used in combination with other consequences. However, use of extinction involves consideration of several potential problems.

First, the effectiveness of any extinction program is dependent on control of reinforcers that are accelerating or maintaining a particular response. Accordingly, individuals using extinction programs must not only accurately analyze reinforcers for a particular behavior, but also gain control over them. The fact that a student may be, at least in part, reinforced for a particular maladaptive response by his or her peer group, parents, or others often makes the procedure a significant challenge. Second, extinction programs that gain only partial or intermittent control over a behavior may end up making the behavior pattern more immune to extinction (Mathis, Cotton, & Sechrest, 1970). Third, extinction procedures often result in a short-term increase in the target behavior or occurrence of other more intense maladaptive responses. For example, if a child who tends to talk out to attract attention from his teacher is exposed to an extinction schedule, the student's initial response will probably be to increase his talk-outs in order to obtain the contingent attention that is being denied. Under such circumstances, at least periodically, some students may then turn to behaviors that are so unacceptable that ignoring is impossible. For example, the child who starts hitting others for attention after being denied contingent attention would likely require an intervention program other than extinction. Finally, for students who do not demonstrate behaviors for the purpose of obtaining attention, extinction programs are unsuitable.

In spite of such weaknesses, extinction is an appropriate intervention for some individuals with autism. For example, Lovaas, Freitag, Gold, and Kassorla (1965) used an extinction program to demonstrate the power of attention in promoting self-injurious responses; Wolf, Risley, and Mees (1964) successfully used an extinction program to eliminate bedtime problems. As with other interventions, individual circumstances must be considered to determine whether extinction is the most desirable option for managing behavior.

Punishment Programs

Punishment involves presenting undesired consequences or withdrawing reinforcement (e.g., loss of privileges) contingent upon specified undesired behaviors. As mentioned, although proven capable of changing behavior, punishers are recommended *only* when positive alternatives, such as positive reinforcement and extinction, have been found or are considered to be ineffective. The rationale for limited and conservative use of punishers is that such consequences may inadvertently reduce certain desired behaviors, and that persons administering punishment programs may themselves become punishers. Moreover, some students with autism have difficulty distinguishing between positive and negative attention and may display inappropriate behaviors to get attention regardless of whether it is positive or negative. Nonetheless, when used prudently and under appropriate circumstances, punishment represents a significant part of an individual's intervention options. Moreover, it is our contention that it is unacceptable to withhold punishment when it is deemed the most acceptable intervention option. The use of punishment procedures is recommended

- when positive reinforcement procedures and/or extinction have proven to be unsuccessful, or when it is determined that such procedures are unacceptable;
- if the desired behavior is so frequent that there is little or no incompatible behavior to reinforce; or
- if the behavior is so intense that the individual is a danger to self or others.

For punishment procedures to be effective, the teacher (and all other involved staff) should do the following:

- Pair the procedure with positive reinforcement for appropriate behavior.
- Systematically and consistently carry out the punishment.
- Deliver the punishment promptly.
- Implement the procedure in a nonemotional fashion.
- Pair the punishment with a warning signal (the warning signal, administered prior to punishment, permits the warning to become a conditioned punisher, thus leaving the warning as the control mechanism).

- Obtain prior written approval from parents, administrators, and other appropriate persons.

- Develop a detailed description of the program, including exactly what is to be done, who will do it, how long the procedure will continue before formal reassessment of the program, and the method to be used in collecting data to document program success or failure.

- Make frequent contact with parents to communicate progress.

Punishment options include response-cost programs, time-out, overcorrection, and differential reinforcement. *Response cost,* or cost contingency, consists of removing a reinforcer contingent on a specific undesired behavior. Tokens, free time, and privileges may be withdrawn contingent on display of specific behaviors. *Time-out* involves removing an individual from reinforcement contingent on display of a maladaptive response. This strategy has been successfully used to decelerate a variety of unacceptable behaviors. Time-out programs should be structured so that students with whom this procedure is used understand that (a) the time-out procedure is used contingent on specific unacceptable behaviors, and (b) removal from reinforcement is for brief periods of time. Although time-out programs may be effective with some behaviors of individuals with autism, other behaviors will likely require other interventions. For example, some time-out methods may be ineffective with self-stimulation and other unacceptable behaviors that operate independently of attention from others.

According to Foxx and Azrin (1973), *overcorrection* has two objectives: (a) to overcorrect the environmental effects of a maladaptive behavior and (b) to require the disrupting individual to practice a correct form of an appropriate behavior. The procedure for achieving the first objective, *restitutional overcorrection,* requires "the disrupter to correct the consequences of his misbehavior by having him restore the situation to a state vastly improved from that which existed before the disruption" (Foxx & Azrin, 1973, p. 2). A child who soils the classroom, for example, might be made to clean the affected area. *Positive practice overcorrection,* used to achieve the second objective, requires the child who soils to practice picking up items in the classroom. Restitutional overcorrection is applicable only when a maladaptive response disrupts the environment. For example, because self-stimulatory behaviors do not disrupt the environment, only positive practice overcorrection procedures are used with such responses.

Overcorrection is designed not only to reduce unacceptable behavior, but also to facilitate an individual's learning an acceptable alternative. Although further research is needed to document the long-term value of overcorrection, it appears to be a method that assists in both eliminating maladaptive behavior and providing the individual with an appropriate alternative behavior.

Differential reinforcement of other behaviors (DRO) involves attending to and rewarding responses that have been identified as incompatible or appropriate alternatives to an undesired behavior (Skiba, Pettigrew, & Alden, 1971). Thus, unacceptable behaviors are weakened (and as much as possible, ignored) by reinforcing appropriate alternative behaviors. This process involves several options, including reinforcing a student for engaging less frequently in an undesired behavior, reinforcing a student for engaging in behavior that is incompatible with the undesired response, and reinforcing a student for engaging in behavior that is more acceptable than the undesired one.

An example of a DRO procedure for a student who was frequently out of his seat without permission consisted of reinforcing him for in-seat behavior. This program, paired with his teacher's socially praising the child for staying in his seat and attending to his assigned task, resulted in a significant reduction in his being away from his desk without permission.

Antecedent Interventions

Students with autism react to a variety of environmental stimuli as well as adult and peer contingencies, which is frequently revealed by functional analysis of individual students' responses. As a result, manipulation of these factors can help improve students' functioning.

Individuals who teach and otherwise work with children and youth with autism routinely use antecedent manipulation, including removing a child from an area where toys are stored in a classroom or modifying the curriculum. Manipulation of antecedent conditions, however, is an effective management tool when the antecedent stimuli that control an individual's behavior are properly understood and can be controlled. That is, removing a child from a distracting area of the room to reduce self-stimulation does not mean that the student will not engage in self-stimulatory behaviors in other areas; and moving a student up next to the teacher's desk in an effort to increase attention to task does not necessarily result in improved attention if the basic issue is that the curriculum fails to fit a student's needs. A variety of potentially significant variables may be manipulated, including (a) modeling, (b) curriculum modification, (c) educational planning, and (d) social stories.

Modeling involves providing individuals with appropriate models for desired behaviors (Bandura, 1969). A variety of researchers and practitioners have reported on the benefits of modeling, including O'Connor (1969), who assessed the impact of modeling on preschool children's social behavior. In O'Connor's investigation, 6 socially withdrawn students improved their social behaviors by viewing a film of a model child observing the social interactions of other children. Although modeling is ineffective when used independently of other procedures (e.g., practice, reinforcement of desired responses), it appears to be a procedure that can facilitate desired behavior among students with autism.

Anyone who has ever worked with students with autism can attest to the important role of effective *curriculum modification* and planning in managing children and youth with autism. Indeed, careful educational planning and implementation are crucial for developing functional skills and replacing nonfunctional and deviant behaviors with more appropriate responses.

Educators of students with autism have routinely expressed concern over the difficulty of selecting curricula to meet the needs of their students. One reason for this uncertainty is that optimal curricular choices for students with autism are less well defined than for many other students with disabilities. Moreover, children and youth with autism who are also severely impaired may receive little benefit from instructional programs based on the established curriculum for students without disabilities. In addition, educators have failed to reach consensus on the proper instructional methods for students with autism. As a result, educators of students with autism routinely draw from a variety of curricular and instructional methods.

Although the curricular and instructional procedures used with students with autism vary according to the unique needs of individual students, six major skill areas should receive primary consideration: social and behavioral functioning; motor; self-help; speech and language; preacademic/academic; and prevocational/vocational. Careful attention to these areas, along with use of suitable instructional methods, bodes well for students with autism and their behavioral and social success.

Effective *educational planning* and scheduling involve creating an acceptable learning environment for students with autism. Characteristics of effective classrooms for students with autism include the following:

- carpeted floors

- window blinds

- designated areas for such activities as academic work, free time, and vocational/prevocational tasks

- individual study carrels (constructed to allow the sides to be easily dismantled to increase social interactions and accommodate students who require less physical structure)

- a toilet

- a refrigerator

- a sink with running water

- an observation area with a one-way mirror

- a closed storage space

- adequate lighting, heating, and ventilation

- a time-out area

- individual student desks and chairs

- group work tables and chairs

- teacher desk and chair

- bulletin boards and chalkboards

- a screen that blocks unwanted visual stimuli
- an intercommunication system between the classroom and main office
- portable room dividers
- an individual work section
- a small-group area
- an ancillary therapy section
- a free-time section
- a prevocational training area
- a general-use area
- a self-help and hygiene area

Careful scheduling of curricula and experiences for students with autism can also serve as an important management tool. In keeping with the intent of having educational and treatment programs assist children and youth with autism in gradually moving toward independent functioning and improved social behavior, each student should be programmed to receive individual, independent, and small- and large-group experiences. Thus, based on a careful review of the objectives for each pupil, staff must determine which objectives can most appropriately be met within each of the three above-mentioned instructional arrangements. We believe that students should not be excluded from a given scheduling format simply because they experience difficulty. For example, students accustomed to one-to-one instruction may never adapt to a group format if they are not exposed to this option. Thus, in spite of student resistance to group arrangements, provision of only one-to-one instruction would not support the goal of developing behavior control and student independence in various settings.

Use of *social stories* is a relatively new intervention method for individuals with autism (Gray & Gerand, 1993; Swaggart et al., 1995). A social story describes social situations in terms of specific social cues and appropriate social responses. These stories are individualized for each student, usually in the form of two to five sentences. Sentences include descriptive information about a setting, individuals, and actions; *directive* statements describe appropriate behavioral responses and *perspective* sentences describe the feelings and reactions of others in the situation.

Several preliminary studies have suggested that social stories are a promising method for students with autism. For example, Swaggart et al. (1995) increased socially appropriate greeting behaviors and decreased aggression in a severely impaired child with autism and significantly improved social play responses in two 7-year-old boys with autism. Although the efficacy of social story programs remains to be established, the method seems to be worthy of consideration. Swaggart et al. observed:

There is no question that future research is needed to further validate the effectiveness of using social stories with children with autism. Indeed, the

exact role the social stories played in enhancing subjects' social skills, in relation to other variables, is unclear. Nonetheless, based on preliminary findings,
it appears that this technique may have utility in individual and group settings for students with autism who function at a variety of levels. (p. 13)

Generalization, Maintenance, and Follow-Up Activities

As noted, individuals with autism are well known for their difficulty in generalizing and transferring skills from one setting and other certain conditions to
other environments and conditions. For example, a child who has learned to
monitor and control her self-stimulatory behavior in the classroom with her
teacher cannot be assumed to have the same control when with her parent or
when at a local shopping mall. Accordingly, effective management planning
involves attention to generalization planning.

Follow-up and maintenance procedures involve evaluation of intervention
efforts to make any necessary procedural changes. Because students with
autism may be slow to respond even to effective programs, it is important not
to change an intervention too soon, even if it initially fails to produce a desired
behavior change.

Finally, it is recommended that support staff, including classroom aides,
related services staff, and other personnel working with children and youth
with autism be properly trained, supported, and reinforced for their efforts.

Summary

Effective management of children and youth with autism is a foundational
activity. Indeed, in the absence of utilitarian management programs, students
with autism will likely make minimal progress. This chapter provides information regarding several management options, including reinforcement, extinction, behavior reduction, and antecedent manipulation interventions. These
behaviorally based program options offer flexible and broad potential for application with students with autism in various settings.

References

Alberto, P. A., & Troutman, A. C. (1990). *Applied behavior analysis for teachers* (3rd. ed.). Columbus, OH: Merrill.

Azrin, N. H., Besalel, V. A., Jamner, J. P., & Caputo, J. N. (1988). Comparative study of behavioral
methods of treating self injury. *Behavioral Residential Treatment, 3,* 119–152.

Bandura, A. (1969). *Principles of behavior modification.* New York: Holt, Rinehart & Winston.

Bersoff, D., & Grieger, R. (1971). An interview model for the psychosituational assessment of children's behavior. *American Journal of Orthopsychiatry, 41,* 483–493.

Clark-Hall, M., Collier, H., Fayman, K., Grinstead, J., Kearns, P., Robie, D., & Rotton, M. (1976). *Responsive parent training manual.* Lawrence, KS: H & H Enterprises.

Farrar-Schneider, D. (1994). Aggression and noncompliance: Behavior modification. In J. L. Matson (Ed.), *Autism in children and adults* (pp. 183–191). Pacific Grove, CA: Brooks/Cole.

Foxx, R., & Azrin, N. (1973). The elimination of outside self-stimulatory behavior by overcorrection. *Journal of Applied Behavior Analysis, 6,* 1–12.

Gardner, W. I., & Cole, C. L. (1990). Aggression and related conduct difficulties. In J. L. Matson (Ed.), *Handbook of behavior modification with the mentally retarded* (pp. 225–251). New York: Plenum.

Gray, C., & Gerand, J. D. (1993). Social stories: Improving responses of students with autism with accurate social information. *Focus on Autistic Behavior, 8*(1), 1–10.

Groden, G., & Baron, M. G. (1988). *Autism: Strategies for change.* New York: Gardner.

Hall, R. V. (1970). *Behavior modification: The measurement of behavior.* Lawrence, KS: H & H Enterprises.

Hall, R. V., Hawkins, R. P., & Axelrod, S. (1975). Measuring and recording student behavior: A behavior analysis approach. In R. A. Weinberg & F. E. Wood (Eds.), *Observation of pupils and teachers in mainstream and special education: Alternative strategies* (pp. 18–27). Minneapolis: University of Minnesota, Leadership Training Institute.

Iwata, B. A., Pace, G., Kalsher, M. J., Cowdery, G. E., & Cataldo, M. F. (1990). Experimental analysis and extinction of self-injurious escape behavior. *Journal of Applied Behavior Analysis, 23,* 11–27.

Koegel, R. L., & Koegel, L. K. (1995). *Teaching children with autism.* Baltimore: Brookes.

LaVigna, G. W., & Willis, T. J. (1992). A model for multielement treatment planning and outcome measurement. In D. E. Berkell (Ed.), *Autism: Identification, education and treatment* (pp. 135–149). Hillsdale, NJ: Erlbaum.

Lovaas, O. I. (1987). Behavioral treatment and normal intellectual functioning in autistic children. *Journal of Consulting and Clinical Psychology, 55,* 3–9.

Lovaas, O. I., Freitag, G., Gold, V. J., & Kassorla, I. C. (1965). Recording apparatus and procedure for observation of behaviors of children in free play settings. *Journal of Experimental Child Psychology, 2,* 108–120.

Mathis, B. C., Cotton, J. W., & Sechrest, L. (1970). *Psychological foundations of education.* New York: Academic Press.

Mitchell, W. S., & Stoffelmoyer, B. E. (1973). Application of the Premack principle to the behavioral control of extremely inactive schizophrenics. *Journal of Applied Behavior Analysis, 6,* 419–424.

Myles, B. S., & Quinn, C. (1995). *Behavior analysis form.* Kansas City: University of Kansas Medical Center, Department of Special Education.

Newman, R., Whorton, D., & Simpson, R. (1977). The modification of self-stimulatory verbalizations in an autistic child through the use of an overcorrection procedure. *AAESPH Review, 2,* 157–163.

O'Connor, R. D. (1969). Modification of social withdrawal through symbolic modeling. *Journal of Applied Behavior Analysis, 2,* 15–22.

O'Leary, K., & Becker, W. (1968). The effects of the intensity of a teacher's reprimands on children's behavior. *Journal of School of Psychology, 7,* 8–11.

Powers, M. D. (1992). Early intervention for children with autism. In D. E. Berkell (Ed.), *Autism: Identification, education and treatment* (pp. 225–252). Hillsdale, NJ: Erlbaum.

Risley, T. R. (1968). The effects and side-effects of punishing the autistic behaviors of a deviant child. *Journal of Applied Behavior Analysis, 1,* 21–34.

Sasso, G. M., & Reimers, T. M. (1988). Assessing the functional properties of behavior: Implications and applications for the classroom. *Focus on Autistic Behavior, 3*(5), 1–15.

Simpson, R. L. (1977). *Behavior modification with the severely emotionally disturbed* (Working paper no. 5. Severe Personal Adjustment Project). Washington, DC: U.S. Office of Education, Department of Health, Education, and Welfare, Bureau of Education for the Handicapped.

Simpson, R. L. (1996). *Working with parents and families of exceptional children and youth.* Austin, TX: PRO-ED.

Simpson, R. L., Myles, B. S., Sasso, G. M., & Kamps, D. M. (1991). *Social skills for students with autism.* Reston, VA: Council for Exceptional Children.

Simpson, R. L., & Regan, M. (1988). *Management of autistic behavior.* Austin, TX: PRO-ED.

Skiba, E. A., Pettigrew, L. E., & Alden, S. W. (1971). A behavioral approach to the control of thumb-sucking in the classroom. *Journal of Applied Behavior Analysis, 4,* 121–125.

Skinner, B. F. (1953). *Science and human behavior.* New York: Macmillan.

Swaggart, B., Gagnon, E., Bock, S., Earles, T., Quinn, C., Myles, B., & Simpson, R. (1995). Using social stories to teach social and behavioral skills to children with autism. *Focus on Autistic Behavior, 10*(1), 1–16.

Williams, C. D. (1959). The elimination of tantrum behavior by extinction procedures. *Journal of Abnormal and Social Psychology, 59,* 269.

Wolf, M., Risley, T., & Mees, H. (1964). Application of operant conditioning procedures to the behavior problems of an autistic child. *Behavior Research and Therapy, 1,* 305–312.

Zimmerman, E. H., & Zimmerman, J. (1962). The alteration of behavior in a special classroom situation. *Journal of Experimental Analysis of Behavior, 5,* 59–60.

The Communicative
Context of Autism

5

Billy T. Ogletree

Although behavioral manifestations of autism vary greatly, certain characteristics are commonly associated with children and adults diagnosed as autistic or autistic-like. One of these is impaired communicative abilities. Persons with autism can be expected to present a wide spectrum of communication impairments ranging from mutism to higher order social deficits. For decades these impairments have frustrated both professionals and parents.

This chapter provides professionals and parents with a theoretical framework and practical knowledge to assist persons with autism in attaining functional communicative abilities. It begins with the presentation of a conceptual model for understanding communicative impairments in autism and follows with a practical overview of this population and its communicative abilities and limitations. The chapter also discusses guidelines for assessment and intervention, with particular emphasis upon persons with nonverbal or emergent verbal communicative abilities. This subgroup is emphasized due to the challenges they pose for most providers. This chapter concludes with a case study illustrating assessment and intervention with a child with autism.

A Conceptual Model for Understanding Communication and Language Impairments in Individuals with Autism

Typical communication and language has been thought to emerge as a result of innate "hard wiring" that enables children to function in early social exchanges with caregivers. These interactions provide the basis for cognitive, affective, and social growth that is central to communication and later language development.

Knowledge of this typical process provides insight into possible sources of communication and language impairment in autism. First, if we define "hard wiring" as neural integrity, it would be fair to assume a causative relationship between atypical central nervous system functioning and communication and language impairments. For example, in a review of etiologies, Locke, Banken, and Mahone (1994) reported numerous structural and functional central nervous system abnormalities in persons with autism. As a result, these hard wiring differences may contribute to learning styles/strategies that interfere with the typical emergence of communication and language.

Schuler (1995) provided an extensive review of learning differences in autism. Citing a variety of literature, she noted at least three distinct learning characteristics: (1) Persons with autism can demonstrate central deficits with information processing rooted in deficient coding and categorization abilities (i.e., the input and organization of information); (2) persons with autism tend to prefer static (i.e., nonmoving) rather than transient visual stimuli; and (3) learners with autism exhibit stimulus overselectivity, a "tendency to tune in to a single stimulus component" (p. 14).

It is easy to imagine how these learner characteristics may affect early communication and the emergence of language. Consider, for example, the following typical caregiver–infant exchange. A baby looks at his mother who smiles, shakes her head, and talks softly to the child. The baby responds by smiling and vocalizing. In this scenario, the mother's stimulus is largely transient, which places the child with autism at risk because of his preference for static stimuli. Furthermore, the child who exhibits stimulus overselectivity may miss the entire event because of attention only to the mother's clothing or jewelry.

As children age, typical caregiver exchanges play a vital role in establishing referential and relational meaning. For example, a child shows her mother a ball. The mother responds by labeling the ball and expanding her utterance in a descriptive manner—"It's a big blue ball." Due to overselectivity (e.g., preoccupation with the ball), the child with autism may fail to even establish the joint attention necessary to participate in this exchange. If she does participate, her processing limitations may prevent the coding and categorization of information critical for establishing meaning.

The learner characteristics of persons with autism may continue to interfere with typical communication and language emergence throughout childhood and adolescence. For example, as successful communication becomes more dependent upon the processing of subtle transient stimuli such as speech, facial expressions, and body postures, persons with autism may be at increasingly greater risk for communicative failure.

A conceptual model for understanding communication and language impairments in individuals with autism, then, begins with the assumption of obvious or imperceptible central nervous system differences that contribute to atypical learner styles/strategies. Initially, these characteristics compromise early caregiver–child exchanges central to typical sociocommunicative and cognitive growth. Subsequently, they place the individual with autism at increasing risk for communicative failure due to the complexities inherent in higher order communication and language.

The model described above is clearly simplistic. That is, other factors can be implicated in the communication and language impairments of persons with autism. These include motor limitations (DeMyer, 1975; Rogers & Pennington, 1991) and apparent preferences for object-referenced rather than people-referenced thought (Schuler, 1995). Needless to say, communication and language impairments in autism are the result of multifactored causation.

Communication and Language Characteristics of Persons with Autism

The following discussion of the communication and language of persons with autism focuses on those who communicate either through nonverbal or emergent verbal means or through productive speech and language. The section concludes with a discussion of the development of comprehension across these subgroups.

Nonverbal Communication

For the purposes of this review, *nonverbal communication* is defined as "intentional nonsymbolic communication," described as persistent signaling offered with a knowledge of its effects on a listener (Bates, 1979). An example might be a child's persistent reach toward an object while gazing back and forth between the object and a nearby caregiver who could help get the object for the child. Intentional communication originates from infant behaviors and emerges within the infant–caregiver communicative exchange as a result of the child's acquisition of social skills and the caregiver's ability to interpret the signals. In typically developing children, initial intentional nonsymbolic communication takes the form of conventional gestures and vocalizations.

In recent years, the intentional nonsymbolic communicative behaviors of persons with autism have received considerable study. Primarily, findings relate to this population's conventional and unconventional use of communicative forms (e.g., gestures, vocalizations, and behaviors) and the functions these forms express. Rate and reciprocity of nonsymbolic communication have also received increased attention. Table 5.1 provides a summary of the communicative forms and functions most often observed in persons with autism.

Table 5.1

Communicative Forms and Functions Used Most Often by Persons with Autism Who Communicate Nonsymbolically

Communicative forms

Conventional

    Gestures

        Isolated gestures characterized by contact with objects/persons

    Vocalizations

        Limited sophistication characterized by infrequent use of consonants

Unconventional

    Excess behavior

        Aberrant

        Self-injurious

Communicative functions

Behavior regulation

    Requests

    Protests

    Escapes

Social interaction[a]

    Showing off

    Greeting

Joint attention[a]

    Commenting

[a]Infrequently observed.

Conventional Communicative Forms

Studies of the use of conventional communicative forms have emphasized this population's use of gestures and vocalizations. For example, persons with autism have been reported to gesture less frequently and with less sophistication than children who are typically developing or persons with other developmental disabilities (Bartak, Rutter, & Cox, 1975; Ricks & Wing, 1976; Wetherby & Prutting, 1984; Wetherby, Yonclas, & Bryan, 1989). With respect to sophistication, isolated gestures involving contact with others or objects (e.g., hand-over-hand leads) have been frequently reported.

Findings specific to vocalizations have been less prevalent. Wetherby and Prutting (1984) noted substantial vocal behavior from their 2 participants, who were not using words or other symbols flexibly. In a subsequent, more detailed study, Wetherby et al. (1989) reported significant vocal immaturity (the lack of consonants) from 3 prelinguistic individuals with autism.

Persons with autism who use intentional gestures and vocalizations have been reported to express a narrow range of communicative functions. This is in stark contrast to normally developing children, who communicate preverbally for a variety of purposes. Curcio (1978), who provided the initial description of purposes served by the communicative behaviors of children with autism, reported gestures serving requesting, protesting, and greeting functions. In more recent studies, Wetherby and Prutting (1984) and Wetherby et al. (1989) reported that their participants communicated to regulate the behavior of others, primarily requesting objects, requesting actions, and protesting. Interestingly, social and joint attention functions (e.g., showing-off behaviors or comments) were not observed or were observed infrequently.

Drawing from the literature, Wetherby (1986) speculated that functions serving regulatory purposes (e.g., requests) emerge first, followed by social (e.g., greetings) and, in some cases, joint attention (e.g., showing) functions. She theorized that the ability to attract attention to self (an early social function) may serve as a bridge to the less frequent, and later emerging, functions of directing attention to objects or events. These findings have received support from naturalistic observations of the spontaneous communication of children with autism (Stone & Caro-Martinez, 1990).

Unconventional Communicative Forms

Studies of the unconventional expression of communication in nonverbal persons with autism have examined the potential communicative value of aberrant or self-injurious behavior. The literature is replete with examples of excess behavior serving communicative purposes for persons with autism or other severe developmental disabilities (Durand & Carr, 1991; Horner & Budd, 1983; Horner, Day, Sprague, O'Brien, & Heathfield, 1991; Lovaas, Freitag, Gold, & Kassorla, 1965; Schuler & Goetz, 1981; Vollmer, Marcus, & Rigdahl, 1995).

Doss and Reichle (1991) described excess behavior as "behavior . . . that results in self-injury or injury of others, causes damage to the physical environment, interferes with the acquisition of new skills, and/or socially isolates the learner" (p. 215). Excess behavior has been reported to serve a variety of functions, including attention getting, requesting, escaping, and protesting (Carr & Durand, 1985; Durand & Carr, 1987). Doss and Reichle speculated that learners often engage in excess behavior as a result of positive and negative reinforcement. For example, individuals may engage in behaviors to obtain positive or avoid undesirable consequences.

Finally, Wetherby et al. (1989) examined communicative rate and reciprocity. *Communicative rate* is defined as the number of intentional communicative acts occurring per minute. Their study revealed that the communicative rates of their 3 participants with autism were consistent with those observed in children who were typically developing.

Wetherby et al.'s (1989) description of *reciprocity,* or "discourse structure," refers to the use of either initiated or respondent communicative acts. *Initiated acts* are defined as those offered by the child without an adult's speaking prior to the act, whereas *respondent acts* are defined as those intended to maintain a topic or imitate a previous act. These investigators reported that initiated communicative acts significantly exceeded respondent acts. This pattern can contribute to inflexibility within communicative interactions (i.e., limited turn taking) and is inconsistent with the use of discourse structure by children who are typically developing.

In summary, a variety of nonverbal communicative abilities may be observed in persons with autism. These may take the form of intentional communicative acts offered through conventional or unconventional means. Persons capable of intentional nonsymbolic communication can be expected to rely heavily upon isolated gestures and to express somewhat limited ranges of communicative functions. They also may present themselves as inflexible turn takers in interactions.

Emergent Verbal Communication

The emergent verbal communicative abilities of persons with autism have received limited attention in the professional literature. Two divergent theories of their early language acquisition prevail. One suggests that language emerges in a manner that is largely consistent with normal acquisition. Supporting this view are limited longitudinal data and several studies detailing early speech/sign use in persons with autism. A second perspective suggests that language development in persons with autism is atypical and heavily dependent upon extreme gestalt processing styles, whereby language is learned through memorization and repetition with limited comprehension.

The Normal Acquisition Position

Tager-Flusberg et al. (1990) followed the language acquisition patterns of 6 high-functioning children with autism over a 1- to 2-year period. Participants presented mean lengths of utterance (MLU) between 1 and 4 morphemes. Analysis of speech samples collected bimonthly revealed MLU gains in 4 of 6 participants. In general, participants also appeared to acquire grammatical structures and experience changes in lexical growth/diversity in a manner consistent with normative expectations. Atypical patterns of language emergence included a decline in MLU by 1 participant and reliance upon an increasingly narrow range of grammatical structures by participants with MLUs above 3.

Numerous investigators have documented somewhat typical language emergence patterns in persons with autism after the introduction of sign language (Fulwiler & Fouts, 1976; Layton & Baker, 1981; A. Miller & E. E. Miller, 1973; Ogletree, 1992; Webster, McPherson, Sloman, Evans, & Kuchar, 1973; Yoder & Layton, 1988). For example, Layton and Baker reported findings of an 18-month sign language training effort with a child who was mute. Posttraining, the child used a core vocabulary of single signs and some signed phrases. Although a somewhat typical pattern of word emergence was reported, the child's rate of sign acquisition was slow and his creativity with signs was limited (i.e., his use of language was limited to expressing immediate needs or describing objects present in this environment). In addition, Fulwiler and Fouts reported specific findings from their use of total communication training with a nonverbal child with autism. After only 20 hours of training, the child was reported to use several single signs and some signed phrases. Interestingly, soon after signs emerged, some intelligible speech was also observed. Fulwiler and Fouts reported the following emergence of word classes (signed and verbal) from the child: nouns, verbs, pronouns, and adverbs. Signed phrases were observed to consist of verb–object and adverb–noun combinations. These investigators noted that the child's word class frequencies and phrasal structures were consistent with early normative expectations.

Ogletree (1992) also trained signs to a nonverbal child with autism. At the initiation of training, the child was described as a nonsymbolic intentional communicator. After 52 training sessions using naturalistic procedures, 13 signs were observed spontaneously, including eight nouns and five verbs. By the midpoint of training, sign combinations were reported reflecting verb–object phrasing. Unlike Fulwiler and Fouts (1976), however, Ogletree observed no verbalizations. Ogletree's findings, like those of Fulwiler and Fouts, appear consistent with early patterns of normal language emergence.

The Atypical Acquisition Position

Several theorists have suggested that initial language emergence in persons with autism is the product of atypical cognitive and linguistic growth. Central to this position is the role of *echolalia* (i.e., a class of speech repetitions) in the acquisition of language form and function for persons with autism (Baltaxe & Simmons, 1977; Prizant, 1983, 1987; Simon, 1975). Specifically, echolalia has been suggested to be the product of a gestalt processing preference. *Gestalt processors* are thought to learn language through memorization and repetition, which initially occurs with limited comprehension (Peters, 1983). Persons with autism, then, may progress from echoing whole chunks of language to echoing and combining smaller segments of language, to using a generative language system (Baltaxe & Simmons, 1977). This idea has received particular support from Prizant and Rydell (1984), who reported evidence of the increasingly productive and sophisticated use of echolalia among study participants with autism.

In addition to its speculative role in the emergence of language form, echolalia has also been reported to contribute to the emergence and expression of language function (Prizant, 1983). Two broad categories of echolalia—immediate and delayed—have been identified on the basis of the temporal latency between the echo and the original utterance (Rydell & Prizant, 1995).

Prizant and his colleagues (Prizant & Duchan, 1981; Prizant & Rydell, 1984) suggested that some forms of immediate and delayed echolalia serve *noninteractive functions*. Examples include *nonfocused echolalia* (i.e., speech devoid of relevance given the context in which it is offered) and *situational echolalia* (i.e., speech triggered by objects, actions, or events). Prizant and colleagues also reported several *interactive functions* expressed through immediate and delayed echolalia, including turn taking, labeling, affirming, completing, calling, protesting, and requesting. McEvoy, Loveland, and Landry (1988) confirmed these findings, reporting many of the same interactive functions from their participants with autism. Types and examples of echolalia are provided in Table 5.2.

I believe that the typical and atypical positions regarding early verbal development in autism are compatible. For example, if one assumes a continuum of normalcy with respect to language emergence, persons at the "less normal end" might be expected to depend heavily upon echolalia as a means of developing productive language. In contrast, persons at the "more normal end" of the continuum might demonstrate patterns of typical emergence aided less visibly by a gestalt cognitive and linguistic processing style. Regardless of the position taken, it is clear that although the language form of persons with autism can appear typical, their use of language in social contexts is usually impaired.

Table 5.2
Types and Examples of Echolalia

Immediate echolalia

Speech repetitions occurring immediately following original utterances.

Example: Original utterance—"How are you today?" Immediate response—"How are you today?"

Delayed echolalia

Speech repetitions occurring after a clear period of temporal delay.

Example: Original utterance offered by a child's parent at breakfast—"Would you like a drink?" Delayed response during afternoon snack when provided with a choice between milk or juice—"Would you like a drink?"

Productive Speech and Language

Clearly, many persons with autism develop sophisticated speech and language abilities. Any review of these abilities must include attention to both speech and language structure and function.

Speech

The articulatory or phonologic abilities of persons with autism are often a relative strength compared to other areas of communication and language. For example, investigators have reported speech clarity comparable to or exceeding that of control populations with disability (Bartolucci, Pierce, Streiner, & Eppel, 1976; Boucher, 1976). Interestingly, in some cases the echolalia of persons with autism has been observed to be more articulate than their generative speech (Prizant, 1978).

However, most aspects of voice can be impaired in persons with autism, including abnormalities of pitch, volume, timing, and stress. According to Baltaxe and Simmons (1975), intonation, stress, and timing are most often impaired, leading to speech that is staid and invariant.

Language

Expressive language can be described in terms of form (i.e., morphology and syntax), content (i.e., semantics), and use (i.e., pragmatics; Bloom & Lahey, 1978). Over the past 20 years, a wealth of data have been reported regarding the language form of higher functioning persons with autism. In general, findings have supported a "delayed but not different" conclusion (Bartolucci, Pierce, & Streiner, 1980; Swisher & Demetras, 1985). That is, morphological and syntactic abilities have been thought to emerge in a slow but typical pattern. Prizant (1988) questioned this conclusion because echolalic utterances were not included in the analyses upon which it was based.

Higher order impairments of language content in autism were recently reviewed by Brook and Bowler (1992). They noted numerous semantic differences, including the following:

- problems encoding meaning relevant to conversation
- literal interpretations of verbal messages
- semantic confusion specific to temporal sequencing
- poor senses of semantic relationships

Brook and Bowler speculated that these, among other deficits, place persons with autism at significant risk for communicative failure.

Language use, or *pragmatics,* has been described as the primary area of communication impairment in persons with high-functioning autism. L. K. Koegel

(1995) reviewed three categories of pragmatics: paralinguistic/extralinguistic features, linguistic intent, and social competence (see Table 5.3).

In summary, persons with autism possessing productive speech and language demonstrate a variety of communicative abilities and impairments. Although they may speak clearly and use fair sophistication with respect to language form, they usually exhibit a variety of semantic and/or pragmatic deficits that place them at significant risk for communicative failure.

Comprehension in Persons with Autism

Comprehension of communication and language is a developmental process that continues into early adulthood. Hallmarks include (a) "context-assisted" comprehension of nonsymbolic and emergent symbolic communication (e.g., comprehension aided by gestures, vocal tone/stress); (b) comprehension of word order; and (c) comprehension of higher order language content, form, and use.

The following is an abbreviated review of comprehension in persons with autism. An attempt is made to address comprehension abilities across the communication/language subgroups of individuals with autism discussed here: (a) nonverbal and emergent verbal communication and (b) productive speech and language.

Nonverbal and Emergent Verbal Communication

Little is known specific to the communication or language comprehension of persons with autism who are nonverbal. Impaired comprehension, however, seems probable given this population's frequent affective deficits (e.g., speech tone/stress abnormalities). The normal language literature emphasizes the relationship between affect and emergent comprehension in infants and toddlers (Bloom & Lahey, 1978; Stern, 1985). Specifically, children who are typically developing rely upon paralinguistic and extralinguistic information during communicative exchanges. Simply stated, it is the emotion of "no" or the extended palm offered in conjunction with "give it to me" that conveys meaning to typical infants and toddlers.

Regardless of probable deficits, parents and other communicative partners frequently report at least context-assisted comprehension in children with autism who are nonsymbolic. Furthermore, some researchers have reported anecdotal data supporting comprehension. For example, Ogletree (1992) stated that his nonverbal study participant was capable of following some single-step commands.

Comprehension in persons with autism who are capable of emergent verbalizations has been considered primarily in its relationship to echolalia. Initially it was assumed that limited comprehension caused echolalia (Stengel, 1964). A more developmental view describes echolalia as a transitional process by which some children with autism acquire functional language. In support of

Table 5.3

Paralinguistic/Extralinguistic Categories of Language Use

Category	Features
Paralinguistic	Those aspects of speech (e.g., stress, volume, intonation, and pitch) that are used to map implied meaning to messages. Their essential nature becomes apparent when one recognizes the multiple intentions paralinguistic features can convey. For example, "my turn" can be a question or imperative, depending upon how features are used to "color" the phrase (e.g., intonation).
Extralinguistic	Those nonlinguistic aspects of messages that typically provide illustration, emphasis, or clarification. Examples of these include depictive or indicative gestures, facial expressions, and body posturing. L. K. Koegel (1995) has suggested, as noted earlier in this review, that both paralinguistic and extralinguistic features are often impaired in persons with autism.
Linguistic intent	"The use of utterances in the context of social discourse" (Koegel, 1995, p. 20). The expression of linguistic intent, then, is a process of constant evaluation by modifying the message according to a speaker's perceptions of both listener knowledge and communicative success. An example might be a comment about a ball game. The comment, if responded to with a puzzled look or question, might be followed by a more specific reference to the game and play of interest. As is clear from this example, linguistic intent is closely related to the paralinguistic and extralinguistic pragmatic features mentioned above. Koegel has suggested that inattention to communicative partners and limited expressive language abilities can prevent successful expression of linguistic intent by persons with autism.
Social competence	Those verbal and nonverbal speaker skills used within interactions. According to Koegel, verbal aspects of social competence include establishing and maintaining a topic and proper interactive turn taking. Nonverbal social competence is apparent in physical behaviors used to regulate conversation, such as eye gaze, proxemics, physical closeness, and posturing. Impairment of both verbal and nonverbal social competence is a widely recognized characteristic of persons with high-functioning autism (Brook & Bowler, 1992; Koegel, 1995).

this position, many investigators have reported inverse relationships between echolalia and comprehension abilities (Fay, 1969; Howlin, 1982; Rutter & Lockyer, 1967). Specifically, they have suggested that echoic utterances decrease over time as comprehension and productive language increase. Recent efforts have furthered this position, reporting qualitative changes in echolalia during the move to functional language. For example, *mitigated echolalia,* a more sophisticated nonexact echo, has been observed in children with autism as their comprehension and expressive language abilities become increasingly complex (Roberts, 1989).

Productive Speech and Language

Recent investigations of higher order speech and language comprehension in persons with autism have primarily considered word meaning, morphology, and syntax. Results indicate that comprehension of simple words and concepts such as color, number, and form does not differ substantially from that of language-matched normally developing children (Bryson, 1983; Tager-Flusberg, 1985a, 1985b, 1985c; Ungerer & Sigman, 1987). Eskes, Bryson, and McCormick (1990) extended this conclusion, stating that higher functioning persons with autism are capable of comprehending even more complex concepts such as life and time.

Limited findings specific to morphology and syntax have supported both a normal and a disordered comprehension scenario. For example, Beisler, Tsai, and Vonk (1987) reported no significant differences in performance on an auditory comprehension measure between children with and without autism matched by age, mental age, and sex variables. These researchers also noted similar patterns of errors for both groups. In contrast, using other language measures, Bartak, Rutter, and Cox (1975) reported more severe language-comprehension deficits in children with autism than in children with language delay or psychiatric diagnoses.

As noted, persons with autism who exhibit advanced expressive language abilities often experience communicative failure due to limited sensitivity to partners within social discourse, which could be considered a form of impaired comprehension. For example, communicative exchanges may be jeopardized as a result of literal interpretations of messages or failing to modify messages according to knowledge about the listener (Brook & Bowler, 1992; L. K. Koegel, 1995).

Obviously, additional research is needed to develop a complete understanding of communication/language comprehension in autism. The current knowledge base suggests that, at least for persons who are verbal, language comprehension may be either consistent with or impaired compared to developmental expectations. In contrast, their comprehension and use of semantic/pragmatic subtleties necessary for successful social discourse are often impaired.

Assessment of Communication and Language in Persons with Autism

The ultimate goal of communication or language assessment for persons with autism should be the generation of reliable and representative data useful in treatment planning. This section describes assessment principles and practices vital for achievement of this goal. Practices specific to nonverbal and emergent verbal communicators are emphasized because of the specific challenges they present.

Assessment Principles

In a recent review of assessment in speech–language pathology, Ogletree, Saddler, and Bowers (1995) reported a shift from exclusionary, one-time, client-focused practices to practices that are more inclusive, ongoing, and ecologically valid. They suggested that this shift is the result of four major assessment principles, initially described by Beukelman and Mirenda (1992; see Table 5.4).

Table 5.4
Assessment Principles

Principle 1: *All people communicate.* Communication is a characteristic of all individuals. One might assume that this is a belief generally embraced by individuals serving persons with communication and language impairments. Unfortunately, it is not. In contrast, many service providers practice from the assumption that if persons are not communicative via clear, conventional means, they are not candidates for communication/language assessment. Obviously, this perspective would prevent the assessment of many persons with autism.

Principle 2: *Assessment should be a process.* This principle recognizes the changing nature of communication in persons with disabilities, particularly those with autism. As a result, assessment cannot be a static event, but needs to occur early and often to identify problems, determine directions for treatment, evaluate treatment effectiveness, and project future needs.

Principle 3: *Assessment should be functional.* Communication and language assessment for persons with autism must provide data specific to functional needs. L. K. S. McLean (1990) has encouraged functional assessment in the evaluation of persons with disabilities. Specifically, she has advised against the sole use of procedures that only provide performance comparisons with normative standards.

Principle 4: *Assessment should involve more than the person with disability.* Assessment must focus upon persons with autism and their typical communicative partners and environments. This is in contrast to traditional assessment, which was client centered and occurred in isolated "testing" contexts.

Assessment Practices

During the past two decades, innovative assessment practices have been generated that are consistent with the principles mentioned in Table 5.4. Due to the scope and range of these practices, only those relevant to persons with nonverbal or emergent verbal abilities are reviewed here, with specific attention given to assessment targets and protocols. *Assessment targets* can be any behaviors/observations that provide information about the communicative competence or performance of persons with communication impairments. *Assessment protocols*, in turn, are procedures designed to evaluate targets. According to Ogletree and Burns Daniels (1993), successful assessment protocols reliably identify typical communicative behaviors and needs across communicative environments and provide information to assist with treatment decisions and directions.

The Assessment of Nonverbal and Emergent Verbal Communicators

Ogletree, Fischer, and Turowski (1996) recently posed assessment targets for communicators with profound disabilities, as illustrated in Table 5.5. Targets are specific to both the communicator and his or her environments and are applicable to persons with autism with nonverbal or emergent verbal abilities.

Ogletree et al. (1996) identified the primary communicator-related target for nonverbal communicators as *communicative intent*. According to these authors, a communicative behavior is intentional when it is directed toward a potential partner and a response is awaited (Wetherby, Cain, Yonclas, & Walker, 1988). They cited the following behavioral signs of communicative intent: (a) alternating eye contact between a communicative partner and a goal, (b) gesturing persistently toward a goal, (c) signaling in a ritualized manner, and (d) terminating signaling when a goal is achieved (Bates, 1979; Harding, 1984; Harding & Golinkoff, 1979).

If intentional communication is observed, several other targets specific to its expression are suggested as listed in Table 5.5 (Ogletree et al., 1996). These include the rate (i.e., frequency), forms (i.e., conventional and unconventional means), and functions (i.e., purposes including requests, protests, comments, and greetings among others) of intentional communicative behaviors.

Other communicator-related targets posed by Ogletree et al. (1996) include dyadic interactional skills such as the ability to "attend to others and to the focus of interaction, to initiate and respond within interaction, and to direct the attention of others for the purpose of establishing joint focus on objects or events" (p. 55). A final dyadic interaction target is communication/language comprehension.

Prizant (1988) also included echolalia, suggesting that the assessment of echolalia can provide insight into an individual's knowledge of communicative function and emergent communicative and linguistic abilities. In part, he based this conclusion on the previously discussed notion that echolalia can fol-

Table 5.5

Assessment Targets for Nonverbal and Emergent
Verbal Communicators with Persons with Autism

Communicator-related targets

    Physical competence

      Hearing

      Vision

      Gestural/vocal development

      Oral motor abilities

    Communicative intent

      Rate of communicative acts

      Communicative forms

      Communicative functions

      Echolalia

    Dyadic interaction skills

      Attention to others

      Focus on interaction

      Patterns of initiation and response within interaction

      Ability to establish joint focus on objects or events

    Comprehension of communication

Environmental targets

    Numbers of communicative partners and settings

    Opportunities for communication across partners and settings

    Communicative success across partners and settings

Note. From "Assessment Targets and Protocols for Nonsymbolic Communicators with Profound Disabilities," by B. Ogletree, M. Fischer, and M. Turowski, 1996, *Focus on Autism and Other Developmental Disabilities, 11*(1) p. 54.

low a predictable pattern of emergence leading to productive language for some persons with autism.

    Prizant (1988) noted both the importance of and difficulty with assessing oral motor abilities in persons with autism, suggesting that strong indicators of oral motor impairment can include the lack of intelligible speech in the presence of relatively superior receptive language and cognitive abilities, or oral posturing and groping articulatory movements. The presence of oral motor difficulties or the otherwise unexplained absence of speech should lead investigators to additional assessment targets specific to the applicability of augmentative communication. Initial targets might include imitative gestural behaviors, graphic symbol recognition, and environmental support for nonspeech communication.

Ogletree et al. (1996) identified numerous environmental targets for nonverbal and emergent verbal communicators. These include the number of communicative partners, opportunities for and success with communication, and the number and variety of typical communicative environments. Obviously, these targets are intended to provide information specific to the person with a disability and his or her environment. Table 5.6 provides an assessment protocol (Ogletree et al., 1996) designed to assess the targets discussed above.

Treatment of Communication Disorders in Persons with Autism

Any review of communication or speech and language treatment for persons with autism must include discussions of treatment appropriateness, goal selection, and various treatment approaches/strategies. What follows is a review of these issues and summaries of two current nontraditional approaches. Treatments most appropriate for nonverbal and emergent verbal communicators are emphasized.

Treatment Appropriateness

Most persons with autism present communication or speech and language impairments and, according to discrepancy-based treatment decisions, would therefore be candidates for intervention. In fact, most persons with autism would benefit from communication or speech and language treatment. For example, if treatment is viewed as direct service intended to remediate communication deficits, all persons with autism would be probable candidates. Furthermore, if the only acceptable treatment outcome is "typical" communicative abilities, treatment could continue indefinitely. In contrast, if treatment is viewed along a continuum from direct service to consultation, and if outcomes are functional communicative abilities, one could envision no treatment or limited treatment for some.

According to this perspective, treatment is appropriate for persons with autism when improvements in functional communicative abilities are needed. For some, these improvements may be possible through consultation specific to communication partners and environments. The needs of others may be best addressed through more traditional direct communication or speech and

Table 5.6

Assessment Protocols for Nonverbal and Emergent
Verbal Communications with Persons with Autism

Protocol	Features
1. Caregivers' interview	Collection of data specific to typical communicative behaviors, partners, and environments.
2. Caregivers–communicator interaction	Observations specific to communicator and environmental assessment targets (videotaping may be useful).
3. Structured sampling	The communicator is placed in near-obligatory communicative contexts. Structured sampling should allow specific opportunities for assessing communicator-related targets, including communicative intent, dyadic interaction skills, and comprehension. A typical structured sampling activity might include eating in front of a communicator without offering food. These types of activities have been used effectively in the collection of communication/emergent language samples from persons with autism and other developmental disabilities (Cirrin & Rowland, 1985; J. McLean, L. K. S. McLean, Brady, & Etter, 1991; Ogletree, 1992; Ogletree, Wetherby, & Westling, 1992; Wetherby & Prutting, 1984).
4. Formal assessment measure (if structured sampling is unsuccessful or if a score is desired)	Available instruments include those intended for persons with severe to profound handicaps or infants and young children. Examples include the *Programmed Acquisition of Language with the Severely Handicapped* (Owens, 1982), the *Nonspeech Test of Receptive/Expressive Language* (Huer, 1983), the *Preverbal Communication Schedule* (Kiernan & Reid, 1987), the *Communication and Symbolic Behavior Scales* (Wetherby & Prizant, 1991) and the *Receptive-Expressive Emergent Language Scale–Second Edition* (Bzoch & League, 1991), among others. A more expansive range of informal and formal assessment measures may be used to describe emergent verbal abilities. Specifically, traditional language sampling and analysis procedures may prove helpful as may standardized measures of language content, form, and use.
5. Observations across settings	Provides a vehicle for assessment of both communicator-related and environmental targets. Videotaping by typical partners is recommended to lessen the time and physical demands of these observations.

Note. From "Assessment Targets and Protocols for Nonsymbolic Communicators with Profound Disabilities," by B. Ogletree, M. Fischer, and M. Turowski, 1996, *Focus on Autism and Other Developmental Disabilities, 11*(1) p. 54.

language services. As noted, carefully planned and implemented assessment protocols should provide data to assist with these decisions.

Treatment Goals

The selection of treatment goals for persons with developmental disabilities has historically been based upon developmental information. Assessment data are used to identify unattained developmental milestones, which in turn are selected for treatment targets. Unfortunately, developmentally based goal selection can put persons with autism or other disabilities on a path of prerequisite skill acquisition that may never result in functional abilities.

Ogletree, Saddler, and Bowers (1995) identified at least four variables that are critical in the goal-selection process, as highlighted in Table 5.7.

Treatment Approaches

After goals have been set, treatment approaches must be chosen to address the communicative needs of persons with autism. Choosing an approach begins with a careful consideration of the objectives of treatment.

Consultation

If goals can be addressed through cooperative interactions with partners, consultation may be the best treatment approach. For example, if providing more opportunities for communication is a goal, therapists could work in consultation with partners to identify potential opportunities and facilitate their effective use. Luterman (1996) has suggested that consultative treatment is fast becoming the "approach of the 1990s" as therapists recognize the power of working with significant others.

However, consultation alone is not sufficient to address all treatment objectives. In those instances in which communication or speech and language goals necessitate ongoing contact with the individual with autism, the speech–language pathologist will probably choose from discrete trial or natural training treatment paradigms. Of course, the effectiveness of either of these approaches is often enhanced if they occur in conjunction with partner consultation.

Discrete Trial Training

In discrete trial training, trainers attempt to control all aspects of treatment. Procedures include imitation, prompting, and reinforcement. If desired responses are not obtained, behaviors are shaped to approximate treatment targets. Over the course of treatment, prompting and shaping procedures are faded to

Table 5.7

Treatment Goal Selection Variables

Variable	Description
1. Input of persons with autism and their families	This implies that treatment decisions formerly made and owned by professionals should now be made by persons with disabilities and their families.
2. Immediate and future communicative needs of persons with autism	This means making a conventional protest a treatment priority for the child who has no effective way of escaping undesirable tasks other than head banging or biting. It also means choosing to emphasize pragmatic language abilities for the young adult targeted for employment in a fast-food chain.
3. Functionality	Functional training emphasizes all communication modes and stresses both the improvement of communicative abilities and environments for persons with disabilities. For the nonverbal child with autism, a functional treatment orientation might result in establishing the goals of promoting gestural communication or increasing communicative opportunities across environments, rather than the goal of encouraging oral language forms in narrow treatment contexts.
4. Age appropriateness	Unfortunately, speech–language pathologists and others working from a developmental perspective have often chosen goals and materials according to functioning level. This can lead to activities that foster limited expectations and ultimately have minimal functional outcomes. Instead, goals must also be age appropriate.
5. Strengths of persons with autism and their environments	Recently, there has been a dramatic shift from deficit- to strength-based treatment. For example, a child who frequently gestures to request objects could be encouraged to gesture to express other communicative functions (e.g., requests for action or protests). Likewise, a goal encouraging signed requests for objects would be reasonable given the existing nonsymbolic strength of gestural requests. Incorporating strengths within environments might involve the use of highly motivating communicative partners or settings. For example, one might choose ambitious goals for a classroom or work setting where partners are available to model or encourage communication and language or where environments are otherwise supportive of treatment.

encourage independence. Discrete trial training often relies heavily upon trainer modeling. In fact, listening to, processing, and repeating stimuli can be identified as the primary role of recipients of treatment (Fey, 1986).

During a traditional discrete trial training session, a person with autism and a trainer would sit facing each other to minimize distractions and facilitate behavioral control. If the goal was the production of a specific speech sound, the trainer would produce the sound, request it of the child or adult, and possibly use light physical prompts to assist with production. Productions would then be shaped and reinforced until acceptable to the trainer.

Although discrete trial training has been reported to be effective with persons with autism and other developmental disabilities (Blank & Milewski, 1981; Guess, Sailor, Rutherford, & Baer; 1968; Hewett, 1965; Jeffree, Wheldall, & Mittler, 1973; Lovaas, Schreibman, & Koegel, 1974; Stevens-Long & Rasmussen, 1974), this approach is not without limitations. First, the controlled nature of training can lead to skills not easily generalized across communicative partners and environments (Lovaas, Koegel, Simmons, & Stevens-Long, 1973). Further, discrete trial training appears best suited for teaching specific linguistic forms rather than the functional communication skills frequently targeted for today's client with autism (Ogletree, Saddler, & Bowers, 1995).

Recent developments specific to the long-term effectiveness of discrete trial training have been encouraging. For example, Lovaas (1987) reported positive outcomes for 19 preschool children with autism who had participated in intensive behavioral treatments (i.e., 40 hours per week of one-to-one contact with a therapist in addition to treatment through community and special education sources). When compared to a control group receiving less intensive behavioral treatment (i.e., 10 hours of one-to-one treatment), these children were determined to have less restrictive school placements and higher IQs. A follow up conducted 4 years later by McEachin, Smith, and Lovaas (1993) revealed that 8 of the 9 experimental participants with the best original treatment outcomes were indistinguishable from average children when compared by intelligence and adaptive behavior measures.

Although these findings are positive, Mesibov (1993) noted several potential methodological problems that might prevent their general acceptance. These include a lack of random participant distribution, concern about the representative nature of the participant pool, and variability in assessment protocols used with participant groups. Mesibov also cautioned that McEachin et al.'s (1993) results should not be interpreted as support for "curing" autism, noting that outcomes measured did not address many of the social deficits frequently observed in this population.

Natural Training Paradigms

Trainers using natural training paradigms assume responsibility for the directions and procedures associated with treatment while attempting to maintain a naturalness that is conducive to generalizable learning. Four techniques used during natural training include focused stimulation, vertical structuring and expansion, incidental teaching, and mand model (Fey, 1986; see Table 5.8).

The natural training paradigm techniques are typically employed within a joint action routine format. Snyder-McLean, Solomonson, McLean, and Sack (1984) defined *joint action routines* as ritualized patterns of interaction involving joint action, unified by a specific theme, following a logical sequence, including a clear beginning and end, and consisting of defined roles for participants. Routines can vary in complexity, from rolling a ball or preparing foods to acting out stories/community events. The success of treatment conducted within routines can be attributed, in large part, to the predictable nature of routine sequences.

Table 5.8

Techniques Used in Natural Training Paradigms

Technique	Description
1. Focused stimulation	Trainers arrange the environment in a way to increase the likelihood of target responses and frequently model targets. This occurs in the absence of specific efforts to make the child respond.
2. Vertical structuring and expansion	Stimuli are presented under less natural conditions, and efforts are made to encourage responses.
3. Incidental teaching	Procedurally more like discrete trial approaches (e.g., they use prompts and cues), yet occurs in natural training environments during daily activities. Differs from discrete trial training in that the child initiates training episodes and, if necessary, reinforcers are administered prior to the production of "ideal" responses. For example, an episode may begin when a child reaches for an object that is out of reach. The trainer may subsequently model/prompt a response that would allow the child to obtain the desired object. If the child fails to produce the target after two attempts, the object is provided in an effort to maintain its value as a reinforcer and reduce the child's frustration.
4. Mand model	Procedurally more like discrete trial approaches. Differs from incidental teaching in that the trainer initiates the training sequence. In the example used for incidental training, as the child moves toward the object, the trainer requests a response (e.g., "Tell me what you want.") and models/prompts if necessary.

Though still somewhat in their infancy, natural training paradigms appear to hold significant promise for speech–language pathologists serving persons with autism and other developmental disabilities. Over the past decade, reports of positive changes in communicative abilities after the introduction of these procedures have appeared regularly in the professional literature (Coe, Matson, Fee, Manikan, & Linarelli, 1990; Elliott, Hall, & Soper, 1990; Goldstein & Hockenberger, 1991; R. L. Koegel, L. K. Koegel, & Surratt, 1992; R. L. Koegel, O'Dell, & Dunlap, 1988; Ogletree, 1992; Ogletree, Fischer, & Sprouse, 1995; Warren & Kaiser, 1986; Warren, Yoder, Gazdag, Kim, & Jones, 1993). Many of these reports have not only supported natural training, but have also demonstrated its relative benefits compared to discrete trial training.

Nontraditional Approaches to the Treatment of Communication Impairments in Persons with Autism

During the past decade, numerous nontraditional treatment approaches have emerged to address the communication-related and other needs of persons with autism. Among these, auditory integration training (AIT) and facilitated communication (FC) have received international attention.

AIT was developed by Guy Bernard in the late 1960s as a listening treatment for auditory sensitivity and processing problems in persons with autism and other disorders. According to Berard (1993), middle ear abnormalities and acute hyperactivity of cochlear hair cells can cause auditory distortions/dysfunctions that adversely affect attention and learning. AIT reportedly eliminates auditory abnormalities through modulated and filtered exposure to sound.

AIT begins with an initial assessment to determine areas of hyperacute hearing, which are then targeted with sound exposure under earphones. Subsequent assessments occur to measure treatment effectiveness and to modify sound presentation if necessary. AIT is typically completed in 2 weeks after 10 hours of treatment.

Although anecdotal evidence for AIT has been reported in the popular press and through case studies (Stehli, 1991), little empirical support has surfaced. For example, two recent efficacy studies reported some positive changes in participants' behavioral profiles but no posttreatment sound-sensitivity alterations (Rimland & Edelson, 1992, 1994). Methodological shortcomings such as inadequate subject selection procedures and inappropriate controls make even this marginal support for AIT suspect.

FC has been described as an approach whereby facilitators provide graduated manual support to assist persons in accessing/applying an augmentative communication device (typically a letter board or typewriter/computer keyboard; Crossley, 1988). Biklen and Schubert (1991) described numerous aspects of the approach that reportedly contribute to its successful use. These include user support at the forearm or hand, initial training with simple tasks such as picture pointing or fill-in-the-blank activities, verbal reminders to promote peak performance, alternatives to testing for competence, and gradual fading of physical support.

While using FC, persons with autism with limited or no verbal abilities have reportedly authored sophisticated communication (Biklen, 1990, 1992; Crossley, 1992),which has led some to question the notion of underlying cognitive/social deficits in autism. Biklen (1990) and Crossley (1988), for example, proposed the alternative hypothesis that impaired voluntary motor movements (i.e., global apraxia) cause the expressive deficits of individuals with autism.

A major controversy surrounding FC has been the source of users' communication. That is, do facilitators either consciously or unconsciously influence FC users? Research attempts to empirically validate FC have generally suggested that facilitators are the probable sources of users' communication (Cabay, 1994; Datlow, Smith, Haas, & Belcher, 1994; Ogletree, Hamtil, Solberg, & Scoby-Schmelzle, 1993; Prior & Cummins, 1992; Regal, Rooney, & Wandas, 1994; Wheeler, Jacobson, Paglieri, & Schwartz, 1993).

In contrast, qualitative research efforts have provided observational support for the approach, including the uniqueness of users' typographical errors across facilitators, unusual typed communication such as swearing, typing with minimal support, and users' expressions of information unknown to facilitators (Biklen & Schubert, 1991; Biklen, Winston Morton, Gold, Berrigan, & Swaminathan, 1992; Crossley & Remington-Gurney, 1992).

FC's lack of empirical validation has caused many to question its appropriateness as a treatment alternative for persons with autism. Although it is deserving of continued study, the data currently suggest that FC's broad use as a treatment for communication impairments in autism is unjustified (for further discussion, see Chapter 11).

 ## Johnny: A Case Study

What follows is a brief case illustrating issues common to assessment and treatment of communication disorders in persons with autism. Although these issues will differ somewhat depending upon the communicative functioning of those served, "Johnny's" case is intended to provide an applied overview of major points raised throughout this chapter.

Johnny was diagnosed with autism at age 3. In conjunction with his initial diagnosis, Johnny participated in a team assessment, which included a communication evaluation. In the following year, he participated in speech and language therapy. The progression of assessment and treatment decision making specific to Johnny's case is detailed below.

Prior to Johnny's communication assessment, a speech–language pathologist (SLP) contacted his parents to discuss their expectations of the evaluation and to discuss their perceptions of Johnny's communicative abilities and needs.

Their response suggested that Johnny was a nonverbal communicator who used hand-over-hand gestures and some aberrant behaviors to request/protest within his environment. By report, he was to enroll in a public preschool classroom after his fourth birthday. Johnny's parents conveyed the expectation that evaluation should provide specific information to assist Johnny in reaching his communicative potential. The SLP suggested that Johnny's parents videotape some of his typical interactions and bring the tape with them to his evaluation.

Upon arriving at the evaluation, Johnny and his parents were met by the SLP, who verified Johnny's case history information and provided an overview of the evaluation procedures. Afterward, she asked one of Johnny's parents to play with him to allow for a period of natural interaction. During this time, the SLP recorded Johnny's intentional communicative behavior and observed the interaction patterns of his parent. Following this period of observation, the SLP presented Johnny with structured sampling tasks. Johnny appeared to enjoy the tasks and participated in frequent turn taking. He was observed to initiate communication by taking and directing the SLP's hand. These behaviors were easily interpreted as requests for objects and actions. He protested by hitting and biting himself. Johnny's vocalizations appeared noncommunicative, consisting of repeated consonant-vowel syllable shapes.

Structured sampling was followed by probing specific to comprehension and graphic symbol recognition. Johnny was presented with simple paradigms to measure context-assisted comprehension, including requests to identify body parts and objects (e.g., the SLP extended her hand as she requested a comb from an array of grooming objects). Comprehension probing progressed to similar paradigms, which eliminated contextual assistance and introduced nonsensical commands (e.g., the SLP requested that Johnny "make the ball kiss the car"). Johnny demonstrated consistent performance when contextual assistance was provided but otherwise performed at a chance level. The SLP initiated probes of graphic symbol recognition after Johnny's parents reported that he often seemed to respond to pictures. Matching-to-sample and "point to" paradigms revealed limited recognition or association of color photographs and common objects.

Johnny's on-site evaluation concluded with administration of a standardized measure of communication functioning, which revealed receptive and expressive age equivalents of 14 and 10 months, respectively. Initial findings conveyed to Johnny's parents described him as a child with gestural communicative strengths and context-assisted comprehension. The SLP requested that a more complete staffing and planning take place after she had a chance to view Johnny's video from home and observe him within the preschool setting where he would be attending.

The SLP's review of videotaped interactions confirmed the representative nature of her evaluation sample. That is, in the home setting Johnny was a nonverbal gestural communicator who occasionally used behavior to express his wants and needs. Video observations also revealed that Johnny's parents frequently anticipated his communicative behaviors, reducing the frequency of communicative opportunities and making increasingly sophisticated communication from Johnny unnecessary.

The SLP's observations in the public school preschool class revealed an inclusive setting. The teacher was assisted by one aide and two parents, all of whom expressed a willingness to work with Johnny. Routine activities occurring throughout the day required students to initiate and participate in social, motor, self-help, and leisure routines.

During a final evaluation staffing, the SLP met with Johnny's parents, other representatives of the evaluation team, and representatives of the preschool, including the preschool SLP. In an interdisciplinary discussion, Johnny's communicative strengths were profiled, including his turn taking within activities, gestural requesting, and assisted comprehension. Environmental strengths were noted, including Johnny's supportive home environment and the inclusive nature of the preschool he would be attending. His communicative needs were discussed, including his lack of respondent communicative acts, his narrow use of nonsymbolic signaling (i.e., his restricted expression of communicative functions), his lack of conventional emergent symbolic communication (including limited vocal abilities), and his use of behavior as a means of communication. Johnny's environmental needs included increased communicative opportunities and parental expectations specific to expressive communication. Needs related to his classroom included a more robust communication system to allow him to participate in typical classroom routines.

The SLP who had conducted Johnny's evaluation led the group in a discussion of treatment decisions for Johnny. First, it was determined that Johnny was a candidate for communication treatment given the variety of functional needs revealed during the evaluation process. Second, Johnny's parents were asked what they saw as Johnny's greatest needs in the area of communication. They responded by requesting a reduction in Johnny's behavior as a means of communication. Working from Johnny's gestural strength, the SLP suggested that one goal could be replacing aberrant behavior with nonsymbolic gestures. Other suggested goals included increasing opportunities for respondent communication, expanding Johnny's range of nonsymbolic communicative functions to include greetings and requests for social routines, encouraging generalized requesting signs such as "more," and using graphic symbols (color photographs) to augment communication efforts. Environmental goals included increasing Johnny's opportunities for communication in the home setting and transferring eventual treatment strategies to Johnny's new preschool teachers.

After the evaluation, Johnny began receiving educational and developmental services from the public preschool. His new SLP used evaluation recommendations to create a comprehensive treatment program. She implemented a consultative treatment approach with Johnny's parents and teachers to assist with the creation of communicative opportunities across environments. Natural training approaches were initiated to expand Johnny's nonsymblolic communicative repertoire, replace behavior, and introduce requesting signs and graphic symbols. Specifically, mand-model techniques were used during weekly one-on-one sessions and incidental teaching strategies were applied by the SLP each week during in-class activities. Johnny's teachers and parents were instructed in these approaches and implemented them in the absence of the SLP.

To provide a measure of treatment effectiveness, data specific to Johnny's goals were collected each week. In the classroom and home settings, videos of routine activities provided the source of evaluative data. As a supplement, parents and teachers were asked to keep anecdotal records of changes in Johnny's communicative behaviors.

Two months after the initiation of treatment, Johnny was initiating communication with greater frequency in the home and school settings. In addition, his aberrant behaviors were decreasing as he began to use a gestural nonsymbolic protest. Johnny had also expanded his expression of communicative functions to include greetings and had begun to use the sign "more" as a general request. Finally, he was occasionally requesting in the preschool by offering communicative partners graphic symbols available throughout the classroom. Interestingly, these changes in Johnny's communication were paralleled by an increase in his vocal behavior. In fact, some single-word immediate echolalia had been reported by his parents.

The SLP continued to consult with Johnny's parents and teachers regarding new directions for his treatment, including expansion of nonsymbolic communicative functions and introduction of general and specific requesting signs. Additional attention was placed upon the possible value of graphic symbols as a communication option and the encouragement of echolalia as a potential communicative form.

Summary

Johnny's case was presented in an effort to illustrate the principles and practices presented in this chapter. Some of those included active parental and teacher participation in decision making/strategy implementation, an emphasis upon strengths rather than weaknesses, a focus upon functional skills, and the presentation of assessment and treatment decision making as an ongoing process.

Johnny, like many persons with autism, presents speech–language pathologists and other service providers with complex assessment and treatment scenarios that require flexible and creative solutions. This chapter has attempted to provide insight specific to some of those solutions. I hope that this information has enhanced readers' understanding of communication impairments/abilities in autism and, in turn, will positively influence service delivery to this population and their families.

References

Baltaxe, C., & Simmons, J. (1975). Language in childhood psychosis: A review. *Journal of Speech and Hearing Disorders, 40,* 439–458.

Baltaxe, C., & Simmons, J. (1977). Bedtime soliloquies and linguistic competence in autism. *Journal of Speech and Hearing Disorders, 42,* 376–393.

Bartak, L., Rutter, M., & Cox, A. (1975). A comparative study of infantile autism and specific developmental receptive language disorder: The children. *British Journal of Psychiatry, 126,* 127–145.

Bartolucci, G., Pierce, S., & Streiner, D. (1980). Cross-sectional studies of grammatical morphemes in autistic and mentally retarded children. *Journal of Autism and Developmental Disorders, 10,* 39–50.

Bartolucci, G., Pierce, S., Streiner, D., & Eppel, P. (1976). Phonological investigation of verbal autistic and mentally retarded subjects. *Journal of Autism and Developmental Disorders, 6,* 303–316.

Bates, E. (1979). *The emergence of symbols: Cognition and communication in infancy.* New York: Academic Press.

Beisler, J. M., Tsai, L. Y., & Vonk, D. (1987). Comparisons between autistic and non-autistic children on the *Test for Auditory Comprehension of Language. Journal of Autism and Developmental Disorders, 17,* 95–101.

Berard, G. (1993). *Hearing equals behavior.* New Caanan, CT: Keats.

Beukelman, D. R., & Mirenda, P. (1992). *Augmentative and alternative communication: Management for severe communication disorders in children and adults.* Baltimore: Brookes.

Biklen, D. (1990). Communication unbound: Autism and praxis. *Harvard Educational Review, 60,* 291–314.

Biklen, D. (1992). Typing to talk: Facilitated communication. *American Journal of Speech and Language Pathology, 1*(2), 15–17, 21–22.

Biklen, D., & Schubert, A. (1991). New words: The communication of students with autism. *Remedial and Special Education, 12*(6), 46–57.

Biklen, D., Winston Morton, M., Gold, D., Berrigan, C., & Swaminathan, S. (1992). Facilitated communication: Implications for individuals with autism. *Topics in Language Disorders, 12*(4), 1–28.

Blank, M., & Milewski, J. (1981). Applying psycho-linguistic concepts to the treatment of an autistic child. *Applied Psycholinguistics, 2,* 65–84.

Bloom, L., & Lahey, M. (1978). *Language development and language disorders.* New York: Wiley.

Boucher, J. (1976). Articulation in early childhood autism. *Journal of Autism and Developmental Disorders, 7,* 177–187.

Brook, S. L., & Bowler, D. M. (1992). Autism by another name? Semantic and pragmatic impairments in children. *Journal of Autism and Developmental Disabilities, 22,* 61–82.

Bryson, S. E. (1983). Interference effects in autistic children: Evidence for the comprehension of single stimuli. *Journal of Abnormal Psychology, 92,* 250–254.

Bzoch, K. R., & League, R. (1991). *Receptive-expressive emergent language scale–Second edition.* Austin, TX: PRO-ED.

Cabay, M. (1994). Brief report: A controlled evaluation of FC using open-ended and fill in questions. *Journal of Autism and Developmental Disabilities, 24,* 517–528.

Carr, E., & Durand, V. M. (1985). Reducing behavior problems through functional communication training. *Journal of Applied Behavior Analysis, 18,* 111–126.

Cirrin, F. M., & Rowland, C. M. (1985). Communicative assessment of nonverbal youths with severe and profound mental retardation. *Mental Retardation, 23,* 52–62.

Coe, D., Matson, J., Fee, V., Manikan, R., & Linarelli, C. (1990). Training nonverbal and verbal play skills to mentally retarded and autistic children. *Journal of Autism and Developmental Disorders, 20,* 177–188.

Crossley, R. (1988, October). *Unexpected communication attainments by persons diagnosed as autistic and intellectually impaired.* Paper presented at the annual meeting of the International Society for Augmentative and Alternative Communication, Los Angeles.

Crossley, R. (1992). Getting the words out: Case studies in facilitated communication training. *Topics in Language Disorders, 12*(4), 29–45.

Crossley, R., & Remington-Gurney, J. (1992). Getting the words out: Facilitated communication training. *Topics in Language Disorders, 12*(4), 46–59.

Curcio, F. (1978). Sensorimotor functioning and communication in mute autistic children. *Journal of Autism and Childhood Schizophrenia, 2,* 1–8.

Datlow, B., Smith, M., Haas, P. J., & Belcher, R. G. (1994). FC: The effects of facilitator knowledge. *Journal of Autism and Developmental Disorders, 24,* 357–368.

DeMyer, M. K. (1975). The nature of neuropsychological disability in autistic children. *Journal of Autism and Childhood Schizophrenia, 8,* 181–189.

Doss, S. L., & Reichle, J. (1991). Replacing excess behavior with an initial communicative repertoire. In J. Reichle, J. York, & J. Sigafoos (Eds.), *Implementing augmentative and alternative communication: Strategies for learners with severe disabilities* (pp. 193–214). Baltimore: Brookes.

Durand, V. M., & Carr, E. (1987). Social influences on "self-stimulatory" behavior: Analysis and a treatment application. *Journal of Applied Behavior Analysis, 20,* 119–132.

Durand, V. M., & Carr, E. (1991). Functional communication training to reduce challenging behavior: Maintenance and application in new settings. *Journal of Applied Behavior Analysis, 24,* 251–264.

Elliott, R. O., Hall, K. L., & Soper, V. (1990). Analog language teaching versus natural language teaching: Generalization and retention of language learning for adults with autism and mental retardation. *Journal of Autism and Developmental Disorders, 21,* 433–448.

Eskes, G. A., Bryson, S. E., & McCormick, T. A. (1990). Comprehension of concrete and abstract words in autistic children. *Journal of Autism and Developmental Disorders, 20,* 61–73.

Fay, W. (1969). On the basis of echolalia. *Journal of Communication Disorders, 2,* 38–49.

Fey, M. E. (1986). *Language intervention with young children.* Austin, TX: PRO-ED.

Fulwiler, R., & Fouts, R. (1976). Acquisition of American sign language by a noncommunicating autistic child. *Journal of Autism and Childhood Schizophrenia, 6,* 43–51.

Goldstein, H., & Hockenberger, E. H. (1991). Significant progress in child language intervention: An 11-year retrospective. *Research and Developmental Disabilities, 12,* 401–424.

Guess, D., Sailor, W., Rutherford, G., & Baer, D. M. (1968). An experimental analysis of linguistic development: The productive use of the plural morpheme. *Journal of Applied Behavior Analysis, 1,* 297–306.

Harding, C. (1984). Acting with intention: A framework for examining the development of the intention to communicate. In L. Feagans, C. Garvey, & R. Golinkoff (Eds.), *The origins and growth of communication* (pp. 123–135). Norwood, NJ: Ablex.

Harding, C., & Golinkoff, R. (1979). The origins of intentional vocalizations in prelinguistic infants. *Child Development, 50,* 33–40.

Hewett, F. (1965). Teaching speech to an autistic child through operant conditioning. *American Journal of Orthopsychiatry, 35,* 927–936.

Horner, R. H., & Budd, C. M. (1983). *Teaching manual sign language to a nonverbal student: Generalization of sign use and collateral reduction of maladaptive behavior.* Eugene: University of Oregon Center on Human Development.

Horner, R. H., Day, H. M., Sprague, J. R., O'Brien, M., & Heathfield, L. T. (1991). Interspersed requests: A nonaversive procedure for reducing aggressive and self-injury during instruction. *Journal of Applied Behavior Analysis, 24,* 265–278.

Howlin, P. (1982). Echolalia and spontaneous phrase speech in autistic children. *Journal of Child Psychology and Psychiatry, 23,* 281–293.

Huer, M. (1983). *The nonspeech test of receptive/expressive language.* Lake Zurich, IL: Don Johnson Developmental Equipment.

Jeffree, D., Wheldall, I., & Mittler, P. (1973). Facilitating two-word utterances in two Down syndrome boys. *American Journal on Mental Deficiency, 78,* 117–122.

Kiernan, C., & Reid, B. (1987). *Preverbal communication schedule.* Manchester, U.K.: Hester Adrian Research Centre.

Koegel, L. K. (1995). Communication and language intervention. In R. L. Koegel & L. K. Koegel (Eds.), *Teaching children with autism: Strategies for initiating positive interactions and improving learning opportunities* (pp. 17–32). Baltimore: Brookes.

Koegel, R. L., Koegel, L. K., & Surratt, A. (1992). Language intervention and disruptive behavior in preschool children with autism. *Journal of Autism and Developmental Disorders, 22,* 141–154.

Koegel, R. L., O'Dell, M. C., & Dunlap, G. (1988). A natural language teaching paradigm for nonverbal autistic children. *Journal of Autism and Developmental Disorders, 17,* 187–200.

Layton, T. I., & Baker, P. S. (1981). Description of semantic-syntactic relations in an autistic child. *Journal of Autism and Developmental Disorders, 11,* 385–399.

Locke, B. J., Banken, J. A., & Mahone, C. H. (1994). The graying of autism: Etiology and prevalence. In J. L. Matson (Ed.), *Autism in children and adults: Etiology, assessment, and intervention* (pp. 37–58). Pacific Grove, CA: Brooks/Cole.

Lovaas, O. I. (1987). Behavioral treatment and normal educational and intellectual functioning in young autistic children. *Journal of Consulting and Clinical Psychology, 55,* 3–9.

Lovaas, O. I., Freitag, G., Gold, V. J., & Kassorla, I. C. (1965). Experimental studies in childhood schizophrenia: Analysis of self-destructive behavior. *Journal of Experimental Child Psychology, 2,* 67–84.

Lovaas, O. I., Koegel, R. L., Simmons, J. Q., & Stevens-Long, J. (1973). Some generalization and follow-up measures on autistic children in behavior therapy. *Journal of Applied Behavior Analysis, 6,* 131–166.

Lovaas, O. I., Schreibman, L., & Koegel, R. L. (1974). A behavior modification approach to the treatment of autistic children. *Journal of Autism and Childhood Schizophrenia, 4,* 11–129.

Luterman, D. M. (1996). *Counseling persons with communication disorders and their families* (3rd ed.). Austin, TX: PRO-ED.

McEachin, J., Smith, T., & Lovaas, O. I. (1993). Long-term outcomes for children with autism who received early intensive behavioral treatment. *American Journal on Mental Retardation, 98,* 359–372.

McEvoy, R., Loveland, K., & Landry, S. (1988). The functions of immediate echolalia in autistic children: A developmental perspective. *Journal of Autism and Developmental Disorders, 18,* 657–668.

McLean, J., McLean, L. K. S., Brady, N. C., & Etter, R. (1991). Communication profiles of two types of gesture using nonverbal persons with severe to profound mental retardation. *Journal of Speech and Hearing Research, 34,* 294–308.

McLean, L. K. S. (1990). *Transdisciplinary issues in early communicative intervention.* Paper presented at the Social Use of Language: Pathways to Success Conference, Nashville, TN.

Mesibov, G. B. (1993). Treatment outcome is encouraging. *American Journal on Mental Retardation, 98,* 379–388.

Miller, A., & Miller, E. E. (1973). Cognitive developmental training with elevated boards and sign language. *Journal of Autism and Childhood Schizophrenia, 3,* 65–85.

Ogletree, B. (1992). Communication intervention for a preverbal child with autism: A case study. *Focus on Autistic Behavior, 7*(1), 1–12.

Ogletree, B., & Burns Daniels, D. (1993). Communication-based assessment and intervention for prelinguistic infants and toddlers: Strategies and issues. *Infants and Young Children, 5*(3), 22–30.

Ogletree, B., Fischer, M., & Sprouse, J. (1995). An innovative language treatment for a child with high functioning autism. *Focus on Autistic Behavior, 10*(3), 1–10.

Ogletree, B., Fischer, M., & Turowski, M. (1996). Assessment targets and protocols for nonsymbolic communicators with profound disabilities. *Focus on Autism and Other Developmental Disabilities, 11,* 53–58.

Ogletree, B., Hamtil, A., Solberg, L., & Scoby-Schmelzle, S. (1993). Facilitated communication: Illustration of a naturalistic validation method. *Focus on Autistic Behavior, 8*(4),1–10.

Ogletree, B., Saddler, Y., & Bowers, L. (1995). Speech pathology. In B. Thyer & N. P. Kropf (Eds.), *Developmental disabilities: A handbook for interdisciplinary practice* (pp. 217–233). Cambridge, MA: Brookline.

Ogletree, B., Wetherby, A., & Westling, D. (1992). Profile of the prelinguistic intentional communicative behaviors of children with profound mental retardation. *American Journal on Mental Retardation, 97,* 186–196.

Owens, R. (1982). *Programmed acquisition of language with the severely handicapped.* San Antonio, TX: Psychological Corp.

Peters, A. (1983). *The units of language acquisition.* Cambridge, U.K.: Cambridge University Press.

Prior, M., & Cummins, R. (1992). Questions about facilitated communication and autism. *Journal of Autism and Developmental Disorders, 22,* 331–337.

Prizant, B. M. (1978). *The functions of immediate echolalia in autistic children.* Unpublished doctoral dissertation, State University of New York, Buffalo.

Prizant, B. M. (1983). Language and communication in autism: Toward an understanding of the "whole" of it. *Journal of Speech and Hearing Disorders, 48,* 296–307.

Prizant, B. M. (1987). Clinical implications of echolalic behavior in autism. In T. Layton (Ed.), *Language and treatment of autistic and developmentally disordered children* (pp. 65–68). Springfield, IL: Thomas.

Prizant, B. M. (1988). Communication problems in the autistic client. In N. J. Lass, L. V. McReynolds, J. L. Northern, & D. E. Yoder (Eds.), *Handbook of speech–language pathology and audiology* (pp. 1014–1089). Philadelphia: B. C. Decker.

Prizant, B. M., & Duchan, J. F. (1981). The functions of immediate echolalia in autistic children. *Journal of Speech and Hearing Disorders, 46,* 241–249.

Prizant, B. M., & Rydell, P. J. (1984). An analysis of the functions of delayed echolalia in autistic children. *Journal of Speech and Hearing Research, 27,* 183–192.

Regal, R. A., Rooney, J. R., & Wandas, T. (1994). FC: An experimental evaluation. *Journal of Autism and Developmental Disabilities, 24,* 345–356.

Ricks, D. M., & Wing, L. (1976). Language, communication and the use of symbols. In L. Wing (Ed.), *Early childhood autism* (pp. 191–221). Oxford, U.K.: Pergamon.

Rimland, B., & Edelson, S. (1992). *Auditory integration training in autism: A pilot study.* (Available from the Autism Research Institute, 4182 Adams Ave., San Diego, CA 92116)

Rimland, B., & Edelson, S. (1994). The effects of auditory integration training on autism. *American Journal of Speech–Language Pathology, 3*(2), 16–24.

Roberts, J. M. A. (1989). Echolalia and comprehension in autistic children. *Journal of Autism and Developmental Disorders, 19,* 271–282.

Rogers, S. J., & Pennington, B. F. (1991). A theoretical approach to the deficits in infantile autism. *Development and Psychopathology, 3,* 137–167.

Rutter, M., & Lockyer, L. (1967). A 5 to 15 year follow-up study of infantile psychosis. II: Social and behavioral outcome. *British Journal of Psychiatry, 113,* 1183–1199.

Rydell, P. J., & Prizant, B. M. (1995). Assessment and intervention strategies for children who use echolalia. In K. A. Quill (Ed.), *Teaching children with autism: Strategies to enhance communication and socialization* (pp. 105–132). New York: Delmar.

Schuler, A. (1995). Thinking in autism: Differences in learning and development. In K. A. Quill (Ed.), *Teaching children with autism: Strategies to enhance communication and socialization* (pp. 11–32). New York: Delmar.

Schuler, A. A., & Goetz, C. (1981). The assessment of severe language disabilities: Communicative and cognitive considerations. *Analysis and Intervention in Developmental Disabilities, 1,* 333–346.

Simon, N. (1975). Echolalic speech in childhood autism: Consideration of possible loci of brain damage. *Archives of General Psychiatry, 32,* 1439–1446.

Snyder-McLean, L., Solomonson, B., McLean, J., & Sack, S. (1984). Structuring joint action routines: A strategy for facilitating communication and language in the classroom. *Seminars in Speech and Language, 5*(3), 213–228.

Stehli, A. (1991). *The sound of a miracle: A child's triumph over autism.* New York: Doubleday.

Stengel, E. (1964). Speech disorders and mental disorders. In A. U. S. de Reuck & M. O'Connor (Eds.), *Disorders of language* (pp. 285–287). Boston: Little, Brown.

Stern, D. (1977). *The first relationship.* Cambridge, MA: Harvard University Press.

Stern, D. (1985). *The interpersonal world of the infant.* New York: Basic Books.

Stevens-Long, J., & Rasmussen, M. (1974). The acquisition of simple and compound sentence structure in an autistic child. *Journal of Applied Behavior Analysis, 7,* 473–479.

Stone, W. L., & Caro-Martinez, L. M. (1990). Naturalistic observations of spontaneous communication in autistic children. *Journal of Autism and Developmental Disorders, 20,* 437–453.

Swisher, L., & Demetras, M. (1985). The expressive language characteristics of children with autism compared with mentally retarded or specific language impaired children. In E. Schopler & G. B. Mesibov (Eds.), *Communication problems in autism* (pp. 147–161). New York: Plenum.

Tager-Flusberg, H. (1985a). Basic level and superordinate level categorization in autistic, mentally retarded, and normal children. *Journal of Experimental Child Psychology, 40,* 450–469.

Tager-Flusberg, H. (1985b). The conceptual basis for referential word meaning in children with autism. *Child Development, 56,* 1167–1178.

Tager-Flusberg, H. (1985c). Constraints on the representation of word meaning: Evidence from autistic and mentally retarded children. In Barrett & S. A. Kuczaj (Eds.), *The development of word meaning* (pp. 69–82). New York: Springer-Verlag.

Tager-Flusberg, H., Calkins, S., Nolin, T., Baumberger, T., Anderson, M., & Chadwick-Dias, A. (1990). A longitudinal study of language acquisition in autistic and Down children. *Journal of Autism and Developmental Disorders, 20,* 1–21.

Ungerer, J., & Sigman, M. (1987). Symbolic play and language comprehension in autistic children. *Journal of the American Academy of Child Psychiatry, 20,* 318–337.

Vollmer, T. R., Marcus, B. A., & Rigdahl, J. E. (1995). Noncontingent escape as treatment for self-injurious behavior maintained by negative reinforcement. *Journal of Applied Behavior Analysis, 28,* 15–26.

Warren, S. F., & Kaiser, A. P. (1986). Incidental language teaching: A critical review. *Journal of Speech and Hearing Disorders, 51,* 291–299.

Warren, S. F., Yoder, P. J., Gazdag, G. E., Kim, K., & Jones, H. A. (1993). Facilitating prelinguistic communication skills in young children with developmental delay. *Journal of Speech and Hearing Research, 36,* 83–97.

Webster, C. D., McPherson, H., Sloman, L., Evans, M. A., & Kuchar, E. (1973). Communication with an autistic boy by gestures. *Journal of Autism and Childhood Schizophrenia, 3,* 337–346.

Wetherby, A. M. (1986). Ontogeny of communicative functions in autism. *Journal of Autism and Developmental Disorders, 16,* 295–316.

Wetherby, A. M., Cain, D., Yonclas, D., & Walker, V. (1988). Analysis of intentional communication of normal children from the prelinguistic to the multiword stage. *Journal of Speech and Hearing Research, 32,* 240–252.

Wetherby, A. M., & Prizant, B. (1991). *Communication and symbolic behavior scales.* Chicago: Riverside.

Wetherby, A. M., & Prutting, C. (1984). Profiles of communicative and cognitive-social abilities in autistic children. *Journal of Speech and Hearing Research, 27,* 364–377.

Wetherby, A. M., Yonclas, D., & Bryan, A. (1989). Communicative profiles of preschool children with handicaps: Implications for early identification. *Journal of Speech and Hearing Research, 54,* 148–159.

Wheeler, D. L., Jacobson, J. W., Paglieri, R. A., & Schwartz, A. A. (1993). An experimental assessment of facilitated communication. *Mental Retardation, 31*(1), 49–60.

Yoder, P. J., & Layton, T. I. (1988). Speech following sign language training in an autistic child with minimal verbal language. *Journal of Autism and Developmental Disabilities, 18,* 433–448.

Social Competence of Individuals with Autism: An Applied Behavior Analysis Perspective

6

Gary M. Sasso, Linda Garrison-Harrell,
Colleen M. McMahon, and Janine Peck

lthough a number of behavioral, environmental, and biological variables are associated with the autistic disorder (Phelps & Grabowski, 1991; Schopler & Mesibov, 1995), it is generally accepted that there are three major defining features that are specific to autism: (a) profound difficulty or failure in development of social relationships; (b) impairments or failure in development of functional communicative language; and (c) ritualized, stereotypic, and/or compulsive behavior (American Psychiatric Association, 1994). These characteristics, in combination and to varying degrees, refer to symptoms that appear to be present in all individuals with autism.

In recent years, the first characteristic, impairments in social interaction, has increasingly been viewed as the primary defining characteristic of autism (Sasso, 1987). Socially, individuals with autism differ from their normally developing peers in a number of critical ways. The failure of the child with autism to develop social relationships begins in early infancy, with parents often reporting that their infant does not do what "normal babies" do (Rosenberg, Wilson, Maheady, & Sindelar, 1997). That is, these infants often do not respond to familiar faces with a smile, do not exhibit an anticipatory posture to being picked up, and lack the attachment behaviors common to their peers. Further, during childhood, individuals with autism rarely develop reciprocal affection bonds and do not turn to the parent or caregiver for assistance when hurt. Indeed, they rarely exhibit pleasure in the presence of those who care for them, avoid direct eye contact, and often treat others as if they did not exist (Kasari, Sigman, & Yirmiya, 1993; Sigman, Mundy, Sherman, & Ungerer, 1986). As children with autism grow older, this impairment in social functioning is evidenced in a number of other ways. For example, the development of friendships, normative play patterns, and expressions of empathy are often problematic, and aberrant behavior is often evident during instructional and other demanding activities (Ferster, 1961; R. L. Koegel, L. K. Koegel, & Surratt, 1992).

From a behavior-analytic standpoint, these characteristic responses can be viewed as a sign that the social events that have inherent reinforcing value for most of us are not pleasurable for many individuals with autism. Simply stated, responding increases when it produces reinforcers. If individuals with autism fail to engage in responses related to social interaction, we must assume that the consequences for these behaviors are not preferred stimuli (Ferster & Skinner, 1957; Skinner, 1981).

In addition, antecedent stimuli present in these environments (e.g., parent/caregiver, smiles, physical contact) that prompt or signal the social behavior of most children because they are associated with pleasurable consequences often do not act in the same manner for children with autism. These stimulus events can be viewed as positive (i.e., signaling a pleasurable event), aversive (i.e., signaling a punishing event), or neutral (Catania, 1992). However, each stimulus must be evaluated relative to all other stimuli that are present at the same time in the environment. Therefore, persons, events, and physical arrangements that may signal a response compete in a context that contains many other possible signaling stimuli. For example, a child who walks into a roomful of other children who are playing with different toys will most often choose to play with a person and toy that have a pleasurable past history.

In the four decades since Kanner's (1944) original clinical observations of 11 children at Johns Hopkins University, we have learned a number of important things about social learning and the cognitive difficulties of individuals with autism. It is becoming increasingly clear, for example, that even higher functioning children with autism often have problems with perceptual organization and relating stored information to incoming sensory experiences. In the context of communication, these problems are manifested in deficits in the ability to differentiate speech sounds and speech functions or in limitations regarding communicative intent and a restricted range of communicative functions (Curcio, 1978; Wetherby & Prutting, 1984).

These cognitive and communication problems are also displayed in the social behavior of children with autism. Recent research suggest that they often do not understand people's social intentions, with concurrent difficulties comprehending even simple social scenarios (L. K. Koegel & Kern-Koegel, 1994; Mundy, Sigman, & Sherman, 1987). For example, children with autism will sometimes interpret bids from peers to play a game as aggression. Likewise, these children sometimes fail to interpret the differential demands of events such as birthday parties or sporting events. In practical terms, this suggests that social environments do not provide the support or reinforcement necessary to sustain interactions for many of these children.

An accumulating body of behavior-analytic research involving children with autism demonstrates that social interaction can be taught and learned through careful arrangement of antecedents and consequences (Bauman & Kemper, 1994; Kennedy & Shukla, 1995). Much of the early research focused on establishing behavior–environment relationships through the arrangement of very specific and clear reinforcement contingencies to establish prerequisite social responses, followed by efforts to establish more complex social responses (Baer & Sherman, 1964; Lovaas, 1977). In this way, the behavior-analytic model has been shown to be perhaps the most effective form of instruction for helping children with autism acquire social behavior.

Much of the early and current work using applied behavior-analytic techniques to increase social responding has used discrete trials (Donnellan-Walsh, Gossage, LaVigna, Schuler, & Traphagen, 1976; Lovaas, 1987). Under highly structured conditions, this model involves the development of specific antecedent (i.e., discriminative stimulus), response, and consequence (either positive or negative) conditions. This technique is designed to gain stimulus control over the response, increasing (as noted) the probability that a specific stimulus will be followed by a specified response.

However, by its very success, this process can hinder our efforts to achieve generalized and durable responses across persons and settings (Sasso, Shores, Wehby, & Denny, 1994). The discrete trial (i.e., stimulus control) format is designed to gain consistent responding in the presence of distinct stimulus and consequence events. Therefore, any responses outside of these specific stimuli represent a training error, a loss of stimulus control. To put this another way, if we are doing our jobs well as behavior analysts, responding should always occur in the presence of the discrete discriminative stimuli and consequences we have chosen and trained, and never occur in other environments, with other persons, or with nontraining stimuli.

In an effort to overcome or "finesse" this problem, behavior analysts have devoted a considerable amount of time to issues involving stimulus control and transfer of skills. Procedures such as using sufficient exemplars, mediating generalization, and training loosely (Stokes & Baer, 1977), as well as general case programming (Becker, Englemann, & Thomas, 1975) and peer mediation (Ragland, Kerr, & Strain, 1978; Strain, Kerr, & Ragland, 1979) have all been developed in an effort to expand the stimulus class (i.e., circumstances under which behavior will be reinforced) to achieve generalized and durable performance of acquired skills.

From a behavior-analytic standpoint, there is a series of events that must occur if an acquired social behavior is to be generalized across environments and persons and maintained over time. Additionally, there are a number of ways this process can break down or fail. The following sections present a social interaction success and failure model based on principles of applied behavior analysis.

A Social Interaction Transfer Model

Generally, we can assume that a newly acquired behavior following treatment is durable and will transfer if it maintains over time, appears in a wide variety of environments, or spreads to a wide variety of behaviors within the same response class (Baer, Wolf, & Risley, 1968). For the social behavior of individuals with autism, generality can be viewed as a process that includes several crucial events that must occur to ensure that acquired social responses are maintained and transferred. Figure 6.1 presents a model describing events that must take place if acquired social behavior is to generalize to other persons and settings and maintain over time.

The highlighted area represents the desired path—that is, one that leads to the transfer of learned skills that maintain over time. The first step involves the presence of some type of *stimulus event* that can signal to the child the opportunity to use a learned social response or set of responses. This stimulus or prompt can be related to another person; for example, another child approaches the student and says, "Hi"; or "Let's play kickball." Or the stimulus might be contextual (Kennedy, Sasso, Shukla, & Meyer, 1996), an event or setting that serves as the stimulus for differentiated social responses, such as a birthday party in the classroom or a cooperative learning task in which several students are charged with completing a project. Whatever the case, a successful social interaction always begins with a stimulus prompt that orients the student toward possible responses.

To be successful in the next step, *recognition,* the student with autism must perceive the initial stimulus. Applied behavior analysts have traditionally had difficulty describing perception because it is a covert rather than an overt process. That is, since cognition is impossible to view directly, we have always measured cognitive processes indirectly through the resulting behavior. This method is correlational at best, but it is clear that some form of recognition of an event must occur that acts as a prompt or cue followed by a process that allows the child to choose from a repertoire of possible interactional responses (Kolers & Roediger, 1984; Skinner, 1945).

In addition, perception of this stimulus must be accurate. That is, the child must correctly recognize the stimulus and choose from an array of possible learned responses that are appropriate to that stimulus. To use a very simplistic example, if the child is approached by another and asked to play a game, the child may have in his or her repertoire a number of appropriate and socially facilitative responses, including "No thanks, I don't want to play now," or "OK, that sounds like fun," from which to choose. However, the child also has a number of other possible responses that would be inappropriate and might terminate the interaction, such as "I watched the Discovery channel last night," or "Do you like Cheerios?"

In the third step, the child must *use the skill.* This sounds simple, but for children and youth with autism it is often very difficult. The research of the past 10 years clearly indicates that these children, even when they perceive the stimulus correctly, often have difficulty with many of the subtleties of a successful social exchange. In even the most basic of social interactions, a number of related variables must receive attention if the exchange is to be successful.

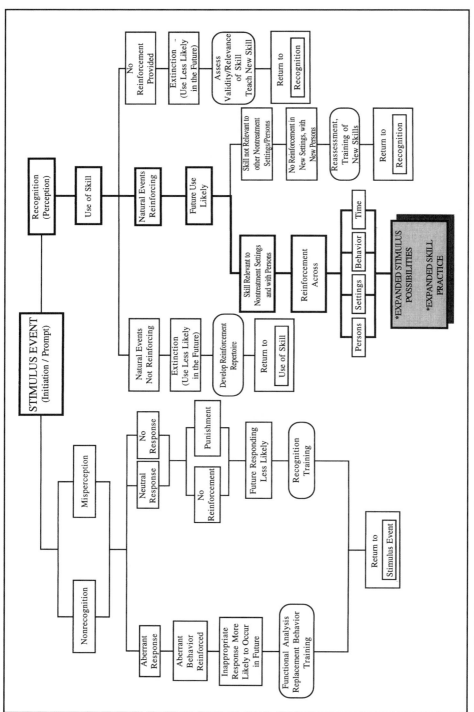

Figure 6.1. Social interaction generalization model.

For example, during a simple greeting, the person must correctly determine the proper physical proximity from the other; if the distance between the two is too close, it may be uncomfortable for the recipient of the greeting. Likewise, if the distance is too great, it can signal aloofness or an unwillingness to engage. In addition, the amount of eye contact during the exchange must be regulated. Maintaining eye contact for too long or failure to establish eye contact during the social interaction is uncomfortable to many people and may result in a failed or misunderstood exchange. The above examples of the additional collateral, often nonverbal, behaviors necessary to the social process are among those that children with autism typically have trouble acquiring and using. However, once the skill is used, successful generalization and maintenance become dependent not on the child with autism, but on the social environment.

In the next two steps, the child's behavior is *reinforced* by persons or events in the environment, which makes future use of the skill more likely. Using the above "greeting" example, if the behavior is to occur again, the student with autism not only must receive acknowledgement of his or her effort, but also must gain access to preferred people or activities through the use of the greeting or obtain praise that he or she values. Therefore, the environmental response to the behavior will determine the value of the greeting. It may be rewarded, ignored, or responded to with behavior that is not valued by the child with autism. Briefly, to be successful and continue the process toward generality, the response to the greeting must be valued by the child and viewed as reinforcing.

Following reinforcement, if the skill that the child has learned is relevant to nontreatment settings and persons, it will allow spread of effect across other persons, settings, behaviors, and time. The child's ability to use learned skills in other environments and with an expanding array of persons is critical to the transfer and durability processes because those new environments allow access to new prompts and cues to respond as well as to expanded forms of reinforcement (Horner & MacDonald, 1982; Mundschenk & Sasso, 1995; Sprague & Horner, 1984).

Much of the recent research in this area suggests several things. First, it is now clear that social behavior must occur in a social context (Simpson, Myles, Sasso, & Kamps, 1991). We can teach some of the responses that will be necessary to successful social interaction, but because of the complexity of social intercourse (i.e., multiple cues, setting-specific behavior, multiple examples of successful social interaction across a number of persons), it is necessary that students be exposed to these environments as early and often as possible. Second, it is unlikely that any social skill program will be able to identify and teach all of the skills that are necessary for social competence. There are simply too many skills that must be learned. As a result, our programs must rely on the environment to encourage and teach new skills through modeling, indirect instruction, and differential reinforcement of appropriate social interactions for the child with autism.

Social Interaction Failure Sequences

Unfortunately, many things can and do go wrong in attempts to transfer a skill across settings, persons, behaviors, and time. These failed attempts occur for a variety of reasons, including an inability by the child with autism to recognize the original stimulus event, misperception of this event, failure of the natural environment to support or reinforce the skill, and lack of relevance of that skill to nontreatment settings and/or persons. This section describes how these failure sequences can occur and describes the steps that can be taken to identify and remediate these problems.

Failures of Recognition

The earliest problems related to generalization and maintenance of social behavior occur at the stimulus level (see Figure 6.2). Failure to identify the stimulus (e.g., social initiation, prompt, contextual cue) always leads to a termination of the social interaction. This *nonrecognition* of a social opportunity can occur for many reasons, but all are related to a failure of the stimulus to be discriminated or understood by the child as an opportunity for use of the learned social behavior.

Another problem at the stimulus level is a *misperception* of the social opportunity, or what Gresham (1986) has termed a "bad read." In this situation, the child is aware of the stimulus but does not view it as an opportunity to use the learned skill. Instead, the child may view the stimulus as aversive, as a cue for a different but inappropriate skill, or as a cue to terminate social interaction.

Both nonrecognition and misperception of the stimulus event lead to a number of related problems. For example, the child may demonstrate no response or a neutral response to the stimulus event. In those cases, two major scenarios are possible. First, the child may receive no reinforcement or may receive punishment for a failure to respond or because of his or her neutral but ineffective response. This in turn creates a situation in which those responses are less likely to occur in the future.

Remediation of this social interaction failure involves teaching the child to correctly respond to social stimulus events in the environment (i.e., recognition training; see Figure 6.2). These are among the most difficult skills to teach individuals with autism for two reasons. First, the number of stimuli that must be addressed is considerable, and the child with autism needs to learn individual stimulus events and events in combination in order to correctly respond with the learned social behavior. Second, because so many of the stimulus events in the natural environment compete in a context of other stimuli, to be successful, the child with autism must determine which stimuli are relevant to the social situation and which are irrelevant.

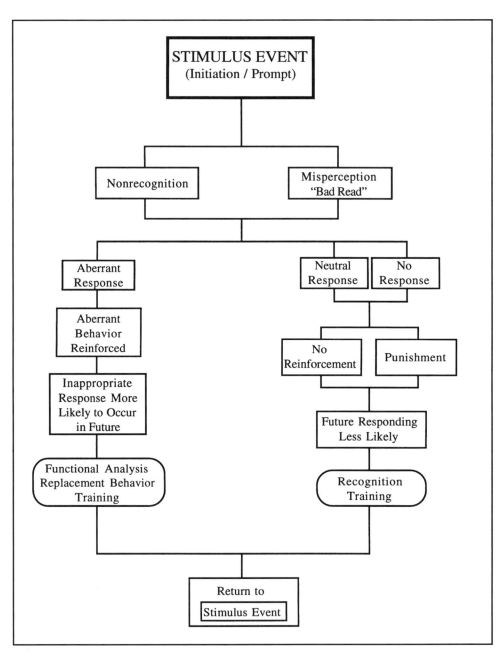

Figure 6.2. Stimulus recognition failure strand.

Given some of problems related to the autistic disorder, such as stimulus overselectivity (Cook, Anderson, & Rincover, 1982) and prompt dependency (R. L. Koegel & Williams, 1980), teaching the child to discriminate correctly is often very difficult. Behavior-analytic remediations related to this training failure most often involve teaching across all of the relevant environments and/or instruction across a number of social stimulus exemplars (Stokes & Baer, 1977; Stokes, Baer, & Jackson, 1974). For example, the child might be taught to use the skill directly at home, in the special education classroom, in the regular education classroom, and across a number of activities within each of these environments. Likewise, in the sufficient exemplars approach, the child with autism is exposed to several other children and their social interaction styles in an effort to encourage social behavior. One other approach to remediating problems due to stimulus recognition failures is social stories (Gray & Garand, 1993). With this intervention, the child with autism is presented with a number of social scenarios and prompted to develop a response or responses, then to go beyond the initial response to an ongoing, more fully developed social interchange. Following intervention, or concurrently with these efforts, the child continues to be exposed to naturally occurring social situations to evaluate the success of the program.

Failures of Reinforcement

The other major area of failure related to transfer and maintenance of social behavior in children with autism stems from the level of reinforcement available in the natural environment. As behavior analysts, we may have been overly fond of stating with conviction that we must turn the child's learned behavior over to naturally occurring categories and schedules of reinforcement in order to achieve transfer and maintenance, a process sometimes known as "entrapment" (Kohler & Greenwood, 1986; McConnell, 1987). However, it is also possible that we have missed a crucial point; that is, we often make the assumption that events occurring in the natural environment will be valued and preferred by the child with autism. If that were the case, then most students with disabilities would not need extensive intervention for both their problem behavior and social skill training. Simply stated, in most cases the natural environment does not support the social behavior of students with autism. There are two potential failure paths related to reinforcement failures (see Figure 6.3).

First, the environment (i.e., persons) may provide no reinforcement for use of the social behavior. In this case, extinction of the response will occur because behavior (particularly newly acquired behavior) will not persist in an environment that does not reward it. In this case, the validity of the social behavior that has been trained is in question (see Figure 6.3). If we teach responses that are not relevant to the social environments of the child, then those responses will be extinguished by that environment.

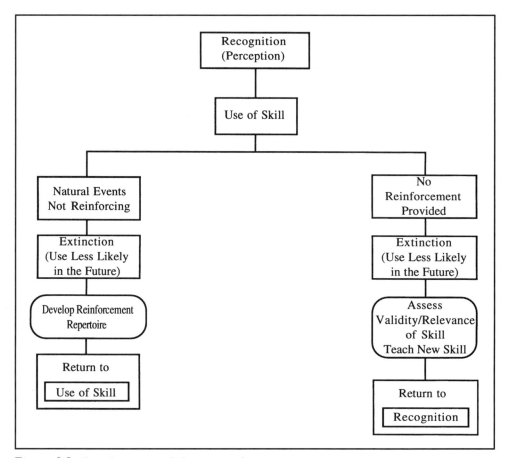

Figure 6.3. Reinforcement failure strand.

Remediation of this problem, then, involves an ecological assessment of the environment (Greenwood et al., 1984; Rogers-Warren, 1984) to determine successful social behavior. This may be accomplished in a number of ways. First, several normative databases are available that describe the most appropriate social behavior at different age levels. For example, Tremblay, Strain, Hendrickson, and Shores (1981) observed the social interactions of children that occur in free-play settings and computed conditional probabilities across social behaviors to demonstrate functional relationships between the behaviors and concurrent positive outcomes in natural settings. The data generated by this and other studies of this type can be used as a guide to the choice of social target skills.

One shortcoming of these types of data is that so much of appropriate social behavior is determined locally (Sasso, Garrison-Harrell, & Rogers, 1994). That is, acceptable and facilitative social behavior in a fourth-grade classroom in New York City is likely to be different in a number of important respects from the effective social behavior of fourth graders in Hays, Kansas. Therefore, normative databases may not always provide the specificity necessary to choose effective social behavior targets.

A second method for determining effective social target behaviors is to develop local normative data related to specific schools, classrooms, and children. One way this has been accomplished has been through informant-based selection of social behaviors thought to be related to social competence and acceptance (Bem & Lord, 1979; Hoier & Cone, 1987). For example, Sasso et al. (1992) used a template-matching procedure with over 300 students across several grade levels in order to determine critical social behaviors across age and gender. This approach required students to choose sets of social behavior that were important from the standpoint of their friends and also those children who were not friends. Responses generated through such a process can then be used as targets for social skill training.

A final and related method of determining social behavior that is relevant to environments is to enter those environments and obtain direct observation data related to the social behaviors that occur most frequently and are reinforced most often in the natural environment (e.g., regular education classroom). This method allows us to identify locally relevant behavior that has a high probability of support.

The second generality problem based on reinforcement occurs when the naturally occurring reinforcers in the environment are not preferred or reinforcing to the child with autism. That is, the social environmental context does not contain the supports necessary to maintain the learned responses and, as with no reinforcement, the behavior cannot be maintained in that environment.

In this case, it is the child's reinforcement repertoire that must be addressed. This can be done by first determining what activities, persons, and behaviors the child prefers. There are a number of ways to conduct a reinforcer-preference assessment, including teacher/parent surveys (O'Neill et al., 1997) and direct manipulation across a number of potential reinforcers (Fisher, Chris Ninnes, Piazza, & Owen-DeShryver, 1996).

Once current preferences are established, the behavior-analytic model provides a technology for developing new reinforcers. This involves pairing a person, event, or activity that we wish to be reinforcing with a person, event, or activity that is known to be preferred by the child with autism. Over time and with repeated exposure, the second person, event, or activity will then become reinforcing. For example, Sasso, Shores, Strain, Garrison-Harrell, and Gresham (1996) paired nonpreferred peers with highly preferred activities within a peer-mediated social intervention for children with autism. Over the course of the investigation, the peers took on the reinforcing properties of the preferred activities. That is, they became reinforcing to the child.

Nonrelevance Failures Across Environments

One final problem that affects the generality of learned social responses in children with autism occurs when the skill is not relevant to other nontreatment settings and persons (see Figure 6.4). In this scenario, the skill has been

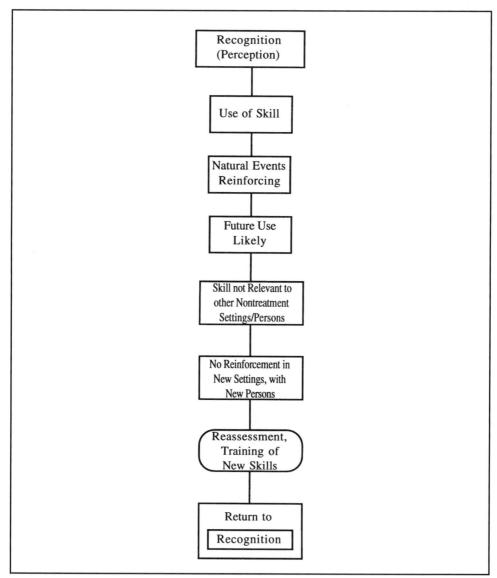

Figure 6.4. Skill relevance failure strand.

used and reinforced by the environment in one setting, but is not reinforced across other settings or the people in those settings. Just as in the case when no reinforcement is provided, it is necessary to assess each of those new environments to determine what skills will be rewarded, and then to instruct the child accordingly.

Summary

Although the model presented in this chapter is not meant to be comprehensive, it does provide a behavior-analytic view of many of the variables related to successful social responding for children with autism. More importantly, from the standpoint of interaction, this model presents a successful process for generalization and maintenance of these behaviors and describes the events that must take place if children are to engage in social behavior across a number of environments and persons. Finally, the failure strands in the model provide a look at the ways generality can fail (e.g., recognition of the stimulus, misperception of the stimulus, and failures related to reinforcement across environments) and a process that can be followed to assess these failures and subsequently offer remediation.

Generalizability of Specific Interventions

Over the past 20 years, a number of interventions have been developed and investigated to improve the social behavior of children with autism. Each has attempted to ensure generalization and maintenance of these behaviors in a different manner. However, many of the programs that we use or investigate do not adequately address generality issues.

Direct skill instruction was perhaps the first and most popular method used to help children with autism acquire social skills (Allen, Hart, Buell, Harris, & Wolf, 1964; Kohler & Fowler, 1985). With this procedure, the child is trained to respond in training settings that are essentially analogue in nature. That is, the training environment is contrived. Usually, the teacher provides models of the target social response and subsequently reinforces successive approximations of the behavior to criterion. The major problem with this type of training is that the validity of the skill being trained is low because the training environment does not match or often even approximate the desired environment for use of the skill. Therefore, the path to generalization with this training model has often been to reteach the behavior across all relevant settings and persons (Gaylord-Ross, Haring, Breen, & Pitts-Conway, 1984). This is often a time-consuming and arduous undertaking.

Because of some of the problems related to direct instruction, practitioners and researchers began to seek out more effective methods for delivering social interaction behavior for children with autism. Cognitive-based interventions such as social stories attempt to provide scenarios for social behavior, again in an analogue environment, and practice in the effective use of these skills. Because this technique attempts to address relevant environments and persons in those environments, a number of successes have been reported using this approach. However, this set of procedures cannot be used without prior or prerequisite skills. That is, the child must be communicative, must be able to imagine possible social scenarios, and must be able to transfer cognitive plans into actions in the relevant environment.

A number of peer-mediated interventions have been used for years and with variable success. Specifically, peer tutoring has enjoyed wide use for the purpose of skill development and as a social interaction procedure (Greenwood, Delquadri, & Hall, 1989; Meyer, Sasso, & Pitts-Conway, 1985). Although there is no question that this procedure can be an effective means of skill delivery for children with autism and can provide often dramatic increases in interaction, the quality and durability of these interactions may be suspect. For example, two investigations (McMahon, Wacker, Sasso, & Melloy, 1994; Sasso, Mitchell, & Struthers, 1986) have shown that the interactions generated by peer tutoring are instructional rather than social in nature, with a poor record of generalization and maintenance outside the tutoring environment.

Peer-initiated interventions have enjoyed greater success (Mundschenk & Sasso, 1995; Strain & Odom, 1986). In this approach, peers are initially taught to interact effectively in natural environments with the child with autism (Sasso & Rude, 1987). Following this initial training, peers are paired or placed within a network for the purpose of social interaction. This procedure allows for naturally occurring social interaction in target environments and often across several peers, increasing the opportunity for additional social stimulus events and expanded skill practice.

However, this procedure also has drawbacks. The most apparent problem is that because it does not directly include an instructional component related to the social behavior of the child with autism, and because children with autism often have difficulty learning from modeling, the procedure may have limited effectiveness for many participants.

Conclusions

What remains clear is that there is still a great deal of work to be done to ensure successful social participation of children with autism. As suggested in this chapter, one way to structure future efforts and investigations in this area is to add a number of assessment components to the process of selecting and delivering social interaction interventions. For example, several points of possible failure are related to the generalization and maintenance of social behavior. If the skill does not occur, or if neutral or aberrant behavior occurs in the natural environment, we must first determine if the stimulus has been recognized or misperceived by the child and then provide recognition training or teach the child to perceive stimuli relevant to the prompt or social context. If, on the other hand, problem behavior occurs in place of the social response, a functional or structural analysis of the variables maintaining the behavior can be conducted to allow for effective intervention. Further, if the skill occurs in one generalization setting or with one peer and subsequently is extinguished (i.e., the behavior does not persist), we must begin to suspect that either there is no reinforcement available in that environment or that the child with autism is not reinforced by the environment's attempt to reward. In those cases, the validity of the skill must be assessed and a new skill taught, or the child's preferences must be expanded. Finally, if the skill occurs across one person/setting but not others, then each new setting must be assessed to determine the relevance of the child's learned social behavior.

As practitioners and researchers, we must pay more attention to the social contexts of these children and the availability of social behavior supports in these environments. For example, many proponents of full inclusion claim that all we need to do is place students with autism in the natural environment (i.e., regular education classroom) and problem behavior will drop and prosocial behavior will increase.

Underlying such statements must be a belief in magic—the magic of the natural environment. However, it is not magic but the presence of behavioral supports that determines the success of these children in these settings (Kennedy et al., 1996). For example, a child with autism was placed in a self-contained special education classroom that was highly structured and demanding. In this setting, he engaged in relatively high frequencies of aggressive and disruptive behavior. A functional analysis of these problem responses revealed that they were maintained by negative reinforcement. That is, the student engaged in aggressive and disruptive behavior in order to escape from nonpreferred tasks and activities. He was subsequently "fully included" in a regular education classroom, where these problem behaviors ceased to occur. An examination of the inclusive environment showed that no academic demands were being placed on the child. Therefore, the reason or functional utility of the aggressive and disruptive behaviors was no longer present.

To be successful in arranging social opportunities for children with autism, we need to devote more resources to identifying the setting variables in the natural environments that support interaction attempts by the child with autism. Careful assessment of these environments will tell us the conditions under which the child is likely to do well and whether the natural environment contains any of the variables related to that success. Careful planning for the inclusion of many of these variables, coupled with the training of social behaviors that have relevance to the setting, will allow us to optimize the chances for individuals with autism to be successful and socially competent.

References

Allen, K. E., Hart, B., Buell, J. S., Harris, F. R., & Wolf, M. M. (1964). Effects of social reinforcement on isolated behavior of a nursery school child. *Child Development, 35,* 511–518.

American Psychiatric Association. (1994). *Diagnostic and statistical manual of mental disorders* (4th ed.). Washington, DC: Author.

Baer, D. M., & Sherman, J. A. (1964). Reinforcement control of generalized imitation in young children. *Journal of Experimental Child Psychology, 1,* 37–49.

Baer, D. M., Wolf, M. M., & Risley, T. R. (1968). Some current dimensions of applied behavior analysis. *Journal of Applied Behavior Analysis, 1,* 91–97.

Bauman, M. L., & Kemper, T. L. (1994). *The neurobiology of autism.* Baltimore: Johns Hopkins University Press.

Becker, W., Englemann, S., & Thomas, D. (1975). *Teaching 2: Cognitive learning and instruction.* Chicago: SRA.

Bem, J. D., & Lord, C. G. (1979). Template matching: A proposal for probing the ecological validity of experimental settings in social psychology. *Journal of Personality and Social Psychology, 37,* 833–846.

Catania, C. A. (1992). *Learning,* Englewood Cliffs, NJ: Prentice-Hall.

Cook, A. R., Anderson, N., & Rincover, A. (1982). Stimulus overselectivity and stimulus control: Problems and strategies. In R. L. Koegel, A. Rincover, & A. Egel (Eds.), *Educating and understanding autistic children* (pp. 90–105). San Diego, CA: College-Hill Press.

Curcio, F. (1978). Sensiomotor functioning and communication in mute autistic children. *Journal of Autism and Childhood Schizophrenia, 8,* 181–189.

Donnellan-Walsh, A., Gossage, L. D., LaVigna, G. W., Schuler, A., & Traphagen, J. D. (1976). *Teaching makes a difference: A guide for developing successful classes for autistic and other severely handicapped children.* Santa Barbara, CA: Santa Barbara Public Schools.

Ferster, C. B., & Skinner, B. F. (1957). *Schedules of reinforcement.* New York: Appleton-Century-Crofts.

Fisher, W. W., Chris Ninnes, H. A., Piazzsa, C. C., & Owen-DeSchryver, J. S. (1996). On the reinforcing effects of the content of verbal attention. *Journal of Applied Behavior Analysis, 29,* 235–238.

Gaylord-Ross, R., Haring, T. G., Breen C., & Pitts-Conway, V. (1984). The training and generalization of social interaction skills with autistic youth. *Journal of Applied Behavior Analysis, 17,* 229–247.

Gray, C. A., & Garand, J. D. (1993). Social stories: Improving responses of students with autism with accurate social information. *Focus on Autistic Behavior, 8,* 1–10.

Greenwood, C. R., Delquadri, J., & Hall, R. V. (1989). Longitudinal effects of classwide peer tutoring. *Journal of Educational Psychology, 81,* 371–383.

Greenwood, C. R., Dinwiddie, G., Terry, B., Wade, L., Stanley, S. O., Thibadeau, S., & Delquadri, J. (1984). Teacher vs. peer-mediated instruction: An ecobehavioral analysis of achievement outcomes. *Journal of Applied Behavior Analysis, 17,* 521–538.

Gresham, F. M. (1986). Conceptual and definitional issues in the assessment of children's social skills: Implications for classification and training. *Journal of Clinical Child Psychology, 15,* 3–15.

Hoier, T. S., & Cone, J. D. (1987). Target selection of social skills for children: The template matching procedure. *Behavior Modification, 11,* 137–163.

Horner, R. H., & MacDonald, R. S. (1982). A comparison of single instance and general case instruction in teaching a generalized vocational skill. *Journal of the Association for the Severely Handicapped, 7,* 7–20.

Kanner, L. (1944). Early infantile autism. *Journal of Pediatrics, 25,* 211–217.

Kasari, C., Sigman, M., & Yirmiya, N. (1993). Focused and social attention in interactions with familiar and unfamiliar adults: A comparison of autistic, mentally retarded and normal children. *Development and Psychopathology, 5,* 401–412.

Kennedy, C. H., & Shukla, S. (1995). Social interaction research for people with autism as a set of past, current, and emerging propositions. *Behavioral Disorders, 21,* 21–35.

Kennedy, C. H., Sasso, G. M., & Shukla, S., & Meyer, K. (1996, May). *Empirical outcomes of inclusive education.* Symposium presented at the 22nd annual convention of the Association for Behavior Analysis, San Francisco.

Koegel, L. K., & Kern-Koegel, L. (1994). *Autism.* Baltimore: Brookes.

Koegel, R. L., Koegel, L. K., & Surratt, A. (1992). Language intervention and disruptive behavior in preschool children with autism. *Journal of Autism and Developmental Disorders, 22,* 141–153.

Koegel, R. L., & Williams, J. A. (1980). Direct vs. indirect response reinforcer relationships in teaching autistic children. *Journal of Abnormal Child Psychology, 8,* 537–547.

Kohler, F. W., & Fowler, S. A. (1985). Training prosocial behaviors to young children: An analysis of reciprocity with untrained peers. *Journal of Applied Behavior Analysis, 18,* 187–200.

Kohler, F. W., & Greenwood, C. R. (1986). Toward a technology of generalization: The identification of natural contingencies of reinforcement. *The Behavior Analyst, 9,* 19–26.

Kolers, P. A., & Roediger, H. L., III. (1984). Procedures of mind. *Journal of Verbal Learning and Verbal Behavior, 23,* 425–449.

Lovaas, O. I. (1977). *The autistic child.* New York: Irvington.

Lovaas, O. I. (1987). Behavioral treatment and normal educational and intellectual functioning in young autistic children. *Journal of Consulting and Clinical Psychology, 55,* 3–9.

McConnell, S. R. (1987). Entrapment effects and the generalization and maintenance of social skills training for elementary school students with behavioral disorders. *Behavioral Disorders, 12,* 252–263.

McMahon, C. M., Wacker, D. P., Sasso, G. M., & Melloy, K. J. (1994). Evaluation of the multiple effects of a social skill intervention. *Behavioral Disorders, 20,* 35–50.

Meyer, L. H. Sasso, G. M., & Pitts-Conway, V. (1985, November). *Current research in the integration of students with severe handicaps.* Paper presented at the annual meeting of the Association for Persons with Severe Handicaps, Boston.

Mundschenk, N. A., & Sasso, G. M. (1995). Assessing sufficient social exemplars for students with autism. *Behavioral Disorders, 21,* 62–78.

Mundy, P., Sigman, M., & Sherman, T. (1987). Nonverbal communication and play correlates of language development in autistic children. *Journal of Child Psychology and Psychiatry, 27,* 657–669.

O'Neill, R. E., Horner, R. H., Albin, R. W., Sprague, J. R., Storey, K., & Newton, J. S. (1997). *Functional assessment and program development for problem behavior* (2nd ed, pp. 4–6). New York: Brooks/Cole.

Phelps, L., & Grabowski, J. (1991). Autism: Etiology, differential diagnosis, and behavioral assessment update. *Journal of Psychopathology and Behavioral Assessment, 13,* 107–125.

Ragland, E. U., Kerr, M. M., & Strain, P. S. (1978). Effects of peer social initiations on the behavior of withdrawn autistic children. *Behavior Modification 5,* 347–359.

Rogers-Warren, A. K. (1984). Ecobehavioral analysis. *Education and Treatment of Children, 7,* 283–304.

Rosenberg, M. S., Wilson, R., Maheady, L., & Sindelar, P. T. (1997). *Educating students with behavior disorders.* Boston: Allyn & Bacon.

Sasso, G. M. (1987). Social interaction: Issues and procedures. *Focus on Autistic Behavior, 2*(4), 1–15.

Sasso, G. M., Garrison-Harrell, L. G., & Rogers, L. (1994). Autism and socialization: Conceptual models and procedural variations. In T. Scruggs & M. Mastropieri (Eds.), *Advances in learning and behavioral disabilities* (pp. 161–175). Greenwich, CT: JAI Press.

Sasso, G. M., Hendrickson, J. M., Mundschenk, N. A., Shokoohi-Yekta, M., Kelly, L., & Plagmann, L. A. (1992). Social behavior identified through an informant-based assessment procedure: Normative data across age and gender. *Monograph in Behavior Disorders: Severe Behavior Disorders of Children and Youth, 15,* 44–56.

Sasso, G. M., Mitchell, V. N., & Struthers, E. M. (1986). Peer tutoring versus structured interaction activities: Effects on the frequency and topography of peer initiations. *Behavioral Disorders, 16,* 9–22.

Sasso, G. M., & Rude, H. A. (1987). Unprogrammed effects of training high-status peers to interact with severely handicapped children. *Journal of Applied Behavior Analysis, 20,* 35–44.

Sasso, G. M., Shores, R. E., Strain, P., & Gresham, F. (1996, November). *Current social interaction research issues for children with behavioral disorders.* Paper presented at the meeting for Severe Behavior Disorders of Children and Youth, Tempe, AZ.

Sasso, G. M., Shores, R., Wehby, J., & Denny, K. (1994, November). *Recent trends in social interaction research.* Paper presented at the annual meeting on Severe Behavior Disorders of Children and Youth, Tempe, AZ.

Schopler, E., & Mesibov, G. B. (1995). Introduction to learning and cognition in autism. In E. Schopler & G. B. Mesibov (Eds.), *Learning and cognition in autism* (pp. 3–11). New York: Plenum.

Sigman, M., Mundy, P., Sherman, T., & Ungerer, J. A. (1986). Social interactions of autistic, mentally retarded, and normal children with their caregivers. *Journal of Child Psychology and Psychiatry, 27,* 647–669.

Simpson, R. L., Myles, B. S., Sasso, G. M., & Kamps, D. M. (1991). *Promoting social interactions of children and youth with autism: Issues and procedures.* Reston, VA: Council for Exceptional Children.

Skinner, B. F. (1945). The operational analysis of psychological terms. *Psychological Review, 52,* 270–277.

Skinner, B. F. (1981). Selection by consequences, *Science, 213,* 501–504.

Sprague, J. R., & Horner, R. H. (1984). The effects of single instance, multiple instance, and general case training on generalized vending machine use by moderately and severely handicapped students. *Journal of Applied Behavior Analysis, 17,* 273–278.

Stokes, T. F., & Baer, D. M. (1977). An implicit technology of generalization. *Journal of Applied Behavior Analysis, 10,* 349–367.

Stokes, T. F., Baer, D. M., & Jackson, R. L. (1974). Programming the generalization of a greeting response in four retarded children. *Journal of Applied Behavior Analysis, 7,* 599–610.

Strain, P. S., Kerr, M. M., & Ragland, E. U. (1979). Effects of peer mediated social initiations and prompting/reinforcement procedures on the social behavior of autistic children. *Journal of Autism and Developmental Disorders, 9,* 41–54.

Strain, P. S., & Odom, S. L. (1986). Peer social initiations: Effective intervention for social skill development of exceptional children. *Exceptional Children, 52,* 543–552.

Tremblay, A., Strain, P. S. Hendrickson, J. M., & Shores, R. E. (1981). Social interactions of normal preschool children: Using normative data for subject and target behavior selection. *Behavior Modification, 5,* 237–253.

Wetherby, A., & Prutting, C. (1984). Profiles of communicative and cognitive-social abilities in autistic children. *Journal of Speech and Hearing Research, 27,* 364–377.

Sensory Integration for Students with Autism

7

Debra Galvin Cook
and Winnie Dunn

There are many ways to look at behavior. This chapter provides a framework for considering the contribution that a neuroscience perspective can offer to a fuller understanding of the behaviors of children with autism. From a neuroscience point of view, even the most aberrant behavior can be viewed as an attempt to reestablish homeostasis (i.e., the internal state of equilibrium for an individual; Kupferman, 1991). For individuals with autism, the range of homeostasis is usually quite narrow, so the nervous system is intrinsically motivated to react more frequently to seek a comfortable level of operation. This internal motivation can generate behaviors that seem unusual to others, but that serve a purpose for the child's nervous system.

Sensory integration theory and techniques represent an application of well-established neuroscience principles to the needs of children with various disabilities. Knowledge about neuroscience and applications of neuroscience in sensory integration literature has contributed to our understanding of the behavioral characteristics that define autism spectrum disorder, including impaired social interest and reciprocity, disordered and/or delayed communication, and restricted and repetitive interests (American Psychological Association, 1994). Families who have children and youth with autism often report that their child's overall functional abilities are negatively affected by their need to seek preferred sensory stimuli or avoid certain types of sensation (Anderson & Emmons, 1996; Angell, 1993; Kientz, 1996). Likewise, adults with autism describe how sensory processing deficits have adversely affected their lives (Grandin & Scariano, 1986; Williams, 1992, 1994). A neuroscience and sensory integrative perspective offers insights about how we might interpret the sensory basis of challenging behaviors and design interventions that support more functional ways to engage in life.

Occupational therapists have the in-depth training and expertise in applying sensory integrative and neuroscience knowledge to the needs of children who have autism. However, the overall focus of occupational therapy is *not* sensory integration, but to help children and families conduct their daily lives in a more satisfying and functional manner. In this effort, sensory integration and neuroscience knowledge are *tools* that enable us to understand what might be supporting or interfering with children's ability to function in their daily lives. The purpose of this chapter is to introduce the principles of neuroscience and provide the tools for incorporating neuroscience and sensory integrative knowledge as part of assessment and intervention with children with autism. On the basis of the information presented in this chapter, parents and service providers will be better prepared to seek out a collaborator, such as an occupational therapist, when they wish to include neuroscience and sensory integrative knowledge in program planning for specific children. To facilitate this effort, the chapter concludes with a discussion of ways to collaborate with others using sensory integrative knowledge.

Researchers, educators, parents of children with autism, and individuals with autism have reported the impact that difficulties in processing sensory information can have on functional performance. Not surprisingly, the diagnostic criteria of autism spectrum disorder recognize the contribution of sensory processing difficulties because such difficulties contribute to restricted, repetitive interests and impaired social reciprocity.

Sensory integration refers to both a neurological process and a theory of the relationship between the neurological process and behavior; thus, it is a theory of brain–behavior relationships (Fisher & Murray, 1991). The theoretical base of sensory integration originates in neuroscience and the social sciences. In her pioneering work, Ayres (1972, 1979) articulated sensory integration theory to better understand the mechanisms involved when individuals have difficulty processing sensory information from their environments. On the basis of this understanding, Ayres applied the theoretical constructs of sensory integration to develop specific intervention strategies for individuals with a variety of disorders.

Sensory integration is the organizing and processing of sensory information from different sensory systems for specific use (Ayres, 1972). The application of sensory integration theory has been prescribed for a variety of individuals who have difficulty processing sensory information, such as children with learning disabilities (Ayres, 1972), individuals with chronic mental illness (King, 1974), and children with regulatory disorders (National Center for Clinical Infant Programs/Zero to Three [NCCIP], 1994). Since knowledge about how the brain functions is critical to understanding how we might apply sensory integration information to the functional performance needs of children who have autism, the following sections examine basic neurological principles and the sensory system.

The nervous system operates to support performance. By selecting and designing activities compatible with central nervous system (CNS) functions, we can facilitate children's performance; that is, "We may use our knowledge of sensory integration theory to help in determining what will be reinforcing and what will not" (Murray & Anzalone, 1991, p. 364). The brain has complementary functions that enable parts of the brain to be responsible for increasing activity level, while other parts provide inhibitory control. Some parts of the brain initiate movement, and other parts stop or control the amount of movement that occurs. Normally, there is a balance of power, enabling the CNS to finely tune responses to meet all environmental demands.

In order to achieve this balance of power, the brain must regulate its own input (centrifugal control) by receiving and processing information that is the most useful for its own functioning. For example, the brain can screen out certain stimuli so that other stimuli receive more careful attention (i.e., suppression). We are all bombarded with an array of sensory stimuli throughout the day; through suppression, the brain determines which stimuli warrant attention and response and which stimuli can be ignored safely (Dunn, 1997b).

When the balance of power is disrupted, as it is in children who have autism, the CNS experiences a release phenomenon. For example, when there are disruptions in brain functions, arousal mechanisms are released from inhibitory control, which in turn can lead to hyperactivity and distractibility. These behaviors do not reflect dysfunction in the arousal mechanisms themselves, but represent a disconnection of arousal systems from other centers that typically modulate responses. A release phenomenon can occur in any part of the CNS related to any function. Many of the abnormal behaviors observed and documented in children with spectrum disorders such as autism can be attributed to a release phenomenon, or poor modulation in the CNS. For example, children who are distractible are experiencing a release phenomenon. They may have difficulty engaging in purposeful behavior because they are constantly attending to all the other stimuli available in the environment (i.e., they have poor suppression). Alternatively, other children may screen out more important stimuli and attend to less important ones; for example, children who have autism may latch on to one sound or one object to inspect, while becoming oblivious to other stimuli, such as someone calling their name. Children who have autism may also display a release phenomenon by screening out or attending to stimuli based on rigid or ritualistic patterns rather than in response to specific life demands; this can result in the child's engaging in inappropriate or even dangerous behaviors (Dunn, 1997b).

A critical aspect of the functioning of the brain is *intersensory integration,* or the brain's ability to organize information from several sources. When children respond to single sensory modalities, they can appear overreactive; with intersensory integration, the brain waits for verification from other senses before responding. For example, children typically look toward someone who touches them before they create a response; this is to add visual input to the touch input so that the response can be more appropriate to the whole context, and not just reactive to one sensation. Children who have autism sometimes react too quickly in a situation, perhaps because they are responding without the benefit of modulated intersensory integration. Intersensory integration supports the development of multidimensional maps of self and environment that enable the child to interact appropriately in various situations.

The Sensory Systems

The sensory systems supply the brain with information. For example, the touch and body position senses (i.e., somatosensory and proprioceptive systems) provide information about the child's body to form the body scheme. Seeing, hearing, smelling, and tasting (i.e., visual, auditory, olfactory, and gustatory systems) provide information about the environment to form maps of the world. The movement sensations (i.e., vestibular system) provide us with information about how our bodies interact with the world (Dunn, 1991a, 1997b). The brain maps that are formed from this information enable us to be oriented in space and time and to make decisions about appropriate actions to take.

How the Sensory Systems Operate

Although each sensory system has its particular functions, all sensory systems develop and function in some basic ways. First, each sensory system brings information from the world to the brain for processing. Second, each sensory system processes its own information at several brain levels. Third, even though each sensory system is named as if it involved only one kind of information, each sensory system has multidimensional features that help us understand children's responses. Fourth, each sensory system has two reasons for transmitting information to the brain: (a) to generate awareness (i.e., arousal/alerting) and (b) to gather information to construct maps of self and environment, which help organize and plan responses (i.e., discrimination/mapping; Dunn, 1991a).

Under typical circumstances, the arousal/alerting and discriminating/ mapping functions complement each other to form a balance of power. This allows us to interact with the environment and gather information for discrimination and mapping under most conditions, while always being able to notice (i.e., arouse to) potentially harmful stimuli. This delicate balance of power requires constant assessment of sensory input so that all potentially important stimuli are noticed without interfering with ongoing purposeful activity (Dunn, 1991a). In children who have autism, this balance is frequently disrupted, which precipitates unusual behaviors as they try to respond and interferes with functional behavior and learning.

In the following sections, we examine how the general neurological principles and the sensory system operations work in each sensory system.

Chemical Senses

Smelling (olfaction) and tasting (gustation) are primal sensory inputs because they evolved earliest in the human repertoire of survival mechanisms. Early in evolution, the gustatory system became the final checking system for food that was to enter the body, whereas the olfactory system became the chemical sense that could determine the location or direction of stimuli (e.g., food or predators) from a distance. The primal nature of these systems is illustrated when we observe the strong responses we have to tastes and smells.

The tongue displays a characteristic pattern of responses to sweet, salty, bitter, and sour tastes, but from a functional standpoint, how we respond to various foods is the major consideration. Our unique responses to tastes is presumably a combination of genetic makeup and experience. For children who have autism, it is not uncommon to see strong preferences and dislikes in food tastes, textures, and temperatures. Strong responses indicate a higher rate of arousal/alerting reactions, suggesting that this part of the system is overriding the discriminating/mapping part. Children who are continuously being alerted tend to react as if they are being threatened; this is the brain's way of saying "this is too much to handle." During such a condition, children are not available for other cognitive processes or for social interactions. In the next section, we discuss how to deal with this situation, so that children can be available for learning. It is also important to remember that when children have very restrictive tastes, their nutritional status can be negatively affected. In these cases, strategies for maintaining adequate nutrition must be included in planning.

The olfactory system is even more sensitive than the gustatory system. However, researchers have been unable to discover basic categories of smell, as they have been able to do with taste. The olfactory system is complex and responds to so many types of odors that classification becomes extremely difficult. Our interest is related to children's responses to smells and how these responses affect daily life. With specific connections to the primitive emotional centers of the brain, the olfactory system has the potential to establish memories and associations. Because of the direct connections with arousal networks, the olfactory input also can quickly increase our level of responsiveness (e.g., using smelling salts with a person who passes out).

We must be vigilant about the possible impact of the olfactory sensory system on children's responses. All of us emit specific odors, and children may recognize family and professionals not only from visual, auditory, and tactile cues, but also from olfactory cues. This may be one factor that contributes to children with autism displaying disorientation and agitation when unfamiliar persons try to engage them. As a result, children may be viewed as noncompliant or as having temper tantrums when, in fact, these behaviors indicate that the brain is overloaded or threatened by an unfamiliar stimulus. The olfactory system is frequently overlooked as a stimulus for these negative reactions because typically smells remain in the background for most of us, but we must consider it as a possibility for children who have autism. Additionally, we must be careful about adding odors such as shampoos, perfumes, and laundry detergents. Although these smells tend to go unnoticed by others, a child with a vulnerable system may react in unpredictable ways.

Tactile System

The tactile (somatosensory) system responds to stimuli from the skin surface. The unique placement of these receptors enables us to know where our bodies end and where the world begins (Dunn, 1991a, 1997b). There are many tactile stimuli, some of which create an arousal state in us. For example, a light touch on the surface of the skin causes the brain to be alerted—we pay attention to what might have caused this stimulus. For example, when someone brushes lightly against a child's arm when passing the desk, the child will take a moment to notice this action. For children who are overly sensitive to touch, this small stimulus can precipitate a bigger response, such as getting up, pushing the person away, or making a negative comment. These bigger responses may interrupt ongoing activity and can be disruptive to group activities as well. Because the tactile system covers such a large area (i.e., the entire surface of the body), children may also respond on the basis of an accumulation of tactile input. In such situations, it might be the addition of several tactile encounters, rather than a single encounter, that leads to a negative reaction. It is important to note that the mouth, hands, and genitalia have the greatest density of touch receptors; this is why children frequently mouth objects, play with small toys, and calm themselves with something to chew.

Conversely, other children do not notice touch enough. These children have absent or delayed responses to touch and frequently do not register stimuli that others would perceive as painful. This explains why behaviors we characterize as "self-injurious" do not seem to be hurtful to the child who is engaging in the behavior (e.g., biting one's arm to the point of breaking the skin). From a neuroscience point of view, these children are displaying very high thresholds for responding and are demonstrating their need for very intense input in order to achieve a response. Because humans have a great need for remaining aware of their bodies and orientation in space, it is not surprising that a child with a very high tactile threshold would go to extreme lengths to try to provide the brain with input.

Other parts of the tactile system enable us to build a map of our bodies (i.e., discriminating/mapping). When we touch somebody firmly (e.g., patting on the back, rubbing, hugging), the brain receives information about what body parts are being touched, which helps build a body map. The map can then be used to plan movements and actions that will be precise and useful for engaging in activities of interest. If we do not have accurate body maps, the result may be inaccurate movements (e.g., clumsiness), too much movement to gain additional input (e.g., children engaging in repetitive actions such as biting or banging), or lack of movement because the movements do not generate useful information. For example, children are engaging in "too much movement" when we observe stereotypic behaviors such as licking or mouthing objects. From a neuroscience point of view, the purpose of these behaviors is to provide additional, intense input about a given object; we hypothesize, therefore, that the child needs more sensory input than is usual. We refer to these patterns of behavior as "sensory-generating" behaviors rather than stereotypic for two reasons. First, "stereotypic" has a clinical quality that implies pathology and conveys a negative connotation, whereas "sensory-generating" is more neutral and descriptive of what we see and the child's purpose for engaging in the behavior. Second, the phrase "sensory-generating" not only honors the child's purpose—satisfying a nervous system need for input—but it also suggests a course of action that respects the child's needs. In a later section, we discuss how to create interventions on the basis of this approach.

Movement System

Whereas the other sensory systems provide information primarily about self or environment, the movement (vestibular) system provides constant and ongoing information about how the body interacts in the environment (i.e., person–environment fit). The vestibular system enables us to remain oriented in space and time.

> In the final analysis, one may have a well-developed sensory map of the external world and a well-developed motor map of movement from one place to another, but if one does not know where they are with respect to that map, they are virtually incapable of using that spatial mapping information. And the vestibular system appears to be the system that gives information about the individual's location in the overall spatial map. (Cool, 1976, p.3)

Children who have autism frequently seek out additional vestibular information, for example, by rocking, swinging, or tilting the head. Although we sometimes consider these behaviors aberrant, from a neuroscience perspective we would hypothesize that by means of these behaviors, children are attempting to orient themselves in space and time. If the brain's homeostasis for this information requires greater amounts of information, more of these behaviors are necessary to feel oriented. From this point of view, therefore, these unusual behaviors have an important role in the child's performance. By understanding this, we can honor the child's need by finding ways to incorporate movement input into daily routines.

Body Position Information

Body position (proprioception) is determined from sense receptors that are housed within the muscles, tendons, and joints. These muscle receptors play an important role in initial learning or relearning of motor movements because they support the muscles to retain the appropriate amount of tension through-out the movement (Crutchfield & Barnes, 1984).

Postural control is a primary function of the vestibular and the proprioceptive systems. Children are able to remain in their desks at school, enter the bus, and manage their lunch trays because they have postural control to keep their bodies upright against gravity as they move through space. The vestibular and proprioceptive systems serve as silent partners during task performance, maintaining postural control while our attention is focused on something else (Dunn, 1991a; Kornhuber, 1974). As other systems are providing information to the brain about a given task, the vestibular and the proprioceptive systems must automatically maintain the body's dynamic orientation in space to support task performance (Dunn, 1991a, 1997b). When children who have autism are focused on maintaining their own bodies in space, they may seem preoccupied and less available to engage in a cognitive activity or social interchange. It is important to understand that if a child must expend a lot of energy to maintain postural control, cognitive processing will inevitably be disrupted.

Visual System

Vision is the most prominent sensation; indeed, there are more fibers in the optic nerve than in all the sensory tracts in the rest of the body (Kandel & Schwartz, 1985). The visual system serves to support the other sensory systems by providing verification of sensory experiences from another point of view. For example, the visual system is designed to recognize contrasts; when the visual environment is less distinct, the cells of the visual system have difficulty responding. The eyes continuously change position with very tiny movements to activate new cells in the retina. In this way, the brain gets ongoing information about the object and can keep the image clear. Busy visual environments can be difficult for the visual system to handle. With too many competing images, the visual system cannot isolate significant high-contrast locations to generate the nerve impulses. For example, think of how difficult it is to find something in the "junk drawer" in the kitchen. This is because there are many overlapping objectives of varying shapes, sizes, and colors, which makes the competition so great that clarity is frequently lost.

We can improve a child's orientation in a busy environment by increasing the contrasts of the images and focusing visual attention (e.g., through the use of a visual schedule). Some children who have autism create strategies to increase visual input (e.g., light filtering or moving close to objects to see details). That is, they are seeking additional ways to get the retinal cells to send information to the brain by increasing the number of times the cells will fire. For example, with light filtering, the children are creating a strobe effect, in which the light source (e.g., bright, bleached) and the hand (e.g., dark, dense) contrast to each other. Occurring over and over as the child moves the hand, this high contrast forces the retinal cells to send repeated messages to the brain, thereby keeping the environmental map distinct and clear. Unfortunately, this interferes with ongoing functional behavior because light filtering requires the child to stop attending to whatever else is happening. We discuss ways to provide ongoing and functional visual contrast in the next section.

Auditory System

The auditory system processes sound primarily for communication, but also as a means of environmental orientation. Thus, direction, distance, and quality of sound all contribute to the ability to orient within our environment from an auditory perspective (Kiang, 1984). The auditory system also participates in a screening process similar to that of the visual system, in which more important sounds receive attention and less important ones are screened out (this process is called "auditory figure–ground perception"). This mechanism allows children to filter out such noises as rustling paper and shuffling feet in the classroom so they can hear the teacher's voice more clearly.

With respect to sound, children who have autism may seem oblivious, may generate their own sounds for orientation, or may be overly attentive to or fearful about sounds in the environment. When oblivious, they appear not to hear what is going on around them, which contributes to the perception that they are in their own world. From a neuroscience viewpoint, such obliviousness indicates the child's greater need for more intensity of input. Children who generate sounds for themselves seem to do so to obtain additional input to keep the arousal state at a level that enables interaction. Still other children seem overly sensitive to sounds; they tend to look fearful, perhaps because they have difficulty sorting out regular environmental sounds from sounds that might signal potential harm. As Temple Grandin (1995) stated about her experiences with autism, "I now realize that because of the autism, my nervous system was in a state of hypervigilance. Any minor disturbance could cause an intense reaction. I was like a high-strung cow or horse that goes into instant antipredator mode when it is surprised by an unexpected disturbance" (p. 111).

Summary

This section has provided foundational information about how the brain receives and processes sensory input as a prerequisite for understanding sensory integrative approaches. The sensory systems provide the brain with all the information it needs to organize a map of self and environment. The brain then uses these maps to design and execute motor acts, including complex actions used in the routines of daily life. Intersensory integration enables the brain to organize input so that the behaviors we create are modulated to fit the situation at hand. When the balance of power in these systems is disrupted, we exhibit unusual behaviors. These behaviors can be interpreted in terms of our need to regulate input to create functional responses. This difficulty negatively affects our ability to learn, perform daily tasks, and interact with others.

In the next section, we discuss the role of the motivational system. Children who have autism have difficulty regulating their own input to produce functional responses, so the contribution of the motivational system becomes a salient factor for designing appropriate interventions.

The Motivational System

Motivation is a complex process that requires consideration of both internal and external actions. To perform a given task, the brain must internally recognize some need (e.g., hunger, cold, desire, social interest), while externally the environment must provide adequate cues and supports to enable the desired performance. Additionally, we must have had opportunities to understand the relationship between the cue to perform and the desired performance (i.e., learning; Dunn, 1991b). Table 7.1 contains a worksheet for identifying the motivational aspects of performance.

Internal motivation may be the most unfamiliar to educators who study learning, cognitive, and behavioral theories of motivation. Brody (1983) described three factors that determine our tendency to perform a task that can help elucidate internal motivational factors: the incentive, the expectancy, and the need for success. We have *incentive* when we value the goal. We have *expectancy* when we are able to understand that the particular task we are performing will help to reach the goal. Finally, *need for success* refers to our need to complete the task correctly. Table 7.2 contains a list of questions to ask to address these factors in intervention planning.

Parents and professionals are sometimes puzzled as to why a child who has autism would engage in particular types of behaviors that clearly are outside the range of usual performance. Understanding these internal mechanisms of motivation, particularly those related to the brain's need for homeostasis, centrifugal control, and intersensory integration, is critical to accurate interpretation of the behavior and performance of children who have autism.

For example, when children who have autism smear feces, we might react by being disgusted. Although this is a disgusting behavior, with neuroscience knowledge, we can interpret it in a way that enables us to understand the child's motivation. We are then more likely to be able to move past our negative reactions to create strategies that establish more acceptable and functional

Table 7.1

Worksheet for Reviewing the Motivational Features of an Individual's Performance

Questions regarding motivational state	Ratings: Mark the box that best represents the individual's performance		
	Low	**Medium**	**High**
What is the individual's overall level of motivation for functional performance?			
How does the internal environment interact with level of motivated behavior?	Conflicts with need to perform functional tasks	Neither supports nor conflicts	Supports functional performance
How does the external environment interact with level of motivated behavior?	Conflicts with need to perform functional tasks	Neither supports nor conflicts	Supports functional performance
How much experience has the individual had with the functional task to develop relationships between salient stimuli and appropriate responses?	None	Some experience	Sufficient amount
What are the characteristics of the individual's intrinsic motivation?			
a. need to assert self	Very low need	Moderate need	Very high need
b. need to interact with others	Very low need	Moderate need	Very high need
c. need to feel competent/successful	Very low need	Moderate need	Very high need
d. need to obtain reinforcement	Very low need	Moderate need	Very high need
How is motivated behavior manifested?			
a. ANS output (e.g., flushing, sweating)	Too little	Appropriate	Too much
b. somatic motor output	Too little	Appropriate	Too much
Which task/environmental factors interact with this individual's level of motivation to perform functional tasks?	Difficulty of information that needs to be processed	Necessity for continuous/sustained effort	Highly interfering environment
	Amount of information that needs to be processed	Amount of time the task requires	Environment that provides ongoing support
a. contribute to motivated behavior			
b. interfere with motivated behavior			

Note. From *Neuroscience Foundations of Human Performance, Lesson 12,* p. 13, by W. Dunn, 1991, Bethesda, MD: American Occupational Therapy Association, Inc. Reprinted with permission.

Table 7.2

Questions That Elucidate Contributions of Various
Motivational Factors to Task Performance

Factor in motivation	Definition	Questions that service providers ask to determine the contribution of this factor to motivated performance
Incentive	The person needs or values the goal object	What does this person want to do? What does this person need to do to function in life? What behaviors or activities do family values support? What types of rewards does this person respond to?
Expectancy	The person 1. understands that the task is relevant to goal attainment 2. believes that the act will lead to the goal	Have I made a clear link between the activities we are doing in therapy and the person's desired goals? Does the person accept that what we are doing will lead to goal attainment? Are there ways for me to provide external support (e.g., task adaptation or environmental modification) to make the relationship to goals more apparent?
Success	The person selects the task based on the need to complete the task correctly	What is the person's level of frustration tolerance? Does the person seem to care/notice when a task is incomplete or incorrect? Are task adaptations acceptable to the person, or does the person insist on one particular pattern of performance?

performance. First, when observing children who engage in this behavior, we notice that they are focused and interested, rather than repelled by the activity. Feces have unique and intense sensory features; therefore, the smell and texture provide very strong sensory input. We might hypothesize that children are generating powerful sensory inputs for the brain by smearing feces. The odor makes the environment more noticeable and the sticky, thick texture provides a medium that allows the child to be very aware of the hand surface and shape. Following up on this hypothesis, we would acknowledge the child's behavior as a way to meet an internal motivation to obtain additional sensory input for orientation to self and environment. On the basis of this recognition, then, we can create intervention strategies with the family to provide the child with more acceptable means to meet those internal motivational needs throughout the day. For example, we might experiment with different room freshener odors to make the environment more "olfactory" for the child, or we might suggest cooking activities such as making cookies, which require hand mixing of ingredients. These strategies honor the child's internal drives and facilitate functional performance at the same time.

In serving children who have autism, it is short-sighted to consider only external motivational factors. As illustrated in the above example, it is likely that the child was motivated by the brain's need for intense input. External reinforcers or contingencies would not be sufficient to diminish the behavior because the child's nervous system is indicating a need for input. That is, the child is motivated more strongly by this internal need for input than by the actions we might take in the external environment (e.g., time-out).

When considering the motivational aspects of performance, we must also guard against creating prompt-dependent behavior. If the child stops the undesirable behavior only when adults tell him or her to, the child does not establish internal mechanisms of control for him- or herself. In cases in which children continue a behavior for extended periods of time, a neuroscience perspective leads to the question, "What does the child need from that behavior?" On the basis of the answer to this question, routines can be constructed to provide more intense input so that the child can satiate in a more reasonable time. For example, if a child stays in the shower until someone gets him or her to stop, we might hypothesize that the tactile sensations of the water hitting his or her skin meet a sensory need. We might first observe how long it would take for him or her to get out without a prompt (i.e., to reach threshold). Then we could identify other ways to provide tactile input that would offer a more reasonable time period for personal hygiene and getting ready for the day. We might consider heavier bedding at night because this provides tactile pressure input; we might examine clothing choices and select more tightly fitting clothes (e.g., leggings) to provide more ongoing tactile input throughout the day. If the nervous system can be satiated in these ways, the need for prolonged showering could diminish.

Thresholds for Action as Factors in Daily Life

In the brain, homeostasis can be seen in each neuron, neuronal pattern, and system in the CNS. Although homeostasis represents the stability or comfort point for that cell or system, each nervous system has set points for action or inaction (called "thresholds"; Kandel & Schwartz, 1985). Thresholds in the CNS indicate the amount of stimuli we need to notice or react to stimuli (Dunn, 1997a). A threshold is a point at which an action can occur; input that accumulates below the threshold does not stimulate a response or action (homeostasis remains intact), whereas input that accumulates at or above the threshold leads to an action or response (homeostasis is disrupted). Thresholds are established in the CNS by our genetic endowment, exposure to stimuli, opportunities to have experiences, and both cognitive and emotional learning.

Typical children generally have a broad range for homeostasis, whereas children with autism tend to have a narrower range for homeostasis, which results in more frequent needs to reestablish the steady state. Because each child has a unique set of thresholds in the CNS, we must observe carefully to understand how particular thresholds affect each child's performance range. Additionally, children demonstrate variability within their CNS on particular days (e.g., when more or less rested) and within particular systems (e.g., the somatosensory system is more sensitive than the vestibular system); all of these conditions can affect the child's' performance capacity.

Thresholds enable *modulation* of *all* input to the CNS functions (i.e., the ability to monitor and regulate information in the interest of generating an appropriate response to particular stimuli). Key neurophysiological processes related to modulation of input include habituation and sensitization (Dunn, 1997a; Kandel & Schwartz, 1985).

Habituation

Habituation is a brain function that reflects a form of learning. When cells and systems in the CNS begin to recognize a stimulus or pattern of stimuli, their thresholds shift to accommodate this familiarity (i.e., habituate) and decrease transmission. Habituation is an important brain function because daily life would be constantly interrupted if we had to respond to every stimulus all day long as if it were new and needing our attention. When there is habituation, the thresholds for action are raised, so that the neurons and systems need more or new information before reactions occur.

Sensitization

Sensitization occurs due to learning, but the nature of the stimulus causes the CNS to be more alert to certain stimuli. During sensitization, the brain recognizes the stimulus as important or potentially harmful; the CNS generates a heightened response. Sensitization is an important function because it enables us to remain aware of our contexts and can trigger responses when the situation seems to warrant one.

Modulation of Thresholds

The brain must create a balance between habituation and sensitization (i.e., modulation) for daily life, which consists of a configuration of functional behaviors, to be effective, efficient, and satisfying. Although children typically have thresholds that reflect their overall brain responsiveness, as mentioned, their threshold range shifts based on additional factors such as which system(s) are involved in a task (e.g., touch, movement) or their capacity for that day (e.g., rested or tired).

When habituation and sensitization are poorly modulated, children can exhibit maladaptive behaviors. A tendency toward high neurological thresholds, (i.e., too much habituation) leads to children appearing lethargic or inattentive (i.e., underresponsive). If a child is underresponsive, we consider ways to improve the chances of responding. For example, when a child is lethargic in the classroom, the teacher might speak in a more varied tone, use touch during instruction, or increase the contrast of the worksheet or visual demonstration to increase responsiveness. Each of these strategies increases input to reach higher thresholds. By contrast, a tendency toward low thresholds (i.e., too much sensitization) leads to children appearing to be overly excitable or hyperactive (i.e., overresponsive; Dunn, 1997a). When a child is overly sensitized, we design interventions that may reduce the frequency of that pattern. For example, if a child is overly sensitive to voices at school, and this keeps her from completing her seatwork, we might consider ways to reduce the auditory input so that her sensitivities would be triggered less, and work productivity could increase. From a functional perspective, these strategies might be considered methods for establishing more effective modulation for productive living. Throughout the first part of this chapter, we have provided several examples of how understanding and knowledge of neuroscience can help facilitate more normalized daily functioning of individuals with autism. In the following section, we present a comprehensive model for how to incorporate neuroscience principles into our work with individuals with autism on a consistent basis.

A Conceptual Model for Incorporating Neuroscience Principles

To gain insight about the how the brain is operating, we must observe behavior. For example, we know that flushing or blanching of the skin, sweating, and goose bumps are indications that the autonomic nervous system (ANS) is operating. But the more subtle aspects of the neuroscience–behavior links sometimes escape our consideration; it is these subtleties that can enable us to refine our assessment and intervention planning skills with children who have autism.

Dunn (1977a) outlined a behavioral response continuum that reflects the motivation to act in relation to the neurological thresholds described above (i.e., habituation to sensitization). Figure 7.1 contains a diagram of this proposed interaction, with the vertical axis depicting the neurological thresholds and the horizontal axis depicting the behavioral response continuum. At one end of the continuum, children might respond in *accordance* with their neurological

Neurological Threshold Continuum	Behavioral Response Continuum	
	responds in ACCORDANCE with threshold	responds to COUNTERACT the threshold
HIGH (habituation)	Poor Registration	Sensation Seeking
LOW (sensitization)	Sensitivity to Stimuli	Sensation Avoiding

Figure 7.1. Relationships between behavioral responses and neurological thresholds. *Note.* From "The Impact of Sensory Processing Abilities on the Daily Lives of Young Children and Their Families: A Conceptual Model," by W. Dunn, 1997, *Infants and Young Children, 9*(4), p. 24. Copyright 1997 by Aspen Publishers. Reprinted with permission.

thresholds. Children with generally high thresholds would respond infrequently because their thresholds for action would rarely be met, and they would not seek additional input (i.e., they have poor registration). Children with low neurological thresholds, on the other hand, would respond to many stimuli because their thresholds would be met frequently (i.e., they are sensitive to stimuli). At the other end of the behavioral response continuum, children would respond to *counteract* their typical neurological thresholds. In this condition, children with high thresholds would find ways to generate more stimuli so that their thresholds would be met more often (i.e., they would seek sensation), whereas children with low neurological thresholds would find ways to avoid triggering their thresholds (i.e., they would avoid sensation).

When we consider this proposed interaction between the neurological threshold and behavioral response continua, we see that the neuroscience frame of reference enhances our ability to observe and interpret children's behavior. For example, we can consider potential effects of high or low neurological thresholds on performance during daily life and can subsequently construct effective interventions that honor the brain's actions. Below, we examine these interactions as part of daily life routines in children who have autism (see Dunn, 1997a, for original presentation of this work).

Poor Registration

Children who have high neurological thresholds and act in accordance with those thresholds have a difficult time recruiting responses in a timely manner. As a result, they tend to have a dull or uninterested appearance (Dunn, 1997a). They may not have adequate neural activation to establish or maintain focus on important or necessary tasks in their lives. They might be withdrawn, difficult to engage, or seem self-absorbed; they may also be easily exhausted and appear apathetic (NCCIP, 1994). Children who demonstrate poor registration need highly salient stimuli to engage them in functional tasks.

When working with children with poor registration, we need to find ways to intensify the task and contextual features so that the brain gets more information and, therefore, has a better chance to reach the high thresholds. Meeting the thresholds for action also means that the brain is receiving information for learning; some children who have autism may seem "out of it" because their high thresholds keep them from displaying the capacity to recognize stimuli that other children routinely notice and respond to.

When addressing poor registration needs, we *increase* the contrast and *reduce* the predictability of events, thereby creating more opportunities for the sensory systems to send input to the brain. For example, we might make objects weigh more to increase proprioceptive input, change an item's color or background color to make the item more noticeable on the table, or add a movement to the task routine to increase vestibular system activity. For example, if a parent is having trouble getting his daughter to get dressed because she is so lethargic, we might suggest that he play music in her room in the morning, spray air freshener in the room, hang her clothes against an opposite-colored background, and have her bend down to get socks and shoes on. Each of these changes adds sensory input to the dressing task (i.e., auditory, olfactory, visual, and vestibular inputs, respectively), and the accumulation of inputs increases the chances that the daughter will reach her thresholds and become more responsive. Through ongoing dialogue with the parent, we would be able to adjust the routine to achieve even more sensory input or a little less, depending on how the daughter responds. When the amount of sensory input is too great, children become irritable or overly excited. We are striving to reach the middle ground of enough arousal to be involved in the task without so much arousal that the child becomes agitated or distracted from performance.

Sensitivity to Stimuli

Some children who have low thresholds are sensitive to stimuli. Acting in accordance with those thresholds, they tend to be hyperactive and distracted (Dunn, 1997a). Children who are sensitive to stimuli may have difficulty completing tasks because they are interrupted as they attend to the new stimuli that occur during the natural course of the day. They may also have difficulty learning from their experiences because routines are disrupted frequently, so that the continuity required to develop habits is lacking. Some children may display excessive fear or caution, and others may be easily upset (NCCIP, 1994).

When serving children with sensitivity to sensory stimuli, we must emphasize the discriminating features of sensory systems (see Dunn, 1991a; Dunn & DeGangi, 1992) because these do not increase arousal. Tables 7.3 and 7.4 outline which features of each sensory system are more discriminatory. Touch-pressure stimuli (i.e., firm contact with the skin) travels to the brain without exciting the reticular formation (a generalized arousal center in the brain stem); this type of input allows the person's CNS to receive input without increasing arousal (Dunn, 1991a). Children with sensory sensitivity can receive touch-pressure input to obtain information about their bodies without experiencing more generalized arousal. Input that contains a more alerting or arousing quality may more easily draw them away from the task at hand. The more organizing (i.e., not arousing) input these children can obtain, the better their chances for completing tasks and learning from them. Care providers must be flexible yet assertive when serving these persons. We must also be respectful about the affective and emotional responses they display in response to what we consider the routine events of the day; these children may be more sensitive to task and contextual events than other children.

Sensation Seeking

Children who have high neurological thresholds and who develop responses to counteract them find ways to increase the intensity of their sensory experiences. They add movement, touch, sound, and visual stimuli to every life event. Sensation seekers make noises continuously, fidget in their seats, touch everything, feel objects, touch and hang on to others, or chew on things. Each of these actions intensifies the sensory input for the child, which, in turn, increases the child's chances of meeting high thresholds. Children who seek sensation might also be observed to lack caution in play, display excitability, and engage in impulsive behavior (Dunn, 1997a).

(text continues on page 214)

Table 7.3

Arousal/Alerting and Discrimination/Mapping Descriptions of the Sensory System

Sensory system	Arousal/alerting descriptors	Discrimination/mapping descriptors
For all systems	Unpredictable: The task is unfamiliar; the child cannot anticipate the sensory experiences that will occur in the task	Predictable: Sensory pattern in the task is routine for the child, such as diaper changing—the child knows what is occurring and what will come next.
Somatosensory	Light touch: Gentle tapping on skin; tickling (e.g., loose clothing making contact with skin).	Touch pressure: Firm contact on skin (e.g., hugging, patting, grasping). Occurs both when touching objects or persons, or when they touch you.
	Pain: Brisk pinching; contact with sharp objects; skin pressed in small surface (e.g., when skin is caught in between chair arm and seat).	Long-duration stimuli: Holding, grasping (e.g., carrying a child in your arms).
	Temperature: Hot or cold stimuli (e.g., iced drinks, hot foods, cold hands, cold metal chairs).	Large body surface contact: Large body surfaces include holding, hugging; also include holding a cup with the entire palmar surface of hand.
	Variable: Changing characteristics during the task (e.g., putting clothing on requires a combination of tactile experiences).	
	Short-duration stimuli: Tapping, touching briefly (e.g., splashing water).	
	Small body surface contact: Small body surfaces, as when using only fingertips to touch something.	
Vestibular	Head position change: The child's head orientation (e.g., pulling the child up from lying on the back to sitting).	Linear head movement: Head moving in a straight line (e.g., bouncing up and down, going down the hall in a wheelchair).
	Speed change: Movements change velocity (e.g., teacher stops to talk to another teacher when pushing the child to the bathroom in his wheelchair).	Repetitive head movement: Movements that repeat in a simple sequence (e.g., rocking in a rocker).
	Direction change: Movements change planes, such as bending down to pick something up from the floor while carrying the child down the hall.	
	Rotary head movement: Head moving in an arc (e.g., spinning in a circle, turning head side to side).	

(continues)

Table 7.3 *Continued.*

Sensory system	Arousal/alerting descriptors	Discrimination/mapping descriptors
Proprioception	Quick stretch: Movements that pull on the muscles (e.g., briskly tapping on a muscle belly).	Sustained tension: Steady, constant action on the muscles pressing or holding on the muscle (e.g., using heavy objects during play). Shifting muscle tension: Activities that demand constant change in the muscles (e.g., walking, lifting, and moving objects).
Visual	High intensity: Visual stimulus is bright (e.g., looking out the window on a bright day). High contrast: A lot of difference between the visual stimulus and its surrounding environment (e.g., cranberry juice in a white cup). Variable: Changing characteristics during the task (e.g., a TV program is a variable visual stimulus).	Low intensity: Visual stimulus is subdued (e.g., finding objects in the dark closet). High similarity: Small differences between visual stimulus and its surrounding environment (e.g., oatmeal in a beige bowl). Competitive: The background is interesting or busy (e.g., the junk drawer, a bulletin board).
Auditory	Variable: Changing characteristics during the task (e.g., a person's voice with intonation). High intensity: The auditory stimulus is loud (e.g., siren, high-volume radio).	Rhythmic: Sounds repeat in a simple sequence/beat (e.g., humming, singing nursery songs). Constant: The stimulus is always present (e.g., a fan noise). Competitive: The environment has a variety of recurring sounds (e.g., the classroom, a party). Noncompetitive: The environment is quiet (e.g., the bedroom when all is ready for bedtime). Low intensity: The auditory stimulus is subdued (e.g., whispering).
Olfactory/ gustatory	Strong intensity: The taste/smell has distinct qualities (e.g., spinach).	Mild intensity: The taste/smell has nondistinct or familiar qualities (e.g., Cream of Wheat).

Note. From "The Sensorimotor Systems: A Framework for Assessment and Intervention," by W. Dunn. In F. P. Orelove and D. Sobsey (Eds.), *Educating Children with Multiple Disabilities: A Transdisciplinary Approach* (2nd ed., p. 42), 1991, Baltimore: Paul H. Brookes. Copyright 1991 by Paul H. Brookes. Reprinted with permission.

Table 7.4
Reasons for Incorporating Various Sensory Qualities into Integrated Intervention Programs

Sensory system	Arousal/alerting descriptors	Discrimination/mapping descriptors
For all systems	Unpredictable: To develop an increasing level of attention to keep the child interested in the task/activity (e.g., change the position of the objects on the child's lap tray during the task).	Predictable: To establish the child's ability to anticipate a programming sequence or a salient cue; to decrease possibility of being distracted from a functional task sequence (e.g., use the same routine for diaper changing every time).
Somato-sensory	Light touch: To increase alertness in a child who is lethargic (e.g., pull cloth from child's face during peek-a-boo).	Touch pressure: To establish and maintain awareness of body parts and body position; to calm a child who has been overstimulated (e.g., provide a firm bear hug).
	Pain: To raise from unconsciousness; to determine ability to respond to noxious stimuli when unconscious (e.g., flick palm of hand or sole of foot briskly).	Long-duration stimuli: To enable the child to become familiar and comfortable with the stimulus; to incorporate stimulus into functional skill (e.g., grasping the container to pick it up and pour out contents).
	Temperature: To establish awareness of stimuli; to maintain attentiveness to task (e.g., use hot foods for spoon eating and cold drink for sucking through a straw).	Large body surface contact: To establish and maintain awareness of body parts and body position; to calm a child who has been overstimulated (e.g., wrap child tightly in a blanket).
	Variable: To maintain attention to or interest in the task (e.g., place new texture on cup surface each day so child notices the cup).	
	Short-duration stimuli: To increase arousal for task performance (e.g., tap child on chest before giving directions).	
	Small body surface contact: To generate and focus attention on a particular body part (e.g., tap around lips with fingertips before an eating task).	
Vestibular	Head position change: To increase arousal for an activity (e.g., position child prone over a wedge).	Linear head movement: To support establishment of body awareness in space (e.g., carry child around the room in fixed position to explore its features).
	Speed change: To maintain adequate alertness for a functional task (e.g., vary pace while carrying the child to a new task).	Repetitive head movement: To provide predictable and organizing information; to calm a child who has been overstimulated (e.g., rock the child).
	Direction change: To elevate level of alertness for a functional task (e.g., swing child back and forth in arms prior to positioning him or her at the table for a task).	
	Rotary head movement: To increase arousal prior to functional task (e.g., pick child up from prone [on stomach] facing away to upright facing toward you to position for a new task).	

(continues)

Table 7.4 *Continued.*

Sensory system	Arousal/alerting descriptors	Discrimination/mapping descriptors
Proprioception	Quick stretch: To provide additional muscle tension to support functional tasks (e.g., tap muscle belly of hypotonic muscle while providing physical guidance to grasp).	Sustained tension: To enable the muscle to relax, elongate, so body part can be in more optimal position for function (e.g., press firmly across muscle belly while guiding a reaching pattern; add weight to objects being manipulated). Shifting muscle tension: To establish functional movements that contain stability and mobility (e.g., prop and reach for a top; reach, fill, and lift spoon to mouth).
Visual	High intensity: To increase opportunity to notice object; to generate arousal for task (e.g., cover blocks with foil for manipulation task). High contrast: To enhance possibility of locating the object and maintaining attention to it (e.g., place raisins on a piece of typing paper for prehension activity). Variable: To maintain attention to or interest in the task (e.g., play rolling catch with a clear ball that has movable pieces inside).	Low intensity: To allow the visual stimulus to blend with other salient features; to generate searching behaviors, because characteristics are less obvious (e.g., find own cubbyhole in back of the room). High similarity: To establish more discerning abilities; to develop skills for naturally occurring tasks (e.g., scoop apple sauce from beige plate). Competitive: To facilitate searching; to increase tolerance for natural life circumstances (e.g., obtain correct tools from equipment bin).
Auditory	Variable: To maintain attention to or interest in the task (e.g., play radio station after activating a switch). High intensity: To stimulate noticing the person or object; to create proper alerting for task performance (e.g., ring a bell to encourage the child to locate the stimulus).	Rhythmic: To provide predictable and organizing information for environmental orientation (e.g., sing a nursery rhyme while physically guiding motions). Constant: To provide a foundational stimulus for environmental orientation; especially important when other sensory systems (e.g., vision, vestibular) do not provide orientation (e.g., child recognizes own classroom by fan noise and calms down). Competitive: To facilitate differentiation of salient stimuli; to increase tolerance for natural life circumstances (e.g., after child learns to look when his or her name is called, conduct activity within busy classroom). Noncompetitive: To facilitate focused attention for acquiring a new and difficult skill; to calm a child who has been overstimulated (e.g., move child to quiet room to establish vocalizations).

(continues)

Table 7.4 *Continued.*

Sensory system	Arousal/alerting descriptors	Discrimination/mapping descriptors
Auditory		Low intensity: To allow the auditory stimulus to blend with other salient features; to generate searching behaviors if stimulus is less obvious (e.g., give child a direction in a normal volume).
Olfactory/ gustatory	Strong intensity: To stimulate arousal for task (e.g., child smells spaghetti sauce at lunch).	Mild intensity: To facilitate exploratory behaviors; to stimulate naturally occurring activities (e.g., smell of lunch food is less distinct, so child is encouraged to notice texture, color).

Note. From "The Sensorimotor Systems: A Framework for Assessment and Intervention," by W. Dunn. In F. P. Orelove & D. Sobsey (Eds.), *Educating Children with Multiple Disabilities: A Transdiciplinary Approach* (2nd ed., pp. 39–40), 1991, Baltimore: Paul H. Brookes. Copyright 1991 by Paul H. Brookes. Reprinted with permission.

In working with children who seek sensation, it is imperative to observe them carefully first to determine what sensations they prefer in their routines. We can be most effective with those who seek sensation when we incorporate the sensations they need into the routines of daily life. For example, some children with autism seek movement input by rocking, running, and jumping, but these actions interfere with personal hygiene routines and socialization. In these instances, we would want to reconstruct the important tasks so the child gets high-intensity movement as part of the activities of interest. At home, we might place the toothpaste and soap under the sink so the child gets to bend down to get the items (bending moves the head upside down, which provides the vestibular system with very strong input). We would then watch to see how much of this type of vestibular input would satisfy the child so that he or she would no longer need to stop brushing his or her teeth to go spin around or rock on the floor. Similarly, at school, we might pair the child with a friend to erase the chalkboards and encourage jungle gym play at recess. These tasks inherently include movement input, so that the child can receive the movement input he or she seeks without having to stop ongoing activity with peers.

Respecting the input children need also reduces the anxiety that is often associated with working to meet high thresholds; that is, when threshold needs are met, the child can focus on the functional aspects of life tasks more readily. The objective of effective intervention is to support creative and purposeful exploration during daily life so that the sensation-seeking rituals do not interfere with functional performance.

Sensation Avoiding

Children who have low thresholds and wish to counteract their thresholds work to reduce input. We see these children as being resistant and unwilling to participate in activities, particularly unfamiliar ones. They experience discomfort in meeting their neurological thresholds, and to keep from feeling this discomfort, they reduce their activity and withdraw. For example, a child who is a sensation avoider may feel overwhelmed at the grocery store with all the items densely filling the visual environment and all the unpredictable sounds; such a child might become irritable or aggressive as a way to get someone to take him out of this setting.

One predominant strategy among these children is the development of rituals for conducting daily life tasks and intolerance of adaptations in these rituals. Rituals provide comfort because they stimulate a familiar pattern of neural activity; this familiarity increases the chances for habituation responses in the brain and reduces the possibility of triggering their low thresholds. Changes in rituals increase sensory stimulation due to the newness of the task, which generates anxiety, since triggering thresholds may be uncomfortable. These children's behavior may be characterized as stubborn and controlling. They might also seem inattentive to some stimuli, along with being preoccupied with others. These behaviors control input, but may be perceived by adults as self-absorption (NCCIP, 1994). The self-absorption might be related to the vigilance that the child must display to keep control over possible "assaults" from unfamiliar inputs.

We must first and foremost honor the discomfort these children experience. Through careful observation, we can determine the characteristics of their rituals (i.e., what is it that they include or exclude from the ritual?). Some frames of reference might suggest that we bombard these children with input so they "get used to it." This strategy can lead to more and more withdrawal, however, as the children attempt to maintain some sense of homeostasis and control. From a neuroscience viewpoint, it is preferable to introduce stimuli in a systematic manner to enable the child to accommodate the new input as part of the familiar routines. We select a ritual, usually one that is most important to the family or the child's welfare, such as eating. After understanding the characteristics of the ritual, we can expand it in some small way so that there is a blending of familiar and new stimuli (Dunn & DeGangi, 1992). This enables the child to incorporate the new stimuli into a comfortable pattern. For example, many children who have autism express strong preferences not only for foods they will eat, but also for the rituals surrounding eating and preparing the food. If the child is focused on the taste of the food, we can add a color or texture to the food to broaden the ritual's sensory qualities (e.g. we can put pink food coloring into applesauce, or we can add finely ground nuts to it). This creates an opportunity for the child to arouse to the new stimulus and perhaps accept it into the ritual, broadening the ritual without causing an aggressive or withdrawing response. Disrupting a ritual too swiftly usually leads to more avoidance behaviors and further decline of functional performance (Dunn, 1997a). There is a great risk with these children of entering into power struggles (NCCIP, 1994); the neuroscience perspective provides a behavioral paradigm for explaining the defiant behaviors we might observe.

Children who avoid sensation may appear disengaged, which can be confused with poor registration. There is a difference, however. Children who avoid sensory experiences notice and withdraw from activities, whereas children with poor registration are not aware of what is going on around them. Mistaking withdrawal behaviors for the lack of awareness of one's environment can lead to ineffective intervention choices.

Summary

When characterizing children's behaviors into these categories, it is important to remember that these are not static states. All of us can shift along the threshold and response continua from one day to the next, or from one situation to the next, even though we may have stronger tendencies for certain responses. Skilled observation of children's behaviors is the best indicator of status.

Application of Sensory Integration Theory to Daily Life Routines

In applying sensory integration knowledge to the needs of children who have autism, three primary goals are relevant: (a) to develop and maintain coping and attention skills, (b) to develop and maintain social reciprocity in relationships, and (c) to develop specific functional skills for daily life. As noted, the role of motivation is inherently linked to an individual's unique way of processing sensory information and can be observed in corresponding performance.

Incorporating a sensory approach into our problem solving for children who have autism requires a basic understanding of centrifugal control in the brain (see above) and an understanding of each individual's continuum of need for sensory input to provide an optimal level of alertness (i.e., internal state) to engage in social interactions and perform functional tasks. Each individual's nervous system sets the tone for how information is perceived and serves as the foundation for how the individual responds. We must consider level of alertness (e.g., tired, rested, interested), the requirements of the task (e.g., whether the skills required are in the individual's repertoire), and the features of the environment (e.g., noisy, emotionally supportive; Dunn, Brown, & McGuigan, 1994). We will discuss ways to consider and include these factors as part of comprehensive planning.

Applying a Sensory Approach to Yourself

The first step to applying sensory processing strategies as positive supports for students with autism is to know your own threshold and sensory preferences and how these personal characteristics affect your coping, social relationships, and functional skills. All of us seek or avoid different kinds of sensory input in order to increase or decrease our own state of alertness. Review the examples in Table 7.5 as a means of identifying the sensory preferences that assist you in achieving or maintaining an optimal level of arousal or alertness. Characterize what types of sensation you seek and avoid to be comfortable and productive in your daily life.

Now consider how these preferences affect your life. Let's say you have a low threshold for sensory input and thus tend to be sensitive to a barrage of sights, sounds, activities, and smells. This might manifest itself in your being a person who enjoys quiet time, prefers that things run on schedule, likes to make lists of all your "things to do," enjoys crossing them off the list once the tasks are completed, and has a small, close group of friends. Each of these behavioral choices is a coping strategy that limits the sensory input you would typically receive in your daily routine. The quieter the day, with few distractions and people interrupting you, the better you feel. With regard to social

Table 7.5

Examples of Sensory Preferences

Listen (auditory)	Look (visual)	Move (vestibular)	Oral (taste/ smell/touch)	Touch (tactile)
Work in a quiet room	Fluorescent lighting	Shift frequently in a chair	Chew gum	Apply lotion to hands and other body areas
Work while listening to music	Flames of a fire	Stretch	Bite nails	Take a hot/ warm shower or bath
Sing or talk to self	Animated videotapes	Rock in a rocking chair	Suck on hard candy	Pet an animal
Go to sleep to the sound of a vaporizor or fan	Dim lighting	Jiggle crossed legs while sitting	Chew on pens, toothpicks	Fidget with objects while talking
Listen to the squeak of a wheel on your shopping cart	View through sunglasses	Dance	Crunch and/or suck on ice	Twist own hair
Listen to continuous dog barking	Bright sunlight coming through the car window	Practice aerobic or isometric exercise	Lick, bite, and/or suck on lips or inside of cheek	Keep hands in pockets

relationships, you tend to choose close relationships with individuals who are more like you (quiet, reserved), avoiding close relationships with individuals who are most unlike you (loud, boisterous) because these choices are most compatible with your sensory threshold needs. From a functional performance perspective, you create a lot of order to manage your own need for predictability in the sensory input you receive.

Applying a Sensory Approach to Children with Autism

Selecting these patterns of behavior and performance are your ways to honor your nervous system's needs for modulating input and not overloading you. Children who have autism need our help to construct their lives to be manageable for them because they cannot do for themselves what you do for yourself. Now let's examine how this might work.

Developing and Maintaining Coping and Attention Skills

Coping refers to the process of making adaptations to meet personal needs and to respond to the demands of the environment (Williamson, Szczepanski, & Zeitlin, 1993). Children with autism who have difficulty processing sensory information often become upset about changes in routines that are not predictable; are overwhelmed by the intensity, frequency, and duration of sensations in particular environments; or may seem unaware of what is going on around them because they have "tuned out" external stimuli. In response, they may develop coping strategies that appear strange to others. Although we might initially perceive these strange behaviors as maladaptive, from a coping point of view the behaviors serve some purpose for the child (e.g., reestablish homeostasis, obtain needed sensory input). Coping strategies may include seeking preferred sensations (e.g., rocking) or avoiding less preferred or even painful sensations (e.g., someone touching your skin).

Attention is the ability to self-regulate and direct interest to learn about the self and the environment. Learning is compromised when children who have autism are unavailable to attend to instruction because they spend a good deal of their time seeking or avoiding particular types of sensory input.

Developing and Maintaining Social Reciprocity in Relationships

When children with autism have difficulty processing sensory information, they correspondingly have difficulty regulating their own and others' emotional responses. Children with autism are more likely to be interested in and thus pursue social relations with others who can respond in *accordance* with *their* processing needs. This social interest is sometimes described in the literature as *bonding* or *attachment*. Classic benchmark studies like Harlow and Harlow's (1966) research on the power of tactile contact as comfort was pioneer evidence that enhanced our understanding of the need for sensory experiences that drive how social relations are formed and maintained. For example, the child who seeks tactile input throughout the day across various environments by "touching everything in sight" will engage the social reciprocity of his or her mother, who provides play materials that include the child's preferred textures. Children with autism can and do form close relations, albeit in different ways than do children who are typically developing. Children with autism are like their peers in that they form social attachments to caregivers who are sensitive and responsive to their needs—particularly their sensory needs.

Developing Specific Functional Skills

When students have difficulty or are unable to perform functional skills, such as dressing, writing, or using utensils to eat, it is because of a breakdown in processing sensorimotor information. The close relationship between the sensory and motor systems cannot be overemphasized (Dunn, 1991a). That is, the motor parts of the brain can only activate from incoming sensory information. When children have difficulty developing functional skills, several factors may be operating. First, the sensory systems may have difficulty collecting relevant information or may bombard the brain with too much information. Second, the sensory information that is collected may be distorted as it is processed in the brain. In either case, the child has inaccurate or unreliable information for designing and carrying out age-related functional skills (i.e., motor acts; Dunn, 1991a). Unfortunately, many teachers and therapists do not realize that the sensory systems "fuel" the motor system. As a result, the sensory processing features are ignored while the motor response becomes the focus of intervention; interventions based on motor performance alone will most likely be unsuccessful because they do not resolve the underlying problem of poor sensory input for the motor planning process. For example, children who have difficulty brushing their teeth (a motor performance act) often have adverse responses to the many sensory features of tooth brushing, such as the taste and smell of toothpaste, the visual distraction of a mirror over the sink, the sound of running water, or the feel of hard plastic and nylon bristles in the mouth. All of these sensory features may be overwhelming to a child with autism. Thus, practicing the toothbrushing motor acts will not improve performance in this case. Instead, first we would have to address the sensory features of the task to determine which ones were interfering with performance. We could then decide whether we need to reduce the sensory feature (e.g., turn off the water) or work to increase the child's sensory processing capacity (e.g., use finger to "brush," then a soft cloth, then a soft brush).

Similarly, imitating simple to complex motor movements is often difficult for individuals with autism. The degree to which imitation abilities are impaired is often a good indicator of how disorganized the sensory processing abilities are. Sometimes individuals with autism appear to have very well developed motor skills, such as the ability to climb and jump. Often parents whose children have great balance and coordination skills report that their children also have no fear when it comes to climbing, jumping, and otherwise exploring. The parents may also report that even though their child's balance and coordination skills appear exceptional, the child is unable to fasten buttons, cut with a knife, or ride a bicycle. Understanding the sensory processing features that underlie the discrepancy is the key to assisting individuals with autism in either developing their sensory processing capabilities or changing the demands/features of the task to promote the desired independence in performance.

Assessment of Sensory Aspects of Functional Performance

Often we are asked to help with a child's sensory processing problems. There is no "one-size-fits-all recipe," but there *is* a logical framework that can be used to design a "recipe" that fits the individual needs of the child who has autism. The recipe comes from knowing how the nervous system works. As noted, each child's nervous system contains maps constructed by genetic and environmental influences. Trained professionals and sensitive, responsive caregivers (mothers, fathers, siblings, grandparents) can learn ways to create opportunities to meet the sensory needs of their family members with autism. Designing the "just-right recipe" is a dynamic process that changes over time in response to the child and the environment.

The first step in creating sensory-based intervention strategies is to collect data that identify the child's current level of performance in relation to the status of each of the sensory systems. Data are collected from various sources (parent, teacher, child) across naturally occurring environments (home, school, community). Methods for data collection include skilled observation of performance, questionnaires, and interviews. Formal, standardized assessments of sensory integration are not appropriate for children with autism because they cannot meet the required standards for testing behavior. We generally consider the child's sensory responses, cognitive and communication features, the environmental supports and barriers to performance, and the impact of these factors on function.

The Sensory Profile: A Measure of Sensory Processing in Daily Life

Sometimes professionals get caught up in their own methods of gathering data about children, such as formal testing and skilled observation of performance, and they neglect parents and teachers as critical sources of information. Parents and teachers spend the most time with the children and therefore can provide information about the impact of children's assets and liabilities on their daily life performance. After all, it is not the children's diagnosis that matters; it is the effects on daily life that must be central to intervention planning. Children with autism are not homogeneous; they must cope with different contexts, such as different types of home life, different teacher temperaments, and different daily expectations and interests. Parents and teachers provide us with information about how the objective features of the child's autism play themselves out in the daily life routines and therefore point the way for us. For example, not all parents are bothered by a child's narrow food choices; therefore, we would deal with narrow food choices only if it were disruptive to the family's mealtime patterns.

For two decades, occupational therapists have collected information from parents and teachers about children's responses to sensory experiences during their daily routines by taking sensory histories. In sensory histories, we ask the informant to tell us how the child responds to various external sensory events and internal states, such as the water and towel during bath time or the sound of the vacuum cleaner, or if the child has unusual fears. In order to establish a more systematic way to collect this information, Dunn and colleagues (Dunn,

1994; Dunn & Westman, 1997) compiled items from these sensory histories and created the *Sensory Profile*, a 125-item questionnaire in which the parent or teacher tells how frequently the child displays the behaviors described. Further on the basis of a series of studies, Dunn and colleagues have identified the best use of the items on the *Sensory Profile* for groups of children with various disabilities, including autism, Tourette syndrome, and attention-deficit/hyperactive disorder (ADHD; Bennett & Dunn, in press; Dunn & Brown, 1997; Ermer & Dunn, in press; Kientz & Dunn, 1997).

Table 7.6 contains a list of the items from the *Sensory Profile* that children who have autism are more likely to display than are children without disabilities and children who have ADHD. The items comparing children with autism to children without disabilities (the top of the table) include the aloofness or separateness that children who have autism demonstrate in daily life (e.g., stubborn, uncooperative, difficulty tolerating changes in routines, lack of emotional expression). This inability to engage successfully with one's surroundings is one of the most powerful identifying features of children who have autism; the *Sensory Profile* enables parents to characterize this difference. At the bottom of the table, where the children who have autism are contrasted with children who have ADHD, a different pattern emerges. Items in this section are directed more at oral sensory needs (e.g., experiences discomfort at dental work, is picky eater, gags easily). Perhaps another identifying feature of children who have autism is their difficulty with the primary orientation that oral input provides; infants map their world through sucking, biting, and chewing, and then expand their body perception from the mouth to the hands and to other body parts as they are able to explore more (i.e., move about in the environment). If children who have autism have difficulty with this first level of orienting to self, perhaps what we are observing is their continued attempts to achieve this orientation. In other words, they have difficulty processing oral sensory input, so their behavior toward oral experiences turns out to be negative (e.g., decreased awareness or oversensitivity). In contrast, we might hypothesize that children who have ADHD are able to successfully orient orally, but have difficulty when they try to move about in space.

In summary, the *Sensory Profile* (Dunn & Westman, 1997) offers an effective way to solicit critical information from care providers about the effects of sensory processing on daily life. The research completed to date indicates that parents who live with children who have autism report a different experience with their children than do parents who have children without disabilities or parents of children with other disabilities. These differences in the life experiences occur *regardless* of the parents' backgrounds or parenting styles and thus constitute compelling evidence that must be considered in comprehensive assessment.

Cognitive and Communication Features

Assessment of current level of performance must be holistic and include cognitive and communication status. The many aspects of cognition must be

Table 7.6

Sensory Profile Items Related to Children Who Have Autism

1. Items on the *Sensory Profile* that were more likely to be displayed by children who have autism than by children without disabilities:

    Seeks all kinds of movement, which interferes with daily routines

    Displays emotional outbursts when unsuccessful at tasks

    Has difficulty tolerating changes in routines

    Is stubborn or uncooperative

    Has difficulty making friends

    Seems to have weak muscles

    Has weak grasp

    Cannot lift heavy objects

    Limits self to particular food textures/temperatures

    Has difficulty paying attention

    Doesn't express emotions

    Looks away from task to notice all actions in the room

    Writes illegibly

    Looks carefully or intensely at objects/people

    Stares intensely at objects/people

    Avoids eye contact

    Walks on toes

    Expresses distress during grooming (e.g., hair cutting, face washing, fingernail cutting)

    Has fears that interfere with daily routines

2. Additional items that children who have autism display more frequently than children who have attention-deficit/hyperactivity disorder:

    Avoids getting "messy" (i.e., paste, sand, fingerpaint, glue, tape)

    Expresses discomfort at dental work or toothbrushing

    Limits self to particular food textures/temperatures

    Picky eater, especially regarding textures

    Gags easily with food textures, food utensils in mouth

    Displays unusual need for touching certain toys, surfaces, or textures

    Mouths objects frequently (i.e., pencil, hands)

    Shows decreased awareness of pain and temperature

    Has fears that interfere with daily routines

    Does not perceive body language or facial expression

considered, including imitation, perception, fine and gross motor, eye–hand integration, and verbal and performance abilities. Communication status includes verbal and nonverbal performance. The *frequency* of communicative acts, the various *forms* of communication (such as contact, gestures, and echolalia), and the *functions* of communication strategies (such as requesting, protesting, and social greeting) should be well understood. Additionally, unconventional verbal behavior, communication partners, and opportunities across various settings are important data to incorporate when designing sensory-based interventions.

Environmental Supports and Barriers

We must also consider the features of the child's *performance environments*. The performance environment includes three considerations: the objects, the people, and the expectations. We can characterize a particular classroom in all three ways: (a) The classroom might be characterized as visually busy if there are many learning materials on the walls and hanging from the ceiling (objects); (b) we could characterize the classroom as friendly if the teachers and children spend time greeting one another; and (c) the classroom rules would tell us about the environmental expectations (e.g., everyone must raise his or her hand to be excused to use the bathroom). For children who have autism, these environmental features can determine success or failure. Because they are more self-absorbed and cannot always derive salient meaning from the environment, these children are more vulnerable to failure in mismatched contexts.

Functional Analysis

After the child's current level of performance in context is understood, behaviors that include concerns and strengths are investigated and recorded across home, school, and community settings. Three outcome goals are the targets of the functional analysis: (a) determining the degree to which the concern or problem behavior(s) interfere with functional performance, (b) identifying what ecological factors support performance or interfere with performance, and (c) identifying what purpose or function the behaviors serve.

A sequence of guiding questions to ask when one is completing the three outcome goals of the functional analysis is found in Table 7.7. The degree to which the problem behavior(s) interfere with functional performance is interpreted differently by different individuals.

Not all sensory-seeking and sensory-avoiding behaviors interfere with performance. In fact, such behaviors often support performance. The frequency, intensity, and duration of problem/concern behaviors determine the degree of interference. Additionally, other people such as parents or teachers may not report the seeking or avoiding of behaviors as interfering. It is important to

(*text continues on page 227*)

Table 7.7

Functional Analysis Worksheet

What are the questions to ask? Briefly describe behavior of concern:	Focus your answers by considering:	Answers to questions for the home setting	Answers to questions for the school setting	Answers to questions for community settings
1. How much does the problem behavior(s) interfere with functional performance?	Consider what skills/opportunities are unavailable/competing.			
2. Is the behavior reported as a concern by *all* people across the child's life environments?	Consider all persons: peers, parents, siblings, professionals.			
3. Are internal motivations such as hunger, thirst, fatigue, or pleasure factors?	Consider the motivational power.			
4. Have there been sudden changes in the person's life (medications, change in family status, stress)?	Consider drug/diet interaction effects, consistency and predictability of daily routines.			
5. Are there opportunities for choice making?	Consider the frequency and complexity for making choices daily.			

(continues)

Table 7.7. Continued.

What are the questions to ask? Briefly describe behavior of concern:	Focus your answers by considering:	Answers to questions for the home setting	Answers to questions for the school setting	Answers to questions for community settings
6. What is the balance between active and sedentary activities?	Consider time of day, duration of sedentary and active times.			
7. How many transitions occur between active and sedentary activities, environments, and people?	Consider the predictability of transitions.			
8. What are the person's expectations for support and independence with daily performance?	Consider what the person with autism wants and needs to do.			
9. What are others' expectations and matching behaviors for support and independence with daily performance?	Consider what others expect.			
10. What is the nature of curricular instruction (materials used for learning, teaching style of adults, meaningful content, interesting teaching strategies)?	Consider the child's developmental level, functional relevance, and learning style.			
11. Are there environmental pollutants (noise, sights, and smells that are disorganizing)?	Consider how predictable/unpredictable pollutants are.			

(continues)

Table 7.7. *Continued.*

What are the questions to ask? Briefly describe behavior of concern:	Focus your answers by considering:	Answers to questions for the home setting	Answers to questions for the school setting	Answers to questions for community settings
12. What purpose or function does the behavior serve?	Consider escape avoidance or attainment.			
13. Is the purpose of the behavior to obtain internal stimulation (e.g., endorphin release)?	Consider what type of stimulation is gained.			
14. Is the purpose of the behavior to obtain external stimuli (e.g., attention, objects, activities)?	Consider what type of attention, object, or activity is gained.			
15. Is the purpose of the behavior to avoid/ escape internal stimuli (e.g, pain, hunger, fatigue, irritation)?	Consider what internal sensory state is avoided.			
16. Is the purpose of the behavior to avoid/ escape external stimuli (e.g., attention, tasks, events)?	Consider what/who is avoided.			

consider that others' tolerance or interference may be relevant to consider for intervention.

For example, Lucas, a 13-year-old junior high student, seeks deep pressure and tactile input at high frequencies across environments throughout the day. He meets these sensory needs by wearing his favorite jacket over his clothes every day at school. At home, he watches television with his favorite quilt wrapped around himself and uses the same quilt to wrap up in when going to sleep at night. Lucas's teachers and parents recognize that jacket wearing and quilt wrapping provide important calming, orienting sensations for Lucas. Neither of these sensory-seeking behaviors interferes with performance at school or home. Rather, the sensory input supports performance and attention for other tasks (academic instruction and recreational/leisure time).

Applying sensory processing strategies also requires consideration of other ecological factors that can have a subtle to profound impact on functional performance. For example, physiological variables that affect internal motivation are often overlooked. Hunger, thirst, fatigue, and pleasure are among the strong motivators that often cannot compete with external reinforcers. Remember, sensory-generating behaviors that produce pleasure have strong physiological underpinnings that are not easily replaced or extinguished. Typically, the sensory-generating behavior takes on another form, while still producing the same function (to gain preferred sensation).

Sudden changes in a person's life can have situational or long-term effects on performance. Children with autism often cannot communicate the negative impact that changes such as medications, changes in family status, or stress have on their daily performance. Likewise, opportunities for choice making influence how a child might be motivated to attempt or complete a task. When opportunities for choice making are not embedded within natural routines, children with autism become prompt dependent or engage in challenging, disruptive behaviors; most importantly, they miss opportunities to practice social reciprocity or turn taking.

Choice making can be expanded to include the child's sensory needs by considering the configuration of activities across daily schedules and routines. The combination, duration, and time of day for active and sedentary activities are powerful variables that influence daily performance. The number of transitions across active and sedentary activities, environments, and people can be expanded or reduced to meet the sensory needs of the child.

A functional analysis also considers an individual's expectations for him- or herself, as well as others' expectations. Honoring the sensory needs that a child with autism has by creating appropriate, naturally occurring opportunities to have sensory needs met is critical to successful outcomes.

The nature of curricular instruction, materials used for learning, and the teaching style of adults should also be considered. Meaningful content that is appropriate for the child's developmental age and sensory needs is a necessary part of effective, engaging teaching strategies.

Environmental pollutants that can have a pervasive effect include noise, sights, and smells that are disorganizing. The oversensitive child with autism may be predictably "undone" by the smell of lunch cooking in the school cafeteria.

A functional analysis also considers the motivation for a given behavior. Behaviors serve two basic functions. First, the behavior may be performed or avoided to *obtain desirable events*. Obtaining desirable events, in turn, can be categorized as a means of *obtaining internal stimulation* (sensory-generating behaviors that provide an endorphin release) and/or as a means of *obtaining external stimuli* (attention, objects, or activities). Both functions (to obtain internal and external stimuli) can be operating simultaneously. Second, the behavior may be performed or avoided to *avoid or escape undesirable events*—avoiding/escaping *internal stimulation* (pain, hunger, irritation, or fatigue) or *external stimuli* (attention, tasks, or events).

The outcomes of this type of systematic, contextual investigation create a foundation for effective communication across individuals who provide service to the child with autism. The following outcomes provide a baseline for intervention strategies:

1. A clear profile of the child's threshold for sensory preferences and avoidance across all sensory systems.

2. The topography and intensity of the target (concerns and strengths) behaviors. These behaviors may include sensory-generating behaviors, avoiding behaviors, or challenging behaviors, such as tantrums.

3. The functions of the target behavior. The functions of the behavior serve a primary communicative intent. The child may be trying to communicate in a nonverbal or verbal way that he or she is trying to reach or maintain homeostasis. The target behavior is observed by others as seeking desired sensory input or avoiding undesirable sensory input.

4. The efficiency of the target behavior. The proficiency the child demonstrates in recruiting the stimuli needed for the behavior is considered.

5. The stimulus situations that set the occasion for the target behavior to occur.

6. The potential setting events associated with the target behavior.

7. The potential events, actions, and objects that are reinforcing for the individual.

8. The alternative, desirable behaviors that serve the same function as the target behavior.

9. The child's learning characteristics (e.g., tactile, visual, or auditory).

Creating Intervention Plans

The information gained from the functional analysis provides the content needed for designing effective interventions. The functional analysis systematically identifies and describes a child's interaction with sensory input throughout the day; considers the timing, duration, and intensity of various sensory events; and targets behaviors that are functional and organized in contrast to behaviors that are disorganized and keep the child from being successful in various activities of daily living. Matching the family's needs, preferences, and style is an essential component of the guiding vision that directs the intervention planning.

The focus of intervention is a collaboration between the person, family, and service providers. Effective intervention considers the specific sensory needs of the child across various contexts. The term "sensory diet," coined by Wilbarger (1971, 1984, 1995), is compatible with our goal of planning a well-rounded program that considers the child's preferences and dislikes. This metaphor involves using a nutritional diet for the "just-right" combinations of sensory input to maintain an optimal level of arousal and performance (Kientz, 1996; Wilbarger, 1995; Zuckerman, 1994). Creating a sensory diet requires efficient, accurate, and sensitive data collection based on an understanding of the child's current level of performance and a functional analysis of that individual's performance. The sensory diet concept should be applied to daily life as a dynamic approach that is regulated according to sensitive observation, not preestablished protocol. As Wilbarger (1995) noted, some activities are like snacks in that they fill us up until mealtime. We believe that homeostasis is the ultimate objective of creating an appropriate sensory diet for each individual, with sensory deprivation and sensory overload anchoring the extremes on the continuum of an individual's homeostasis. Creating a sensory diet, then, is dictated by the individual child's need to achieve and maintain homeostasis.

In considering the configuration of daily routines at home, at school, and in other community environments, our options for creating a personalized sensory diet include providing frequent opportunities for preferred sensation while minimizing chances for undesired sensations. We make sure that all the opportunities are present as part of naturally occurring activities so that we can support functional performance while meeting sensory needs. Otherwise, the child ends up engaging in sensory-generating behaviors that interrupt ongoing performance, leading to dysfunction. We also consider the difficulty of a particular task, making sure that we reduce the demands of coping with difficult sensory input when the task is harder. We can gradually introduce more challenging sensory qualities into simpler routines (e.g., a new clothing texture when the child will be engaging in a preferred play activity).

The power of sensory interventions is greatest as part of predictable routines that are a natural part of everyday life. Tasks the child must engage in, such as routines for arrival, transition, and departure at school, are important targets because the child's negative responses and inability to complete these tasks are very disruptive to everyone. We can enhance success in these tasks by adding preferred sensations to the routines and removing as much of the undesired sensations as possible. For example, if a child becomes agitated by unpredicted tactile stimuli, we would want to make sure that he or she goes to the bus ahead of other children to reduce the possibility of the children bumping into him or her. At home, this same child might need to have an established pattern of drying off after bath time so that his or her nervous system can begin to anticipate what the tactile sensations will feel like and not feel uncomfortable or threatened by them. The routines around sleeping, grooming, dressing, eating, playing, interacting, and completing chores also provide rich opportunities for embedding sensory interventions.

Sensory Task Analysis

We can observe children's performance from a variety of perspectives; in this section we consider the sensory features of performance. Through skilled observation, you can determine the child's level of sensitivity to stimuli (hypersensitivity/defensiveness vs. hyposensitivity/lack of sensory awareness).

Figure 7.2 is a completed worksheet for face washing that helps analyze a daily routine from a sensory point of view. First, record the routine performance of the task and which sensory experiences would naturally occur during task performance. Then record the special additional sensory features that occur because of the particular place where the task has to be completed. Finally, indicate changes that might be made in the performance routine to reduce sensory experiences that might be interfering with performance and to enhance other sensory aspects that might improve performance.

Tables 7.3 and 7.4 contain definitions of terms that can assist in completing the sensory task analysis. Specifically, Table 7.3 provides a brief definition of each word and a short daily life example illustrating when that particular sensory experience might occur. Table 7.4 contains the same words, but gives a reason why each sensory stimulus might be used therapeutically in daily life. The words are organized into two columns. The arousal/alerting descriptors column contains sensations that are more likely to generate arousal in the CNS, whereas the discriminating/mapping descriptors column includes sensations that are more likely to provide organized information for the internal and external maps housed in the brain for use in planning motor responses.

Table 7.8 provides a list of examples of observations you could make during a particular life task (see column headings) that would indicate difficulties with the sensory system. This information can be used to construct a screening or referral checklist.

(text continues on page 236)

ROUTINE/TASK ___Washing face___ SENSORY CHARACTERISTICS		What Does the Particular Environment Hold? (e.g., classroom sink)	What Adaptations are Likely To Improve Functional Outcome?
Somato-sensory	light touch (tap, tickle)		Turn water off to decrease splashing
	pain		
	temperature (hot, cold)		Try alternative water temperatures
	touch pressure (hug, pat, grasp)		Pat face instead of rubbing cloth on face
	duration of stimulus (short, long)		
	body surface contact (small, large)		Try washing one part only; begin with chin area
	predictable		
	unpredictable		(NOTE: make sure routine is consistent day to day)
Vestibular	head position change		Alter water source so don't have to bend head down
	speed change		(e.g., in a pan or tub)
	direction change		Keep head up so don't have the down–up pattern
	rotary head movement		
	linear head movement		Keep head up; if need arousal, place items on
	repetitive head movement–rhythmic		counter to encourage more head turning
	predictable		
	unpredictable		
Proprio-ceptive	quick stretch stimulus		Move objects to decrease head control requirements
	sustained tension stimulus		
	shifting muscle tension		

Figure 7.2. Sample completed form for analyzing sensory characteristics of face washing. *Note.* From "The Sensorimotor Systems: A Framework for Assessment and Intervention," by W. Dunn. In F. P. Orelove & D. Sobsey (Eds.), *Educating Children with Multiple Disabilities: A Transdisciplinary Approach* (2nd ed., p. 67), 1991, Baltimore: Paul H. Brookes. Copyright 1991 by Paul H. Brookes. Reprinted with permission.

ROUTINE/TASK ___Washing face___

SENSORY CHARACTERISTICS		What Does the Particular Environment Hold? (e.g., classroom sink)	What Adaptations are Likely To Improve Functional Outcome?
Visual	high intensity		
	low intensity		
	high contrast		
	high similarity (low contrast)	X Other objects	Use dark wash cloths & light soap; use dark
	competitive	X on sink	containers on light counter; remove extra
	variable	X Counter changes day to day	items from counter
	predictable	X	If arousal is needed, vary placement of items
	unpredictable		
Auditory	rhythmic		Prepare wet cloth; don't have running tap water
	variable		Use tub of water instead of running water
	constant		
	competitive	X Other students	Move child to the bathroom alone
	noncompetitive		
	loud	X Teacher's voice	Provide physical prompts and decrease talking
	soft		
	predictable		
	unpredictable	X Unplanned	
Olfactory/ Gustatory	mild		If arousal is needed, use strong smelling soap
	strong		
	predictable		
	unpredictable		

Figure 7.2. Continued.

Table 7.8

Examples of Observable Behaviors That Indicate Difficulty with Sensory Processing During Daily Life Tasks

Personal hygiene	Dressing	Eating	Homemaking	School/work	Play
Withdraws from splashing water	Tolerates a narrow range of clothing items	Only tolerates food at one temperature	Avoids participation in tasks that are wet or dirty	Cries when tape or glue gets on skin	Selects a narrow range of toys, textures
Pushes washcloth/towel away	Prefers tight clothing	Gags with textured food or utensils in mouth	Seeks to remove batter that falls on arms	Overreacts to pats, hugs; avoids these actions	Can't hold onto toys/objects
Cries when hair is washed and dried	More irritable with loose-textured clothing	Winces when face is wiped		Only tolerates one pencil, one type of paper, only wooden objects	Rubs toys on face, arms
Makes face when toothpaste gets on lips, tongue	Cries during dressing	Hand extends and avoids objects and surfaces (finger food, utensils)		Hands extend when attempting to type	Mouths objects
Tenses when bottom is wiped after toileting	Pulls at hats, head gear, accessories				
Can't lift objects that are heavier, such as a new bar of soap	Can't support heavier items (e.g., belt with buckle, shoes)	Uses external support to eat (e.g., propping)	Drops equipment (e.g., broom)	Drops books	Unable to sustain movements during play
Can't change head position to use sink and mirror in same task	Fatigues prior to task completion	Tires before completing meal	Uses external support such as leaning on counter to stir batter	Becomes uncomfortable in a particular position	Tires before game is complete
	Misses when placing arm or leg in clothing	Can't provide force to cut meat	Has difficulty in pouring a glass of milk	Hooks limbs on furniture to obtain support	Drops heavy parts of a toy/game
		Tires before completing foods that need to be chewed		Moves arm, hand in repetitive patterns (self-stimulatory)	

(continues)

Table 7.8 *Continued.*

Personal hygiene	Dressing	Eating	Homemaking	School/work	Play
Becomes disoriented when bending over the sink Falls when trying to participate in washing lower extremities	Gets overly excited/distracted after bending down to put on socks Cries when moved around a lot during dressing	Holds head stiffly in one position during mealtime Gets distracted from meal after several head position changes	Avoids leaning to obtain cooking utensil Becomes overly excited after moving around the room to dust	Avoids turning head to look at persons; to find source of a sound After being transported in a wheelchair, more difficult to get on task Moves head in repetitive pattern (self-stimulatory)	Avoids play that includes movement Becomes overly excited or anxious when moving during play Rocks excessively Craves movement activities
Can't find utensils on sink Has difficulty in spotting desired item in drawer Misses when applying paste to toothbrush	Can't find buttons on patterned or solid clothing Overlooks desired shirt in closet or drawer Misses armhole when donning shirt	Misses utensils on the table Has trouble getting foods onto spoon when they are a similar color to plate	Can't locate correct canned item in the pantry Has difficulty finding cooking utensils in the drawer	Can't keep place on the page Can't locate desired item on communication board Attends excessively to bright or flashing objects	Has trouble with matching, sorting activities Has trouble locating desired toy on cluttered shelf

(continues)

Table 7.8 *Continued.*

Personal hygiene	Dressing	Eating	Homemaking	School/work	Play
Cries when hair dryer is turned on Becomes upset by running water Jerks when toilet flushes	Is distracted by clothing that makes noise (e.g., crisp cloth, accessories)	Is distracted by noise of utensils against each other (e.g., spoon in bowl, knife on plate) Can't keep eating when someone talks	Is distracted by vacuum cleaner sound Is distracted by TV or radio during tasks	Is distracted by squeaky wheelchair Is intolerant of noise others make in the room Overreacts to door closing Notices toilet flushing down the hall	Play is disrupted by sounds Makes sounds constantly
Gags at taste of toothpaste Jerks away at smell of soap	Overreacts to clothing when it has been washed in a new detergent	Tolerates a narrow range of foods Becomes upset when certain hot foods are cooking	Becomes upset when house is being cleaned (odors of cleansers)	Overreacts to new person (new smells) Intolerant of scratch-n-sniff stickers Smells everything	Tastes or smells all objects before playing

Note. "The Sensorimotor Systems: A Framework for Assessment and Intervention," by W. Dunn. In F. P. Orelove & D. Sobsey (Eds.), *Educating Children with Multiple Disabilities: A Transdisciplinary Approach* (2nd ed., p. 42), 1991, Baltimore: Paul H. Brookes. Copyright 1991 by Paul H. Brookes. Reprinted with permission.

Incorporating a sensory approach into intervention and problem solving for children who have autism requires a basic understanding of centrifugal control in the brain and an understanding of each individual's continuum of need for sensory input. Such understanding can help to ensure that an optimal level of alertness (i.e., internal state) is present so that the child is able to engage in social interactions and perform functional tasks. Each individual's nervous system sets the tone for how information is perceived and serves as the foundation for how the individual responds. We first determine an optimal level of alertness (e.g., tired, rested, interested), the requirements of the task (e.g., whether the skills required are in the individual's repertoire), and the features of the environment (e.g., noisy, emotionally supportive; Dunn et al., 1994). We next discuss ways to consider and include these factors as part of comprehensive planning.

How To Use Consultants with Expertise in Sensory Integration Theory

Parents and educators often inquire about the use of consultants to assist in the evaluation and intervention process of sensory processing issues that affect the performance of children with autism. The following list of frequently asked questions and responses may be useful to parents and educators considering using consultants with expertise in sensory integration theory with children with autism.

1. *What are the qualifications for expertise in using sensory integration theory for individuals with autism? What professionals can provide expertise in this area?* Occupational therapists are uniquely qualified because of their entry-level training in neurological, biological, and social sciences. Occupational therapists, who have particular expertise in applying neuroscience principles and sensory integration theory, typically have completed continuing education and/or graduate training, combined with applied experience. Professionals from other disciplines, such as education, psychology, physical therapy, and speech–language pathology, may also have interest and training in sensory integration theory and applications. Additionally, parents are a rich source of information about sensory features that support or interfere with the performance of their children. Even though parents may not have specialized training, very often they are excellent observers of their child's behavior and interested in ways to meet the needs of their child.

Qualifications for consultants include effective communication skills that provide a forum for collaboration with all relevant parties. The consultant should be able to define and describe what sensory integration is and articulate how this theory can be applied in people's daily lives. The differences that parents and educators can expect to see in the child are part of the communication process in goal setting. Parents and teachers will notice improved sensory processing abilities through the child's ability to tolerate transitions, self-direct and self-monitor, form social relations, and perform skills in daily life.

A good consultant has knowledge of content area, demonstrates effective communication skills, and considers the possibilities for support and carryover across other environments.

2. *What are appropriate assessments tools?* Consultants use data from a variety of sources. Standardized tests for sensory processing are inappropriate for children with autism. Assessment is viewed as a dynamic process that creates a profile for the child with autism from which an intervention plan can be designed.

3. *Where and how frequently should intervention services be provided?* Autism is a pervasive spectrum disorder. Addressing the sensory needs of the child requires an integrated approach in which interventions are embedded within the context of daily routines. Sometimes children benefit from regular, designated times to have focused sensory play as part of their daily routines.

References

American Psychiatric Association. (1994). *Diagnostic and statistical manual of mental disorders* (4th ed.). Washington, DC: Author.

Anderson, E., & Emmons, P. (1996). *Unlocking the mystery of sensory dysfunction.* Arlington, TX: Future Horizons.

Angell, R. (1993). A parent's perspective on the preschool years. In E. Schopler, M. E. Van Bourgondien, & M. M. Bristol (Eds.), *Preschool issues in autism* (pp. 17–37). New York: Plenum Press.

Ayres, A. J. (1972). *Sensory integration and learning disorders.* Los Angeles: Western Psychological Services.

Ayres, A. J. (1979). *Sensory integration and the child.* Los Angeles: Western Psychological Services.

Bennett, D., & Dunn, W. (in press). Comparison of children with and without attention deficit hyperactivity disorder on the sensory profile. *American Journal of Occupational Therapy.*

Brody, N. (1983). *Human motivation.* New York: Academic Press.

Cool, S. J. (1987). A view for the "outside": Sensory integration and developmental neurobiology. *Sensory Integration Newsletter, 10*(2), 2–3.

Crutchfield, C. A., & Barnes, M. R. (1984). *The neurophysiologic basis of patient treatment: Volume III, Peripheral components of motor control.* Atlanta, GA: Stokesville.

Dunn, W. (1991a). Assessing human performance related to brain function. Neuroscience foundations of human performance. *AOTA Self Study Series, 12,* 3–38.

Dunn, W. (1991b). Motivation. Neuroscience foundations of human performance. *AOTA Self Study Series, 7,* 3–36

Dunn, W. (1994). Performance of typical children on the *Sensory Profile*: An item analysis. *American Journal of Occupational Therapy, 48,* 967–974.

Dunn, W. (1997a). The impact of sensory processing abilities on the daily lives of young children and their families: A conceptual model. *Infants and Young Children, 9*(4), 23–25.

Dunn, W. (1997b). Implementing neuroscience principles to support habilitation and recovery. In C. Christiansen & C. Baum (Eds.), *Occupational therapy: Enabling function and well-being* (pp. 182–233). NJ: Slack.

Dunn, W., & Brown, T. (1997). Factor analysis on the *Sensory Profile* from a national sample of children without disabilities. *American Journal of Occupational Therapy, 51*(7), 490–495.

Dunn W., Brown, C., & McGuigan, A. (1994). The ecology of human performance: A framework for considering the effect of context. *American Journal of Occupational Therapy, 48,* 595–607.

Dunn, W., & DeGangi, G. (1992). Sensory integration and neurodevelopmental treatment for educational programming. *AOTA Self Study Series, 2,* 5–55.

Dunn, W., & Westman, K. (1997). The *Sensory Profile:* The performance of a national sample of children without disabilities. *American Journal of Occupational Therapy, 51,* 25–34.

Ermer, J., & Dunn, W. (in press). The *Sensory Profile:* A discriminant analysis of children with and without disabilities. *American Journal of Occupational Therapy.*

Fisher, A. G., & Murray, E. A. (1991). Introduction to sensory integration theory. In A. Fisher, E. Murray, & A. Bundy (Eds.), *Sensory integration theory and practice* (pp. 3–27). Philadelphia: F. A. Davis.

Grandin, T. (1995). *Thinking in pictures and other reports from my life with autism.* New York: Doubleday.

Grandin, T., & Scariano, M. (1986). *Emergence: Labeled autistic.* Novato, CA: Arena.

Harlow, H. F., & Harlow, M. K. (1966). Learning to love. *American Scientist, 54,* 244–272.

Kandel, E. R., & Schwartz, J. H. (1985). *Principles of neural science.* New York: Elsevier.

Kiang, N. Y. S. (1984). Peripheral neural processing of auditory information. In I. Darian-Smith (Ed.), *Handbook of physiology, Section 1: The nervous system, Volume II: Sensory processes, Part 2* (pp. 639–674). Bethesda, MD: American Physiological Society.

Kientz, M. A. (1996). Sensory-based needs in children with autism: Motivation for behavior and suggestions for intervention. *Developmental Disabilities Special Interest Section Newsletter, 19*(3), 1–3.

Kientz, M. A., & Dunn, W. (1997). Comparison of children with autism and typical children using the *Sensory Profile. American Journal of Occupational Therapy, 51*(7), 530–537.

King, L. J. (1974). A sensory integrative approach to schizophrenia. *American Journal of Occupational Therapy, 28,* 529–536.

Kornhuber, H. H. (1974). The vestibular system and the general motor system. In H. H. Kornhuber (Ed.), *Handbook of sensory physiology, Volume V, Vestibular system Part 2: Psychophysics, applied aspects and general interpretations* (pp. 581–620). New York: Springer-Verlag.

Kupfermann, I. (1991). Hypothalamus and limbic system: Peptidergic neurons, homeostasis, and emotional behavior. In E. R. Kandel, J. H. Schwartz, & T. M. Jessell (Eds.), *Principles of neural science* (3rd ed., pp. 735–749). New York: Elsevier.

Murray, E. A., & Anzalone, M. E. (1991). Integrating sensory integration theory and practice with other intervention approaches. In A. Fisher, E. Murray, & A. Bundy (Eds.), *Sensory integration: Theory and practice* (pp. 354–381). Philadelphia: F. A. Davis.

National Center for Clinical Infant Programs/Zero to Three. (1994). *Diagnostic classification of mental health and developmental disorders of infancy and early childhood.* Arlington, VA: Author.

Wilbarger, P. (Ed.). (1971). *The identification, diagnosis and remediation of sensorimotor dysfunction in primary school children* (Title 111 ESEA Project Report 5127). Sacramento: California State Department of Education, Goleta Union School District.

Wilbarger, P. (1984). Planning an adequate sensory diet: Application of sensory processing theory during the first year of life. *Zero to Three, 5*(1), 1–3.

Wilbarger, P. (1995). The sensory diet: Activity programs based on sensory processing theory. *Sensory Integration Special Interest Section Newsletter, 18*(2), 1–4.

Williams, D. (1992). *Nobody nowhere.* Toronto: Doubleday.

Williams, D. (1994). *Somebody somewhere.* Toronto: Doubleday.

Williamson, G. G., Szczepanski, M., & Zeitlin, S. (1993). Coping frame of reference. In P. Kramer & J. Hinojosa (Eds.), *Frames of reference for pediatric occupational therapy* (pp. 395–435). Baltimore: Williams & Wilkins.

Zuckerman, M. (1994). *Behavioral expressions and biosocial bases of sensation seeking.* New York: Cambridge University Press.

Inclusion of Students with Autism in General Education Classrooms: The Autism Inclusion Collaboration Model

8

Brenda Smith Myles
and Richard L. Simpson

One of the major provisions of the Individuals with Disabilities Education Act (IDEA), 1997 reauthorization, is an appropriate education for students with exceptionalities in the least restrictive environment. That is, IDEA stipulates that students with autism, just like other children and youth with disabilities, are entitled to appropriate educational services in settings that best meet their individual needs and that offer the greatest opportunities for contact with students without disabilities.

Although the majority of children and youth with disabilities receive at least a portion of their education in general education settings, this does not hold true for most students with autism. Only 4.7% of students with autism are served in the general education classroom, and 6.9% are educated in resource rooms. Increasingly, however, these students are being placed in general education settings, a trend that is anticipated to continue and, in fact, dramatically increase over the next few years. Many professionals consider this trend to be positive (Kellegrew, 1995; Sailor et al., 1989), and even those who have voiced concerns about the direction of current inclusive policies and practices have acknowledged that the trend is not likely to be discontinued in the near future (Lieberman, 1992; Vergason & Anderegg, 1992; Ysseldyke, Algozzine, & Thurlow, 1992). In spite of the trend toward general education placement of students with autism, few models and procedures are available to guide inclusion-related policies and practices. The Autism Inclusion Collaboration Model is one of the few models designed to support general educators in their work with students with autism through collaboration with special educators and ancillary staff. The purpose of this chapter is to examine the individual components of this model and illustrate their use and importance for successful inclusion and integration of students with autism.

The Autism Inclusion Collaboration Model is designed to support general educators who assume responsibilities for teaching children and youth with autism. As such, the following proactive assumptions regarding the appropriateness of many students with autism for general education placement form the philosophical core of the model:

- Students with autism and their nondisabled peers benefit from planned contact with one another.

- Given appropriate support and resources, the majority of general education teachers, staff members, and administrators are agreeable to having qualified students with autism in their classrooms.

- General educators are willing and able to effectively assume primary teaching responsibility for many students with autism, contingent on special educator and ancillary staff support and other resources.

The underpinning of the model is *collaboration*; thus, it emphasizes shared responsibility and shared decision making among general educators, special educators, and support personnel. The model also considers both learner behaviors and instructional factors (Koegel et al., 1995; Salend, 1990; Warger & Pugach, 1996).

The Autism Inclusion Collaboration Model has four major components:

- environmental and curricular modifications and general education classroom support

- attitudinal and social support

- coordinated team commitment

- home–school collaboration (see Figure 8.1)

Each model component is presented as a discrete item; however, components are interwoven. Thus, each component significantly affects the others and cannot operate effectively in isolation.

Environmental and Curricular Modifications and General Education Classroom Support

For years researchers, policymakers, and administrators have called for appropriate inclusive modifications and other supports for general education teachers who assume primary instructional responsibility for children and youth with disabilities (K. J. Miller & Savage, 1995; Myles & Simpson, 1989, 1990). For children and youth with autism, such modifications and support are particularly important due to their unique needs, including availability of appro-

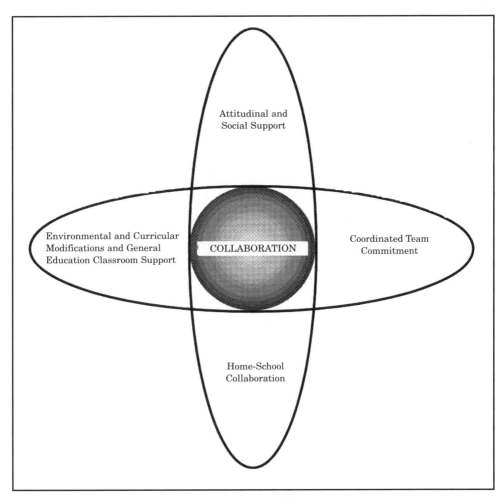

Figure 8.1. Autism Inclusion Collaboration Model.

priately trained support personnel, reduced class size, access to collaborative problem-solving relationships, adequate teacher planning time, availability of paraprofessionals, and inservice training. Each of these areas is discussed in more detail below.

Availability of Appropriately Trained Support Personnel

The accessibility of knowledgeable and collaboratively oriented support service personnel is essential to successful placement of students with autism and other disabilities in general education settings. That is, general education teachers who teach students with autism should be able to call on professionals from various disciplines to help implement educational programs and demonstrate best-practice methods. Professionals from a variety of disciplines have determined that availability of support services positively affects student performance and teacher attitude (Kellegrew, 1995; Salend, 1990). Indeed, general education teachers have been found not to be supportive of inclusion for students with disabilities unless they receive assistance from qualified resource personnel (Simpson & Myles, 1991). Further, parents and support service personnel themselves seem to agree that support services facilitate successful inclusion. For example, Myles and Simpson (1990) and Simpson and Myles (1991) noted that more than one half of parents and three fourths of ancillary staff surveyed indicated that support staff availability was a necessary ingredient in successful inclusion. In addition, general education teachers rated support services (along with class size) as the most important variable for successful inclusion of students with disabilities in general education classrooms (Simpson & Myles, 1991). Because of the complex needs of students with autism, team support is particularly necessary. For example, speech–language, motor, sensory, behavioral, and academic problems evident in these children and youth necessitate a multiperson, multifaceted approach to planning and implementing a comprehensive program. When this occurs, general education teachers tend to be willing to accept students with autism in their classrooms. Accordingly, the model presented here strongly recommends that general education teachers who assume primary responsibility for students with autism receive assistance from social workers, psychologists, speech pathologists, special educators, occupational therapists, physical therapists, counselors, and other professionals as needed.

Reduced Class Size

As a means of improving schools, many have observed that the efficiency of our educational system could be significantly improved by a reduction of the size of the average general education class. Smaller class sizes are often seen to be extremely important for students' academic achievement, social and personal development, and teacher job satisfaction. Thus, several researchers have established that reduced class size facilitates increased student success, particularly for children and youth with disabilities (Cates & Yell, 1994; Vaughn, Schumm, Jallad, Slusher, & Saumell, 1996). Specifically, teachers who have fewer students are often able to (a) better individualize instruction for students and use a wider variety of instructional methods and (b) more effectively manage their classes and thereby experience fewer discipline problems.

For students with autism, reduced class size is a paramount importance because they typically require high levels of teacher–student interaction and classroom structure. Researchers have found that these students learn best when teacher-to-student ratios are small. In addition, behavioral excesses and deficits are most easily controlled when the student has access to adequate teacher support. These elements are typically unavailable in classrooms containing large numbers of students. Research and professional opinion suggest that a class size of 15 to 19 students is appropriate for including 1 student with a disability, such as autism (Myles & Simpson, 1992).

There appears to be little question that reduced class size bodes well for students' success, including children and youth with autism in general education settings. Accordingly, an integral feature of the Autism Inclusion Collaboration Model is a class size that permits general education teachers to respond effectively to the individual needs of all students.

Accessibility to Collaborative Problem-Solving Relationships

As more and more students with disabilities are being served in regular education classes, the need for collaborative relationships designed to assist general education teachers plan for these students is increasingly being recognized (Idol & West, 1987; Warger & Pugach, 1996). In fact, the majority of states have policies that mandate consultation. When asked to select classroom modifications minimally needed to include a student with a disability, 65% of the regular class teachers polled by Myles and Simpson (1989) selected consultation, suggesting that this is an important factor for teachers working with included students with autism.

Data-based findings also support teachers' perceptions of the importance of consultation. For example T. L. Miller and Sabatino (1978) reported that student performance gains were equivalent for students with mild exceptionalities in a resource room and those who were served through a consultation model. Commenting on their findings, the authors noted "the consultation model was surprisingly effective, since academic gains were on par with the direct service approach. That is, regular teachers seemingly became as effective in delivering instruction to special children within their classes as resource teachers were in intensive, 'out of mainstream' classes" (p. 89).

Although the terms *consultation* and *collaboration* are often used interchangeably, Pugach and Allen-Meares (1985) have contended that there are important differences between them. That is, *consultation* may denote unequal status between professionals, with specialists providing advice to classroom teachers, whereas *collaboration* implies equal status among team members who share information, provide consultative support to one another, and jointly problem solve.

The Autism Inclusion Collaboration Model emphasizes *collaborative consultation*. Educators vary in their desire for "expert advice," but it is our experience that collaborative consultation is the most efficient and effective means of supporting general education teachers working with students with autism and preparing general education teachers to generalize and sustain problem-solving programs learned in collaborative consultative relationships. Future collaborative approaches will likely discontinue the use of models in which consultation flows exclusively from expert to teacher, in favor of more transdisciplinary approaches (Peterson, 1987). As a result, consultants will increasingly be expected not only to provide expert advice, but also to seek expertise from a variety of sources and to coordinate the application of such expertise.

Since students with autism present multiple needs that transcend traditional "educator" roles, educators who work with students with autism must be able to collaborate with nonschool systems such as medicine, mental health, daycare, and so forth. Accordingly, they must be knowledgeable about the services and expertise each system can provide, how to access them, and how to coordinate services and expertise to best serve students.

Adequate Teacher Planning Time

With regard to placing students with autism in general education classes, teacher planning time is extremely important. Similarly, Myles and Simpson (1989) and Simpson and Myles (1991) reported that approximately one half of general educators and ancillary staff (e.g., school psychologists and speech pathologists) noted that additional planning is necessary for one student with a disability to be placed full-time in an inclusionary setting with the majority preferring about 1 hour of daily planning time.

Additional planning time is needed to permit teachers to individualize academic tasks, plan alternative or additional activities, and develop appropriate, individualized instructional methods. This time is also needed for them to be able to collaborate with others. Hence, the Autism Inclusion Collaboration Model incorporates adequate planning time as an essential component.

Availability of Paraprofessionals

As of 1980, over 80,000 paraprofessionals worked in public school special education programs (Pickett, 1980). This number has continued to rise (Blalock, 1991; Goodlad, 1990). Although paraprofessionals are seen far less frequently in general education programs, they are considered to play an important role in supporting students with disabilities (Jones & Bender, 1993; Simpson & Myles, 1990), including children and youth with autism. In this regard, Karagianis and Nesbit (1983) noted that paraprofessionals are "a necessary adjunct to the regular classroom where the teacher has a defined responsibility for handicapped children" (p. 19). Regular class teachers seem to concur with this assessment: Myles and Simpson (1989) found that 65% of the general educators in their survey perceived paraprofessionals to be minimally necessary to support students with disabilities in inclusive settings.

An important element of the Autism Inclusion Collaboration Model is that, to the extent necessary, paraprofessionals must be available in general education settings to support children and youth with autism. Emphasis should be placed on training paraprofessionals to work with students with autism. Paraprofessionals require knowledge regarding (a) characteristics, (b) communication skills, (c) behavior management techniques, (c) instructional methods, and (d) arrangement of the educational environment (French & Cabell, 1993). Once trained, paraprofessionals may assist with a variety of tasks, including (a) helping students practice previously taught academic and social skills; (b) documenting student performance and progress; and (c) assisting teachers with daily planning, materials development, and curriculum modification (Boomer, 1994).

We do not consider it appropriate for paraprofessionals to exclusively and constantly be assigned to a student with autism for the purpose of translating teachers' instructions and implementing all programs. In many instances, part-time assignment of a paraprofessional and use of a paraprofessional with all students in a classroom is preferred. On some occasions, students with autism can complete tasks without paraprofessional assistance; when this occurs the student should be allowed to work independently. While the student with autism works in this manner, the paraprofessionals can support other students in the classroom on an as-needed basis. Nonetheless, we consider availability of paraprofessionals to be an essential resource for effectively serving students with autism in regular classrooms.

Inservice Training

It is often difficult for general educators to teach children and youth with autism because they do not have the necessary training in understanding the characteristics of this exceptionality, communicating with persons with limited verbal skills, or implementing academic procedures that have been proven effective for this population (Koegel, Rincover, & Egel, 1982).

Accordingly, the Autism Inclusion Collaboration Model supports continued inservice programs for general educators who work with students with autism. Both group and individual inservice formats are used within this model. Group inservices may be used to provide a general body of information regarding characteristics and needs of students with autism; individual training may focus on specific instructional techniques, intervention methods, and so forth (French & Cabell, 1993). Further, both special and general educators require collaboration and consultation skill training to prepare them for their new roles and, ultimately, to ensure that students with autism receive the best possible services.

A number of studies have revealed that inservice training programs for teachers may be desirable in implementing inclusionary programs. For example, Myles and Simpson (1989, 1990) and Simpson and Myles (1991) found that parents of children with disabilities, support service staff, and general educators were supportive of inservice programs as a vehicle to enhance inclusion efforts. Indeed, approximately one half of those surveyed selected this option as minimally necessary for supporting students with disabilities in general education settings. Educators recognize the complex needs of students with disabilities, including those with autism, and have stipulated that training programs should provide continuous support and education; one-shot workshops or inservice programs are generally considered ineffective (Cates & Yell, 1994).

Attitudinal and Social Support

It is widely recognized that students with autism require attitudinal and social support in order to be truly integrated into a general education classroom (e.g., Mesibov, 1992; Sasso, Simpson, & Novak, 1985; Wing, 1992). Even before enactment of P.L. 94-142, and thus prior to IDEA's specific language of least restrictive environment, integration was a goal for a number of disability organizations. In 1973, for instance, the Association for Retarded Citizens called for placement of individuals with disabilities in settings "as close to normal as possible" (National Association of Retarded Citizens, 1973, p. 72). Moreover, even at relatively early stages of special education program development, notes of caution were expressed regarding the need to carefully prepare environments to accommodate students with disabilities. For example, Martin (1974) warned that unless educators developed strategies to create an accepting environment for students with disabilities, "we will be painfully naive, and I fear we will subject many children to a painful and frustrating educational experience in the name of progress" (p. 150).

In spite of cautionary notes, however, limited attention has been paid to preparing general classroom settings to accommodate students with disabilities, including those with autism. Thus, in spite of the recognized importance of teachers, school staff, and students being aware and supportive of students with autism (Newman & Simpson, 1983; Sasso et al., 1985), few guidelines are available for creating educational environments in which children and youth with disabilities will thrive and experience acceptance. For example, guidelines for teachers' and students' roles in facilitating social interaction of students with autism have not been defined. Research has validated several interventions that enhance the social skills of persons with autism (i.e., direct, adult-mediated, and peer-mediated instruction), yet those who interact with these students in a school setting are often unaware of their roles in initiating and sustaining these programs. Indeed, many are unaware that these programs even exist.

The attitudes of the persons associated with a given school—including administrators, teachers, parents, and students—in large measure determine the extent to which the Autism Inclusion Collaboration Model (or any other inclusion strategy) will be effective (Gersten & Woodward, 1990). If school personnel are not supportive of inclusion, it is likely that the inclusion experience will be short-lived for the student with autism. Persons of the attitude that students with autism are not well suited for inclusion will create a self-fulfilling prophecy, and the student will not profit from the inclusive environment.

With respect to administrator attitudes, O'Rourke (1980) found a significant relationship between teaching personnel's and building principals' attitudes toward students with disabilities. That is, building principals' attitudes set the tone for the overall school's attitude, including the attitudes of teachers and staff. Accordingly, positive principal attitudes, as well as administrative support for working with all students (including those with autism), are a prerequisite for optimal educational benefits for all students, including students with disabilities in regular education classes (Heller & Schilit, 1987; Vaughn et al., 1996). Indeed, we strongly recommend that administrative personnel be selected on the basis of their attitudes toward individuals with disabilities and, specifically, their willingness to accommodate these students in their classes. Although it is possible to modify administrators' attitudes toward children and youth with disabilities (Donaldson, 1980), it is far more efficient to initially select educational leaders who have positive attitudes toward inclusion and students with autism than attempting to modify less than favorable attitudes.

Positive teacher attitudes are also determinants of success for students with disabilities in regular classes. General education teachers typically see themselves as ill-equipped to deal with students with disabilities (L. Miller, 1990; Vaughn et al., 1996). Nevertheless, they tend to perceive inclusion as a positive educational practice, contingent on appropriate teacher training and support (Knoff, 1985; Moore & Fine, 1979; Reynolds, Martin-Reynolds, & Mark, 1982; Stephens & Benjamin, 1981; Williams & Algozzine, 1979). Myles and Simpson (1989) reported that 86% of the general educators they surveyed were willing to accept a student with a disability in their classrooms on a full-time basis if appropriate support and training were provided. Without such support and training, on the other hand, fewer than 33% of the teachers were willing to accept the same student. Other studies have revealed different findings. Some general education teachers have indicated that they do not want to work with students with special needs, including those with autism (Vaughn et al., 1996). Given the impact of teacher attitude on student academic, social, and behavioral success, school personnel must carefully consider teacher attitudes when placing students with autism in general education settings.

Parents of both normally developing children and children with disabilities are also important stakeholders in the inclusion process; thus, successful integration of students with autism also hinges on their support (Heller & Schilit, 1987; Vaughn et al., 1996). Such a claim is best understood by examining the historical role of parents in the development of special education programs; that is, it was their activities and lobbying that brought about virtually every important special education system reform, including passage of

P.L. 94-142. In fact, as mentioned, many parents of children with disabilities appear willing to place their children in general classrooms, contingent on appropriate support (Abelson & Weiss, 1984; Abramson, Wilson, Yoshida, & Hagerty, 1983).

Inclusion programs must feature methods and procedures that facilitate adults' awareness and acceptance of students in general education settings as necessary in order for social and psychological integration to be achieved. In recognition of this important element, the Autism Inclusion Collaboration Model advocates disseminating information about individuals with autism to students, parents, teachers, administrators, and others. Such information should include not only facts about the rationale and advantages of inclusion, but also information about autism.

Development of positive attitudes also requires that inclusion stakeholders (e.g., teachers, administrators, and parents) be permitted to discuss their roles, attitudes, and feelings about inclusion, particularly as it relates to students with autism. Thus, development of a supportive general education climate for students with autism is best accomplished by combining information with opportunities for further discussion.

As is the case of adults who interact with students with autism, nondisabled peers also require information and experiences designed to familiarize them with the characteristics and needs of students with autism, to foster more accepting attitudes toward individuals with autism and to promote more positive peer interactions (Hurley-Geffner, 1995). Positive attitudes toward students with disabilities, including those with autism, do not occur automatically. Accordingly, this frequently overlooked component of inclusion must be considered in planning.

Use of curricula and experiences designed to facilitate better understanding and sensitivity toward included students with disabilities have proven effective (Fiedler & Simpson, 1987). Several resources are available for disseminating information about autism to general education students as well as structuring integration activities involving students with and without disabilities. For example, Simpson and Regan (1988) developed a curriculum for nondisabled students on such topics as human differences and similarities, characteristics of autism, and making friends with students with autism. This resource also identifies methods of structuring interactions between students with autism and their peers. Similarly, Quill (1990) has provided guidelines for integrating students with autism into a school, and Tomchek, Gordon, Arnold, Handleman, and Harris (1992) have offered suggestions for facilitating inclusion of preschool children with autism. Regardless of the degree to which the educational and social needs of students with autism may vary, their peers must receive information and experiences to allow individuals with autism to be successful and accepted.

Generally, children and youth with autism will lack social skills needed for assimilation and acceptance in general education classrooms unless they receive proper training and attention. Thus, a significant feature of the Autism Inclusion Collaboration Model is an emphasis on best-practice social interaction training methods. These include the following (Simpson, Myles, Sasso, & Kamps, 1991):

- direct skill instruction (students receive instruction and social skills needed for various settings, including general education)

- antecedent prompting methods (students are prompted by adults to engage in specified interactive behavior with peers)

- peer-initiated training strategies (socially competent peers are instructed in methods for initiating and encouraging social interactions with children with autism in natural settings)

- peer tutoring (socially competent peers are instructed to use effective teaching techniques with their classmates with autism)

These methods are not only very useful but also extremely flexible (Sasso, 1987). Hence, they may vary from setting to setting, depending on students' needs, while still addressing the important issue of fostering positive and accepting relationships between children with autism and their normally achieving peers. Without such support, students with autism are vulnerable to rejection and isolation, which could destine for failure an otherwise successful inclusion program.

Coordinated Team Commitment

Special education and general education have historically functioned as independent systems. Thus, special educators have assumed responsibility for students with disabilities in special education settings, whereas general educators have been expected to assume primary responsibility for students with disabilities in inclusive settings in addition to "traditional" regular education students.

Often to the distress of general educators, special educators have also historically assumed primary responsibility for determining (a) if and when the needs of students with disabilities can appropriately be met in general education settings, (b) which regular education programs and teachers will best meet integrated students' needs, and (c) how inclusion may most effectively be accomplished. Not surprisingly, this system, in combination with other imprudent inclusion policies and activities, has weakened many general educators' motivation to participate in inclusion efforts. Knoff (1985), for instance, reported that many general educators feel imposed on by inclusion, consider themselves unprepared to teach students with disabilities, and feel put upon by inclusive practices.

Improvements in the way students with autism are integrated into general education can be expected only with the support of and a close working relationship between general and special educators. Thus, a major component of the Autism Inclusion Collaboration Model involves shared responsibility by general and special educators for students with autism. That is, general educators must accept that integrated students with autism are their responsibility while they are in regular education programs. In return, general educators can expect full participation in decision-making processes associated with inclusion (including input regarding which students are appropriate for inclusion) along with appropriate support (e.g., training, consultation).

Calls for shared ownership are not new (Heller & Schilit, 1987; Hersh & Walker, 1983; Warger & Pugach, 1996). Yet, in spite of a widespread emphasis by both practitioners and researchers on the significance of this variable in developing successful inclusion programs, it continues to present problems (Ysseldyke et al., 1992).

A first step toward coordinated team commitment is to arrange schools so that they require and reinforce coordination and communication among faculty and staff. *Coordination*, in this context, refers to the clear definition of roles for service delivery personnel, especially individuals involved in including students with autism. Recognizing the importance of such reorganization, Judy Schrag (1990), former director of the U.S. Office of Special Education Programs, observed that

> special education program enhancements include better coordination across special programs and general education, increased roles of the building principals, continued exploration of the circumstances under which students with special needs can be educated in the regular classrooms and exploration of refinements in our assessment and classification procedures. (p. 7)

Coordination of special and general education programs requires that individuals be aware of their own responsibilities as well as those of others. It is our contention that much discontent among general education teachers concerning inclusive programs stems from a lack of orchestration (e.g., role clarification) of school personnel responsibilities. Hence a logical step in dealing with this problem is to establish responsibility boundaries more clearly.

Related to achieving coordinated team commitment, *communication* is the basis for developing a collaborative relationship, the philosophical underpinning of the Autism Inclusion Collaboration Model. Communication is the basis for involvement of all inclusion stakeholders, including administrators, parents, teachers, support personnel, and students. Effective communication ensures that involved persons are working toward the same goals and that each person follows established procedures (Vaughn et al., 1996). As has often been stated, effective communication is the *sine qua non* of effective general–special education collaboration.

The need for shared decision making and participatory management has been recognized for some time (Goodlad, 1990). Such organizational systems have increased involvement in decision making, resulting in enhanced well-being of stakeholders and increased organizational efficiency in meeting individual needs. These outcomes have obvious importance for including persons with autism, and thus, as noted by a variety of educators, are worthy of serious consideration (Clune & White, 1988; Mertens & Yarger, 1988; Walberg & Lane, 1989; White, 1989).

Summary

We are not convinced that every student with autism should be included in general education classes. Nonetheless, we recognize that many children and youth with autism can and should be integrated into regular class settings, and that inclusion will likely continue into the 21st century. Moreover, we recognize that societal and school changes will require that general and special educators work together more effectively to serve the needs of *all* students, including those with autism. Indeed, we take very seriously the warnings of legislators and the general public that special education will need to evolve or dissolve.

Effectively and efficiently including students with autism will continue to be a significant challenge for schools in coming decades. The use of structured multifaceted models such as the Autism Inclusion Collaboration Model can significantly assist in this important undertaking.

References

Abelson, A. G., & Weiss, R. (1984). Mainstreaming the handicapped: The views of parents of non-handicapped pupils. *Spectrum, 2,* 27–29.

Abramson, M., Wilson, V., Yoshida, R. K., & Hagerty, G. (1983). Parents' perceptions of their learning disabled child's educational performance. *Learning Disability Quarterly, 6,* 184–194.

Blalock, G. (1991). Paraprofessionals: Critical team members in our special education programs. *Intervention in School and Clinic, 26,* 200–214.

Boomer, L. (1994). The utilization of paraprofessionals in programs for students with autism. *Focus on Autistic Behavior, 9*(2), 1–9.

Cates, D. L., & Yell, M. L. (1994, March). *Service delivery models and students with emotional disabilities and behavior disorders: A rural perspective.* Paper presented at the 14th annual meeting of the American Council on Rural Special Education, Austin, TX.

Clune, W. H., & White, P. A. (1988). *School-based management: Institutional variation, implementation, and issues for further research.* New Brunswick, NJ: Rutgers University, Center for Policy Research in Education.

Donaldson, J. (1980). Changing attitudes toward handicapped persons: A review and analysis of research. *Exceptional Children, 43,* 504–516.

Fiedler, C., & Simpson, R. L. (1987). Modifying the attitudes of nonhandicapped high school students toward handicapped peers. *Exceptional Children, 53,* 342–351.

French, N., & Cabell, E. (1993). Are community college training programs for paraeducators feasible? *Community College Journal of Research and Practice, 17,* 131–140.

Gersten, R., & Woodward, J. (1990). Rethinking the Regular Education Initiative: Focus on the classroom teacher. *Remedial and Special Education, 11*(3), 7–16.

Goodlad, J. I. (1990). *Teachers for our nation's schools.* San Francisco: Jossey-Bass.

Heller, H., & Schilit, J. (1987). The Regular Education Initiative: A concerned response. *Focus on Exceptional Children, 20,* 1–6.

Hersh, R., & Walker, H. M. (1983). Great expectations: Making schools effective for all students. *Policy Review Studies, 2,* 147–188.

Hurley-Geffner, C. M. (1995). Friendships between children with and without developmental disabilities. In R. L. Koegel & L. K. Koegel (Eds.), *Teaching children with autism: Strategies for initiating positive interactions and improving learning opportunities* (pp. 105–126). Baltimore: Brookes.

Idol, L., & West, J. F. (1987). Consultation in special education (Part II): Training and practice. *Journal of Learning Disabilities, 20,* 474–494.

Individuals with Disabilities Education Act of 1990, 20 U.S.C. §1400 *et seq.*

Jones, K., & Bender, W. (1993). Utilization of paraprofessionals in special education: A review of the literature. *Remedial and Special Education, 14*(1), 7–14.

Karagianis, L., & Nesbit, W. (1983). Support services: The neglected ingredient in the integration recipe. *Special Education in Canada, 53*(3), 18–19.

Kellegrew, D. H. (1995). Integrated school placements for children with disabilities. In R. L. Koegel & L. K. Koegel (Eds.), *Teaching children with autism: Strategies for initiating positive interactions and improving learning opportunities* (pp. 127–146). Baltimore: Brookes.

Knoff, H. M. (1985). Attitudes toward mainstreaming: A status report and comparison of regular and special educators in New York and Massachusetts. *Psychology in the Schools, 22,* 410–418.

Koegel, R. L., Koegel, L. K., Frea, W. D., & Smith, A. E. (1995). Emerging interventions for children with autism: Longitudinal and lifestyle implications. In R. L. Koegel and L. K. Koegel (Eds.), *Teaching children with autism: Strategies for initiating positive interactions and improving learning opportunities* (pp. 1–15). Baltimore: Brookes.

Koegel, R. L., Rincover, A., & Egel, A. L. (1982). *Educating and understanding autistic children.* San Diego, CA: College-Hill.

Lieberman, L. M. (1992). Preserving special education . . . For those who need it. In W. Stainback & S. Stainback (Eds.), *Controversial issues confronting special education* (pp. 13–25). Boston: Allyn & Bacon.

Martin, E. (1974). Some thoughts on mainstreaming. *Exceptional Children, 41,* 150–153.

Mertens, S., & Yarger, S. J. (1988). Teaching as a profession: Leadership, empowerment, and involvement. *Journal of Teacher Education, 39*(1), 32–37.

Mesibov, G. B. (1992). Treatment issues with high-functioning individuals with autism. In E. Schopler & G. B. Mesibov (Eds.), *High-functioning individuals with autism* (pp. 143–155). New York: Plenum.

Miller, K. J., & Savage, L. B. (1995, March). Including general educators in inclusion. In *Reaching to the future: Boldly facing challenges in rural communities* (Conference proceedings of the American Council on Rural Special Education, Las Vegas, NV).

Miller, L. (1990). The Regular Education Initiative and school reform: Lessons from the mainstream. *Remedial and Special Education, 11*(3), 17–22.

Miller, T. L., & Sabatino, D. A. (1978). An evaluation of the teacher consultant model as an approach to mainstreaming. *Exceptional Children, 44,* 86–91.

Moore, J., & Fine, M. J. (1979). Regular and special class teachers' perceptions of normal and exceptional children and their attitudes toward mainstreaming. *Psychology in the Schools, 15,* 253–259.

Myles, B. S., & Simpson, R. L. (1989). Regular educators' modification preferences for mainstreaming mildly handicapped children. *The Journal of Special Education, 22,* 479–492.

Myles, B. S., & Simpson, R. L. (1990). Mainstreaming modification preferences of parents of elementary-age children with learning disabilities. *Journal of Learning Disabilities, 23,* 234–239.

Myles, B. S., & Simpson, R. L. (1992). General educators' mainstreaming preferences that facilitate acceptance of students with behavioral disorders and learning disabilities. *Behavioral Disorders, 17,* 305–315.

National Association for Retarded Citizens. (1973). *The right to choose.* Arlington, TX: Author.

Newman, R. K., & Simpson, R. L. (1983). Modifying the least restrictive environment to facilitate the integration of severely emotionally disturbed children and youth. *Behavioral Disorders, 8,* 103–112.

O'Rourke, A. P. (1980). A comparison of principal and teacher attitudes toward handicapped students and the relationship between those attitudes and school morale of handicapped students. *Dissertation Abstracts International, 40*(7-A), 3954.

Peterson, N. L. (1987). *Early intervention for handicapped and at-risk children.* Denver, CO: Love.

Pickett, A. L. (1980). Roles of paraprofessionals in school. *Education Unlimited, 2,* 6–7.

Pugach, M. C., & Allen-Meares, P. (1985). Collaboration at the preservice level: Instructional and evaluation activities. *Teacher Education and Special Education, 8,* 132–143.

Quill, K. A. (1990). A model for integrating children with autism. *Focus on Autistic Behavior, 5*(4), 1–19.

Reynolds, B. J., Martin-Reynolds, J., & Mark, F. D. (1982). Elementary teachers' attitudes toward mainstreaming educable retarded students. *Education and Training of the Mentally Retarded, 17,* 171–176.

Sailor, W., Anderson, J., Halvorsen, A. T., Doering, K., Filler, J., & Goetz, L. (1989). *The comprehensive local school: Regular education for all students with disabilities.* Baltimore: Brookes.

Salend, S. J. (1990). *Effective mainstreaming.* New York: Macmillan.

Sasso, G. M. (1987). Social interactions: Issues and procedures. *Focus on Autistic Behavior, 2*(4), 1–7.

Sasso, G. M., Simpson, R. L., & Novak, C. G. (1985). Procedures for facilitating integration of autistic children in public school settings. *Analysis and Intervention in Developmental Disabilities, 5,* 233–246.

Schrag, V. (1990). Charting the course for the 1990's. In L. M. Bullock & R. L. Simpson (Eds.), *Monograph on critical issues in special education: Implications for personnel preparation* (pp. 2–8). Denton: University of North Texas.

Simpson, R. L., & Myles, B. S. (1989). Parents' mainstreaming modification preferences for children with educable mental handicaps, behavior disorders and learning disabilities. *Psychology in the Schools, 26,* 292–301.

Simpson, R. L., & Myles, B. S. (1990). The general education collaboration model: A model for successful mainstreaming. *Focus on Exceptional Children, 23*(4), 1–10.

Simpson, R. L., & Myles, B. S. (1991). Ancillary staff members' mainstreaming recommendations for students with exceptionalities. *Psychology in the Schools, 28*(1), 26–32.

Simpson, R. L., Myles, B. S., Sasso, G., & Kamps, D. M. (1991). *Promoting social interactions of children and youth with autism.* Reston, VA: Council on Exceptional Children.

Simpson, R. L., & Regan, M. (1988). *Management of autistic behavior.* Austin, TX: PRO-ED.

Stephens, T. M., & Benjamin, L. B. (1981). Measures of general classroom teachers' attitudes toward handicapped children. *Exceptional Children, 46,* 292–297.

Tomcheck, L. B., Gordon, R., Arnold, M., Handleman, J., & Harris, S. (1992). Teaching children with autism and their normally developing peers: Meeting the challenges of integrated education. *Focus on Autistic Behavior, 7*(2), 1–19.

Vaughn, S., Schumm, J. S., Jallad, B., Slusher, J., & Saumell, L. (1996). Teachers' views of inclusion. *Learning Disabilities Research and Practice, 11*(2), 96–106.

Vergason, G. A., & Anderegg, M. L. (1992). Preserving the least restrictive environment. In W. Stainback & S. Stainback (Eds.), *Controversial issues confronting special education* (pp. 45–54). Boston: Allyn & Bacon.

Walberg, H. J., & Lane, J. J. (1989). *Organizing for learning: Toward the 21st century.* Reston, VA: National Association of Secondary School Principals.

Warger, C. D., & Pugach, M. C. (1996). Curriculum consideration in an inclusive environment. *Focus on Exceptional Children, 28*(8), 1–12.

White, P. A. (1989, September). An overview of school-based management: What does the research say? *NASSP Bulletin,* 1–8.

Williams, R. J., & Algozzine, B. (1979). Teachers' attitudes toward mainstreaming. *The Elementary School Journal, 80,* 63–67.

Wing, L. (1992). Manifestations of social problems in high-functioning autistic people. In E. Schopler & G. B. Mesibov (Eds.), *High-functioning individuals with autism* (pp. 129–142). New York: Plenum.

Ysseldyke, J. E., Algozzine, B., & Thurlow, M. L. (1992). *Critical issues in special education.* Boston: Houghton Mifflin.

Successful Transition of Students with Autism

9

Sally Morgan Smith
and Julie A. Donnelly

All too often, books on autism focus only on the needs of children with autism, leaving parents and teachers without proper information on how to support adolescents and young adults in the process of planning for transition as these students move through school to adult life. This chapter discusses transition planning and services for students with autism that will enable the student, the family, and the school to identify skills needed to develop appropriate goals and establish a community network to support these goals. The chapter starts with a review of the factors that illustrate the need for transition planning. As a backdrop for current transition efforts, the evolution of transition and legislation that affects transition are also discussed. The role of transition assessment as an ongoing means of determining student strengths, needs, and preferences, as well as the Individualized Education Program (IEP) process are major highlights of this chapter, followed by a discussion of transition across the life span.

Transition is "life changes, adjustments, and cumulative experiences that occur in the lives of young adults as they move from school environments to more independent living and work environments" (Wehman, 1992, p. 5). As such, transition is not a single event but rather an ongoing process that relates to all roles in life. Transitions, changes, and new circumstances can be particularly difficult for individuals with autism (Wing, 1996). Such planning is particularly critical for students with autism because they often exhibit challenging behaviors, such as self-stimulatory behaviors, social skills problems, behavioral difficulties, and language problems (Kauffman, 1977; Suomi, Ruble, & Dalrymple, 1992).

One aspect of transition—that of students with disabilities moving from school to postschool life—is a growing concern because of the poor adult outcomes many of these young adults face. For example, the need for improved services for secondary students is manifested in the high dropout rate among students with disabilities and the dismal employment prospects of young adults served in special education programs. According to a summary of transition outcomes by Wagner (1989), there is a 38% dropout rate across all students with disabilities compared to an approximate 20% rate for nondisabled peers. Unemployment rates for adults with disabilities is reported to range from 50% to 75% (Louis Harris and Associates, Inc., 1987). Changing these bleak prospects requires that students with disabilities have access to a broader array of options at the secondary level, ranging from academic support to community-based education focused on employment, including functional and independent living skills, personal-social content, and career awareness. These needs can be met only through comprehensive programs that provide a continuum of services based on the specific strengths of the individual student. Educators must understand the importance of dealing with transition planning for students with disabilities to provide a viable curriculum. The main focus of the educational program in general education is the attainment of a specific number of Carnegie units required for graduation. When special education students are fully included in general education classes, this becomes the main focus for their educational program also. During this process, other postschool options may be overlooked.

Factors That Illustrate the Need for Transition Planning

One question that often is raised in the current educational reform effort is whether students are in fact being prepared for a world that no longer exists. For example, many secondary-level special education programs focus on tutorials geared toward success in inclusive classes or remedial programs without preparing students adequately for life after high school. Special education students need to experience life skills and self-determination training, but this may not be included in a general education setting. The U.S. Department of Education (1994) reported that students who spent more of their time in academic courses were significantly more likely to fail courses than students who were involved in vocational training and employment programs. That is, education must be focused on the ultimate goal—well-adjusted adults leading full lives—rather than the intermediate goal of academic success.

Without such preparation, young adults with special needs experience

- high dropout rates;
- high rates of unemployment or underemployment and poor wages;
- inability to live independently;
- unsuccessful attempts at completing postsecondary training and education;
- dissatisfaction with quality of life; and
- limited opportunities for making personal choices.

These six areas are addressed below to illustrate the need for transition planning that focuses on future independence and success in school and employment settings.

High School Dropout Rate

Research shows that more than 30% of students served in secondary special education programs drop out of school. There are no specific numbers for students with autism; however, many students who fit the criteria for autism are classified as having learning disabilities, behavioral disorders, or mental retardation labels (Rutter & Schopler, 1988). When reviewed by individual category, the dropout rates become even more alarming. For example, Wagner (1989) and Wehman (1992) reported the following dropout rates:

- students with learning disabilities, 27% to 54%
- students with behavioral disorders, 39% to 47%
- students with mental retardation, 20% to 25%

Clearly, this high dropout rate implies that secondary special education fails to meet the needs of many students served in these programs.

Unemployment/Underemployment and Poor Wages

Secondary special education programs appear to have little impact on student adjustment to community life. Thus, neither graduates nor dropouts find adequate employment opportunities. According to Wagner (1989), the unemployment rate for young adults with disabilities exceeds 50%. Further, dropouts are generally employed at about one half the rate of graduates (Hasazi, Gordon, & Roe, 1985).

Although data on employment rates vary from study to study, students with learning disabilities generally demonstrate the highest rates. Specifically, Zigmond and Thornton (1985) cited employment rates of 70% for students with learning disabilities, compared to 47% for students with mental retardation (Edgar, 1988).

For individuals with autism, the rates are more dismal. For example, Kanner, Rodriguez, and Ashenden (1972) found that only 10% of a sample of 96 children diagnosed as having autism at Johns Hopkins Hospital prior to 1953 were "sufficiently integrated into the texture of society to be employable" (p. 10). A study by Rumsey, Rapoport, and Sceery (1985) focused on 14 adult men (mean age = 28) with mean verbal IQ scores of 93. Four were employed in menial jobs, 3 were in sheltered workshops, 4 were in vocational training, 2 were unemployed, and 1 was in a state hospital. Szatmari, Bartolucci, Bremner, Bond, and Rich (1989) reported on 12 men and 4 women (mean age = 26) with a mean IQ of 92. Seven were employed, 3 were students (all participants graduated from high school and 7 went on to college), 2 were unemployed, and 4 attended sheltered workshops. In a British study, Newson, Dawson, and Everard (1982) followed the history of 93 more able (IQ normal or above) persons with autism. The 74 who were in the postschool group fared as follows: 10 were in college, 7 were in special training, and 15 were in ordinary training. Twenty were employed, only 5 of whom were in menial jobs, but 22 were in sheltered employment. Of the 93 individuals studied by Newson et al., only 27% were in competitive employment. Wehman (1993) concluded that the majority of reported cases of autism had poor employment outcomes.

In addition to unemployment, underemployment of individuals with disabilities is of grave concern. For example, Edgar (1987) reported that although 60% of high school graduates with disabilities were employed, only 18% earned more than minimum wage. If students with learning disabilities and behavior disorders are not considered in this statistic, the percentage drops to 5%.

Generally, the types of jobs obtained by graduates of special education programs tend to be entry-level jobs with low salaries, few if any benefits, and minimal opportunity for advancement (Edgar, 1988). Even individuals described as high-functioning autistic with postsecondary education degrees often find themselves unable to obtain or retain jobs at their educational level because of social skill deficits. Though they have abilities that might qualify them for higher paying positions, they instead find jobs shelving books at libraries, bagging groceries, or washing dishes (Donnelly, 1996).

Youth with disabilities are unemployed or underemployed for three basic reasons (Okolo & Sitlington, 1988):

- lack of interpersonal skills (e.g., work habits, work attitudes, and social communication skills)

- lack of job-related academic skills

- lack of specific vocational skills to perform more than entry-level personal service jobs

Youth with autism are unemployed or underemployed especially because of communication and social skills deficits, sensory issues, and problem behaviors (Smith, Belcher, & Juhrs, 1996). Therefore, if students with autism are to be prepared for the world of work, specific skills must be identified in each of the above areas, and a delivery system must be developed to ensure relevant instruction and services.

Living Independently

According to the National Longitudinal Transition Study, 82% of young adults with disabilities live at home with their parents (Wagner, 1989). Other studies have reported that from 50% to 69% of persons who had been in special education programs lived with their parents and were financially dependent on them. Rumsey et al. (1985) found that of the 14 adults with autism in their study, only 1 lived independently; 3 were in supervised home settings, 1 was in a state hospital, and the remaining 9 lived with their parents.

These findings clearly indicate that school programs must be designed to address independent living and community survival skills; without such specific training, most individuals with disabilities are unable to achieve the outcome of independent living.

Postsecondary Training or Education

Although a growing number of high-functioning individuals with autism are attending college, a 1991 study by Lord and Venter revealed that only 1 in 18 study participants completed a university degree; 1 other participant had attended college but left without a degree. On a more promising note, Szatmari et al. (1989) found that 7 out of 16 subjects with high-functioning autism were university graduates.

The Rehabilitation Act of 1973 and the Americans with Disabilities Act (ADA) of 1990 require that colleges and universities provide equal opportunity for participation by persons with disabilities. A *person with a disability* is defined as someone with a physical or mental impairment that substantially limits one or more major life activities. Many colleges and universities offer tutoring and support services for typical students; they must provide equal support services to students with disabilities. Although the types of service may vary from school to school, they often consist of providing note takers, test proctors, and auxiliary aides in mainstream classes. In addition, basic skill classes, guidance, and counseling are often available.

Individuals with autism qualify for these services; however, college staff may not have experience or training in providing the unique social supports and the time management, organizational skills, and communication skills that would also benefit these individuals. For example, one high-functioning individual with autism had completed three fourths of a college course when the professor took him aside and asked why he had not completed an assigned task. As they discussed the requirement, the professor realized that he had never directly assigned the task but had assumed that it was understood. The other students followed his implied instructions, but the student with autism had only understood those directions that were literal and clearly stated. Because of his communication difficulties, the student was unable to defend himself or explain his problem and, therefore, was penalized (Donnelly & Levy, 1995).

Many students with autism and other disabilities can qualify for assistance with tuition, books, and living expenses through vocational rehabilitation services. With appropriate support, many individuals with high-functioning autism can earn good grades and therefore prepare themselves to make a contribution to society through postsecondary training.

Quality of Life

Quality of life is a relative concept. That is, because there is no one accepted definition, quality of life must be considered in terms of each individual. According to Halpern (1992), one necessary component of a good quality of life is that people should have an opportunity to make choices. For most people in our society, employment, and the money earned through employment plays a critical role in quality of life, but money does not guarantee satisfaction (Edgar, 1988). For example, Halpern (1985) suggested that social and interpersonal networks are also of utmost importance to personal adjustment. Developing friendships and participating in community activities add a new dimension of fulfillment to life. It is imperative, therefore, that schools offer specific social skills training to support social skills development so that students with autism may have these experiences.

Self-Determination

Quality of life is enhanced through self-determination, that is, the ability and opportunity to make one's own decisions and solve the problems of everyday life. Self-determination, which begins with knowing oneself, identifying one's aspirations, and being aware of one's needs (Fullerton, 1993), makes it possible for the person with autism to make appropriate choices.

The need for self-determination is addressed in the Individuals with Disabilities Education Act of 1990 (IDEA) and its amendments of 1997, as well as the Rehabilitation Act Amendments of 1992. Specifically, IDEA mandates that students participate in their own transition planning meeting. The Rehabilitation Act Amendments, in turn, declare that people with disabilities have the right to self-determination just like their nondisabled peers. Greater importance must be placed on students' learning to have more direction in their lives. This can be accomplished by giving students more opportunities to make choices and live with the consequences. Whether making choices about simple decisions, such as what to wear to school, or more important decisions, such as what classes to take or career to pursue, students have a right to self-determination. They even have the right to fail! In addition, students must have an active role in the development of their IEP. Many schools are providing instruction for their special education students to prepare them to facilitate their own IEP meetings. Direct instruction must take place first to teach the necessary skills; then role playing will provide the practice to enable the students to make these skills part of their repertoire of self-awareness and self-advocacy skills.

Historical Perspective on Transition

To foster a better understanding of the origin and evolution of transition, this section reviews its historical progression. Starting with the school as a foundation and extending to employment in the work/study model of the 1960s, the focus in the 1970s was on career education, evolving in the mid-1980s to the "bridge" concept up until the current global view of transition. Each of these stages is briefly discussed.

The Work/Study Program

The premise behind transition services began over 30 years ago with the work/study programs and the Vocational Education Act of 1963. Originally conceptualized as a cooperative program between the public schools and the local offices of state rehabilitation agencies, the main purpose of the work/study program was to create for students with mild disabilities an integrated academic, social, and vocational curriculum accompanied by appropriate work experiences to prepare them for later community adjustment. The Vocational Education Act of 1963 specified that persons with disabilities be included in ongoing vocational education with nondisabled peers.

The Career Education Movement

When career education was declared a priority by the U.S. Department of Education in 1970, the general population of students was targeted, but soon persons with disabilities were also included, as stipulated in the Education for All Handicapped Children Act of 1975 (P.L. 94-142). During this stage, career education was broadly structured and financed largely through federal money. The disadvantage of these programs was that students were trained for specific skills rather than in work habits that could be used in a variety of settings. Gradually, however, the emphasis changed to training in generally acceptable employee behaviors (i.e., being on time for work, attending to task, getting along well with co-workers, accepting directions from the supervisor).

The "Bridges" Model of Transition

In the early 1980s the transition movement was based on a rather limited definition that conceptualized transition as the "bridge between the security and structure offered by the school and the opportunities and risks of adult life" (Will, 1984, p. 1). Halpern (1992) described this early transition model as the "bridges model," which allowed transition from school to work for special education students. The bridges model was composed of a continuum of services. The first bridge, transition without special services, was available to anyone. The second bridge, transition with time-limited services, provided access to short-term services. Finally, transition with ongoing services was a small component used mainly in demonstration models. Special education students were provided whatever level of support they needed along this continuum. The greatest level of support was provided in model sites established to develop programs that could later be replicated. This transition model, which originally focused solely on employment, has evolved during the past 10 years and now includes all aspects of adult life.

As shown, over a period of 30 years, transition from school to adult living has acquired a broad, life-career focus that includes the student, parent(s), school personnel, and adult service agencies working collaboratively to develop IEPs with adult outcomes. This change to a more global focus on the whole person should be the guiding force behind developing appropriate IEPs and school programs that reflect transition-related outcomes.

Legislation that Affects Transition

Planning and educational programming that address postschool outcomes for students with disabilities are driven by legislation and accompanying mandates and regulations. For example, IDEA mandates that students participate in their own transition planning meetings. According to the Rehabilitation Act Amendments, in turn, people with disabilities have the right to self-determination just like their nondisabled peers. To provide a basic understanding of the legal underpinnings of transition, the following section specifically reviews IDEA, the ADA, and the Rehabilitation Act Amendments.

Individuals with Disabilities Education Act (IDEA)

IDEA (1990, 1997) requires that specific outcomes be identified based on student needs, preferences, and interests, and that educational programs for all students with disabilities, 16 years of age and older, "be supported by transition services language that would include instruction, community experiences, development of employment and other post-school adult living objectives, and if appropriate, the acquisition of daily living skills and functional vocational evaluation" (Section 300.18[b]).

Further, IDEA recognizes a broad definition of transition:

Transition services mean a coordinated set of activities for a student, designed within an outcome oriented process, which promotes movement from school to post-school activities, including post-secondary education, vocational training, integrated employment (including supported employment), continuing and adult education, adult services, independent living, or community participation. (Section 300.18[a])

Americans with Disabilities Act (ADA)

ADA (P.L. 101-336), which was also passed in 1990, offers more choices and options for people with disabilities. As such, it is a form of civil rights legislation that prohibits discrimination against people with disabilities in employment, public accommodations, transportation, and telecommunications. ADA supports transition in that it mandates employment opportunities for persons with disabilities. Further, it mandates that employers and the community at large make accommodations for persons with disabilities so that they can access buildings.

School to Work Opportunities Act of 1994

The School to Work Opportunities Act of 1994 assists in the transition from school to work. It encourages employers to take leadership roles in dealing with school settings. Businesses have provided support in the form of advisory committees, adopt-a-school, and partners-in-education programs. In turn, the employers and businesses have been recognized in their communities for the support and opportunities that they have afforded the students. Ultimately, all participants have benefited from this program. The students have been given real-life work experiences and mentoring from business leaders, and the businesses have helped better prepare their workforce for tomorrow.

Rehabilitation Act Amendments

According to the Rehabilitation Act Amendments,

> disability is a natural part of the human experience and in no way diminishes the right of an individual to (a) live independently, (b) enjoy self-determination, (c) make choices, (d) contribute to society, (e) pursue meaningful careers, and (f) enjoy full inclusion and integration in the economic, political, social, cultural, and educational mainstream of American society. (p. 24)

Together, IDEA, ADA, the School to Work Opportunities Act of 1994, and the Rehabilitation Act Amendments provide federal mandates that have a great impact on people with disabilities. Early career education, vocational preparation, and school programs with an emphasis on transition-related issues will support these mandates. With these federal regulations in place, the states have taken the initiative to develop their own state guidelines to support the federal mandates. The federal mandates, and the ensuing state mandates, hold school districts accountable for providing the transition services needed by each individual student. Ultimately, the school districts will be responsible for meeting these demands.

Current Definition of Transition

In 1994 the Division of Career Development and Transition (DCDT) of the Council for Exceptional Children adopted the following definition of transition:

> Transition refers to a change in status from behaving primarily as a student to assuming emergent adult roles in the community. The roles include employment, participating in post-secondary education, maintaining a home, becoming appropriately involved in the community, and experiencing satisfactory personal and social relationships. The process of enhancing transition involves the participation and coordination of school programs, adult agency services, and natural supports within the community. The foundation for transition should be laid during the elementary and middle school years, guided by the broad concept of career development. Transition planning should begin no later than age 14, and students should be encouraged, to the full extent of their capabilities, to assume a maximum amount of responsibility for such planning. (Halpern, 1994, p. 117)

The mandates of IDEA regarding transition, as well as this DCDT definition, provide a structure that is applicable to all students with disabilities, including students with autism. However, effective transition services are not yet in place in many schools throughout the United States. Although IDEA has specific guidelines for transition, some states have been slow to implement these steps. Also, states have interpreted the federal mandates in different ways. A crucial component that allows states to address transition with only a limited number of students is the IDEA age requirement of 16. Although IDEA states that younger students may be deemed appropriate for transition planning, this age stipulation gives many states a way to avoid dealing with transition planning for students who could have greatly benefited from it. Some states have chosen to lower the age requirement, whereas other states adhere to the age 16. This causes problems because many students with disabilities have either dropped out of school before they turn 16, or they have already decided to drop out. Many people feel that the age requirement is too old. However, that is the age stated in IDEA. Special educators must take a more proactive and assertive role in the implementation of transition services in the development of IEPs and program planning for their students. As time goes on, if the DCDT definition of transition becomes more widely accepted, many of interstate discrepancies will be removed.

IDEA clearly places the initial responsibility for transition planning on the public schools. To be effective, however, transition planning and programming must go beyond the school setting to take place as a collaborative effort involving the student, family, school, rehabilitation counselor, adult service providers, and community members. Without such broad input into the development and implementation of the IEP for the student with disabilities, the student is not likely to acquire the skills necessary to successfully live and work in a complex society.

Transition must look beyond employment, taking into consideration also quality of life and its impact on all aspects of adult adjustment. Identification of postschool outcomes must be the driving force behind developing long-range goals that enable students with autism to achieve their dreams. In this regard, it is important that the process of transition planning involves making decisions *with* each individual student and his or her family, rather than *for* the individual with autism.

There is no one single plan used for all students with a specific disability. For example, students with autism span a spectrum of functioning levels (Wing, 1996), so a transition plan must be developed for each individual student that suits his or her strengths and needs. Further, student choice and preferences are also key factors in transition planning. Table 9.1 presents the steps in a typical transition planning process. These steps are discussed in more detail in the remainder of this chapter.

The first step toward effective planning involves transition assessment to gain insight into the needs, preferences, and interests, as well as the present level of performance of a specific student.

Table 9.1

Transition Planning Process for Students with Autism

Step 1	Provide student with training to be an active participant in the Individualized Education Program (IEP) meeting.
Step 2	Hold IEP meeting to explain transition planning and the roles of the student, parents, and school in the process. Discuss their visions for the future. Obtain their input regarding assessment, appropriate adult outcomes, types of school programs and services needed, student's vocational interests, and adult service providers to include in IEP process.
Step 3	Review student records. Decide what additional assessment needs to be carried out. Conduct formal and informal assessments. Analyze assessment data. Develop portfolio with student. Assessment will be an ongoing process.
Step 4	Reconvene with IEP team. Discuss assessment results with student and parents. Revisit vision for the future. Plan community experiences, including supervised work experiences. Develop goals and objectives reflecting adult outcomes.
Step 5	Implement the transition IEP and monitor student progress.
Step 6	Reconvene the IEP team annually or as needed to modify the IEP.

Transition Assessment

Transition is "a lifelong process that begins at birth and relates to all life roles, not just work" (Szymanski, 1994, p. 402). Therefore, transition assessment must be multifaceted and ongoing, surveying all aspects of one's life throughout the life span. Adult outcomes (e.g., independent living skills, personal–social adjustment, and occupational adjustment) are the foundation for the development of transition assessments (Clark, 1995).

In arriving at a complete picture of the student, effective transition assessment (including career assessment and vocational assessment) starts by determining the student's present level of performance, as well as needs, interests, and preferences. Such information may be collected from reviewing cumulative records, analyzing test information or administering additional assessments, and interviewing the student, as well as gathering data from parents, school personnel, rehabilitation counselors, community members, and others who have an interest in assisting planning for a student's future.

Formal Assessment

Formal transition assessment includes the following:

- achievement tests

- aptitude tests

- interest inventories

- adaptive behavior scales

- transition planning assessment instruments (e.g., The *Transition Behavior Scale*, McCarney, 1989; The *Life Centered Career Education (LCCE) Knowledge Battery*, Brolin, 1992; and the *Transition Planning Inventory*, Patton & Clark, 1996)

- commercial work samples

- a medical evaluation

Informal Assessment

Informal transition assessment includes the following:

- personal interviews with the student, parents, and teachers

- informal questionnaires and inventories with students, parents, and teachers (e.g., the *Enderle-Severson Transition Rating Scale*, Enderle & Severson, 1991; the *Life Centered Career Education Performance Battery*, Brolin, 1992; the *McGill Action Planning System*, Vandercook & York, 1989)

- self-report checklists for students
- functional skills rating scales or checklists (e.g., the *Adolescent and Adult Psychoeducational Profile*, Mesibov, Schopler, Schaffer, & Landrus, 1988)
- interviews and questionnaires with employer and job coach

Through a variety of people who know the student directly and can give their perspectives on the student's capabilities and level of preparedness, information is gathered on independent living skills, personal–social adjustment, ability to access the community, participation in recreation and leisure activities, academic and behavioral issues, dreams for the future, postsecondary training and education interests, and vocational interests. When one is gathering this information, it is more helpful if the student and others are asked similar questions in order to get various perspectives on the same issues.

Functional Assessment

Functional assessment measures daily living activities, skills, behavioral performances, environmental conditions, and needs. This type of assessment is conducted at home, at school, in the community, in the work place, and in other environments where the young adult lives and works. Although similar to informal assessment, functional assessment provides the opportunity to assess the student in actual settings, such as on-the-job assessment of real work skills and habits or the student's ability to access public transportation.

Portfolio Assessment

Portfolio assessment consists of consolidating the assessments mentioned above with additional information about the student. Developing a portfolio to follow the student throughout school is helpful because it provides a complete overview of the student that can constantly be updated. The student helps decide what information is included in the portfolio, but it generally includes

- summaries of formal, informal, and functional assessments;
- summaries of transition planning assessments;
- videos of actual job performance;
- interviews with employers and co-workers, friends, and family;
- videos of participation in recreational and leisure activities;
- videos of daily living and functional living skill performances; and
- letters of reference from friends, school personnel, roommates, employers, and co-workers.

Portfolio transition assessment is ideal for students with autism because it is an ongoing process that illustrates the student's growth, change, and abilities. As the student develops through the years in school, areas of strengths and concerns change, as do areas of interest. Therefore, transition-related areas must continually be assessed and reassessed in order to plan and develop appropriate IEPs and modify the program as necessary to meet changing needs. The importance of transition assessment cannot be overstated. It is the cornerstone of effective transition planning.

Life-Span Approach to Transition Planning for Students with Autism

Transition is viewed as a lifelong process that starts at birth and continues across the life span, with emphasis being placed on the evolution of the whole person.

The life-span approach to transition is based on the premise that transition is not a product but rather an ongoing process that begins at birth and continues throughout life (Clark, Carlson, Fisher, Cook, & D'Alonzo, 1991; Repetto & Correa, 1996; Szymanski, 1994), with career interests and aspirations evolving over time. Schools, therefore, must provide programs that meet the specific needs of the individual student as the student grows and matures.

To encourage transition across the life span, students with disabilities need to participate in age-appropriate activities with same-age peers (with and without disabilities). They also need to be contributing members of the community— for example, by participating in activities that are of interest to them. Thus, mentors from the community or school who share the same interests as the students with autism may help them develop their interests into employable skills. Briefly, in order for students to learn the skills necessary for a successful adult life, schools must provide a comprehensive program that includes academic support, as well as community-based education focused on employment, independent living, social skills, and life skills. Examples of how such a program may be implemented through the school years are provided below.

Academic Support

It is important for students with disabilities to have opportunities to play with nondisabled peers and to have age-appropriate responsibilities. During the preschool years, typical students begin to develop awareness of roles and responsibilities by observing others at work and by playing. Students with autism may not be aware of others or participate in typical play that imitates adult work behavior. As a result, teachers may need to draw to their attention to adults and children doing domestic chores and professional work in their environments. Further, peer social groups could assist them in learning and rehearsing appropriate skills.

In the elementary and junior high school years, students with autism should be taught good work habits and interpersonal skills while they increase their social skills and career awareness. In later school years, areas of special interest to the person with autism can be broadened and molded into employable skills while the ability to live independently is acquired. Program planning and goals need to be flexible to meet the changing abilities and needs of the student with autism.

Community-Based Instruction

Given the intent of transition, a shift from traditional classroom-based education to community-based activities is essential. Community-based instruction provides opportunities for students to practice the skills they have learned in school in the settings in which the skills are naturally required. For students with autism, for whom generalization is often a problem, the opportunity to carry out life skills in the community helps them understand how the skills pertain to their own lives and futures.

Students must realize their potential and be encouraged to work to attain their goals. Finding success in community work experiences, for example, may encourage some students to go on for further training or education after high school graduation. Whatever course of action a student decides to pursue after high school will be smoother if the foundation has been established during school. For example, connections with adult agencies should be made while the student is still in school so that the adult service provider has adequate time to develop a plan of action, thereby avoiding a breakdown in services.

Paid Work Experiences

Paid work experience offers students the opportunities obtain employment during school with support from school personnel and to maintain employment after graduation. Not only does this provide a monetary incentive, but it also enables the student to experiment with a variety of occupations and see first-hand what different jobs entail. In addition, paid work experience allows opportunities for developing relationships and friendships within the community, thereby allowing students with autism to become an integral part of their community. These various work experiences provide a repertoire of skills for the student to present to future employers. It will be greatly beneficial to the student leaving high school to have a portfolio of successful work experiences to share with prospective employers. Paid work experiences also provide the student with spending money that will permit a more fulfilled lifestyle. In addition, paid work experiences during school offer the perfect opportunity for the school to teach skills in budgeting, banking, and comparison shopping.

Because individuals with autism frequently have difficulty generalizing skills learned in a simulated environment, opportunities to participate in a "place-train" model of supported employment is often more successful than more traditional approaches. The place-train model teaches essential work behavior in the natural setting: the actual job. Rather than waiting until the student has learned the required behaviors in a setting that is not motivating, individuals with disabilities have had success learning these skills at the paying job site (Wehman & Moon, 1988).

Functional Curriculum Approach

Although different goals are developed depending upon the individual student's needs and capabilities, a functional curriculum approach could be followed for all students. Functional curriculum for students with more severe disability might entail learning basic daily living skills, such as brushing teeth and dressing independently. Students with high-functioning autism might learn to plan a budget, complete job applications, and use a checking account. Finally, others might be planning to attend college and consequently need to learn how to complete applications and follow deadlines for turning in assignments. The key to success for the functional curriculum is that the instruction takes place in the actual environments in which the skills will be used.

No matter what outcomes have been chosen by a given student, successful transition from school to adult life requires effective planning, appropriate school experiences, and established connections with postschool resources, such as (a) adult service providers (e.g., vocational rehabilitation, independent living centers, and special transportation agencies), (b) vocational/technical school or college representatives (e.g., student service coordinators), and (c) community resources (e.g., recreational facilities, churches, and other organizations).

Developing the Transition-Related IEP

After careful analysis of the results of the transition assessment with input from the student, family, school personnel, rehabilitation counselor, adult service providers, and interested community members, it is time to develop the IEP to ensure that the school will provide the appropriate programs and services to meet the needs of the individual student. This process is quite similar across students regardless of age or level of disability.

The cornerstone of successful transition services begins with the transition planning process, which occurs in the context of the development and implementation of the IEP. In order to accomplish this, the IEP team must consider the needs, interests, and preferences of the student. All members, as stated earlier, should participate, with the student as the facilitator whenever possible, and the parents being equal partners in the process with the school and adult service agency members. Goals and objectives should be related to transition so that they are relevant to the particular student and to the real world. IEP goals should reflect functional curriculum and vocational and life skills. Community-based instruction will be appropriate for some students. At all times, the individual student must be kept in mind and a transition program must be developed that meets the student's specific needs.

Summary

The student and his or her family are the driving force behind creating a vision for the future.

- What goals and dreams does the student have?
- What steps need to be taken to achieve these goals?
- What school programs are needed to enable the student to attain this vision?
- What are the student's strengths and interests that could be directed into an employable skill?

These are all important questions. The student must assume responsibility for important life decisions and must gain a sense of empowerment with respect to transition planning. Long-range outcomes must be identified and goals and objectives developed to enable the student to reach those outcomes. Goals should be outcome driven and reflect the individual student's vision and capabilities. Further, responsibilities must be identified for all parties involved. Delivery of transition services must ensure that the instructional program is based on student needs, preferences, and interests, and that the student is included within the regular school program with community-based learning opportunities provided.

Ongoing evaluation of the transition planning process allows all parties involved to monitor the student's progress and reconvene as needed. Changes will be made. Typically, as the student gets older, new visions and dreams emerge and goals are modified accordingly. This is how life is for most of us—changes occur and adjustments must be made to deal with them. Young adults with autism can cope with the many transitions they will face if they have a strong sense of self-determination and an understanding of their capabilities. Transition planning helps allow the students develop both of these qualities and acquire the skills needed to reach their vision.

References

Americans with Disabilities Act of 1990, 42 U.S.C. § 12101 *et seq.*

Brolin, D. E. (1992). *Life centered career education (LCCE) knowledge and performance batteries.* Reston, VA: Council for Exceptional Children.

Clark, G. M. (1995). *Transition planning assessment for students with learning disabilities.* Paper presented at the PRO-ED symposium on Transition for Students with Learning Disabilities, University of Kansas.

Clark, G. M., Carlson, B., Fisher, S., Cook, I., & D'Alonzo, B. (1991). Career development for students with disabilities in elementary schools: A position statement of the Division on Career Development. *Career Development for Exceptional Individuals, 14*(2), 110–120.

Donnelly, J. A. (1996, September). *Jobs we've lost and ones we've kept.* Panel of individuals with autism presented at the MAAPing the Future Conference, Chicago.

Donnelly, J. A., & Levy, S. M. (1995, July). *Strategies for assisting individuals with high-functioning autism and/or Asperger's.* Paper presented at the annual meeting of the Autism Society of America, Greensboro, NC.

Edgar, E. (1987). Secondary programs in special education: Are many of them justifiable? *Exceptional Children, 53,* 555–561.

Edgar, E., (1988). Transition from school to community. *Teaching Exceptional Children, 20*(2), 73–75.

Education for All Handicapped Children Act of 1975, 20 U.S.C. § 1400 *et seq.*

Enderle, J., & Severson, S. (1991). *Enderle-Severson transition rating scale.* Moorehead, MN: Practical Press.

Fullerton, A. (1993). *Development of a life decisions strategies curriculum to promote self-determination.* Unpublished manuscript, Portland State University.

Halpern, A. S. (1985). Transition: A look at the foundations. *Exceptional Children, 51,* 479–486.

Halpern, A. S. (1992). Transition: Old wine in new bottles. *Exceptional Children, 58,* 202–211.

Halpern, A. S. (1994). The transition of youth with disabilities to adult life: A position statement of the Division on Career Development and Transition, the Council for Exceptional Children. *Career Development for Exceptional Individuals, 17*(2), 115–124.

Hasazi, S. B., Gordon, L. R., & Roe, C. A. (1985). Factors associated with the employment status of handicapped youth exiting high school from 1979 to 1983. *Exceptional Children, 51,* 455–469.

Individuals with Disabilities Education Act of 1990, 20, U.S.C. § 1400 *et seq.*

Individuals with Disabilities Education Act Amendments of 1977.

Kanner, L., Rodriguez, A., & Ashenden, B. (1972). How far can autistic children go in matters of social adaptation? *Journal of Autism and Childhood Schizophrenia, 9,* 9–33.

Kauffman, J. M. (1977). *Characteristics of children's behavior disorders.* Columbus, OH: Merrill.

Lord, C., & Venter, A. (1992). Outcome and follow-up studies of high-functioning autistic individuals. In E. Schopler & G. B. Mesibov (Eds.), *High-functioning individuals with autism,* (pp. 187–200). New York: Plenum.

Louis Harris and Associates, Inc. (1987). *The ICD survey of disabled Americans: Bringing disabled Americans into the mainstream.* New York: International Center for the Disabled.

McCarney, S. B. (1989). *Transition behavior scale.* Columbia, MO: Hawthorne Educational Service.

Mesibov, G. B., Schopler, E., Schaffer, B., & Landrus, R. (1988). *Adolescent and adult psychoeducational profile.* Austin, TX: PRO-ED.

Newson, E., Dawson, M., & Everard, P. (1982). *The natural history of able autistic people: Their management and functioning in social context.* Nottingham, England: University of Nottingham, Child Development Research Unit.

Okolo, C., & Sitlington, P. (1988). Mildly handicapped learners in vocational education: A statewide study. *Journal of Special Education, 22,* 220–230.

Patton, J. R., & Clark, G. M. (1996). *Transition planning inventory.* Austin, TX: PRO-ED.

Rehabilitation Act of 1973, 29 U.S.C. § 701 *et seq.*

Rehabilitation Act Amendments of 1992, 29 U.S.C. § 701.

Repetto, J. B., & Correa, V. I. (1996). Expanding views on transition. *Exceptional Children, 62,* 551–563.

Rumsey, J. M., Rapoport, M. D., & Sceery, W. R. (1985). Autistic children as adults: Psychiatric, social and behavioral outcomes. *Journal of the American Academy of Child Psychiatry, 24,* 465–473.

Rutter, M., & Schopler, E. (1988). Autism and pervasive developmental disorders: Concepts and diagnostic issues. In E. Schopler & G. B. Mesibov (Eds.), *Diagnosis and assessment in autism* (pp. 15–36). New York: Plenum.

School to Work Opportunities Act of 1994, 20 U.S.C. § 6101 *et seq.*

Smith, M. D., Belcher, R. G., & Juhrs, P. D. (1996). *A guide to successful employment for individuals with autism.* Baltimore: Brookes.

Suomi, J., Ruble, L., & Dalrymple, N. (1992). *Let community employment be the goal for individuals with autism.* Bloomington: Indiana Resource Center for Autism.

Szatmari, P., Bartolucci, G., Bremner, R. S., Bond, S., & Rich, S. (1989). A follow-up study of high-functioning autistic children. *Journal of Autism and Developmental Disorders, 19,* 213–226.

Szymanski, E. M. (1994). Transition: Life-span and life-space considerations for employment. *Exceptional Children, 60,* 402–410.

U.S. Department of Education. (1994). *Sixteenth annual report to Congress on achieving better results for children and youth with serious emotional disturbance.* Washington, DC: U.S. Government Printing Office.

Vandercook, T., & York, J. (1989). The McGill Action Planning System (M.A.P.S.): A strategy for building vision. *Journal of the Association for the Severely Handicapped, 14,* 205–215.

Vocational Education Act of 1963, 26 U.S.C. § 5.

Vocational Education Act Amendments of 1968, U.S.C. § 2310.

Wagner, M. (1989, March). *The transition experiences of youth with disabilities: A report from the National Longitudinal Transition Study.* Paper presented at the annual meeting of the Division of Research, Council for Exceptional Children, San Francisco.

Wehman, P. (1992). *Life beyond the classroom: Transition strategies for young people with disabilities.* Baltimore: Brookes.

Wehman, P. (1993). Natural supports: More questions than answers? *Journal of Vocational Rehabilitation, 3,* 1–3.

Wehman, P., & Moon, M. S. (1988). *Vocational rehabilitation and supported employment.* Baltimore: Brookes.

Will, M. (1984). *OSERS programming for the transition of youth with disabilities: Bridges from school to working life.* Washington DC: U.S. Department of Education, Office of Special Education and Rehabilitative Services.

Wing, L. (1996). *The autistic spectrum.* London: Constable.

Zigmond, N., & Thornton, H. (1985). Follow-up of postsecondary age learning disabled graduates and dropouts. *Learning Disabilities Research, 1,* 50–55.

Medical Interventions for Students with Autism

10

Luke Y. Tsai

Whereas previous chapters have primarily addressed clinical and educational features and interventions of autism, the focus of the present chapter is medical intervention. The chapter is written for parents and professionals to help them to understand when and how medications can be used as part of a comprehensive intervention with children and youth with autism. Specifically, this chapter concentrates on autistic disorder, Pervasive Developmental Disorder Not Otherwise Specified (PDDNOS)/atypical autism, and Asperger Syndrome because they share many clinical features and interventions. The term *autism spectrum disorder* (ASD) is used to cover the three subtypes of Pervasive Developmental Disorders (PDDs).

Although both behavioral and biological studies have generated sufficient evidence suggesting neurobiologic etiologies of ASD, at present no specific biological markers have been identified. In the absence of a complete understanding of the causes of ASD, attempts at intervention have been haphazard and poorly organized. To date, no single intervention modality has been shown to be effective in *curing* any of the subtypes of ASD. However, as discussed elsewhere in this book, a comprehensive nonmedical approach comprising parental counseling, behavior modification, and special education in a highly structured environment has demonstrated significant treatment effects in many individuals with ASD. Parents and others who work with students with ASD rarely have any grave concern about this type of intervention approach. However, they often feel uneasy about medical intervention, particularly medication treatment (pharmacotherapy) for their children/students. In the eyes of many parents and other caretakers, medication therapy is a treatment of last resort, to be used only when other types of intervention have yielded only very limited results. Such feelings, no doubt, stem from past abuses of psycho-tropic medications in persons with developmental disabilities.

Despite such parental reaction, solid evidence shows that certain medica-tions are effective as a first-line treatment of some neuropsychiatric disorders (e.g., depression, obsessive-compulsive disorders, tic disorders, etc.) that may develop in some students with ASD. Effective treatment of additional neuro-psychiatric disorders ameliorates the psychiatric or behavioral symptoms that interfere with students' abilities to participate in educational, social, work, and family systems, and also enhances their positive response to other forms of intervention. Like most drugs, psychotherapeutic medications correct or compensate for some malfunction in the body. They do not cure ASD, but they do lessen its symptoms.

The primary aim of medical intervention of children and youth with ASD is to ensure their physical and psychological health. To accomplish this goal, preventive medical care is crucial. In general, a good preventive health care system should include scheduling regular physical check-ups to monitor phys-ical growth and development, vision, hearing, and blood pressure; administer-ing immunization according to schedule; arranging regular visits to the den-tist; and paying attention to diet and hygiene.

The secondary aim of medical intervention of students with ASD is early detection and treatment of various behavior problems, including sleep and eat-ing problems. These problematic behaviors may be clinical manifestations of coexisting neuropsychiatric disorders or medical/dental conditions associated with ASD. In any case, effective treatment will significantly improve the qual-ity of these students' lives.

To be effective, the medical intervention should be driven by a multidisci-plinary treatment plan that integrates the perspectives and recommendations of medical physicians (developmental neurologist, developmental/behavioral pedia-trician, or psychiatrist), psychologists, special education teachers, speech and lan-guage pathologists, occupational and physical therapists, and parents. Further, medication should be prescribed and managed by a specialized physician work-ing closely with the student, the student's family, and other professionals.

Assessment

Baseline Medical Assessment

Effective medical intervention begins with a thorough medical assessment, including a comprehensive physical and neurological examination, extensive neurochemical assessments, and an intensive speech and language assess-ment. The pretreatment assessment is essential for detecting many medical conditions such as seizure disorder, meningitis, lead poisoning, brain tumors, endocrinological disorders, and chromosomal abnormalities that can cause or exacerbate behavioral, emotional, or cognitive problems. The pretreatment assessment is also essential for establishing the baseline physical status prior to medication therapy.

Physical and Neurological Examinations

A responsible physician should perform a physical examination and collect other information by using behavioral/developmental rating scales, as well as directly and carefully observing the student. Particular attention should be paid to vocal and motor tics before the initiation of stimulants. Symptoms of tardive dyskinesia such as lip licking, tongue thrusting, and puffing or pouting of the lips must be taken into account when neuroleptics are being considered.

Biochemical Assessment

Other information should be collected by using various tests such as electro-encephalogram (EEG; e.g., to evaluate seizure disorders); electrocardiogram (EKG; e.g., to monitor side effects caused by antidepressants); and neuroradi-ological imaging (e.g., to evaluate medication treatment effects). Other laboratory tests, when appropriate, include

- chromosome studies;
- amino acid screening on blood and urine;
- thyroid function tests (e.g., for diagnostic evaluation of depression or for monitoring lithium side effects);
- liver function tests (e.g., for monitoring side effects caused by pemoline);
- viral antibodies;
- blood lead levels; and
- complete blood count (CBC) and differential blood count (e.g., for monitoring side effects caused by neuroleptics).

In addition, simple measures such as recording standing and supine blood pressure, pulse, height, and weight (e.g., weight loss caused by stimulant and weight gain caused by neuroleptics) should not be ignored.

Complete documentation of present illness, past medical history (including immunizations and hospitalizations), medical review of body systems (e.g., nerve system, endocrine system), history of allergies, other prescribed or illicit drug or alcohol use, and family neuropsychiatric history should also be collected. Finally, it should be emphasized that assessment procedures are continuous throughout the course of the treatment.

Speech and Language Assessment

Psychotherapeutic medications and anticonvulsants may alter speech and language development and/or performance (e.g., neuroleptics, stimulants, and tricyclic antidepressants can alter speech production, rate, volume, and coherence). As a result, it is important that baseline speech and language assessment be carried out by a qualified and experienced speech pathologist.

Problems Encountered During Medical Assessment

In some students with ASD, administering these assessments can be a challenge. For example, because of their rather low cognitive and communicative functioning, it may be impossible to explain the examination procedure to them. Also, some students with ASD may resist any physical contact and may even react violently to the usual examination procedure. The assistance of a parent or therapist who is familiar with the student's behavior patterns and means of communication can be most helpful. Further, sometimes the physician will have to determine how many assessment procedures are essential rather than doggedly following the standard examination procedure (Dalldorf, 1983).

General Approaches to Pharmacotherapy

Pharmacotherapy begins with establishing a relationship between behavioral abnormalities (i.e., symptoms) and underlying biochemical abnormalities (e.g., certain neurotransmitters' depletion). The goal of pharmacotherapy is to correct both of these with an effective chemical agent (i.e., medication).

Based on contemporary definition and classification systems, ASD is viewed as heterogeneous both behaviorally and biochemically (Tsai & Ghaziuddin, 1996). Until the cause–effect relationship in ASD becomes clear, the aim of pharmacotherapy of ASD will be to effectively control symptoms or behavioral problems. To achieve this goal, it is essential to learn about the basic principles of pharmacotherapy; the workup for use of various medications; the basic categories of medications, their indications, contraindications, and side effect profiles; and measuring medication effects. These topics are addressed in this chapter with particular reference to individuals with autism.

Basic Principles of Pharmacotherapy

1. Medication treatment must be based upon a sound diagnosis. In this connection, it should be kept in mind that students with autism may develop the full range of neuropsychiatric disorders. Therefore, when the symptom/behavior reflects an underlying organic brain syndrome/neurological disorder (e.g.,

Tourette syndrome), medication selection must be based on the presence of *specific* types of psychopathology (e.g., motor tics).

2. Medication treatment should be reserved for individuals with severe symptoms after the forms of nonmedical intervention have proven ineffective. A complete functional behavioral analysis must be carried out by a qualified and experienced behavioral therapist before initiation of a psychotherapeutic medication. The medication should be used to alter specific symptoms and should be carefully evaluated for these effects using reliable measures, described in the next section. This approach will provide a realistic expectation of the extent to which the chosen medication will be effective.

3. Medication should never be used as the sole intervention, but only as part of a comprehensive intervention program that includes psychosocial, behavioral, and special education interventions. Without additional therapy, the improvement associated with the medication usually disappears after the medication is discontinued.

4. Children differ significantly from adults in their pharmacokinetic capacities due to their relatively large liver size in proportion to body weight. Hence, children tend to need higher doses relative to body weight than do adults. On the other hand, children usually have less connecting tissue (adipose) and less protein binding than adults and, therefore, may have more medication available for bioactivity and, potentially, more side effects (Rapoport & Mikkelsen, 1978).

5. Appropriate medication selection requires comprehensive information about the individual, including current functioning, family history, and medical history. It is crucial that the parents or caretakers maintain an up-to-date medical record because the prescribing physician needs to know whether the individual has seizures, which medications were previously used and what responses they produced, and which medications the individual is currently taking. Many medications may lower the threshold for seizure or may interact with anticonvulsants to either potentiate or diminish their individual effectiveness.

6. Students should be involved in the treatment process as much as possible, regardless of age and level of functioning. Consequently, every effort should be made to help the student understand the reason and purpose for taking the medication(s). Sensitive counseling can help overcome any fears of taking medication that the child may have and prevent students from developing negative attitudes toward or misperception regarding the use of medication. Instead, the student becomes a useful and helpful ally in the intervention.

7. The student's family or responsible care provider (e.g., school or residential group home) must also be included in the process. Their attitude toward the use of medication and their ability to work with the physician and the student is extremely important for the success of the intervention. A parent or caretaker is a necessary source of information about the individual's functioning and response to medication. The parent or caretaker needs to be informed about the reasons for medication therapy, the likely therapeutic effects, side effects, and so forth.

8. During the initial phases of medication therapy, the individual should be seen at least once a week. Once he or she has been stabilized, usually after several weeks, a medication maintenance program can begin. Individuals can then be seen less frequently, such as monthly or bimonthly, to review therapeutic response and development of side effects.

9. In general, if an individual has not responded to a medication within 4 weeks while in the therapeutic range, it is unlikely that he or she will respond at a later date. When therapeutic response is demonstrated, medication treatment should proceed at optimal dosage for periods of at least 1 to 2 months. Moreover, a medication holiday should be planned to permit evaluation of the need for continued treatment as well as assessment of the development of side effects, such as growth changes or development of dyskinesias (impairment of voluntary movements resulting in jerky motions).

10. Placebo effects often exist and should be weighed carefully to determine whether the medication should be confirmed. The placebo effect can be produced by the individual taking the medication, the family members, or the caretakers, including the prescribing physician. Therapeutic gains need to be weighed carefully against side effects, and all efforts must be made to minimize risks to the individual.

Measures of Medication Effects

Like any other type of medication, psychotherapeutic medications do not produce the same effect in everyone. Some people respond better to one medication than another. Some need larger dosages than others. Age, sex, body size, body chemistry, habits, and diet are some of the factors that can influence a medication's effect.

To determine the optimal dosage, many researchers and clinicians prefer to titrate dosage for each patient. Usually, this entails starting with a low dosage and raising it by standardized increments every 3 or 5 days until the "optimal" clinical effect is seen or the therapeutic range is reached, or until the side effects begin to interfere with desired changes. Others prefer to employ standardized doses based on the subject's body weight. Certain medications can be measured in the blood to guide their clinical use. However, there is disagreement in the research literature as to whether there is a clear relationship between medication concentration in the blood and clinical response to that medication (Curry, 1978). Another concern with regard to the use of blood level is the lack of agreement on the clinically useful range of blood concentration indicative of therapeutic change. Nonetheless, measurement of blood levels may provide a medication index that can be related to changes in specific behaviors in order to prevent serious side effects and to identify nonresponders.

Dosage regulation of any medication depends on reliable measurement of changes or improvements of targeted behaviors. However, this is not always easily achievable in students with autism, many of whom are unable to accurately report their symptoms or their response to treatment. Furthermore, a positive treatment effect may be a decrease in the frequency or severity of long-standing maladaptive behavior, which may not be readily apparent in the clinician's office. Therefore, measurement of treatment response must rely on objective techniques that are *reliable* (i.e., repeatable over time or across observers) and *valid* (i.e., reflective of what is actually being measured) for data collection by caretakers.

Various measurement techniques can be employed. These techniques include global impression, direct behavioral observations, behavioral rating scales, self-reports, standardized tests, learning and performance measures, mechanical movement monitors, and monitoring of other drug effects. Finally, it is crucial that the assessment strategies be sensitive to changes produced by the medication and are practical, economic, safe, and ethical.

1. *Global impression*—An individual's overall behavior is judged by global impression. This is the most frequently used but least reliable method of evaluating medication efficacy because it fails to capture day-to-day variability and cannot be replicated across time or clinicians. *Clinical Global Impressions* (Campbell & Palij, 1985) and *Nurse's Global Impression* (Campbell et al., 1978) are examples of scales that have been used.

2. *Direct behavioral observations*—Behavior is recorded as it occurs, with frequent reliability checks; assessment results are often graphed to aid interpretation. This type of assessment can be carried out either in an artificial situation (e.g., a child taking an intelligence test) or in a natural situation (e.g., a child's home or classroom). The major limitation with this procedure is that it is expensive in terms of staff time.

3. *Behavioral rating scales*—These are generally problem-oriented checklists completed by parents or caretakers who are familiar with the student taking medication. It is a quick, efficient, inexpensive, and practical procedure used in almost all clinical settings. Many rating scales have established reliability, validity, and sensitivity to medication changes; for example, Conners' (1976) checklist and the *Ritvo-Freeman Real Life Rating Scale for Autism* (Freeman, Ritvo, Yokota, & Ritvo, 1986).

4. *Self-reports*—This procedure has a limited application in the population with autism due to general difficulties in cognitive and communicative functioning. In addition, self-report tends to have low agreement with other forms of evaluation of a given behavior.

5. *Standardized tests*—All the standardized clinical tests such as intelligence tests, school-achievement tests, language and speech tests, and specific psychological tests (e.g., visual–motor integration test) have been used to assess medication efficacy. However, these tests are generally insensitive to behavioral changes produced by medications.

6. *Learning and performance measures*—These include assessments of short-term memory, task completion, and rate of performance before and after administration of certain medication. Such measurements are appropriate for

short-term medication trials. For long-term studies, standardized intelligence tests may be used.

7. *Mechanical monitors*—These devices (e.g., computerized activity monitor and videotapes) are used primarily to measure the changes of functions and activities of the autonomic nervous system (governs involuntary actions such as secretion) caused by certain medication. However, most devices are presently too cumbersome and expensive for routine clinical use.

8. *Monitoring of other drug effects*—Periodic laboratory screening should be done on a regular basis during the entire duration of medication therapy. For example, it is judicious practice to repeat complete blood count (CBC) and differential, urinalysis, and basic chemistry screening at 3 months and every 6 months for each medication. Blood pressure and pulse rate should be checked weekly. Serial EKG should take place whenever medication with significant cardiovascular effects is prescribed. Finally, weight and height should be recorded on a monthly or quarterly basis.

Side Effects of Pharmacotherapy

Psychotherapeutic medications and anticonvulsants do not produce the same side effects in everyone. Some people experience annoying side effects, while others do not. Many of the side effects of psychotherapeutic medications and anticonvulsants seen in adult patients can also be seen in children and adolescents.

Possible side effects of tricyclic antidepressants include short-term anticholinergic (constipation, tremors, sweating, insomnia, irritability) and cardiovascular (tachycardia, hypotension, arrhythmias) effects. Possible side effects of neuroleptics include cognitive effects (e.g., cognitive blunting), extrapyramidal effects (e.g., acute dystonia, dyskinesia), Parkinsonian reactions (e.g, akathisia, rabbit syndrome), and long-term abnormal involuntary movements (e.g., tardive dyskinesia, withdrawal dyskinesia). Also, many medications have effects on height, weight, blood counts, and liver function. In addition, due to cognitive and communicative impairments, students with ASD often become frightened or suspicious if a sudden change or dysfunction occurs following the administration of medication(s). Such feelings, in turn, may trigger tantrums or interfere with compliance.

It is important to alert and educate parents and caretakers to the potential side effects of the chosen medication as well as the therapeutic benefits. When a psychotherapeutic medication or anticonvulsant is prescribed, the student, the student's family members, and other caretakers should ask the following questions, which have been recommended by the U.S. Food and Drug Administration (FDA).

- What is the name of the medication, and what is it supposed to do?

- How and when should it be taken and stopped being taken?

- What foods, drinks, other medications, or activities should one avoid while taking the prescribed medication?
- What are the side effects and what should one do if they occur?
- Is there any written information available about the medication?

Prevention of Side Effects

The clinician must be knowledgeable about the full range of potential side effects of the medication(s) being prescribed and know how to manage any side effect that might arise. Nevertheless, the best approach to managing adverse effects is prevention. The following are general guidelines for avoiding possible side effects:

1. Obtain a complete family history, including medication treatments and responses and a complete medical history of the patient (including responses to previous medication treatment).
2. Begin treatment with *one* medication.
3. Avoid giving any medication that has resulted in previous side effects in the individual.
4. Avoid giving *preventive* anti-side-effect medication such as an anti-parkinsonian agent.
5. If the patient does not respond to the medication of first choice, discontinue it gradually while a second medication is instituted and its dosage is increased.
6. Use the lowest possible maintenance doses in the therapeutic range once dosage has been established.
7. Regularly monitor the blood level of the medication, blood counts, blood pressure, pulse rate, EKG, liver function, height, and weight.
8. Regularly perform a complete physical and neurological examination and monitor side effects using published side effects rating scales such as the *Dosage Record and Treatment Emergent Symptoms Scale* (DOTES; Guy, 1976b), *Abnormal Involuntary Movement Scale* (AIMS; Guy, 1976a), and *NIMH Systematic Assessment for Treatment Emergent Events* (SAFTEE-GI; Campbell & Palij, 1985).
9. Give periodic drug holidays at least once every 6 months.
10. In most cases, taper and withdraw medications gradually.

Classes of Commonly Used Medications in ASD

It is important for persons who use both medical and mental health services to be well informed about medications for neuropsychiatric disorders. The following section briefly describes classification, indication of use, and common side effects of some commonly used medications in ASD.

Neuroleptics

Description

Neuroleptics, or tranquilizers, include six major classes: (a) phenothiazines (e.g., chlorpromazine or Thorazine; thioridazine or Mellaril), (b) thioxanthenes, (c) butyrophenones (e.g., haloperidol or Haldol), (d) dihydro-indolones, (e) dibenzoxazepines, and (f) diphenylbutylpiperidines (pimozide or Orap). In adults, neuroleptics are prescribed almost exclusively for treatment of schizophrenia and other psychoses. In children, neuroleptics are used less specifically, and agreement over indications for the use of neuroleptics in children is not uniform (Rutter, 1985). They have been used in reducing hyperactivity, stereotypies, tics, and aggressiveness. Low-potency neuroleptics, such as chlorpromazine, have little, if any, therapeutic effect because they yield excessive sedation, even at low doses. On the other hand, haloperidol, a high-potency neuroleptic, has demonstrated both short-term and long-term efficacy.

Side Effects

Side effects of neuroleptics include excessive sedation, acute dystonic reactions (i.e., abrupt, frightening muscular contractions usually involving the head and neck and causing oculogyric crises, facial grimacing, torticollis, opisthotonos, and speech and swallowing difficulties); Parkinson-like movements (i.e. tremor, cogwheel rigidity, excessive salivation, masklike face, and stiffness of voluntary movement); akathisia (i.e., motor restlessness); weight gain; withdrawal dyskinesia; and tardive dyskinesia. Symptoms of dyskinesia include slow involuntary movements of facial, buccal, and lingual muscles, and choreoathetoid movements of the trunk, limbs, or facial muscles. Withdrawal dyskinesia usually occurs within 2 weeks of haloperidol or other neuroleptic withdrawal and lasts for 4 months or less (Polizos & Engelhardt, 1978). Tardive dyskinesia may be permanent; currently no satisfactory treatment is available.

Stimulants

Description

Stimulants including dextroamphetamine (Dexedrine), methylphenidate (Ritalin), and magnesium pemoline (Cylert) have gained widespread usage in treating children with behavior disturbances. For example, it is now generally accepted that stimulants are efficacious in decreasing restless, impulsive behaviors and in improving attention span. However, stimulants have demonstrated relatively little effect on academic achievement and interpersonal functioning.

Although a sizable number of studies of the stimulants in children with hyperactivity/behavior disorder have been published from many medical centers, the effects of stimulants have not been extensively studied in individuals with ASD. Campbell et al. (1976) found that stimulants had only a mildly positive effect on improving attention, but showed clinically and statistically significant increases in stereotypic behavior in children with autism. Aman (1982) reviewed stimulant effects in developmental disorders, concluding that there is no role for the use of stimulants in children with autism. These studies included mostly lower functioning children with autism.

There are now many anecdotal reports of positive effects of stimulants in certain children with autism, particularly those who are higher functioning. I have prescribed methylphenidate to several higher functioning children with autism who have all responded positively. In summary, stimulants may be considered in a higher functioning child with autism who does not have seizure or other neurological disorders, but in whom short attention span, distractibility, impulsivity, and excitability are significant symptoms.

Side Effects

Short-term side effects of stimulants include decreased appetite, insomnia, anxiousness, irritability, proneness to crying, stomachaches, and headaches. Most of the side effects are of mild severity and diminish within 1 to 2 weeks after beginning the medication. All short-term side effects disappear upon ceasing stimulant treatment. A number of follow-up studies have not found any significant long-term side effects caused by stimulants.

Although it is not clear whether stimulants cause tic disorders, including Tourette syndrome, stimulants may exacerbate symptoms in patients who already exhibit tic disorders. If children without prior history of tic disorders develop tics during stimulant treatment, the stimulant should be discontinued immediately. The tics usually subside within 7 to 10 days. If treatment of attention-deficit/hyperactivity disorder (ADHD) is still needed, an alternative medication such as an antidepressant should be used.

Antidepressants

Description

There are two major classes of antidepressants: the monoamine oxidase inhibitors (MAOIs) and the tricyclics. No solid evidence has been found of MAOIs' therapeutic efficacy or of their safety in children (for a review, see Annell, 1972). The tricyclic antidepressants such as amitriptyline (Elavil), imipramine (Tofranil), desipramine (Norpramin), and nortriptyline (Pamelor) presumably act on the central nervous system (CNS) by inhibiting the update of neuro-transmitters at adrenergic nerve terminals, resulting in an increase of mono-amine neurotransmission. Imipramine (Tofranil) is the tricyclic most frequently used in children. A correlation between response and plasma concentration has been demonstrated in certain psychiatric disorders. Studies in children with behavior disorders show that clinical response roughly parallels the plasma level (Winsberg, Yepes, & Bialer, 1976). Tricyclics, specifically imiprimaine, have been shown to be effective in enuresis (Rapoport et al., 1980), in ADHD (Werry, Aman, & Diamond, 1980), and in school phobia (Gittleman-Klein & Klein, 1971). Onset of clinical response varies with the condition treated. In the treatment of enuresis, for example, an effect can be seen within hours to a few days, whereas in school phobia, a response may not be apparent for 3 to 6 weeks.

Side Effects

Side effects of tricyclics include dry mouth, nausea, anorexia, constipation, lethargy, tremors, sweating, insomnia, irritability, rapid heartbeat, irregular heartbeat, and hypotension. When tricyclics are used with amphetamines, hypertensive crises may develop (Kupfer & Detre, 1978). When tricyclics are used with Ritalin, serum level of the tricyclic may increase (Rapoport & Mikkelsen, 1978).

Trazodone (Desyrel) is an antidepressant that is chemically unrelated to other antidepressants. Although its efficacy in the treatment of depression in children and adolescents has not been investigated, it has been recommended for treatment of sleep disturbance and aggression in persons with developmental disabilities (Gualtieri, 1991). Common side effects of trazodone include drowsiness, dizziness/lightheadedness, dry mouth, blurred vision, fatigue, headache, nervousness, nausea/vomiting, and constipation. One potentially serious side effect of trazodone is priapism (prolonged penile erection), which may require surgical treatment.

In recent years, several nontricyclic antidepressants (e.g., fluoexetine [Prozac], sertraline [Zoloft], paroxetine [Paxil], and fluvoxamine [Luvox]) have been introduced in the United States. These medications are serotonin reuptake inhibitors (SRIs) and appear to be as effective as tricyclic antidepressants for treatment of depression in adults. Some reports suggest that some SRIs (e.g., Prozac, Luvox, and Zoloft) are effective in decreasing symptoms of obsessive-compulsive disorder (OCD; Cook, Rowlett, Jaselskis, & Leventhal, 1992; Fontaine & Chouinard, 1986) and Tourette syndrome (Riddle, Hardin, King, Scahill, & Woolson, 1990).

Common adverse effects of SRIs include nausea, nervousness, headache, insomnia, dry mouth, constipation, urinary retention, and urticaria or other skin rash. However, fluoxetin rarely precipitates seizures in patients with convulsive disorders.

Another recently approved antidepressant, bupropion (Wellbutrin), is chemically unrelated to the other antidepressants. Its use in individuals with ASD has not been studied.

Tricyclic Antiobsessional Antidepressants

Description

Clomipramine (CMI or Anafranil) is an antiobsessional medication that belongs to the class of tricyclic antidepressants. It is presumed to influence obsessive and compulsive behaviors through its effects on serotonergic neuronal transmission due to its relatively selective capacity to inhibit the reuptake of serotonin (DeVeaugh-Geiss, Landau, & Katz, 1989; Gordon, State, Nelson, Hamburger, & Rapoport, 1993; Leonard et al., 1989).

Side Effects

The most common side effects of CMI are dry mouth, somnolence, tremors, dizziness, constipation, and ejaculatory failure. Lowering the dosage often reduces side effects when these occur, usually without loss of therapeutic benefit. CMI may lower seizure threshold.

Antianxiety Medications

Description

A number of antianxiety medications are currently available. The preferred medications for most anxiety disorders are the benzodiazepines such as alprazolam (Xanax), diazepam (Valium), chlordiazepoxide (Librium or Librax), and lorazepam (Ativan). A nonbenzodiazepine, buspirone (BuSpar), has also been used for generalized anxiety disorders.

Side Effects

Side effects include drowsiness, loss of coordination, fatigue, and mental slowing or confusion. Other side effects are rare. With benzodiazepines, there is a potential for development of tolerance and dependence as well as the possibility of abuse and withdraw reactions.

Opiate Antagonists

Naltrexone, an opiate antagonist, has been reported to have positive effects on hyperactivity, social relatedness, and self-injury (Campbell et al., 1993; Campbell,

Cohen, Perry, & Small, 1989; Kolmen, Feldman, Handen, & Janosky, 1995). However, other investigators have not found such effects (Gillberg, 1995; Zingarelli et al., 1992). Nevertheless, naltrexone merits further study in a larger sample of subjects using a double-blind and placebo-controlled research design.

Sedatives

Description

The sedative-hypnotic group of medications such as benzodiazepines (diazepam or Valium) and diphenhydramine (Benadryl) has been studied for its effectiveness in a variety of childhood conditions, including aggressiveness, hyperactivity, behavior disturbances, and anxiety disorder. In general, these medications have been found to be no better than placebo or psychotherapy without medication. However, they seem to have a role in the treatment of sleep disorders in children.

Side Effects

Side effects of the sedatives include CNS depression, drowsiness, and dizziness. In addition, there have also been reports of "paradoxical" aggressive reaction in some children (Kraft, Aradli, Duffy, Hart, & Pearce, 1965).

Beta Blockers

Description

Propranolol (Inderal) is a ß-adrenergic receptor blocker that tends to decrease heart rate, cardiac output, blood pressure, and maximal exercise tolerance. It can also have an antiarrhythmic effect on the heart. It has been reported as effective in reducing severe and treatment-resistant aggressiveness directed against others or self. However, these reports are based on uncontrolled trials or case reports involving nonautistic subjects. Furthermore, the patients were diagnostically heterogeneous (Campbell et al., 1989). Further studies, therefore, are needed to determine the effects of beta blockers in individuals with autism.

Side Effects

Side effects of propranolol include Raynaud's phenomenon, bradycardia, bronchoconstriction, depression/dysphoria, hallucination, hypotension, vomiting/nausea, diarrhea, insomnia/nightmares, dizziness, and hypoglycemia.

Other Psychotherapeutic Agents

Fenfluramine (an antiserotonergic anorectic) was initially reported to show positive effects, but subsequent data from a multicenter study (Campbell et al., 1988) and another recent investigation failed to show any positive effect (Leventhal et al., 1993). *Lithium* is a monovalent medication and the lightest alkali metal. In the adult literature, lithium reportedly has a mood-reducing effect in manic disorder. It may also reduce aggressiveness and hyperactivity. Its exact mechanism of action in manic disorder is not fully known. In children, however, the role of lithium is unclear. It appears that it is effective in reducing aggressive behavior in children of normal intelligence diagnosed as having conduct disorder (Campbell et al., 1989). Further uncontrolled studies suggest that lithium may have antiaggressive effects in children with mental retardation. To confirm this suggestion, however, controlled studies are needed. Nonetheless, lithium should be considered in the treatment of students with autism who have clear bipolar affective illness, or in students with autism and severe aggressive and/or self-injurious behavior who fail to respond to other antiaggressive medications.

The most common side effects of lithium include stomachache, anorexia, nausea, vomiting, diarrhea, hand tremors, headache, and weight gain. Leukocytosis with lymphocytopenia, a decrease in thyroxine iodine, urinary frequency, and polyuria have also been reported. These side effects are usually minimal within the therapeutic range and often disappear after several weeks of use.

Clonidine (Catapres), an alpha 2-adrenergic receptor agonist, has been reported as having therapeutic value in Tourette syndrome (TS; Leckman et al., 1982). It is less effective in reducing tics than haloperidol and pimozide, but has fewer side effects than haloperidol. Clonidine also seems to be effective in reducing hyperactivity and irritability in some children with autism who have not responded to other psychopharmacological treatments (Jaselskis, Cook, Fletcher, & Leventhal, 1992). However, it causes significant drowsiness and decreased activity (Fankhauser, Karumanchi, German, Yates, & Katumanchi, 1992; Jaselskis et al., 1992). Other common side effects include dry mouth, drowsiness, dizziness, constipation, and sedation. However, most side effects of clonidine are mild and tend to diminish with continued therapy. Larger studies are warranted to determine whether clonidine is also effective in compulsive and aggressive behaviors.

Guanfacine (Tenex) is another 2-adrenoceptor agonist with longer excretion half-life, decreased sedative side effects, and a more selective binding profile than that of clonidine. It has been reported to be effective in treating children with ADHD (Hunt, Arnsten, & Asbell, 1995), and in treating children with both ADHD and TS (Chappell et al., 1995). Further large-scale studies are warranted to determine the efficacy of guanfacine in the treatment of ADHD and TS.

The side effects of guanfacine are similar to those of other medications of the 2-adrenoceptor agonist class: dry mouth, sedation, weakness, dizziness, constipation, and impotence. Although the side effects are common, most are mild and tend to disappear with continued dosing.

Risperidone (Risperdal) is an antipsychotic agent belonging to a new chemical class, the benzisoxazole derivatives, a potent dopamine type 2 (D2) and serotonin type 2 (5HT2) receptors antagonist. It has efficacy against both the positive and negative symptoms of schizophrenia and demonstrates significant advantages over both the conventional dopamine-blocking neuroleptics and the atypical antipsychotic clozapine (Huttunen, 1995). Risperidone has also been reported to be effective in treating tic disorders, including TS (Bruun & Budman, 1996), obsessive-compulsive disorder (McDougle et al., 1995), and pervasive developmental disorder (Purdon, Lit, Labelle, & Jones, 1994).

My preliminary experience with risperidone suggests efficacy in reducing the frequency and intensity of temper outbursts and aggression in children and adolescents with ASD. Further larger studies are needed to determine whether risperidone presents more advantages than other conventional psychotherapeutic medications. Although it is believed that risperidone has a low tendency to produce extrapyramidal side effects (EPS), it can cause side effects of somnolence, increased dream activity, anxiety, dry mouth, dizziness, constipation, micturition disturbances, nausea, dyspepsia, weight gain, rhinitis, rash, and tachycardia.

Vitamins

"Megavitamin" therapy has become a popular form of treatment for a variety of psychiatric disorders. The proponents of orthomolecular psychiatry claim that "mega" doses of certain vitamins ameliorate or prevent mental disorders such as schizophrenia, mental retardation, and autism.

The efficacy of the use of pyridoxine (Vitamin B6) plus magnesium in individuals with autism has been controversial. Some short-term (2 weeks to 30 days) studies have reported positive results (reviewed by Tsai, 1992). However, other investigators have failed to confirm such findings (Tolbert, Haigler, Waits, & Dennis, 1993). Larger and long-term studies are needed to support a final conclusion. It is strongly recommend that megavitamin treatment be undertaken only under the supervision of a knowledgeable and experienced physician because such treatment is not completely free of toxic side effects.

Anticonvulsants

The anticonvulsants of particular relevance are phenobarbital and related barbiturates, phenytoin (Dilantin), carbamazepine (Tegretol), ethosuximide (Zarontin), valproate (Depakene), clonazepam (Clonopin), gabapentin (Neurontin), and felbamate (Felbatol). These anticonvulsants may act through two mechanisms to achieve their effect: direct modification of neuronal membrane function and alteration of neurotransmission (Menkes, 1985).

The objective in the treatment of the seizure disorder is complete control of seizures, or at least a reduction in their frequency to the point where they no longer interfere with physical and social well-being. It is not uncommon that a single anticonvulsant is sufficient to achieve satisfactory seizure control in individuals with seizure disorder. In some cases, complete seizure control may not be possible, however. Acceptance of the occurrence of an occasional seizure is preferable to using multiple anticonvulsants for prolonged periods, which tends to cause cognitive and behavioral side effects in persons with seizure disorder.

The following are general guidelines for anticonvulsant therapy:

1. Treatment should begin with one medication. If the medication does not control seizures, it should be discontinued gradually while a second medication is instituted and its dosage increased.

2. Alterations in medication dosage should be made gradually, usually no more frequently than once every 5 to 7 days.

3. Once seizures are controlled, the medication should be continued for a prolonged period of time.

4. Determination of anticonvulsant blood levels is necessary in all cases.

5. Anticonvulsant medication should be withdrawn gradually.

The following anticonvulsants are the most commonly used for controlling various types of seizure disorders.

Phenobarbital (Luminal) is effective in treating grand mal seizures, at levels of 10 to 30 ug/ml. Toxic levels of phenobarbital vary from one individual to another. However, no permanent sedation has been seen with levels below 35 ug/ml. Phenobarbital and other barbiturate anticonvulsants may cause hyperactivity or drowsiness. They may also cause initial impairment in cognitive function, which disappears after the first year of therapy (Hellström & Barlach-Christoffersen, 1980).

Phenytoin (Dilantin) has been shown to be effective clinically in controlling tonic-clonic (grand mal) seizures at therapeutic levels ranging from 10 to 20 ug/ml. However, it has lost considerable favor as a long-term anticonvulsant for children because of the wide variability in its absorption, the effects of other anticonvulsants, and the relatively high incidence of side effects (Menkes, 1985). About 2% to 5% of patients receiving phenytoin develop fever, a morbilliform rash, and lymphadenopathy within 2 weeks of the start of therapy with blood levels in the therapeutic range. After discontinuation of the medication, the symptoms clear (Dawson, 1973). At therapeutic levels, prolonged phenytoin therapy causes gum hyperplasia, megaloblastic anemia, lower serum folate concentration, disturbed vitamin D metabolism resulting in hypocalcemic rickets, decreased serum calcium and phosphorus, increased alkaline phosphatase (Crosley, Chee, & Berman, 1975), and peripheral neuropathy. At toxic levels, phenytoin may cause sedation, impairment of motor coordination and performance (e.g., ataxia), negative effects on memory and learning, irreversible degeneration of the cerebellar Purkinje cells (Kokenge, Kutt, & McDowell, 1965), and aggravation of underlying behavior disorder.

Carbamazepine (Tegretol) is chemically unrelated to any of the other major anticonvulsants. Individuals with psychomotor and grand mal seizures are most likely to benefit from the drug. Optimal therapeutic levels are between 4 and 12 ug/ml. The most common side effect of carbamazepine is diplopia, which may disappear spontaneously or after reduction of drug dosage (Lesser, Pippenger, Luders, & Dinner, 1984). Other side effects include rashes, hyponatremia, hepatic dysfunction, and leukopenia. Carbamazepine may also cause hyperactivity, irritability, insomnia (Rivinius, 1982), memory impairment, assaultive behavior, agitation, and motor and phonic tics (Evans & Gualtieri, 1985). Such effects may occur at low doses and at low blood levels.

Primidone (Mysoline) is used to control partial seizures, myoclonic seizures, and secondarily generalized seizures. Common side effects include somnolence, ataxia, rash, and depression. *Ethosuximide (Zarontine)* is the most effective medication for treatment of absence (petit mal) seizures. Side effects are rare. They include gastrointestinal upsets, skin rashes, headaches, and occasional reversible leukopenia (Menkes, 1985).

Valproic Acid (VPA) or *Valproate (Depakene, Depakote)* is highly effective in controlling minor motor, grand mal, petit mal, and simple partial seizures. Correlation between blood levels and therapeutic effects or adverse reactions has not been established. Side effects of VPA include gastrointestinal upsets, increased appetite and weight gain, hepatic dysfunction, sedation, tremors, and asterixis. These side effects tend to develop when the patients are receiving polytherapy.

Clonazepam (Clonopine, Klonopin) is an effective anticonvulsant for most types of minor motor seizures, particularly akinetic and atypical petit mal seizures. It appears to be most effective when given in conjunction with phenobarbital or other anticonvulsants (Wilensky, Ojemann, Temkin, Troupin, & Dodrill, 1981). At present, the relationship between blood levels and therapeutic and toxic effects of clonazepam is uncertain. Clonazepam may cause sedation, memory impairment, depression, excessive weight gain, ataxia, dysarthria, and paradoxical excitement or disinhibition (Rivinius, 1982).

Gabapentin (Neurontin) is a new anticonvulsant approved to be used as an add-on treatment in adults for partial seizures and secondary generalized seizures. Common dose-related side effects include dizziness, ataxia, somnolence, and weight gain. Idiosyncratic adverse effect is skin rash.

Felbamate (Felbatol) is another relatively new anticonvulsant for treatment of partial seizures, generalized seizures, secondary generalized seizures, absence seizures, and myoclonic seizures. Common dose-related adverse effects include anorexia, weight loss, headaches, and insomnia. Idiosyncratic side effects include aplastic anemia and liver failure. Use of felbamate is restricted by an FDA advisory because of the risk of idiosyncratic side effects.

Other Medical Treatment: Diet

Food additives have been advanced as causing behavioral problems including hyperactivity and learning difficulties (Feingold, 1975). Feingold reported positive results in treating children with hyperactivity with an elimination diet that excluded artificial flavors and colors, as well as salicylates and other additives. Dietary treatment has become popular, but many clinicians and researchers have reported rather inconsistent results (for a review, see Kruesi & Rapoport, 1986). To date, the majority of researchers in this field believe that dietary treatment is helpful for a very small subgroup of children with hyperactivity.

The effect of diet on individuals with ASD has not been systematically studied, though some parents and professionals enthusiastically advocate its use. Although dietary treatment may be relatively safe, it should be undertaken only under the supervision of a knowledgeable dietician or physician to ensure that the child's nutritional needs are fully met.

Clinical Indications for Pharmacotherapy in ASD

To achieve the most effective use of medications, it is important that parents and professionals working with or taking care of students with ASD learn both the signs and symptoms of neuropsychiatric disorders and the side effects of medications. The following section briefly describes frequently observed or reported behavioral symptoms or problems in individuals with ASD that may be viewed as clinical manifestations of certain diagnosable neuropsychiatric disorders that are potentially medication responsive. In some of the neuropsychiatric disorders, administration of the psychotherapeutic medications is based on well-documented research. However, the efficacy of medication therapy in other disorders requires further research. The following suggestions are based on the limited clinical and empirical experience of the present author and a few other investigators, as little research has been done in this field at this point.

Comorbid Psychiatric Disorders

No medication is available for effective treatment of the two core autistic symptomatologies (i.e., impairment of social interaction and communication).

However, many of the third-core autistic symptomatologies (i.e., restricted, repetitive, and stereotyped patterns of behavior, interests, and activities) and other behavioral and/or psychiatric symptoms that may be considered clinical manifestations of comorbid psychiatric disorders have been shown to respond positively to some psychotropic medications.

Additional behavioral and/or psychiatric symptoms in persons with autistic disorder have been described by many investigators (e.g., Ando & Yoshimura, 1979; Chung, Luk, & Lee, 1990; Fombonne, 1992; Le Couteur et al., 1989; Rumsey, Rapoport, & Sceery, 1985; Rutter & Lockyer, 1967):

Poor attention and concentration	64%
Hyperactivity	36%–48%
Morbid or unusual preoccupation	43%–88%
Obsessive phenomena	37%
Compulsions/rituals	16%–86%
Stereotyped utterance	50%–89%
Stereotyped mannerisms	68%–74%
Anxiety or fears	17%–74%
Depressive mood, irritability, agitation, and inappropriate affect	9%–44%
Sleep problems	11%
History of self-injury	24%–43%
Tics	8%

These investigators did not specifically investigate the incidence of diagnosable psychiatric disorders in their samples because conceptually these additional behavioral and/or psychiatric symptoms have been viewed as associated features (Tsai, 1996). Research on the specific relationship between these associated features and autistic symptoms is sparse. It is not clear whether these emergent behavioral and/or psychiatric symptoms are developmentally related symptoms/behaviors of autistic disorder or if they should be considered as symptoms of comorbid psychiatric disorders.

Because of difficulties in communicating with other people and showing appropriate affect, individuals with autism do not appear to resist their compulsions, to complain about the compulsive acts, or to manifest distress. Hence, they are unable to or incapable of providing diagnostic information via structured or semistructured diagnostic interviews or self-report scales (Tsai, 1996). This problem increases the likelihood that clinicians will hesitate to ascribe additional psychiatric disorder(s) to persons with ASD, particularly in lower functioning and/or nonverbal individuals. Nevertheless, case reports have described other specific types of psychiatric disorders occurring in individuals with autism. These include unipolar and bipolar affective disorders (Ghaziuddin & Tsai, 1991; Gillberg, 1985; Komoto, Usui, & Hirata, 1984; Lainhart & Folstein, 1994; Steingard & Biederman, 1987); obsessive-compulsive disorder (McDougle, Price, & Goodman, 1990; Tsai, 1992); schizophrenia (Clarke, Littlejohns, Corbett, & Joseph, 1989; Petty, Ornitz, Michelman, & Zimmerman, 1984; Volkmar & Cohen, 1991); and Tourette syndrome (Barabas & Matthews, 1983; Comings & Comings, 1991; Realmuto & Main, 1982; Sverd, 1991; Sverd, Montero, & Gurevich, 1993).

Given the relatively high frequencies of the associated features and the increasing number of case reports of autism associated with other major psychiatric disorders, it is conceivable that a significant number of individuals with an ASD have other coexisting major psychiatric disorders. Thus, effective treatment for students with ASD may require modification of the contemporary diagnostic criteria of certain psychiatric disorders. For example, the diagnosis of obsessive-compulsive disorder may be considered in lower functioning students with autism even in the absence of clear ego-dystonicity (intrusiveness), or the diagnosis of major depression may be considered in nonverbal and/or lower functioning students with autism even in the absence of subjectively reported depressed mood, worry, guilty feelings, and suicidal ideation. If these associated behavioral and/or psychiatric symptoms can be viewed as symptoms of various comorbid psychiatric disorders, data suggest that with an appropriate evaluation, predrug workups, a specific diagnosis, and multiple measures of outcome, pharmacotherapy can be a safe and efficacious treatment for these symptoms in persons with autism (Gordon et al., 1993).

Obsessive and Compulsive Disorder (OCD)

Key features of OCD include obsessions (unwanted ideas, thoughts, images, or impulses) that repeatedly well up in the person's mind, persistent fears that harm may come to self or a loved one, an unreasonable belief that one has a terrible illness, or an excessive need to do things correctly or perfectly. These thoughts are intrusive (ego-dystonic), unpleasant, and produce a high degree of anxiety. Often, the obsessions are repeated thoughts about contamination, repeated doubts, a need to have things in a particular order, aggressive or horrific impulses, and sexual imagery. Compulsions are another key characteristic of OCD—repetitive behaviors in response to obsessions. The most common compulsions are washing and checking. Other compulsions include counting, repeating words silently, hoarding, and endlessly rearranging objects in an effort to keep them in precise alignment with each other. These behaviors are intended to ward off harm to the person with OCD. Some people with OCD engage in regimented rituals while others have rituals that are complex and changing. Most of the time, people with OCD know that their obsessive thoughts are senseless and that their compulsions are not necessary and, therefore, struggle to banish their unwanted, obsessive thoughts and to prevent themselves from engaging in compulsive behaviors. As a result, they often attempt to hide their disorder rather than seeking help. Often they are successful in concealing their obsessive-compulsive symptoms from friends and co-workers.

OCD tends to last for years, even decades. Although symptoms may become less severe from time to time, they are usually chronic. As people with OCD struggle against their compulsions, they often develop a dysphoric mood and become irritable, tense, and depressed (American Psychiatric Association [APA], 1994).

Ritualistic or Compulsive Behaviors in Individuals with Autism

In childhood, ritualistic or compulsive behaviors usually involve rigid routines (e.g., insistence on eating particular foods) or stereotyped, repetitive motor acts such as hand clapping or finger mannerisms (e.g., twisting, flicking movements carried out near the face). For example, many children with autism line up toys or objects and become very distressed if these are disturbed. Some children may repetitively flush toilets or turn light switches on and off. There may be a perseverative preoccupation with certain features of objects, such as their texture, taste, smell, color, or shape. Some children with autism follow extreme food fads. Many develop intense attachments to odd objects, such as pipe cleaners, small plastic toys, and so on. The child may carry the object at all times and protest or throw tantrums if it is removed. Some children with autism develop preoccupations, such as spending a great deal of time memorizing weather information, state capitals, or birth dates of family members. In adolescence, some of these behaviors develop into obsessional symptoms (e.g., repeatedly asking the same question, which must be answered in a specific manner) and compulsive behaviors (e.g., compulsive touching of certain objects). Ritualistic or compulsive behaviors are more often displayed by those with normal intelligence than by those with mental retardation.

Bartak and Rutter (1976) noted that about 68% of the children they studied, who had autism and normal intelligence, engaged in ritual behavior. About 80% of these children also had quasi-obsessive behaviors. Difficulty adapting to new situations was found in about 74% of these children. Unusual play activities such as repeating dialogue from radio and television, continually talking about and playing with a single toy, or repetitively writing or drawing numbers, words, maps, and so on, have been observed in higher functioning children with autism (Shea & Mesibov, 1985).

In a follow-up study of adult males with autism, Rumsey et al. (1985) reported that 86% continued to demonstrate stereotyped, compulsive behaviors, including arranging objects. In a study of the reliability and diagnostic validity of the *Autism Diagnostic Interview* (ADI) with 16 individuals with autism, Le Couteur et al. (1989) reported that 88% had unusual preoccupations, 55% demonstrated verbal rituals, 81% showed compulsions/rituals, and

63% had unusual sensory interests. Fombonne (1992) also studied the results of the ADI with 20 French subjects with autism. He found that 53% had unusual preoccupations, 16% showed compulsions or rituals, and 42% had unusual sensory interests. Some of these obsessive and/or compulsive symptoms are similar to those seen in OCD.

As mentioned earlier, because individuals with autism do not seem to resist their compulsions, complain about their compulsive acts, or manifest distress, clinicians may hesitate to make a superimposed OCD diagnosis in person with ASD. However, it is conceivable that in some higher functioning students with autism, quasi-obsessive behaviors may reflect true symptoms of a coexisting OCD. Indeed, several investigators have reported cases featuring both autistic disorder and obsessive-compulsive disorder (McDougle et al., 1990; Rutter, 1985; Tsai, 1992).

Drug of choice

Clomipramine should be considered in students with ASD who exhibit quasi-obsessive and compulsive behaviors and who do not have seizure disorders. For unusual behaviors such as resistance to change, stereotypies, ritualistic/compulsive behaviors, and unusual attachment, haloperidol, clomipramine, or fluoxetine may be considered (Anderson et al., 1984; Bregman, Volkmar, & Cohen, 1991; Gordon et al., 1993; McDougle et al., 1992; Mehlinger, Scheftner, & Pozanski, 1990).

Tic Disorders

A tic is a sudden, rapid, recurrent, nonrhythmic stereotyped motor movement or vocalization It is experienced as irresistible but can be suppressed for varying lengths of time. Tics may be exacerbated by stress and attenuated during absorbing activities. Common types of tics are shown in Table 10.1

Tic disorders can be subclassified based on duration and variety of tics. For example, transient tic disorders include motor and/or vocal tics lasting for at least 4 weeks but for no longer than 12 months. Tourette syndrome and chronic motor or vocal disorder can have a duration of more than 12 months, but are distinguished from the requirement for Tourette syndrome that there be multiple motor tics and at least one vocal tic (APA, 1994).

Many persons with autism display tic-like symptoms such as grimacing, hand flapping or twisting, toe walking, lunging, jumping, darting or pacing, body rocking and swaying, and head rolling or banging. In some cases, these symptoms appear intermittently. In other cases, they are continuously present. They are usually interrupted by episodes of immobility and odd posturing with head bowed and arms flexed at the elbow. Rutter and Lockyer (1967) reported that among 63 children with infantile autism, about 70% had stereotyped mannerisms; 25% had self-injury. Ando and Yoshimura (1979) reported

Table 10.1

Common Types of Tics

Type	Behaviors
Simple motor tics	Eye blinking, neck jerking, shoulder shrugging, facial grimacing, and coughing
Complex motor tics	Facial gestures, grooming behaviors, jumping, touching, stamping, and smelling an object
Simple vocal tics	Throat clearing, grunting, sniffing, snorting, and barking
Complex vocal tics	Repeating words or phrases out of context, using socially unacceptable (frequently obscene) words, palilalia (repeating one's own sounds or words), echolalia
Rare complications	Self-injurious behaviors (head banging, striking oneself, picking skin) and orthopedic problems (knee bending, neck jerking, or head turning)

that among the 47 children with autism they studied, 68% had stereotyped behavior and 43% had self-injury.

In a follow-up study of adult males with autism, Rumsey et al. (1985) found that these males continued to demonstrate stereotyped behaviors and phonic tics. Le Couteur et al. (1989) noted that of 16 individuals with autism, 89% had stereotyped utterances, 69% had hand/finger mannerisms, and 63% had unusual sensory interests. Fombonne (1992) noted that of 20 individuals, 50% had stereotyped utterances, 74% had hand/finger mannerisms, and 42% had unusual sensory interests. In a follow-up of study of 66 children with autism in Hong Kong, Chung et al. (1990) reported that 24% had self-injurious behaviors and 8% exhibited tics. However, these investigators did not specifically investigate the incidence of diagnosable tic disorders based on any commonly used diagnostic criteria.

Some studies have described the development of Tourette syndrome in individuals with autism (Barabas & Matthews, 1983; Comings & Comings, 1991; Realmuto & Main, 1982; Sverd et al., 1993). I have also seen a few cases. However, it is unclear how frequently the two disorders might occur together. Further it is uncertain how this finding might be linked to the etiology of the two disorders.

Drug of choice

In patients with tic-like symptoms or with a clear diagnosis of Tourette syndrome, haloperidol or diphenylbutylpiperidine (Pimozide or Orap) should be tried first because they are more potent than clonidine. In some cases, haloperidol or pimozide with fluoxetine may be needed. Finally, Risperidone may be considered when all other conventional medications have failed to show efficacy.

If self-injurious behaviors such as head banging, finger biting, hand biting, wrist biting, face scratching, or extremities scratching develop as complications of tic disorder or Tourette syndrome, the above medications for Tourette syndrome should be considered first. Naltrexone trazodone may be considered in individuals who do not respond to these medications (Campbell et al., 1988; Tsai & Ghaziuddin, 1996).

Attention-Deficit/Hyperactivity Disorder (ADHD)

The essential feature of ADHD is a persistent pattern of inattention and/or hyperactivity-impulsivity. ADHD symptoms are listed in Table 10.2. Many young children with autism are markedly overactive but tend to become underactive in adolescence. For example, Rutter and Lockyer (1967) reported that among 63 children with infantile autism, 48% were hyperkinetic at the time of first hospitalization. Ando and Yorshimura (1979) found that among 47 children with autism, 36% were hyperactive. Similarly, Chung et al. (1990) noted that 47% of 66 children with autism in Hong Kong were hyperactive and that 64% also had poor attention and concentration.

In cases with severe hyperactivity, attention deficit, and impulsiveness, clonidine (Ghaziuddin, Tsai, & Ghaziuddin, 1992; Jaselskis et al., 1992), guanfacine, or imipramine may be considered in low- or middle-functioning individuals with autism with or without other neurological disorders such as seizure disorders, Tourette syndrome, and so on. In high-functioning individuals without other neurological disorders, stimulants such as methylphenidate may be tried first (Quintana et al., 1995).

Generalized Anxiety Disorder and/or Panic Attack

The essential features of generalized anxiety disorder are anxiety or worry associated with at least one of the following six symptoms:

- restlessness or feeling keyed up or on edge
- being easily fatigued
- difficulty concentrating or mind going blank
- irritability
- muscle tension
- sleep disturbance

The essential feature of a panic attack is a discrete period of intense fear or discomfort accompanied by some of the following somatic or cognitive symptoms: palpitations, pounding heart, or accelerated heart rate; sweating; trembling or shaking; sensation of shortness of breath or smothering; feeling of choking; chest

Table 10.2

Symptoms of Attention-Deficit/Hyperactivity Disorder

Disorder	Characteristics
Inattention	Failure to pay close attention to details
	Careless mistakes in school, work, and other activities
	Failure to listen when spoken to
	Failure to follow through on instructions, finishing school work, etc.
	Avoidance of or reluctance to engage in tasks that require sustained mental effort
	Loss of things necessary to perform task
	Being easily distracted by extraneous tasks or activities
	Distractibility
	Forgetfulness
Hyperactivity	Fidgeting with hands or feet
	Squirming in seat
	Leaving seat in classroom when expected to be seated
	Running/climbing excessively
	Difficulty playing or engaging in leisure activities quietly
	Constantly "on the go"
	Excessive talking
Impulsivity	Blurting out answers before questions have been completed
	Difficulty waiting turn
	Interruption of or intrusion on others

Note. From Diagnostic and Statistical Manual of Mental Disorders (4th ed.), by the American Psychiatric Association, 1994. Copyright 1994 by the American Psychiatric Association.

pain or discomfort; nausea or abdominal distress; feeling dizzy, unsteady, light-headed or faint; derealization (feeling of unreality) or depersonalization (being detached from oneself); fear of losing control or going crazy; fear of dying; paresthesia (numbness or tingling sensations); and chills or hot flashes (APA, 1994).

Rutter and Lockyer (1967) reported that among 63 children with infantile autism, 60% had anxiety or fear. Ando and Yoshimura (1979) found that 17% of 47 children with autism demonstrated fear. Le Couteur et al. (1989) noted that

73% of 16 individuals with autism had separation anxiety. Similarly, Fombonne (1992) reported that 74% of 20 individuals with autism had separation anxiety. Chung et al. (1990) noted that 23% of 66 children with autism in Hong Kong had fear or phobia and 11% had sleep problems.

It is conceivable that some of these individuals might indeed have had general anxiety disorder and/or panic attack. However, due to the clinician's lack of experience in working with this population, the possibility of coexisting general anxiety disorder and/or panic attack was not considered in these study participants or in other individuals with autism with similar clinical features.

The preferred medication for most anxiety disorders is buspirone (BuSpar) or tricyclic antidepressants. The benzodiazepines such as alprazolam (Xanax), diazepam (Valium), chlordiazepoxide (Librium or Librax), and lorazepam (Ativan) are the second line of medications of choice; these drugs have potential for development of tolerance and dependence as well as the possibility of abuse and withdrawal reactions.

Major Depressive Episode and Manic Episode

Symptoms of a major depressive episode are as follows (APA, 1994):

- depressed mood as indicated by either subjective report or observation (in children and adolescents this can be irritable mood)

- diminished interest or pleasure in all, or almost all, activities

- significant weight loss when not dieting, weight gain, or decrease/increase in appetite

- insomnia or hypersomnia

- psychomotor agitation or retardation

- fatigue or loss of energy

- feeling of worthlessness or inappropriate guilt

- diminished ability to think or concentrate, or indecisiveness

- recurrent thoughts of death, recurrent suicidal ideation without a specific plan, or a suicide attempt or a specific plan of committing suicide.

The symptoms of a major manic episode are as follows (APA, 1994):

- inflated self-esteem or grandiosity

- decreased need for sleep

- more talkative than usual or pressure to keep talking

- flight of ideas or subjective experience that thoughts are racing

- distractibility

- increased goal-directed activity or psychomotor agitation

- excessive involvement in pleasurable activities that have a high potential for painful consequences

Affective expression in persons with autism may be flattened, excessive, or inappropriate to the situation. Their mood is often labile; sobbing, crying or screaming may be unexplained or inconsolable; hysterical laughing and giggling may occur for no obvious reason. Major depression may occur during adolescence and adult life. The depression may be a reaction to partial realization of the disability. This is more likely seen in individuals with higher levels of ability. However, depression also can be found in lower functioning individuals. For example, Chung et al. (1990) reported that 9% of 66 children with autism in Hong Kong had depressive moods; 44% demonstrated irritability or agitation; 29% showed inappropriate affect; and 11% had sleep problems. Investigators have reported cases with both autistic disorder and unipolar/bipolar affective disorders (Gillberg, 1985; Komoto et al., 1984; Lainhart & Folstein, 1994; Steingard & Biederman, 1987), and schizophrenia (Clarke et al., 1989; Petty et al., 1984; Volkmar & Cohen, 1991).

In depressed individuals with autism with a strong family history of unipolar affective illness, a tricyclic antidepressant such as desipramine or other serotonin reuptake blockers such a fluoxetine may be considered (Ghaziuddin, Tsai, & Ghaziuddin, 1991). Close monitoring of the drug response is critical; clinical experience indicates that depression episodes may switch to hypomanic episodes in some cases. Lithium may be the drug of choice in manic-like patients with a family history of bipolar affective illness.

Schizophrenia in Childhood and Adolescence

Most individuals with ASD manifest prodromal or residual symptoms of schizophrenia such as social isolations, impairment in role functioning or grooming, inappropriate affect, and so on. Many higher functioning people with ASD exhibit illogical thinking, incoherence, and poverty in content of speech. Their lack of nonverbal communication may be seen in blunt affect. Some individuals with ASD demonstrate inappropriate laughing or weeping due to an inability to comprehend the meaning of events. Such behaviors may be interpreted as labile or abnormal affect. Some higher functioning verbal persons with ASD have strange beliefs (e.g., some believe there is no air in other states); idiosyncratic interests (e.g., spending an enormous amount of time studying dinosaurs); or sensory experiences (e.g., seeing other people's faces in the air when alone in the room) bordering on delusions or hallucinations. However, one well-established finding is that children with autistic disorder almost never develop a thought disorder with delusions and hallucinations. Only a few well-diagnosed children with autism have been reported to have developed schizophrenia during follow-up periods (Petty et al., 1984).

In individuals who develop clear delusions, hallucinations, and bizarre behaviors, including catatonia, haloperidol should be the drug of first choice. Other antipsychotic medications such as thiothixene (Navan), loxapine (Loxitane), risperidone (Risperdal), and clozapine (Clozaril) are the second line of medications of choice (Pool, Bloom, Mielke, Roniger, & Gallant, 1976).

Other Associated Features of ASD

Aggression

Some individuals with autism become aggressive and physically attack others, sometimes due to frustration. However, many aggressive behaviors do not seem to have any clear cause. They are of great concern because of their devastating effect. In students who exhibit frequent aggressive behaviors and who do not respond to behavioral interventions, haloperidol may be the drug of choice. Trazodone, risperidone, carbamazepine, lithium, and propranolol may be considered in patients who fail to respond to haloperidol treatment.

Unusual Sleeping Patterns

Some children develop completely reversed sleep patterns; that is, they sleep during the day and are awake during the night. The key to solving this problem is to reverse the sleep cycle through a well-planned regimen. Some children with autism seem to need much longer to settle down for sleep (i.e., having initial insomnia) and/or need less sleep than other children. These children tend to keep the whole family awake every night because of their sleep disturbances. Melatonin may be the drug of first choice (Jan, Espezel, & Appleton, 1994). Some children with autism may respond to antihistamines such as diphenhydramine and hydroxyzine, or to clonidine. In more severe cases, a tricyclic antidepressant such as imipramine or trazodone (Gualtieri, 1991) may be considered.

Seizure Disorders

Seizure has been noted in between one fourth and one third of individuals with autistic disorder. Several reports have suggested that many individuals with autism develop their first seizures in adolescence (Deykin & MacMahon, 1979; Rutter, 1984). Volkmar and Nelson (1990) reported that the risk of developing seizures in individuals with autism is highest during early childhood. A prospective study of epilepsy in children with autistic disorder or PDDNOS/atypical autism revealed that about 5% of those with an autistic condition had epilepsy. In the majority, onset of seizures was before the age of 1 year (Wong, 1993).

Although the most common type of seizure is the generalized tonic-clonic seizure, various types of seizure have been observed in individuals with ASD (Tsai & Ghaziuddin, 1996). Because the features of different types of seizure disorders may be difficult to differentiate from the features of ASD or other psychiatric disorders, it is critical that the parents and caretakers of students with ASD learn about clinical features and treatments of various seizure disorders.

In general, seizures in individuals with ASD are managed the same way as in epileptic patients with ASD. However, when psychotropic medications are considered in persons with both ASD and seizure disorder, the potential alterations in seizure threshold and the interactions between psychotropic medications and anticonvulsants must be assessed.

The following sections briefly describe the clinical manifestations and medication treatments of the more frequently observed major seizure disorders.

Generalized Tonic-Clonic Seizure

Generalized tonic-clonic seizure is characterized by abrupt onset, with immediate loss or alteration of consciousness, and an abrupt fall. During the tonic phase, forced expiration against partially closed vocal cords often leads to a hoarse cry. The entire musculature tightens, with limb extension, back arching, trismus, apnea, and eyes deviated conjugately upward. Other symptoms include pupillary dilatation, salivation, diaphoresis, and dramatic rises in blood pressure and heart rate to two or three times the normal levels. Often there is urinary incontinence and, in rare instances, fecal incontinence. The tonic phase lasts from several seconds to several minutes, during which time the skin color turns bluish due to insufficient oxygen in the blood.

The tonic phase is followed by clonic jerking, with the head retroflexed, the arms usually flexed, and the lower extremities extended. The clonic phase can continue for minutes, waxing and waning. In most instances, the clonic phase gradually subsides as the jerks decrease in frequency.

After the clonic phase, the patient slowly regains full consciousness and is typically confused and excessively somnolent for minutes to hours after an attack. When fully awake, the patient may complain of headache and muscle pain but is otherwise unaware of the events surrounding the seizure (Lockman, 1989b; Pedley & De Vivo, 1991).

Petit Mal Seizures

Petit mal seizures, also referred to as absence seizures, manifest as momentary lapses in awareness with amnesia. They begin and end abruptly, rarely lasting more than a few seconds. There is no warning, and sometimes attacks are so brief that they escape detection. In a typical absence seizure attack, the patient abruptly loses consciousness, ongoing activity ceases without significant alteration in posture, and the patient's eyes stare vacantly straight ahead or roll upward. There is no movement except possibly some subtle fluttering of the eyelids and twitching of the perioral muscles. Other common features include pupillary dilatation, change in skin color, tachycardia and piloerection, and automatisms (aberrations of behavior). At the end of the seizure, the patient suddenly resumes previous activity as if nothing had happened, without any confusion or drowsiness. Dozens to hundreds of petit mal seizures may occur in a single day (Lockman, 1989a; Pedley & De Vivo, 1991).

Simple Partial Seizures

In simple partial seizures, the consciousness of the affected individual is not impaired, and the individual can interact normally with the environment except for those limitations imposed on specific functions by the seizure. Simple partial seizures can be classified into the following groups:

1. *motor signs* such as focal motor without march (i.e., seizures remain localized until they cease); focal motor with march (i.e., body parts are often initially involved distally, then more proximal portions are involved), versive, postural (the eyes and head turn to one side and at times the patient gazes at the hand of that side); and phonatory (vocalization or arrest of speech)

2. *somatosensory symptoms* (e.g., tingling or pins-and-needles sensation) or special-sensory symptoms (e.g., visual/light flashing taking the forms of zigzag lines, circumscribed circles, squares, stars, or animals that appear smaller than actual size; auditory buzzing, loud swishing noises, and other easily recognized, complex auditory hallucinations; olfactory, gustatory, and vertiginous tornado fits)

3. *autonomic symptoms or signs* (e.g., epigastric sensation, recurrent abdominal discomfort and vomiting, pallor, sweating, flushing, salivation, piloerection, and pupillary dilation)

4. *rare psychic symptoms* (e.g., dysmnesic symptoms including distortion of memory or time, flashback experiences, dejá vù, or occasional experience of a rapid recollection of episodes from life; cognitive disturbances including dreamy states, sensations of extreme pleasure or displeasure involving feelings of fear and intense depression, and, rarely, anger or rage; distortions of time sense; illusions such as objects' appearing deformed in size or shape; and structured hallucinations of sounds of voices, music, or scenes; Dreifuss, 1989; Pedley & De Vivo, 1991).

Complex Partial Seizures

When consciousness is impaired, the seizure is classified as a *complex partial seizure*. Impairment of consciousness is often the first clinical sign of complex partial seizures. However, in some cases, complex partial seizures evolve from simple partial seizures. The main features of the complex partial seizures vary, but they usually include impairment or alteration of consciousness, unresponsiveness, and automatisms (repetitive complex motor activities that are purposeless, undirected, and inappropriate to the situation; e.g., lip smacking; repetitious swallowing or chewing; fidgeting movements of the fingers or hands; gestural movements such as clapping, scratching, or fumbling with clothes or objects; walking or riding a bicycle with an appearance of being either non-goal-directed or completely disorganized; verbal response to stimulation of stereotyped repetitive utterance).

An alteration of consciousness occurs either near the beginning or during the seizure attack. Psychoillusory phenomena may be reported at the onset of an attack, including a sense of detachment or depersonalization, forced thinking, visual distortions and formed hallucinations, visceral sensations, and a feeling of intense emotion such as fear, loneliness, depression, sadness, anger, joy, or ecstasy. At times, fear during a seizure may lead to the affected person's running away.

After the seizure, patients are confused and slowly recover full consciousness. During a time of incomplete awareness they may resist restraint and react aggressively or angrily to objects and persons in their way. However, rage attacks or temper tantrums do not occur as manifestations of epilepsy (Dreifuss, 1989; Pedley & De Vivo, 1991).

Although focal (partial) seizures may remain localized until they cease, it is not uncommon for focal (partial) seizures to become generalized. Many seizures become generalized so quickly that their initial focal manifestations are not noticed. However, other focal seizures become generalized after an appreciable time has elapsed.

The mechanisms that initiate, promulgate, and terminate seizures remain unknown. Nonetheless, effective treatment can be achieved if an accurate early diagnosis of seizure type(s) can be established. Nonphysician caretakers must be able to provide a thorough and accurate history including (a) a description of the characteristics of the attack (age of onset, date and circumstances of first attack, one or more seizure types, manifestations of seizure attack(s), postepisode manifestations, any change of seizure pattern, any recognizable precipitating or associated factors, frequency of attacks, longest seizure-free intervals, etc.); (b) a pertinent past history including details of birth, postnatal course and early development, serious illness, trauma, ingestions or toxic exposures, reactions to immunizations, and school performance; and (c) a relevant family history (e.g., other family members with a seizure history).

The physician will perform a thorough physical examination of the child and order selective laboratory studies. An EEG should be performed on every child who has seizures. Further, CT or MRI scanning will be considered in children with partial seizures, abnormal neurologic examination, or focal slow-wave abnormalities on the EEG. In some uncertain or confusing cases, a period of watchful waiting often clarifies the diagnostic question.

Effective treatment of an individual with both ASD and seizures requires consideration of the interactions among multiple factors, including medical, psychological, and environmental ones. These individuals are likely to require long-term anticonvulsant treatment. The selection of the medication for the treatment depends on the type of seizure.

Summary

This chapter has presented an overview of medical intervention, particularly pharmacotherapy, in individuals with ASD. Recent advances in medication treatment of autism and other childhood psychiatric disorders have been highlighted. Pharmacotherapy does not alter the natural history or course of ASD. However, data suggest that with an appropriate evaluation, predrug workups, a specific diagnosis, and multiple measures of outcome, pharmacotherapy is a safe and efficacious treatment for some symptoms in individuals with autism. Emphasis is placed on minimizing the individual's additional behavioral or neuropsychiatric symptoms (e.g., hyperactivity, stereotypy, self-injury, aggressiveness) that interfere with or are incompatible with functioning and learning.

Medication treatment of ASD is symptomatic. Further, the use of medications in this population must be viewed as one component of a comprehensive intervention plan. The data presented in this chapter were obtained mainly from children with autism who were treated with neuroleptics. A great deal of work remains to be done with other medications as well as with adolescents and adults with ASD. Future research should also put more emphasis on studying the efficacy of combined interventions, such as pharmacotherapy with behavioral therapy or group therapy with medication therapy. It is highly unlikely that certain medication(s) will be developed in the future that would be curative for ASD. However, we are standing on the threshold of a new era in brain and behavioral sciences. Through research, we will learn even more about neuropsychiatric disorders, including ASD. This knowledge will be used to develop new interventions, including pharmacological therapies, that can help promote more typical social and communicative developments in individuals with autism.

References

Aman, M. C. (1982). Stimulant drug effects in developmental disorders and hyperactivity: Toward a resolution of disparate findings. *Journal of Autism and Developmental Disorders, 12,* 385–398.

American Psychiatric Association. (1994). *Diagnostic and statistical manual of mental disorders* (4th ed.). Washington, DC: Author.

Anderson, L. T., Campbell, M., Grega, D. M., Perry, R., Small, A. M., & Green, W. H. (1984). Haloperidol in the treatment of infantile autism: Effects on learning and behavior symptoms. *American Journal of Psychiatry, 141,* 1195–1202.

Ando, H., & Yoshimura, I. (1979). Effects of age on communication skill levels and prevalence of maladaptive behaviors in autistic and mentally retarded children. *Journal of Autism and Developmental Disorders, 9,* 83–93.

Annell, A. L. (1972). *Depressive states in childhood and adolescence.* Stockholm: Almquist & Wiksell.

Barabas, G., & Matthews, W. S. (1983). Coincident infantile autism and Tourette syndrome: A case report. *Journal of Developmental Pediatrics, 4,* 280–281.

Bartak, L., & Rutter, M. (1976). Differences between mentally retarded and normally intelligent autistic children. *Journal of Autism and Childhood Schizophrenia, 6,* 109–120.

Bregman, J., Volkmar, F., & Cohen, D. (1991). Fluoxetine in the treatment of autistic disorder. *Scientific Proceedings of the Annual Meeting of the American Academy of Child and Adolescent Psychiatry, 7,* 52.

Bruun, R. D., & Budman, C. L. (1996). Risperidone as a treatment for Tourette's syndrome. *Journal of Clinical Psychiatry, 57,* 29–31.

Campbell, M., Adams, P., Perry, R., Tesch, L. McV., & Curren, E. L. (1988). Naltrexone in infantile autism. *Psychopharmacology Bulletin, 24,* 135–139.

Campbell, M., Adams, P., Small, A. M., Curren, E. L., Overall, J. E., Anderson, L. T., Lynch, N., & Perry, R. (1988). Efficacy and safety of fenfluramine in autistic children. *Journal of the American Academy of Child and Adolescent Psychiatry, 27,* 434–439.

Campbell, M., Anderson, L. T., Meier, M., Cohen, I. L., Small, A. M., Samit, C., & Sachar, E. (1978). A comparison of haloperidol and behavior therapy and their interaction in autistic children. *Journal of the American Academy of Child Psychiatry, 17,* 640–655.

Campbell, M., Anderson, L. T., Small, A. M., Adams, P., Gonzalez, N. M., & Ernst, M. (1993). Naltrexon in autistic children: Behavioral symptoms and attentional learning. *Journal of the American Academy of Child and Adolescent Psychiatry, 32,* 1283–1291.

Campbell, M., Cohen, I. L., Perry, R., & Small, A. M. (1989). Psychopharmacological treatment. In T. H. Ollendick & M. Hersen (Eds.), *Handbook of child psychopathology* (2nd ed., pp. 123–147). New York: Plenum.

Campbell, M., & Palij, M. (1985). Measurement of side effects including tardive dyskinesia. *Psychopharmacology Bulletin, Rating Scales and Assessment Instruments for Use in Pediatric Psychopharmacology Research, 21,* 1063–1066.

Campbell, M., Small, A. M., Collins, P. J., Friedman, E., David, R., & Genieser, N. (1976). Levodopa and Levoamphetamine: A crossover study of young schizophrenic children. *Current Therapeutic Research, 19,* 70–86.

Chappell, P. B., Riddle, M. A., Scahill, L., Lynch, K. A., Schultz, R., Arnsten, A., Leckman, J. F., & Cohen, D. J. (1995). Guanfacine treatment of comorbid attention-deficit hyperactivity disorder and Tourette's syndrome: Preliminary clinical experience. *Journal of the American Academy of Child and Adolescent Psychiatry, 34,* 1140–1146.

Chung, S. Y., Luk, S. L., & Lee, P. (1990). A follow-up study of infantile autism in Hong Kong. *Journal of Autism and Developmental Disorders, 20,* 221–232.

Clarke, D. J., Littlejohns, C. S., Corbett, J. A., & Joseph, S. (1989). Pervasive developmental disorders and psychosis in adult life. *British Journal of Psychiatry, 155,* 692–699.

Comings, D. E., & Comings, B. G. (1991). Clinical and genetic relationship between autism-pervasive developmental disorder and Tourette syndrome: A study of 19 cases. *American Journal of Medical Genetics, 39,* 180–191.

Conners, C. K. (1976). *Conners' parent and teacher rating scales.* Toronto, Ontario: Multi-Health Systems.

Conners, C. K. (1985). Methodological and assessment issues in pediatric psychopharmacology. In J. M. Wiener (Ed.), *Diagnosis and psychopharmacology of childhood and adolescent disorders* (pp. 69–110). New York: Wiley.

Cook, E. H., Jr., Rowlett, R., Jaselskis, C., & Leventhal, B. L. (1992). Fluoxetine treatment of children and adults with autistic disorder and mental retardation. *Journal of the American Academy of Child and Adolescent Psychiatry, 31,* 739–745.

Crosley, C. J., Chee, C., & Berman, P. H. (1975). Rickets associated with long-term anticonvulsant therapy in a pediatric outpatient population. *Pediatrics, 56,* 52–57.

Currey, S. H. (1978). Pharmacokinetics and psychotropic drugs. *Psychological Medicine, 8,* 177–180.

Dalldorf, J. S. (1983). Medical needs of the autistic adolescent. In E. Schopler & G. B. Mesibov (Eds.), *Autism in adolescents and adults* (pp. 149–168). New York: Plenum.

Dawson, K. P. (1973). Severe cutaneous reactions to phenytoin. *Archives of Disease in Childhood, 48,* 239.

DeVeaugh-Geiss, J., Landau, P., & Katz, R. (1989). Treatment of obsessive-compulsive disorder with clomipramine. *Psychiatry Annals, 19,* 97–101.

Deykin, E. Y., & MacMahon, B. (1979). The incidence of seizures among children with autistic symptoms. *American Journal of Psychiatry, 126,* 1310–1312.

Driefuss, F. E. (1989). Focal and multifocal cortical seizures. In K. F. Swaiman (Ed.), *Pediatric neurology—Principles and practice* (pp. 393–411). St. Louis, MO: C. V. Mosby.

Evans, R. W., & Gualtieri, C. T. (1985). Carbamazepine: A neuropsychological and psychiatric profile. *Clinical Neuropharmacology, 83,* 221–241.

Fankhauser, M. P., Karumanchi, V. C., German, M. L., Yates, A., & Karumanchi, S. D. (1992). A double-blind, placebo-controlled study of the efficacy of transdermal clonidine in autism. *Journal of Clinical Psychiatry, 53,* 77–82.

Feingold, B. F. (1975). *Why your child is hyperactive.* New York: Random House.

Fombonne, E. (1992). Diagnostic assessment in a sample of autistic and developmentally impaired adolescents, *Journal of Autism and Developmental Disorders, 22,* 563–581.

Fontaine, R., & Chouinard, G. (1986). An open clinical trial of fluoxetine in the treatment of obsessive-compulsive disorder. *Journal of Clinical Psychopharmacology, 6,* 98–101.

Freeman, B. J., Ritvo, E. R., Yokota, A., & Ritvo, A. (1986). A scale for rating symptoms of patients with the syndrome of autism in real life settings. *Journal of the American Academy of Child Psychiatry, 25,* 130–136.

Ghaziuddin, M., & Tsai, L. Y. (1991). Depression in autistic disorder. *British Journal of Psychiatry, 159,* 721–723.

Ghaziuddin, M., Tsai, L. Y., & Ghaziuddin, N. (1991). Fluoxetine in autism: More useful in the presence of depression. *Journal of the American Academy of Child and Adolescent Psychiatry, 31,* 567.

Ghaziuddin, M., Tsai, L. Y., & Ghaziuddin, N. (1992). Clonidine for autism. *Journal of Child and Adolescent Psychopharmacology, 2,* 1–2.

Gillberg, C. (1985). Asperger's syndrome and recurrent psychosis—A case study. *Journal of Autism and Developmental Disorders, 15,* 389–397.

Gittleman-Klein, R., & Klein, D. F. (1971). Controlled imipramine treatment of school phobia. *Archives of General Psychiatry, 25,* 204–207.

Gordon, C. T., State, R. C., Nelson, J. E., Hamburger, S. D., & Rapoport, J. L. (1993). A double-blind comparison of clomipramine, desipramine, and placebo in the treatment of autistic disorder. *Archives of General Psychiatry, 50,* 441–447.

Gualtieri, C. T. (1991). *Neuropsychiatry and behavioral pharmacology.* New York: Springer-Verlag.

Guy, W. (1976a). Abnormal involuntary movement scale. In *ECDEU assessment manual for psychopharmacology* (Rev. ed., Publication ADM 76-338, pp. 534–537). Washington, DC: U.S. Department of Health, Education and Human Welfare.

Guy, W. (1976b). Dosage record and treatment emergent symptoms scale. In *ECDEU assessment manual for psychopharmacology* (Rev. ed., Publication ADM 76-338, pp. 223–244). Washington, DC: U.S. Department of Health, Education and Human Welfare.

Hellström, B., & Barlach-Christoffersen, M. (1980). Influence of phenobarbital on the psychomotor development and behaviour in preschool children with convulsions. *Neuropädiatrie, 11,* 151.

Hunt, R. D., Arnsten, A. F., & Asbell, M. D. (1995). An open trial of guanfacine in the treatment of attention deficit hyperactivity disorder. *Journal of the American Academy of Child and Adolescent Psychiatry, 34,* 50–54.

Huttunen, M. (1995). The evolution of the serotonin-dopamines antagonist concept. *Journal of Clinical Psychopharmacology, 15* (1, Suppl. 1), 4S–10S.

Jan, J. E., Espezel, H., & Appleton, R. E. (1994). The treatment of sleep disorders with melatonin. *Developmental Medicine and Child Neurology, 36,* 97–107.

Jaselskis, C. A., Cook, E. H., Fletcher, K. E., & Leventhal, B. L. (1992). Clonidine treatment of hyperactive and impulsive children with autistic disorder. *Journal of Clinical Psychopharmacology, 12,* 322–327.

Kokenge, R., Kutt, H., & McDowell, F. (1965). Neurological sequelae following dilantin overdose in a patient and in experimental animals. *Neurology, 15,* 823.

Kolmen, B. K., Feldman, H. M., Handen, B. L., & Janosky, J. E. (1995). Naltrexon in young autistic children: A double-blind, placebo-controlled crossover study. *Journal of the American Academy of Child and Adolescent Psychiatry, 34,* 223–231.

Komoto, J., Usui, S., & Hirata, J. (1984). Infantile autism and affective disorder. *Journal of Autism and Developmental Disorders, 14,* 81–84.

Kraft, I. A., Ardali, E., Duffy, J. H., Hart, J. T., & Pearce, P. (1965). A clinical study of chlordiazepoxide used in psychiatric disorders of children. *International Journal of Neuropsychiatry, 1,* 433–437.

Kreusi, M. J. P., & Rapoport, J. L. (1986). Diet and human behavior: How much do they affect each other? *Annual Review of Nutrition, 6,* 113–130.

Kupfer, D. J., & Detre, T. P. (1978). Tricyclic and monoamine oxidase inhibitor antidepressants: Clinical use. In L. L. Iverson, S. D. Iverson, & S. H. Snyder (Eds.), *Handbook of psychopharmacology* (Vol. 14, pp. 199–232). New York: Plenum.

Lainhart, J. E., & Folstein, S. E. (1994). Affective disorders in people with autism: A review of published cases. *Journal of Autism and Developmental Disorders, 24,* 587–601.

Leckman, J. F., Cohen, D. J., Detlor, J., Young, J. G., Harcherick, D., & Shaywitz, B. A. (1982). Clonidine in the treatment of Tourette syndrome: A review of data. In A. J. Friedhoff & T. N. Chase (Eds.), *Advances in neurology, Gilles de la Tourette Syndrome* (Vol. 35, pp. 391–401). New York: Raven.

Le Couteur, A., Rutter, M., Lord, C., Rios, P., Robertson, S., Holdgrafer, M., & McLennan, J. D. (1989). Autism Diagnostic Interview: A standardized investigator-based instrument. *Journal of Autism and Developmental Disorders, 19,* 363–387.

Leonard, H. L., Swedo, S. E. Rapoport, J. L., Koby, E. V., Lenane, M. C., Cheslow, D. L., & Hamburger, S. D. (1989). Treatment of obsessive-compulsive disorder with clomipramine and desipramine in children and adolescents. *Archives of General Psychiatry, 46,* 1088–1092.

Lesser, R. P., Pippenger, C. E., Luders, H., & Dinner, D. S. (1984). High-dose monotherapy in treatment of intractable seizures. *Neurology, 34,* 707–711.

Leventhal, B. L., Cook, E. H., Morford, M., Ravitz, A. J., Heller, W., & Freedman, D. X. (1993). Clinical and neurochemical effects of fenfluramine in children with autism. *Journal of Neuropsychiatry and Clinical Neuroscience, 5,* 307–315.

Lockman, L. A. (1989a). Absence seizures. In K. F. Swaiman (Ed.), *Pediatric neurology—Principles and practice* (pp. 413–416). St. Louis, MO: C. V. Mosby.

Lockman, L. A. (1989b). Nonabsence generalized seizures. In K. F. Swaiman (Ed.), *Pediatric neurology—Principles and practice* (pp. 417–420). St. Louis, MO: C. V. Mosby.

McDougle, C. J., Fleischmann, R. L., Epperson, C. N., Wasylink, S., Leckman, J. F., & Price, L. H. (1995). Risperidone addition in fluvoxamine-refractory obsessive-compulsive disorder: Three cases. *Journal of Clinical Psychiatry, 56,* 526–528.

McDougle, C. J., Price, L. H., & Goodman, W. K. (1990). Fluvoxamine treatment of coincident autistic disorder and obsessive-compulsive disorder: A case report. *Journal of the Autism and Developmental Disorders, 20,* 537–543.

McDougle, C. J., Price, L. H., Volkmar, F. R., Goodman, W. K., Ward-O'Brien, D., Nielsen, J., Bregman, J., & Cohen, D. J. (1992). Clomipramine in autism: Preliminary evidence of efficacy. *Journal of American Academy of Child and Adolescent Psychiatry, 31,* 746–750.

Mehlinger, R., Scheftner, W. A., & Poznanski, E. (1990). Fluoxetine and autism. *Journal of the American Academy of Child and Adolescent Psychiatry, 29,* 985.

Menkes, J. H. (1985). *Textbook of child neurology.* Philadelphia: Lea & Febiger.

Pedley, T. A., & De Vivo, D. C. (1991). Seizures disorders in infants and children. In A. M. Rudolph, J. I. E. Hoffman, & C. D. Rudolph (Eds.), *Rudolph's pediatrics* (19th ed., pp. 1767–1794). Norwalk, CT: Appleton & Lange.

Petty, L. K., Ornitz, E. M., Michelman, J. D., & Zimmerman, E. G. (1984). Autistic children who become schizophrenic. *Archives of General Psychiatry, 41,* 129–135.

Polizos, P., & Engelhardt, D. (1978). Dyskinetic phenomena in children treated with psychotropic medications. *Psychopharmacology Bulletin, 14,* 65–68.

Pool, D., Bloom, W., Mielke, D. H., Roniger, J. J., & Gallant, D. M. (1976). A controlled evaluation of loxitane in seventy-five adolescent schizophrenic patients. *Current Therapeutic Research, 19,* 99–104.

Purdon, S. E., Lit, W., Labelle, A., & Jones, B. D. (1994). Risperidone in the treatment of pervasive developmental disorder. *Canadian Journal of Psychiatry, 39,* 400–405.

Quintana, H., Brimaher, B., Stedge, D., Lennon, S., Freed, J., Bridge, J., & Greenhill, L. (1995). Use of methylphenidate in the treatment of children with autistic disorder. *Journal of Autism and Developmental Disorders, 25,* 283–294.

Rapoport, J. L., & Mikkelsen, E. J. (1978). Antidepressants. In J. S. Werry (Ed.), *Pediatric psychopharmacology: The use of behavior modifying drugs in children* (pp. 208–233). New York: Brunner/Mazel.

Rapoport, J. L., Mikkelsen, E. J., Zavadil, A., Nee, L., Gruenau, C., Mendelson, W., & Gillin, J. C. (1980). Childhood enuresis: 2. Psychopathology, tricyclic concentration in plasma and antienuretic effect. *Archives of General Psychiatry, 37,* 1146–1152.

Realmuto, G. M., & Main, B. (1982). Coincidence of Tourette's disorder and infantile autism. *Journal of Autism and Developmental Disorders, 12,* 367–372.

Riddle, M. A., Hardin, M. T., King, R., Scahill, L., & Woolson, J. L. (1990). Fluoxetine treatment of children and adolescents with Tourette's and obsessive-compulsive disorders: Preliminary clinical experience. *Journal of the American Academy of Child and Adolescent Psychiatry, 29,* 45–48.

Rivinius, T. M. (1982). Psychiatric effects of the anticonvulsant regimens. *Journal of Clinical Psychopharmacology, 2,* 165–192.

Rumsey, J. M., Rapoport, I. L., & Sceery, W. R. (1985). Autistic children as adults: Psychiatric, social and behavioral outcomes. *Journal of the American Academy of Child Psychiatry, 24,* 465–473.

Rutter, M. (1984). Autistic children growing up. *Developmental Medicine and Child Neurology, 26,* 122–129.

Rutter, M. (1985). The treatment of autistic children. *Journal of Child Psychology and Psychiatry, 26,* 193–214.

Rutter, M., & Lockyer, L. (1967). A five to fifteen year follow-up study of infantile psychosis: Description of sample. *British Journal of Psychiatry, 113,* 1169–1182.

Shea, V., & Mesibov, G. B. (1985). The relationship of learning disabilities and higher-level autism. *Journal of Autism and Developmental Disorders, 15,* 425–435.

Steingard, R., & Biederman, J. (1987). Lithium responsive manic-like symptoms in two individuals with autism and mental retardation. *Journal of American Academy of Child and Adolescent Psychiatry, 26,* 932–935.

Sverd, J. (1991). Tourette syndrome and autistic disorder: A significant relationship. *American Journal of Medical Genetics, 39,* 173–179.

Sverd, J., Montero, G., & Gurevich, N. (1993). Cases for an association between Tourette syndrome, autistic disorder, and schizophrenia-like disorder. *Journal of Autism and Developmental Disorders, 23,* 407–413.

Tolbert, L., Haigler, T., Waits, M. M., & Dennis, T. (1993). Brief report: Lack of response in an autistic population to a low dose clinical trial of pyridoxine plus magnesium. *Journal of Autism and Developmental Disorders, 23,* 193–199.

Tsai, L. Y. (1992). Medical treatment in autism. In D. E. Berkell (Ed.), *Autism: Identification, education, and treatment* (pp. 151–184). Hillsdale, NJ: Erlbaum.

Tsai, L. Y. (1996). Cormorbid psychiatric disorder of autistic disorder. *Journal of Autism and Developmental Disorders, 26,* 159–163.

Tsai, L. Y., & Ghaziuddin, M. (1996). Autistic disorder. In J. Weiner (Ed.), *The comprehensive textbook of child and adolescent psychiatry* (2nd ed., pp. 219–254). Washington, DC: American Psychiatric Association.

Volkmar, F. R., & Cohen, D. J. (1991). Comorbid association of autism and schizophrenia. *American Journal of Psychiatry, 148,* 1705–1707.

Volkmar, F. R., & Nelson, D. S. (1990). Seizure disorders in autism. *Journal of the American Academy of Child and Adolescent Psychiatry, 29,* 127–129.

Werry, J. S., Aman, M. G., & Diamond, E. (1980). Imipramine and methylphenidate in hyperactive children. *Journal of Child Psychology and Psychiatry, 21,* 27–35.

Wilensky, A. J., Ojemann, L. M., Temkin, N. R., Troupin, A. S., & Dodrill, C. B. (1981). Chlorazepate and phenobarbital as antiepileptic drugs: A double-blind study. *Neurology, 31,* 1271–1276.

Winsberg, B. G., Yepes, L., & Bialer, I. (1976). Pharmacological management of children with hyperactive/aggressive/inattentive behavior disorders. *Clinical Pediatric, 15,* 471–477.

Wong, V. (1993). Epilepsy in children with autistic spectrum disorder. *Journal of Child Neurology, 8,* 316–322.

Zingarelli, G., Ellman, G., Hom, A., Wymore, M., Heldorn, S., & Chicz-Demet, A. (1992). Clinical effects of naltrexone on autistic behavior. *American Journal on Mental Retardation, 97,* 57–63.

Controversial Therapies and Interventions with Children and Youth with Autism

11

Richard L. Simpson and
Brenda Smith Myles

Perhaps more than any other disability, autism is enigmatic. Children and youth identified as having autism are characterized by unique characteristics, which even by disability standards are highly unusual (Olley, 1992). Some children with autism demonstrate highly advanced splinter skills and other distinctive abilities; others have esoteric preferences and interests that appear to be far in advance of their overall estimated abilities.

Controversial interventions and unauthenticated treatments—unvalidated methodology or treatments, especially those promising extraordinary results—have been closely associated with autism (Simpson, 1995). Indeed, autism appears to offer fertile ground for even the most unusual and implausible treatments (Biklen, 1993). Although the exact reasons or reasons for such an association are unknown, one likely explanation is that autism is the disability about which there is the least understanding and the disability most closely associated with individuals demonstrating highly developed splinter skills and other nonfunctional abilities, which are often misinterpreted as signs of advanced functioning capacity. For instance, when permitted to communicate via facilitated communication, persons with autism are purportedly able to demonstrate advanced cognitive, social, and communication skills and abilities (Biklen, 1993).

It is not surprising that some parents and professionals are willing to consider or even fully embrace unproven interventions in an effort to improve the lives of individuals with autism. As observed by Oliver Wendell Holmes, "There is nothing people will not do, there is nothing they have not done, to recover their health and save their lives." Others have also noted the widespread appeal of untested treatments. Trachtman (1994), for example, reported that one of every three persons living in the United States uses unconventional therapies for illnesses, and that in excess of $14 billion is spent annually on unproven treatments. In Trachtman's words, "Millions of Americans are turning to [medical] therapies many consider bizarre. Still more millions are turning to less spectacular forms of alternative medicine" (p. 112).

It should come as no surprise, therefore, that many professionals and parents are willing to advocate, promote, and/or experiment with unvalidated interventions, which typically offer hope for improvement that is well beyond that of traditional and proven options. This tendency to tolerate and/or support implausible and nonvalidated treatments is particularly strong among individuals associated with persons with autism. Indeed, the history of programs and interventions for individuals with autism is characterized by a never-ending search for a treatment or method that will restore a person with autism to normalcy. Such treatments include auditory integration training, rhythmic and music-based treatments, vitamin intervention, vision therapies, tinted lenses, and so forth.

Because facilitated communication represents the classic example of a controversial intervention, we initially focus our attention on this particular approach. Later in the chapter we generalize beyond this one intervention method to other nonvalidated procedures.

Facilitated Communication: The Quintessential Controversial Intervention for Individuals with Autism

Crossley (1988, 1992a) and Biklen (1990, 1992) are widely known for their claim that facilitated communication (FC) permits individuals with autism and other severe disabilities to engage in unanticipated and even extraordinary communication. Specifically, when provided hand-over-hand or other types of physical support from a nondisabled person, individuals with autism and other disabilities who are thought to have limited communication ability are purportedly able to type highly advanced thoughts and ideas using FC. Even after only minimal experience with FC, individuals with autism have reportedly typed that they are socially competent and that they have normal intelligence. FC has purportedly allowed persons with severe disabilities to communicate that they are trapped within a body that prohibits them from effectively communicating with others (Biklen & Schubert, 1991; Calculator, 1992). Biklen (1992) asserted that individuals with such severe disabilities actually have a condition known as global apraxia. In actuality, persons with global apraxia appear to have severe cognitive and language deficits, in spite of having normal language processing abilities and intelligence. When permitted to communicate via FC, they are able to demonstrate normal abilities.

Crossley, an Australian who has received widespread credit for developing facilitated communication, worked at an institution in Australia with individuals who were thought to be severely retarded. Here, Crossley worked with a young woman, Anne, who had athetoid cerebral palsy. Even though Anne was unable to effectively communicate, feed herself, or walk, Crossley believed that she had more ability than she was given credit for, and that under the right conditions she was capable of communicating with others. By supporting Anne's index finger, Crossley discovered she was able to assist her in communicating through pointing. By shaping this initial response into a form that is similar to what is now known as FC, Crossley (1992a) was able to help Anne read and write. Several years later, Crossley became affiliated with the Dignity through Education and Language Communication Centre (DEAL), an organization committed to assisting individuals with severe communication disorders. While affiliated with DEAL, Crossley reportedly used FC successfully with clients whose intellectual impairments and physical disabilities made it difficult for them to use sign language and standard augmentative communication devices (Biklen, 1990; Crossley, 1992a).

Biklen is credited with introducing FC in the United States (Biklen, 1990, 1993). Based on his preliminary reports (Biklen, 1990), word of FC's phenomenal success quickly spread. Rimland (1992a), for instance, reported that "facilitated communication workshops spread throughout the country and virtually every major newspaper, news magazine and news show ran stories on facilitated communication" (p. 1). As a result, many parents and professionals involved with persons with autism perceived this novel procedure to be "the miracle intervention" that would permit persons with autism to lead normal lives. However, because of its dubious interactive features and lack of scientific support, FC was almost immediately surrounded by controversy (Calculator, 1992; Rimland, 1992a, 1993; Schopler, 1992).

Fueling much of the early controversy over FC were extraordinary claims regarding FC's effectiveness. For example, in describing the utility of FC with a child with a serious impairment, Biklen (1992) reported, "Without facilitation, Mark has no effective means of communicating, save to grab objects, pull people to objects or events that might be of interest to him, or throw tantrums. With facilitation, he can say what is on his mind, he can converse with other students, and he is doing school work at and above the grade level norm for his age" (p. 15). Biklen (1990) also advanced the claim that most individuals with serious impairments with autism are literate, and that after brief FC training they are capable of advanced communication on a variety of highly sophisticated subjects.

Based on anecdotal evaluation methods, Biklen and Schubert (1991) reported positive results with 21 students with whom they used FC. In defense of informal and anecdotal research methodology, they contended that FC should not be subjected to robust scientific evaluation (Biklen & Schubert, 1991; Crossley, 1988, 1992b), arguing that objective scientific methods would violate the trust bond between communicator and facilitator by suggesting that the individual with a disability was incapable of advanced communication. They also asserted that traditional scientific evaluations would be ineffective if they required an individual to communicate with more than one facilitator.

Not surprisingly, doubts about the efficacy of FC quickly surfaced (e.g., Prior & Cummins, 1992). The newsletter of the Autism Society of America, Inc., for instance, noted that "hard evidence for the authenticity of FC is nearly nonexistent" (Autism Society of America, 1992–1993, p. 19); and Calculator (1992) characterized FC as nothing more than a "Ouija board" phenomenon. Subsequent to its initial introduction, FC was the subject of a number of scientific validation studies, virtually all of which concluded that when facilitators lack information needed to respond to queries posed to the individuals being facilitated, they are unable to independently communicate (Hudson, Melita, & Arnold, 1993; Intellectual Disability Review Panel, 1989; Mulick, Jacobson, & Kobe, 1993; Myles & Simpson, 1994; Myles, Simpson, & Smith, 1996; Prior & Cummins, 1992; Rimland, 1992b, 1993; Simpson & Myles, 1995a; Szempruch & Jacobson, 1993; Wheeler, Jacobson, Paglieri, & Schwartz, 1993).

Further, reports of erroneous allegations of abuse based on FC communication began to occur. For example, Rimland (1992a) referred to the case of a 29-year-old Australian woman with mental retardation who was removed from her home after communicating through FC that she wanted to leave home to escape sexual abuse. Because she became distraught after being removed from her home, an evaluation of her ability to communicate by means of FC was undertaken. The woman's FC-assisted reports of abuse came under question when she was unable to answer a series of questions to which she reportedly knew the answers. The questions were taped by the facilitator with whom she worked, and this person assisted the woman in answering 40 questions under four separate conditions: (1) Both the person with the disability and the facilitator were permitted to hear the questions; (2) while wearing earphones, the facilitator and the person with the disability heard the same questions; (3) while wearing earphones, the facilitator and the person with the disability heard different questions; and (4) while wearing earphones, the facilitator heard only music, whereas the person with the disability heard the questions. Under Condition 1 the person with the disability correctly knew 8 to 9 out of 10 items; under Condition 2 she correctly answered 4 of 10 items; under Condition 3 she was unable to correctly answer her own questions, but correctly answered 4 questions that only the facilitator heard. Finally, under Condition 4 the person with the disability incorrectly answered every question. Based on these results, it was concluded that the woman was unable to independently communicate.

In spite of evidence to the contrary, magazines and radio and television shows have regularly presented reports of extraordinary results based on FC. Predictably, these reports were viewed by many families and professionals as offering the best hope for significant improvement for persons with autism. As a result, many professionals and families have requested that FC be made an integral part of students' educational programs. Equally predictable is the reluctance of many professionals and school districts to commit resources to FC without clear evidence of its efficacy. Not surprisingly, conflicts between parents and families have regularly occurred related to the use of FC in schools.

On the one hand, it is understandable that families would want their child with autism to have an opportunity to use the most current and promising procedures. On the other hand, many professionals and families associated with persons with autism are committed to using validated, best-practice procedures. Thus, conflict over the use of FC, as well as other unvalidated treatments, will likely continue until agreement on their role and educational validity can be established.

We believe that FC and other currently unproven methods must undergo scientific validation prior to being widely used with individuals with autism. In this context, we agree with Calculator (1992) that "in the absence of empirical evidence, [facilitated communication] is characterized by its ambiguity, mystique, recurring anecdotes, and spiritual underpinnings" (p. 18). We also believe that this admonition is equally applicable to other unproven interventions. Thus, we consider it unprofessional and reckless to introduce an unvalidated procedure such as FC with the stipulation that it not be subjected to scientific evaluation, as Biklen and Schubert (1991) advocated. Instead, we believe that such evaluation is necessary to determine whether FC or other controversial procedures can be effectively and legitimately used with persons with autism.

Evaluation of Controversial and Unvalidated Methods

A great deal of controversy surrounds the issue of how to evaluate the effectiveness of controversial and unvalidated methods.

Opposing Camps

Proponents of controversial procedures such as FC often support their methods by means of anecdotal reports and "qualitative" evidence (Biklen, 1993), whereas their critics argue that evaluation must be based on traditional scientific procedures, including robust quantitative methods (Simpson & Myles, 1995b; Wheeler et al., 1993). As a result of these differing approaches, inconsistent findings, models, and methods are common.

The evaluation debate essentially falls along two battle lines—those who argue for strict adherence to the traditional scientific inquiry methods and those favoring a more qualitative and anecdotal approach. Traditionally, claims that unique treatments are effective in educating and treating individuals with disabilities have been considered valid only when supported by objective, scientific evidence (Freed, Ryan, & Hess, 1991). *Scientific evidence* in this context refers to objective, verifiable, and reproducible documentation of the effects of an intervention. At the core of this approach is adherence to scientific method protocol. That is, a systematic, standard process based on measurable outcomes, established research designs, empirical data collection procedures, and quantitative data analysis is used to control for extraneous variables and to ensure that claims of effectiveness are objectively supported (Freed et al., 1991; Popper, 1961).

Over the years, traditional scientific methodology associated with education and social sciences has been both praised (Nagel, 1961) and attacked (Poplin, 1987). Criticisms of the use of traditional scientific methods to validate the effectiveness of a novel treatment relate to alleged model deficiencies and overall poor utility. For example, some have argued that research methods based on traditional scientific models such as logical positivism are impractical, that they require researchers to adhere to cumbersome and outdated methodology, and that they fail to permit researchers to respond to important questions (Voeltz & Evans, 1983). Further, Hanson (1958) contended that methodology based on logical positivism does not ensure objectivity because an individual's beliefs, theoretical position, and experiences influence his or her perceptions.

On the other hand, some have argued that naturalistic observation methods, detailed interviews, and other qualitative research procedures can assist researchers in overcoming problems related to logical positivism and traditional research methods (Harre, 1981; Lincoln & Guba, 1985; Taylor & Bogdan, 1984). Indeed, several professionals have used qualitative strategies to evaluate FC (e.g., Biklen, 1993; Bogdan & Biklen, 1991; Crossley, 1992a), contending that this strategy is less intrusive and more effective than traditional procedures in assessing whether individuals benefit from a particular treatment. Others, however, have questioned whether or not these researchers actually adhered to accepted qualitative research methodological standards (Simpson, 1995; Simpson & Myles, 1995b). At least some self-described qualitative research (e.g., Biklen, 1993; Biklen, Winston, Gold, Berrigan, & Swaminathan, 1992) has failed to follow accepted qualitative protocol (Miles & Huberman, 1984) and is actually anecdotal or case study in its methodology. For instance, purported evaluations of the efficacy of FC have relied on poorly defined and highly subjective outcomes that allegedly confirm the independent communication skills of persons with severe disabilities who use FC: unique typographical errors that occur during use of FC; FC-assisted idiosyncratic spelling errors across different facilitators; use of unusual and idiosyncratic phrasing during FC use; divulging of information unknown to facilitators; communication that reveals the unique personality and values of the person being facilitated; and communication that occurs under decreasing levels of physical contact.

We believe that the scientific method is the basic standard by which interventions should be judged. Indeed, other proponents of the scientific method have argued that this model is the most efficient and effective way to establish the efficacy of new treatments and methods (Feigl & Brodbeck, 1953; Kerlinger, 1986), and many professionals view it as a necessary safeguard to protect both professionals and consumers from ineffective or inferior strategies and treatments. Accordingly, those who support robust scientific validation contend that use of controversial methods such as auditory integration training, FC, and so forth, should be made contingent upon demonstration of empirical efficacy based upon objective procedures; some of these supporters have also criticized qualitative research methodology as unscientific and unreliable. In our opinion, both quantitative and qualitative methods can be used to establish efficacy.

We believe that professionals must be willing to acknowledge the benefits of both qualitative and quantitative research in establishing the validity of unsupported and controversial interventions, recognizing that when correctly and professionally used, each approach can be useful and valid. At the same time, however, we support Simpson's (1992) assessment that "although quantitative research methodology is far from perfect, it remains the best way to document the effectiveness of special education in a manner that provides the greatest degree of confidence in the validity and reliability of conclusions" (p. 242).

General Issues

Several general intervention assessment issues have been raised with regard to FC; these issues are also applicable to the assessment of other intervention methods. One argument used to oppose objective, scientific evaluation of the efficacy of FC relates to purported self-concept problems of individuals who are made to participate in such investigations (Biklen, 1993). For example, Crossley (1988) and Biklen and Schubert (1991) have argued that individuals who use FC should not be asked to function in settings wherein there is significant doubt as to their ability to perform. According to these authors, such an atmosphere further undermines these individuals' already fragile self-concepts, that is, self-perceptions damaged by a lifetime of experience with individuals who have considered them unable to perform. These FC supporters reason that exposing these individuals to persons who doubt their independent communication abilities (i.e., objective researchers) significantly impairs their ability to perform.

Opponents of using traditional evaluation strategies to assess FC efficacy have also argued that such methods cause the persons being assessed to experience significant psychological pressure and anxiety. They also claim that such methodology reduces facilitators' performance expectations, thus introducing into the evaluation process an attitude of skepticism that may neutralize the potentially positive effects of the FC procedure. Finally, opponents of using objective, scientific evaluation of FC have argued that formal evaluation causes participants to experience negative feelings (e.g., excessive test anxiety, apprehension about being evaluated) that interfere with communication.

Notwithstanding these concerns, most professionals and parents involved with persons with autism have contended that FC and other purported interventions must be evaluated objectively. Without scientific validation, controversial and other unvalidated methods are supported only by mystique, ambiguity, and often spiritual underpinnings (Calculator, 1992; Schopler, 1992). As a result, controversial interventions are likely to remain vulnerable to allegations that they are based on mysterious processes that are somehow beyond reasonable human understanding. Indeed, some have noted similarities between FC and Ouija boards and other occult phenomena (Green, cited in Rimland, 1993; Calculator, 1992). Cummins and Prior (1992) compared FC to the "Clever Hans" phenomenon, in which a horse named Hans appeared to communicate by tapping his hoof until an investigation revealed that the horse's trainer was cuing the animal. We contend that the mysterious and preternatural associations often linked with controversial interventions will disappear only as a result of vigorous scientific investigations.

Scientific validation of unsupported and other controversial interventions will also help alleviate users' vulnerability to pressure to obtain desired outcomes and the criticism and social ostracism of persons who fail to demonstrate desired results. Simpson and Myles (1995b) reported experiencing a number of situations in which individuals who had failed to obtain the same level of FC-assisted communication success as others were "severely criticized for 'not believing,' 'not doing it [facilitated communication] right,' or otherwise being subjected to emotional blackmail for failing to demonstrate the same degree of success with the procedure as others" (p. 7). These researchers went on to observe the difficult experiences of one particular teacher:

> She underwent a "gut wrenching" self-examination of her beliefs and procedures related to using facilitated communication with one of her students at home each evening for an entire semester, because she was unable to obtain the same degree of communication success as several of her colleagues and the students' parents. She went on to say that her colleagues and the students' parents questioning of her belief in facilitated communication and her utilization of "correct methods" did little to assist her in responding to this dilemma. (p. 7)

From our perspective, reliance on objective, scientific validation interventions is the most efficient and appropriate solution to the problem of socially pressuring individuals to obtain desired outcomes.

Objective, scientific evaluation is also needed to ensure that a given intervention is used in a consistent and appropriate manner. With regard to FC, some facilitators receive little or no training in methods, routines, and guidelines. Moreover, colleges, universities, public schools, and other legitimate training programs are reluctant to train individuals to use methods that have not been subjected to empirical validation methods. Ultimately, it is unlikely that a procedure will be widely adopted and used in mainstream settings such as public schools until it has been objectively shown to be efficacious. Thus, users of undocumented controversial methods can expect to find themselves having to do so only on the margins of mainstream institutions and settings.

There are also significant procedural and ethical issues associated with the failure to objectively evaluate undocumented, controversial methods such as FC, rhythmic and music-based treatments, vision therapies, and so forth. Failure to objectively and scientifically evaluate these methods is likely to delay their legitimate acceptance and use, which, in the event that a particular tool proves to be effective, could negatively affect individuals with autism and their families. Equally important, if an *ineffective* intervention is not objectively evaluated, families and professionals may erroneously assume that it is effective on the basis of anecdotal reports. In such a case, these individuals might pursue the untested, ineffective intervention, ignoring less dramatic, but ultimately more effective avenues. Such shortsighted choices could delay students' development of knowledge and skills required for independent functioning, increase frustration of persons with autism and their families by using inappropriate curricula and procedures, and promote unrealistic and inaccurate expectations.

In the final analysis, we contend that there is no acceptable alternative to objective, scientific evaluation of unvalidated and controversial intervention methods. We also believe that it is irresponsible for professionals to advance intervention procedures as valid tools in the absence of objective, replicable, scientific evidence. We find it particularly reckless for professionals who introduce undocumented and controversial methods to declare that their procedure is unfit for traditional evaluation, as is often the case with FC. Such a stand has the potential to hamper the development and professional use of best-practice procedures, thereby significantly impeding the development of effective programs for individuals with autism.

Use of Controversial Interventions with Children and Youth with Autism

Convincing arguments exist both for use and prohibition of controversial treatment methods with individuals with autism. On the one hand, use of any method that has the potential to assist individuals with autism to live a more independent and normal existence, regardless of whether legitimate researchers have given it their approval, can be easily defended. On the other hand, investing time and other limited resources in using a method that may prove to be ineffective or even harmful, and that may result in reduced use of alternative, proven procedures, is equally problematic. Thus, deciding whether or not to use a controversial method poses a serious dilemma. Many families and professionals are rightfully requesting that individuals with whom they live and work be exposed to the newest and most innovative methods and tools. Thus these individuals are regularly requesting that any one of a number of undocumented methods be made a regular part of their children's educational programs. A number of organizations, families, and professionals, however, are reluctant to commit significant resources to any intervention that has not been shown to be effective.

Making rational and prudent decisions related to the use of controversial methods is not easy. Though not a solution to this challenge, guidelines in the form of questions suggested by Freeman (1993) should be of assistance. Freeman has recommended that individuals contemplating use of a controversial procedure with an individual with a disability pose to themselves the question of whether the treatment has the potential to do harm. Thus, a primary decision relates to whether or not adoption of the procedure will impair or detract from individuals' overall educational and treatment programs. For example, even though FC may be perceived as a relatively benign tool, it has been implicated in several false allegations of physical and sexual abuse and other wrongdoing made by children and youth with the assistance of a facilitator.

Further, as with any treatment method, individual children and youth with autism may encounter needless difficulty as a result of using a particular procedure. For instance, moving a student from a special education classroom to a general education program solely on the basis of claims related to an unsupported technique is clearly not in a child's best interests (e.g., expecting a child previously thought to have a severe disability to master an age-appropriate regular curriculum based on his purported FC-discovered cognitive giftedness). Thus, prior to making major programming changes such as moving a student to a different placement and curriculum because of unsupported claims related to a controversial technique, one should carefully consider the student's potential for significant frustration and regression. Further, when contemplating use of a controversial individual method, one must objectively consider what a student will be required to give up in order to use an unvalidated procedure, and whether the potential gains outweigh the risks. For example, if a student's entire program is changed in order to allow use of an unvalidated method, and such modifications require that documented, effective programs are eliminated, the risks are significant.

Freeman (1993) has also recommended that potential users of controversial methods consider the potential impact on persons and their families if the intervention proves ineffective. Parents and families of children and youth with autism have been particularly vulnerable in situations in which "new treatments" are purported to reveal the presence of or potential for normal functioning, advanced social skills, age-level communication abilities, and so forth. When these claims fail to live up to their expectations, individuals with autism, along with the families and professionals with whom they are involved, often suffer. It may be argued, on the other hand, that not every family and professional associated with an individual for whom a controversial method is unsuccessful will experience a significant negative emotional reaction, that development of creative and novel approaches are keys to improving services for persons with autism, and that experimental trials of novel intervention and treatment approaches must therefore be supported. At the same time, however, it is important to keep in mind families' and professionals' emotional reactions to individuals' failure to achieve unrealistic outcomes associated with the use of controversial methods.

Freeman (1993) has also advocated that the manner in which a controversial procedure will be integrated into an individual's program be thoroughly discussed. In cases in which a controversial method is considered to be appropriate for implementation and evaluation, we advise that families and professionals ask themselves whether the procedure's use will be balanced with other methods and curricula. It is particularly important not to become so infatuated with a controversial procedure that we lose sight of other intervention approaches and curricula. Specifically, we caution that existing functional curricula, vocational, life, and social skill programs not be abandoned or underused in preference for methods lacking in validated efficacy. Parents, family members, and professionals who are involved in planning for individuals with autism are advised to ask themselves the following question related to use of a controversial method: If the effects of a controversial method prove to be minimal or ineffectual, will that individual be potentially harmed because the standard, ongoing program was dramatically altered?

We also think it is important that individuals who are contemplating use of a controversial method with an individual with autism clearly identify appropriate outcomes and assessment markers prior to implementing the procedure. It is particularly important to evaluate these methods using objective formal and informal assessment strategies. Formal assessment strategies include direct observation methods targeted at evaluating those variables purported to be affected by the intervention. Informal assessment of a controversial method involves monitoring a variety of outcomes related to the use of the procedure. For FC, for example, it would be important to determine

- whether or not the facilitator is able to fade physical contact with an individual over time,

- whether or not the individual using FC shows behavioral and social interaction improvements,

- whether or not the individual being facilitated gives evidence of wanting to independently use FC,

- whether or not the individual being facilitated is able to effectively use the procedure with more than one facilitator, and

- whether or not the individual who uses FC is able to complete basic academic tasks such as write his or her name, address, and phone number; and identify letters of the alphabet.

The key consideration in this process is to select and systematically monitor meaningful outcome variables associated with use of the controversial procedure, including those identified on students' Individualized Education Programs.

We also think that a number of life-span issues deserve serious consideration. These factors relate to the implications of long-term use of controversial methods, especially postschool preparation and life-span success. In this context, consideration of the resources needed to hire, train, and maintain personnel to implement a procedure, including whether human and nonhuman resources are available over the long term and whether the controversial method in question effectively promotes long-term goals for individuals with autism have obvious importance. In particular, we think that controversial methods must be objectively evaluated on the basis of whether or not they promote independent functioning of persons with autism in a cost-efficient manner across the life span. Simply stated, if an individual with autism is unable to demonstrate increased independence and capacity to function after a reasonable period of experiencing an intervention program, the long-term growth and developmental potential of such a treatment must be seriously questioned.

A second life-span consideration relates to the impact of a given controversial procedure on an individual's general quality of life. That is, does the treatment or procedure improve the social behavior and social interaction skills of individuals, assist them in finding appropriate employment and living options, create leisure and recreational opportunities, and enhance their overall life satisfaction and happiness and the happiness of their families? Evaluation of these factor presents a daunting challenge for families and professionals. Nonetheless, the potential impact of purportedly useful tools must ultimately be judged on their capacity to affect an individual's functioning and overall satisfaction over the life span.

Major Questions To Ask When Deciding To Use Controversial Interventions

We recommend using the following questions to guide selection and use of controversial methods.

1. Will the intervention impair or detract from the overall educational and treatment program?

2. Will it cause frustration or regression?

3. What happens if the method proves ineffective?

4. Is the controversial method balanced with other program components?

5. Have appropriate outcomes and assessment methods been identified, and can these methods be maintained in the long term with appropriately trained personnel and other resources?

6. Does the method lead to increased independence?

7. What is the impact of the method on an individual's general quality of life?

In summary, we are of the opinion that responsible parents and professionals should be free to decide whether or not to use a controversial intervention procedure prior to a scientific determination of its validity. At the same time, however, users of controversial interventions must keep in mind that *at least some techniques appear to have the potential to do harm*.

Suggestions for Accommodating Controversial Interventions

Given the absence of policies and procedures to guide professionals and parents in making prudent choices about using controversial interventions (Howe & Miramontes, 1992; Lovat, 1994), we recommend that controversial interventions be evaluated primarily using robust, objective scientific methods, and that undocumented treatments be closely monitored until they are fully understood and objectively evaluated.

As we observed earlier, reliance on traditional, robust scientific methods to evaluate controversial interventions is replete with disagreement. In spite of concerns expressed, we see no sensible alternative to using objective scientific methods to establish intervention efficacy. In our opinion, these procedures are the most efficient and effective means of sorting effective from ineffective methods, controlling for positive result biases on the part of originators of new techniques, and ensuring that promising methods are used in a consistent and appropriate fashion. Indeed, for a variety of ethical and procedural reasons, controversial methods must be carefully and fully investigated prior to being presented to the unsuspecting public as an effective intervention.

We hope that adoption of an agreed-upon scientific evaluation strategy will prevent developers of new intervention methods from promoting their undocumented tools as valid and efficacious in the absence of scientific evidence.

Although most individuals involved with persons with autism will undoubtedly agree with the need to evaluate controversial interventions prior to advocating their widespread use, as we have seen, agreement on the means for accomplishing this goal will likely be difficult. One solution to the issue of using controversial treatments would be to use a "best-practice" model. That is, professionals and parents would be advised to rely on practices and procedures that have been proven effective with students with autism and to use alternative methods only when these are implemented under controlled conditions, such as research-based programs. Although this would seem to be a simple and acceptable solution, there is lack of agreement on the meaning of the term "best practice." For example, Peters and Herron (1993) cautioned that the term *best practice* is imprecise, and that it is difficult to distinguish from terms like *most promising practice, exemplary practice,* and *emergent or innovative practice.* They also noted that the imprecision of currently accepted criteria for determining best practice, expert opinion, empirical support, and values contribute to this dilemma, and proposed the following criteria for determining best practice: a sound theoretical base, convincing and compelling methodology and design, connection to existing literature, achievement of desired outcomes, and social validity. Nevertheless, one would be naive to think that achieving agreement on what treatments qualify as best practices would be anything less than a daunting task.

Even if an evaluation strategy similar to the one suggested here were to be agreed upon, this would in no way eliminate the use of controversial interventions prior to being fully understood and evaluated. A deeply ingrained respect and reverence for personal choice and individual freedom can be expected to outweigh the need for empirical validation. Thus, we believe that even if controversial interventions were to be subjected to an agreed-upon evaluation, in all likelihood they would be used prior to widespread agreement on their efficacy and utility. Our recommended guidelines take this into account.

Summary

At the heart of the debate over use of controversial interventions have been issues related to research validation methods (Biklen & Schubert, 1992; Crossley, 1988, 1992b), along with politics and personal values. Thus, in spite of objective research results that have discounted the efficacy of many controversial interventions, such treatments continue to thrive. These methods' promise that individuals with autism who use them can make dramatic cognitive, social, and communication gains makes them symbols of hope. Thus, it is understandable that many professionals and families would perceive undocumented treatments as their best hope for the future. That equally effective traditional interventions are unavailable, and that assessment research based on varying methods has yielded contradictory results, has further fueled this controversy.

The strident debate over use of controversial interventions has left many families and professionals demanding a "bottom line" answer to the question of whether or not a particular controversial intervention is effective. A simple answer to this question will not easily be forthcoming. Rather, values, opinions, and personal perceptions will most likely continue to be the means by which many of these purported treatments are judged. We believe that controversial interventions must be judged on the basis of their outcomes—that is, whether they objectively and scientifically help persons with autism to function more effectively and independently. In our opinion, interventions for persons with autism should bring about scientifically validated gains in language, social, cognitive, motor, vocational, self-help, and independent living skills. Some controversial interventions may prove to be useful tools for some individuals with autism. Thus, we urge professionals and parents to continue their quest to validate objectively the scientific merits of controversial interventions—especially their legitimate educational and training uses. Only through such a process will objective information be made available to guide professionals and families in making responsible choices regarding the use of such interventions.

References

Autism Society of America, Inc. (1992–1993, Winter). Facilitated communication under the microscope. *The Advocate*, pp. 19–20.

Biklen, D. (1990). Communication unbound: Autism and praxis. *Harvard Educational Review, 60*, 291–314.

Biklen, D. (1992). Typing to talk: Facilitated communication. *American Journal of Speech and Language Pathology, 1*(2), 15–17.

Biklen, D. (1993). *Communication unbound: How facilitated communication is challenging traditional views of autism and ability/disability*. New York: Teachers College Press.

Biklen, D., & Schubert, A. (1991). New words: The communication of students with autism. *Remedial and Special Education, 12*(6), 46–57.

Biklen, D., & Schubert, A. (1992, January). *Communication unbound: The story of facilitated communication*. Paper presented at the 1992 national symposium on current issues in the nature and treatment of autism, St. Louis, MO.

Biklen, D., Winston, M., Gold, D., Berrigan, C., & Swaminathan, S. (1992). Facilitated communication: Implications for individuals with autism. *Topics in Language Disorders, 12*(4), 1–28.

Bogdan, R., & Biklen, S. (1991). *Qualitative research for education: An introduction to theory and methods*. Boston: Allyn & Bacon.

Calculator, S. N. (1992). Perhaps the emperor has clothes after all: A response to Biklen. *American Journal of Speech and Language Pathology, 1*(2), 18–20.

Crossley, R. (1988, October). *Unexpected communication attainments by persons diagnosed as autistic and intellectually impaired*. Paper presented at the annual meeting of the International Society for Augmentative and Alternative Communication, Los Angeles.

Crossley, R. (1992a). Communication training involving facilitated communication. In DEAL Communication Centre (Ed.), *Facilitated communication training* (pp. 1–9). Melbourne, Australia: DEAL Communication Centre.

Crossley, R. (1992b). Who said that? In DEAL Communication Centre (Ed.), *Facilitated communication training* (pp. 42–54). Melbourne, Australia: DEAL Communication Centre.

Cummins, R., & Prior, M. (1992). Autism and assisted communication: A response to Biklen. *Harvard Educational Review, 62*, 228–241.

Feigl, H., & Brodbeck, M. (1953). *Readings in the philosophy of science.* New York: Appleton Century Crofts.

Freed, M. N., Ryan, J. M., & Hess, R. K. (1991). *Handbook of statistical procedures and their computer applications to education and the behavioral sciences.* New York: Macmillan.

Freeman, B. J. (1993). Questions to ask regarding specific treatment. *The Advocate, 25*(2), 19.

Hanson, N. R. (1958). *Patterns of discovery: An inquiry into the conceptual foundations of science.* Cambridge, England: Cambridge University Press.

Harre, R. (1981). The positivist-empiricist approach and its alternative. In P. Reason & J. Rowan (Eds.), *Human inquiry: A sourcebook of new paradigm research* (pp. 116–137). New York: Wiley.

Howe, K. R., & Miramontes, O. B. (1992). *The ethics of special education.* New York: Teachers College Press.

Hudson, A., Melita, B., & Arnold, N. (1993). Brief report: A case study assessing the validity of facilitated communication. *Journal of Autism and Developmental Disorders, 23*, 165–173.

Intellectual Disability Review Panel. (1989). *Investigation into the reliability and validity of the assisted communication technique.* Melbourne, Australia: Department of Community Services.

Kerlinger, F. N. (1986). *Foundations of behavioral research* (3rd ed.). New York: Holt, Rinehart & Winston.

Lincoln, Y. S., & Guba, E. G. (1985). *Naturalistic inquiry.* Beverly Hills, CA: Sage.

Lovat, T. J. (1994). The implications of bioethics for teachers and teacher researchers. *British Educational Research Journal, 20*, 187–196.

Miles, M. B., & Huberman, A. M. (1984). *Qualitative data analysis.* Newbury Park, CA: Sage.

Mulick, J. A., Jacobson, J. W., & Kobe, F. H. (1993). Anguished silence and helping hands: Autism and facilitated communication. *Skeptical Inquirer, 17*, 270–280.

Myles, B. S., & Simpson, R. L. (1994). Facilitated communication with children diagnosed as autistic in public school settings. *Psychology in the Schools, 31*, 208–220.

Myles, B. S., Simpson, R. L., & Smith, S. M. (1996). Impact of facilitated communication combined with direct instruction on academic performance of individuals with autism. *Focus on Autism and Other Developmental Disabilities, 11*(1), 37–44.

Nagel, E. (1961). *The structure of science.* New York: Harcourt, Brace & World.

Olley, J. G. (1992). Autism: Historical overview, definitions and characteristics. In D. E. Berkell (Ed.), *Autism: Identification, education and treatment* (pp. 3–20). Hillsdale, NJ: Erlbaum.

Peters, M. T., & Herron, T. E. (1993). When the best is not good enough: An examination of best practice. *The Journal of Special Education, 26*, 371–385.

Poplin, M. (1987). Self-imposed blindness: The scientific method in education. *Remedial and Special Education, 8*(6), 31–37.

Popper, K. R. (1961). *The logic of scientific discovery.* London: Hutchinson.

Prior, M., & Cummins, R. (1992). Questions about facilitated communication. *Journal of Autism and Developmental Disorders, 22*, 331–338.

Rimland, B. (1992a). A facilitated communication "horror story." *Autism Research Review, 6*(1), 1, 7.

Rimland, B. (1992b). Facilitated communication: Problems, puzzles and paradoxes: Six challenges for researchers. *Autism Research Review, 5*(4), 3.

Rimland, B. (1993). Facilitated communication under seige. *Autism Research Review International, 7*(1), 2, 7.

Schopler, E. (1992). Facilitated communication—Hope or hype? *Autism Society of North Carolina, 8*(3), 6.

Simpson, R. (1992). Quantitative research as the method of choice within a continuum model. In W. Stainback & S. Stainback (Eds.), *Controversial issues confronting special education: Divergent perspectives* (pp. 235–251). New York: Allyn & Bacon.

Simpson, R. L. (1995). Children and youth with autism in an age of reform: A perspective on current issues. *Behavioral Disorders, 21*(1), 7–20.

Simpson, R. L., & Myles, B. S. (1995a). Effectiveness of facilitated communication with children and youth with autism. *The Journal of Special Education, 28*, 424–439.

Simpson, R. L., & Myles, B. S. (1995b). Facilitated communication and children with disabilities: An enigma in search of a perspective. *Focus on Exceptional Children, 27*(9), 1–16.

Szempruch, J., & Jacobson, J. W. (1993). Evaluating facilitated communication of people with developmental disabilities. *Research in Developmental Disabilities, 14*, 253–264.

Taylor, S., & Bogdan, R. (1984). *Introduction to qualitative research methods*. New York: Wiley.

Trachtman, P. (1994, September). NIH looks at the implausible and the inexplicable. *Smithsonian*, pp. 110–123.

Voeltz, L. M., & Evans, I. M. (1983). Educational validity: Procedures to validate outcomes in programs for severely handicapped learners. *Journal of the Association for the Severely Handicapped, 6*, 3–15.

Wheeler, D., Jacobson, J., Paglieri, R., & Schwartz, A. (1993). An experimental assessment of facilitated communication. *Mental Retardation, 31*, 49–60.

Author Index

Subject Index